4-12-06

W9-DFS-808

#2006-10

*CIVIL WAR SITES, MEMORIALS,
MUSEUMS AND LIBRARY COLLECTIONS*

Civil War Sites, Memorials, Museums and Library Collections

A State-by-State Guidebook to Places Open to the Public

by Doug Gelbert

McFarland & Company, Inc., Publishers
Jefferson, North Carolina, and London

British Library Cataloguing-in-Publication data are available

Library of Congress Cataloguing-in-Publication Data

    Civil War sites, memorials, museums and library collections : a state-by-state guidebook to places open to the public / by Doug Gelbert.
       p. cm.
    Includes index.
    ISBN 0-7864-0319-5 (case binding : 50# alkaline paper) ∞
      1. United States — History — Civil War, 1861–1865 — Monuments — Guidebooks. 2. United States — History — Civil War, 1861–1865 — Battlefields — Guidebooks. 3. United States — History — Civil War, 1861–1865 — Libraries — Guidebooks.
4. United States — History — Civil War, 1861–1865 — Museums — Guidebooks. I. Title.
E641.G45 1997
973.7 — dc21   97-13087
                                           CIP

Manufactured in the United States of America

McFarland & Company, Inc., Publishers
  Box 611, Jefferson, North Carolina 28640

CONTENTS

INTRODUCTION

Although the exact total can never be known, the number of military actions during the American Civil War has been estimated at more than 10,000. Most of these actions are forgotten today, their sites swallowed up by the American landscape; even those sites still recognized are now endangered by development. This book describes, first, the Civil War *sites* that remain, or are identified, from the conflict of the 1860s; second, the *memorials* that have been erected to commemorate the war; and third, the *collections* that preserve the accounts and artifacts of the war. Sites are defined as the locations of actual military action during the war. Memorials are monuments; more than five hundred are listed individually, and developed battlefield sites contain countless additional memorials and statues. Collections include museums with permanent Civil War displays and libraries with significant collections pertaining to the war.

The book is arranged alphabetically by state. At the beginning of each state's section is a short profile of that state or territory during the Civil War. Under each state the relevant cities are alphabetically listed, and within each city the reader will find an alphabetical listing of attractions with a notation to indicate whether the attraction is a site (site), memorial (mem), or collection (col). If the attraction bears the name of a person, it is alphabetized by that person's last name; for example, the Samuel P. Carter monument in the District of Columbia is listed between Capitol Prison and the Congressional Cemetery. Operating hours and admission policies are given where applicable, along with addresses and telephone numbers. (The author acknowledges that some changes may have occurred since publication and regrets any inconvenience that may result.)

Regular reenactments take place on many Civil War sites. Where possible, these events are noted in the text.

Following the main body of the text the reader will find two reference aids: an appendix listing gravesites of significant Civil War individuals, and a general index.

THE SITES, MEMORIALS AND COLLECTIONS

Alabama

Civil War Status: Confederacy; seceded from the Union on January 11, 1861
1860 Population: 964,201
Troops Provided: 100,000
Known Scenes of Action: 336

Civil War Timeline

August 5, 1864: Battle of Mobile Bay

March 22, 1865: Wilson's raid on Alabama begins

March 27–April 8, 1865: Siege of Spanish Fort

April 2, 1865: Battle of Selma

April 2–9, 1865: Siege and capture of Fort Blakely

April 12, 1865: Surrender of Mobile

May 4, 1865: Surrender of Lieutenant General Richard Taylor's Confederate forces at Citronelle

---

Auburn

1 Davis Monument (mem)

At railroad station.

Jefferson Davis stopped here in February 1861 to review the Auburn Guards on the way to his inauguration as Confederate president in Montgomery. A boulder in the corner of the property commemorates the occasion.

2 Lane House (site)

Sanders Street.

James H. Lane, a native Virginian, was a pupil of Stonewall Jackson at the Virginia Military Institute. He was considered an outstanding officer, but his military career was tarnished when one of his pickets accidentally shot his mentor Jackson at Chancellorsville. After the war Lane spent the last 25 years of his life (1883–1907) as a teacher and was the head of civil engineering at Auburn. Lane is the highest-ranking Confederate veteran in Auburn's oldest burying ground, Pine Hill Cemetery. The Lane House, marked by a United Daughters of Confederacy bronze tablet, has been relocated here from its original site at South College and Thach streets.

Bessemer

3 Bessemer Hall of History Museum (col)

1905 Alabama Avenue, 205-426-1633; Tues–Sat, 10–4. Free.

The Hall of History is housed in a renovated Southern Railroad Terminal, built in 1916. The Civil War collection relates to the 28th Alabama Regiment.

Birmingham

4 Arlington Historical Shrine (site)

331 Cotton Avenue, 205-780-5656; Tues–Sat 10–4, Sun 1–4. Admission charged.

This 1850 Greek Revival antebellum home was the headquarters of General James Harrison Wilson (1837–1925) for a few days in the spring of 1865 while his Federal troops ransacked the area. Wilson was one of the Union "boy wonders" who made major general five years after his graduation from West Point. His orders were to raid through Alabama to Selma, and in 28 days he captured 5 fortified cities, 23 stand of colors, 288 guns, 6820 prisoners — and finally Jefferson Davis on May 10, 1865.

Here he planned the sacking of the University of Alabama. Framed by giant oaks, this historic site offers an authentic picture of the era.

Brierfield

5 Brierfield Ironworks State Park (site)

Route 25, 205-665-1856; Daily, 7–dusk. Admission charged.

In 1862 a group of men banded together to form the Bibb County Iron Company along the Furnace Branch stream. Their notoriety for making high-grade iron quickly attracted the attention of the Confederate government, which purchased the enterprise the following year. On the morning of March 31, 1865, the valuable Bibb Naval Furnaces were left in ruins after a raid by marauding Union Tenth Missouri troops. Attempts to revitalize the ironworks were never fully successful, and the Brierfield furnace blew out forever on Christmas Eve, 1894.

Reenactment: The Battle of Bibb Furnace is reenacted on the last weekend in March. Hiking and nature trails wind through the crumbling red-brick ruins in this 45-acre park; some of the ruins have been restored.

Cedar Bluff

6 Cornwall Furnace Park (site)

Route 9, two miles east of town.

The Noble brothers of Rome, Georgia, constructed this water-powered cold-blast furnace in 1862. It became an important part of the Confederate States of America's ironworks. Local legend maintains that General William Sherman destroyed the blast furnace, but it is more likely that it fell victim to an industrial accident rather than to a Federal torch.

Still, Sherman was especially vitriolic in denouncing Alabama's part in the war, declaring in a letter, "The Government of the United States has in North Alabama any and all rights which they choose to enforce in war, to take their lives, their homes, their lands, their everything because they cannot deny that war exists there, and war is simply power unrestrained by constitution of compact. If they want eternal warfare well and good."

The small 5½-acre park includes a half-mile nature trail amid the ruins, which are among the finest remnants of Civil War industry.

7 Colonel Streight's Surrender Site (site)

Route 9.

Two markers, erected by the United Daughters of the Confederacy, mark the location where Union Colonel Abel Streight's ragged troops capitulated to General Nathan Bedford Forrest after a skirmish on May 3, 1863. The surrender ended Streight's mission to destroy Southern railroads.

Childersburg

8 DeSoto Caverns Park (site)

800-933-2283. Mon–Sat 9–5, Sun 12:30–5. Free.

Sorely lacking in ammunition plants at the beginning of the war, the South used many caves laden with saltpeter deposits as gunpowder plants. Representative of many such caves, DeSoto Caverns display a Confederate gunpowder mining center with original well, leaching trench, and reconstructed vat operation.

Courtland

9 Joe Wheeler Plantation (site)

12280 Highway 20, east of town, 205-637-8513; hours vary. Admission charged.

Fighting Joe Wheeler was a veteran of several Civil War campaigns and served in the Spanish-American War a generation later. His home on 15,000 acres contains artifacts and souvenirs of his military career.

Dauphin Island

10 Fort Gaines Historic Site (site)

East Bienville Boulevard, 334-861-6992; Apr–Aug: daily 9–6; other times: 9–5. Admission charged.

Some type of fortification has been on this site at the east entrance to Mobile Bay since 1717. After it was taken by the Alabama militia on January 5,

1861, the Confederacy completed the present bastion, named for General Edmund P. Gaines. Union forces landed on Dauphin Island early during the Battle of Mobile Bay in August of 1864, but Fort Gaines did not capitulate easily. On August 7 Colonel Charles D. Anderson raised the white flag but was censured by his superiors who felt the fighting should continue and overruled the surrender. Finally Fort Gaines fell the next day.

Battlements, gun mounts, ammunition magazines, and tunnels remain on the island as well as several buildings inside the fort. A self-guided walking tour follows a marked route. Civil War cannons surround the fort. A war museum is on the property. At the entrance is the huge anchor and chain from Admiral David Farragut's flagship, *Hartford*.

Reenactment: Throughout the year, there are ongoing encampments and reenactments at Fort Gaines. The re-creation of the Battle of Mobile Bay is in early June.

Decatur

11 The Old Bank (site)

925 Bank Street Northeast, 205-350-5060; Mon–Fri, 9:30–12 and 1:00–4:30. Free.

The Old State Bank, based on Federal Hall in New York City, opened for deposits in 1833 with Vice President Martin Van Buren in attendance at the dedication. Bank president James Fennell then freed the slaves who had worked on the building. When Federal troops occupied Decatur, the building served as a hospital and guardhouse. Except for the Old Bank, only three other buildings survived the war.

The city of Decatur acquired the Old Bank in 1976 and restored it to its early nineteenth-century appearance. The five limestone columns are nicked and scarred from musket fire; scratched into the column is such Civil War grafitti as "JKC, Co. A, 12th Regt. Indiana Union." The Dancy-Polk House, another of the buildings left standing after the war, is in the historic district.

Reenactment: The September Skirmish takes place each Labor Day at Point Mallard, honoring General John Hunt Morgan, the famed cavalry raider born in nearby Huntsville, and General Joseph "Fighting Joe" Wheeler from Courtland.

Double Springs

12 Looney's Tavern Amphitheater and Park (site)

Route 278, 205-489-5000; Jun–Oct: Thurs–Sat, 8:00 P.M.

In 1862 a band of fiercely independent hill people

from northwest Alabama met at Looney's Tavern in Winston County to consider seceding from the state and the Union. Winston County became known as the Free State of Winston. A drama based on the incident is presented in this 1,500-seat amphitheater overlooking Bankhead National Forest.

Eufala

13 Shorter Mansion (col)

340 North Eufala Avenue, 334-687-3793; Mon–Sat 9–4, Sun 1–4. Admission charged.

This Greek Revival mansion dating back to 1906 houses the visitor center for Eufala, a jumping-off point for a tour of the historical district covering more than 500 registered landmarks. The museum here has a collection of Confederate relics and memorabilia from six Alabama governors. The Shorter family cemetery includes the grave of John Gill Shorter, a governor during the Civil War.

Florence

14 Confederate Monument (mem)

Courthouse lawn, Court and West Tennessee streets.

The gray stone figure is an infantryman in marching gear, sculpted in Italy and dedicated on April 25, 1903.

15 Old Florence Cemetery (site)

East end of Tennessee Street.

The Confederate section of the cemetery contains the graves of 32 soldiers.

16 Peter's Plantation (site)

Gunwaleford Road.

During a skirmish here on April 12, 1864, the Confederates, led by colonels James Jackson and Samuel Ives, surrounded a Union camp, killing four and capturing 42. Their prize booty, however, was 250 beef cattle. A marker commemorates the action.

17 Pope's Tavern Museum (col)

203 Hermitage Drive, 205-760-6439; Tues–Sat, 10–4. Admission charged.

This low, cottage-style structure was a stagecoach stop as far back as 1811 and is one of the earliest buildings in Florence. It was a hospital for the wounded from Forts Henry and Donelson. A museum upstairs is devoted to an extensive Civil War collection.

Gadsden

18 Forrest Cemetery (site)

West side of 15th Street between Walnut and Chestnut.

The church building is based on an English chapel. The Confederate graves sprinkled across the cemetery are marked by iron Maltese crosses.

19 Emma Sansom Monument (mem)

1st and Broad streets.

Union commander Abel Streight sacked Gadsden and burned the main bridge over Black Creek on his way out of town. General Nathan Forrest took up the chase and was guided by 15-year-old Emma Sansom to a shortcut across the creek. The story has it that a bullet ripped by close to her, but she shouted, "They've only wounded my dress." She waved her sunbonnet at the Federals, and both sides cheered her bravery as they held fire until she was safe.

Forrest went on to capture 2,000 Union troops and that night sent "his highest regards to Emma Sansom for her gallant conduct" and asked for a lock of her hair as a keepsake. In 1907 the United Daughters of the Confederacy built a granite-based marble monument, 20 feet high; a bas-relief on its west side shows Emma seated behind General Forrest on his horse, pointing out the ford.

Gulf Shores

20 Fort Morgan Historic Site (site)

Route 180, 334-540-7125; Daily, 8–dusk. Admission charged.

This venerable fort at the west entrance of Mobile Bay was begun in 1819 to control the main shipping channel into Mobile. Its star shape allowed defenders to rain a heavy concentration of artillery fire on an enemy fleet as it approached the fort and to maintain this volume of fire as the enemy force sailed into the bay. Named for Revolutionary War hero General Daniel Morgan in 1833, it was occupied by the Alabama militia on January 4, 1861, taken over from a caretaker in charge of the fortification.

At dawn on August 5, 1864, Admiral David G. Farragut steamed toward Fort Morgan with 14 wooden gunboats and four ironclads. Between his fleet and Mobile were Fort Morgan and its sister defender, Fort Gaines, and three Confederate warships, including the C.S.S. *Tennessee*, considered the most powerful ironclad afloat. The Confederate defenders opened fire, and by half past seven the leading Union ironclad, the U.S.S. *Tecumseh*, had been sunk by an underwater mine, known as a submarine during the Civil War. Ninety-three Union sailors perished with the ship.

The sudden disaster caused precarious confusion under heavy fire in the Union fleet until Farragut issued his famous order, "Damn the torpedoes, full speed ahead!" The fleet maneuvered through the mined waters into Mobile Bay without the loss of another ship. After an 18-day siege Fort Morgan surrendered. Farragut had proved that ships could still handle forts and opened the way for land operations against Mobile.

The five-pointed Fort Gaines is one of America's finest examples of brick architecture. The fort was deactivated after World War II and is now a well-preserved Civil War site. A dry ditch surrounds the fort, which could be swept with deadly cross fire from the guns mounted in the five bastions, or projecting corners of the fort. The barracks — old, weathered farm buildings — were badly damaged in the siege and only the foundations remain. A museum chronicles the fort's history.

Reenactment: On the first weekend in August the Battle of Mobile is reenacted.

Huntsville

21 Church of the Nativity (site)

Southwest corner of Eustis and Greene streets.

Completed in 1859, this Gothic Revival Episcopal church was the only place of worship not occupied by Union troops as a stable, living quarters, or hospital, supposedly because of an inscription on the outside: "Reverence My Sanctuary."

22 Huntsville Depot Museum (site)

320 Church Street, 800-239-8955; Mar–Dec: Tues–Sat 10–4. Admission charged.

Opened in 1860 as the passenger house and eastern division headquarters for the Memphis and Charleston Railroad, this depot is one of the country's oldest railroad structures. Seized by Union invaders in 1862, the depot was a prison for Confederate soldiers. Original grafitti scratched into the walls by both Confederate and Union soldiers is still clearly visible.

Jacksonville

23 Pelham Monument (mem)

Pelham Road.

John Pelham, a Confederate major, was nicknamed the "Gallant Pelham" after Robert E. Lee observed his bravery on the field at Fredericksburg and exclaimed, "It is glorious to see such courage in one so young!" Pelham fought as an artillery commander under J. E. B. Stuart, remaining unscathed through 60 engagements. His commission as a lieutenant colonel was signed and on its way to him when he was killed by a stray shell at the battle of Kelly's Ford, Virginia, on March 17, 1863. When Pelham — blond, blue-eyed, handsome, and described to be "as grand a flirt as ever lived" — was killed, three girls in the Jacksonville area put on mourning. He was only 24.

24 Presbyterian Church Cemetery (site)

South Church and May streets.

The church was pressed into service as a hospital and sustained great damage from invading Federal troops in 1862. Major John Pelham is among those buried here.

Lanett

25 Fort Tyler (site)

Route 29.

At this fort on April 16, 1865, a handful of wounded and convalescent Confederates made a futile attempt to hold a bridgehead against General Wilson's 3,000 troops. It was one of the final conflicts of the war east of the Mississippi. Only an outline of the old earthworks remains.

Leighton

26 LaGrange (site)

Route 157, four miles southwest of town.

Alabama's first chartered college went into operation in LaGrange, a tiny hamlet of 400 people, on January 11, 1830. On the eve of the Civil War 170 students were enrolled in LaGrange College and Military Academy. By 1862, with the cadets and staff away at war, the town was almost deserted and the school doors closed. On April 28, 1863, Colonel Florence M. Cornyn and his "Destroying Angels" swept into the valley and burned LaGrange to the ground forever.

Reenactment: Granite markers are all that remain of the vanished village in the northwest corner of Alabama. A Civil War reenactment is held the weekend after Mother's Day in May, to commemorate the town, the college, and the men who fought in the war.

Livingston

27 Confederate Monument (mem)

Courthouse lawn.

The names of Civil War soldiers from Sumter County are inscribed on the monument.

Marion

28 Judson College (site)

Route 14.

The "Confederate Oak" marks the spot on campus where an original Confederate flag, "Stars and Bars," was presented to the Marion Light Industry. Nicola Marschall, a Prussian portrait painter, who designed the flag, taught music here. A monument to Marschall is at the Perry County Courthouse in town.

McCalla

29 Tannehill Historic State Park (site)

12632 Confederate Parkway, 205-477-5711; Daily, 7–dusk. Admission charged.

Between 1859 and 1863 slaves cut sandstone rocks and transported them by skids to the banks of Roupes Creek and its rich deposits of brown ore. Here Moses Stroup built three tall furnaces, the Tannehill ironworks. Trees on the hillside were felled to provide charcoal for the huge blast furnaces that were soon cranking out 20 tons of pig iron a day for the Confederacy.

On March 31, 1865, it all ended in fire and devastation as three companies of the Eighth Iowa Cavalry swept through the area as part of Union general James Wilson's raid on Alabama war industry sites. At day's end the furnaces were no longer operational, and the foundry, tannery, sawmill, and gristmill were in ruins.

There are nearly 50 historic sites on the 1,500 acres of this state park, including the massive stone furnaces in the furnace area, among the best preserved ironworks of the Civil War period. The solidified, molten metal still lies at the bottom of the furnaces. The Iron and Steel Museum includes Civil War machinery.

Reenactment: A Civil War program and reenactment occur on the Memorial Day weekend.

Mobile

30 Father Ryan Statue (mem)

Spring Hill Avenue, Scott, and St. Francis Street.

The life-size bronze statue depicts the noted priest-poet of the Confederacy.

31 Admiral Raphael Semmes Monument (mem)

City Hall, Government Street.

Ralph Semmes, commandant of the United States navy yard at Pensacola at the time of secession, rose to rear admiral in the Confederate navy. Semmes guided the C.S.S. *Alabama*, the most successful commerce raider of its time. After months of failing to halt her destructive forays, the Federal navy cornered the *Alabama*, convalescing in the French harbor of Cherbourg on June 19, 1864. In the greatest ship-to-ship combat of the Civil War the U.S.S. *Kearsarge*, under Captain John A. Winslow, sank the great nemesis of Union shipping. Semmes is depicted in bronze in uniform with a bas-relief of the steam cruiser *Alabama*.

Montgomery

32 Alabama State Capitol (site)

600 Dexter Avenue, 334-242-3900; Mon–Sat 9–4, Sun 12–4. Free.

This brick building with the 97-foot dome is considered one of the finest Greek Revival buildings in America. The Senate Chamber was the setting for the birth of the Confederacy on February 8, 1861, as Jefferson Davis of Mississippi was chosen as president of the new nation. From here Davis dispatched the ominous telegram, "Fire on Fort Sumter!"

On the front steps is a six-pointed bronze star where Davis stood while Howell Cobb administered the oath of office. Inside, the Senate Chamber has been restored to its Civil War appearance. Trees from battlefields where Alabama men fought grow on the north lawn; the *Confederate Monument* to Alabama sailors and soldiers, with a cornerstone laid by Jefferson Davis on April 26, 1886, was unveiled on December 7, 1898, and designed by Gorda Doud of Montgomery. On the south lawn is a bronze statue of Allen Wyeth, Confederate surgeon, by Gutzon Borglum, and on the terrace off the Capitol steps is a nine-foot bronze of Davis.

33 Alabama War Memorial (mem)

Jackson and Monroe streets, 334-262-6638; Mon–Fri, 8–4:30. Free.

The memorial recognizes the Alabamians who fought in American wars. The Hall of Honor recognizes state natives awarded the Congressional Medal of Honor.

34 First White House of the Confederacy (site)

644 Washington Avenue, 334-242-1861; Mon–Fri, 8–4:30. Free.

President and Mrs. Davis lived in this house, originally at the southwest corner of Bibb and Lee streets, from March 4, 1861, until Richmond became the new capital of the Confederate States of America. The building was moved to its present site, across from the state capitol, in 1921.

The two-story, white frame house is now a Confederate museum with many rare Confederate artifacts, including General Lee's compass. Davis's sword is among the Davis family's personal belongings on display.

35 St. John's Episcopal Church (site)

113 Madison Street, 334-262-1937; Mon–Fri, 8–4 and Sun, 6:45–noon. Free.

After this Gothic-style church was constructed in 1855, the old St. John's (1837) was donated to the Negro Episcopalians, which meant the new St.

John's was built without the usual slave gallery. Confederate president Jefferson Davis rented a pew in the church; a bronze tablet marks his spot of worship. Women met here to sew for soldiers during the war.

36 State Archives and History Museum (col)

624 Washington Avenue, 334-242-4363; Mon–Fri 8–5, Sat 9–5. Free.

The treatment of Alabama history includes many references to the Civil War, including portraits, regimental flags, and the Bible with which Jefferson Davis took the oath of office in becoming president of the Confederacy.

Mountain Creek

37 Confederate Memorial Park (site)

437 County Road 63, just off Route 31, 205-755-1990.

As the nineteenth century closed, Alabama counted over 2,000 survivors of the war that had ended 35 years earlier. Many were living a meager existence and Jefferson Manley Falkner, a Montgomery attorney and Confederate veteran, set out to give more than paltry state pensions to these veterans. Due to his efforts, Alabama's only Confederate veterans home opened in 1902 with a population limited to 100. At Memorial Hall veterans and their wives received housing and medical care, and for many it was a place to die in dignity. In June 1934 the last veteran at the home died, leaving just seven widows as residents. The home was officially closed on October 31, 1939.

In the 102-acre park are two original cemeteries where 313 Confederate soldiers and their wives are buried. A museum houses artifacts from the Old Soldiers' Home and a large collection of uniforms, weapons, and other memorabilia.

Ozark

38 Confederate Soldier (mem)

Dale County Courthouse, Union Avenue.

On the outside lawn is an Italian marble statue of a young soldier facing the north, erected on top of a monument dedicated to the memory of Dale County Confederate soldiers.

Selma

39 Battle of Selma (site)

212 Pine Needle Drive, 800-45-SELMA.

The Selma arsenal, the second largest in the Confederacy, once covered three square blocks and employed 10,000 men. The Confederate navy yard produced the ironclads *Tenneseee, Gaines, Morgan, Selma,* and many other warships. The Union, however, did not reach this tempting target until the war was nearly over when General James H. Wilson and 13,500 cavalry and mounted infantry invaded Alabama. The Selma defense, such as it was, numbered only 2,000—mostly old men and boys. On April 2, 1865, the town was overrun.

Reenactment: Selma's historic district features over 1,250 structures, many with a Civil War story to tell. Walking tours are available. An authentic Civil War camp and reenactments take place for four days each April.

40 Old Depot Museum (col)

Water Avenue and Martin Luther King Jr. Street, 334-874-2197; Mon–Sat 10–4, Sun 2–5. Admission charged.

The artifacts in this 1891 restored brick railroad building include a Civil War room featuring munitions from the Greater Confederate Naval Ordnance Works.

41 Ruins of Cahawba (site)

Route 9, 334-872-8058; Daily, 8–5. Free.

Cahawba was the first state capital of Alabama, serving as the seat of government from 1820 to 1826. Perched at the confluence of the Alabama and Cahawba rivers, the town was plagued by flooding, which prompted the legislature to move to Tuscaloosa. Within weeks Cahawba was nearly abandoned.

A mid-century town renaissance was halted during the Civil War when the Confederate government seized Cahawba's railroad, tore up the iron rails, and used them to extend a nearby rail line. In exchange, a lice-infested prison for 3,000 Union soldiers was established in the center of town. In 1865 a flood inundated Cahawba, turning it into a ghost town once again.

Today nature has reclaimed most of the old capital. There are interpretive signs in the deserted streets marking building sites and ruins. Although the bodies of the prisoners who died here have been disinterred from the old cemetery, their names and regiments are listed on markers. A short, half-mile nature trail explains how native plants were used to survive the Union blockade during the war and even make the Confederate gray dye for uniforms.

Spanish Fort

42 Historic Blakely State Park (site)

33707 State Highway 225, 205-626-0798; Daily, 9–5. Admission charged.

As the Confederacy weakened, Union general Edward R. S. Canby brought 32,000 troops to bear against a force of 2,800 organized by Brigadier

General Randall Lee Gibson. The siege of Mobile began on March 25, 1865, and despite the formidable earthworks around the city, the outcome was inevitable. This last major operation of the Civil War ended on April 9, just hours after Lee had surrendered his army of Northern Virginia.

Reenactment: On the 3,800-acre site are some of the best-preserved Civil War breastworks in the country, alongside earthen forts and old rifle pits. Trails dissect the site, the largest National Register Site east of the Mississippi. The battle, at the second highest point on the coast between Alabama and Maine, is reenacted the first weekend in April.

Stevenson

43 Stevenson Railroad Depot Museum (col)

Route 117, 205-437-3012; Apr–Dec: daily, 9–5; other times: Mon–Fri, 9–5. Free.

With its location at a railroad junction, Stevenson was considered one of the seven most important cities of the South during the Civil War. Military memorabilia is included among the railroad exhibits. Stevenson Depot Days take place in early June.

Tuscaloosa

44 Gorgas House (site)

Capstone Drive, University of Alabama, 205-348-5906. Tues–Fri 10–4, Sat 10–3, Sun 2–4. Free.

The University of Alabama served the Confederacy as a training center for cadets, making it a target for invading Union troops. When the raiders departed, only four buildings were left standing: the President's Mansion, the Round House, the Old Observatory and the Gorgas House. The Gorgas House, built in 1829 and the first permanent building on campus, is the only one open to the public. Today it is a museum.

Union Springs

45 Confederate Monument (mem)

Hardaway and North Prairie streets.

The marble shaft was erected by the United Daughters of the Confederacy.

46 Log Cabin Museum and Confederate Cemetery (site)

Route 82. Free.

The cemetery includes Union and Confederate soldiers next to this 1829 log cabin. Tours are occasionally led by the original builder's descendants.

Valley Head

47 Winston Place (site)

Church Street, 205-635-6381.

The Winston House was built by Dr. John S. Gardner, who attempted to build a silk industry in the area in the early nineteenth century. He planted mulberry trees and imported silkworms, but the climate proved unsuitable for the venture. His home was a headquarters in 1863 for Union colonel Jefferson C. Davis, a cousin of the Confederate president from Kentucky.

Local legend tells us that an old-timer who stumbled into the Union encampment became confused when he learned that Jeff Davis was in charge of the unit. The grizzled veteran cornered the colonel and demanded, "Which pays you the most? Colonelin' the Bluecoats or presidentin' the Confederates?"

The Winston House is now a bed-and-breakfast, but tours can be arranged with the owners.

Arizona

Civil War Status: Part of the New Mexico Territory; Territory of Arizona created 1863
1860 Population: 93,516
Troops Provided: Negligible outside territory
Known Scenes of Action: 75

Fort Defiance

48 Fort Defiance (site)

Route 264.

Fort Defiance, at the mouth of Blue Canyon, was established in 1851 to engage the Navajo nation but was abandoned at the outbreak of the Civil War. The Navajos took advantage of the diminished garrison, and the Navajo wars flared up. Colonel Kit Carson reactivated the fort in 1863 to use it as a base for the Union army. Today the Navajos continue their traditional ways of life on this Indian reservation.

Picacho Peak

49 Battle of Picacho Pass (site)

I-10, Exit 219; northwest of Tucson; 520-466-3183.

In February 1862 a troop of Texas Confederates under Captain Sherod Hunter reached southern-sympathizing Tucson. By April California infantry and cavalry under Federal colonel James H. Carleton were concentrated at Fort Yuma. Meanwhile Hunter was extending his raids deeper into the surrounding desert.

On April 15 a detachment of Union cavalry under Lieutenant James Barrett met the Texans in Picacho Pass. Scarcely a dozen soldiers from each side tangled in the pass. Barrett and two of his men were killed, but the Confederates retreated before advancing Federal reinforcements. The engagement was the only direct confrontation in the territory that would become Arizona. Picacho Pass was the "Farthest Western Battle" of the Civil War.

Reenactment: The battle site is marked by plaques on the site. A Confederate monument is north of the battlefield, dedicated to Captain Hunter's Arizona volunteers. The cavalry clash is restaged on the second weekend in March every year with members of the North and South in costume. Demonstrations of Civil War life are also presented.

Yuma

50 Yuma Quartermaster Depot State Historic Park (site)

2nd Avenue, behind Yuma City Hall; 602-343-2500; Daily 10–5. Admission charged.

From 1864 to 1883, the U.S. Army was supplied from the quartermaster depot located here. Six restored buildings stand on the site that once supplied forts and posts throughout the Southwest, beginning during the Civil War.

Arkansas

Civil War Status: Confederacy; seceded from the Union on May 16, 1861
1860 Population: 435,450
Troops Provided: 50,000
Known Scenes of Action: 771

Civil War Timeline
March 6–8, 1862: Battle of Pea Ridge
December 7, 1862: Battle of Prairie Grove
January 9–11, 1863: Battle of Arkansas Post
March 23–May 3, 1864: Camden Expedition
April 30, 1864: Battle of Jenkins' Ferry
August 29, 1864: Price's raids begin

Arkadelphia

51 Iron Kettle (mem)
Henderson State University.

An old Indian salt works was obtained in barter by John Hemphill in 1811. He worked the mine until better deposits found in Louisiana led to its abandonment in 1850. The salt works were resurrected by the urgent Confederate need for salt. New wells were drilled and drying pans were made out of old steamboat boilers with slaves working day and night. Still, the supply was not adequate, and the operation ended with Union General Frederick Steele's occupation of the area. An old iron kettle used in the Hemphill Salt Works sits on the Henderson State campus.

Cabot

52 Confederate Monument (mem)
Camp Nelson Cemetery; Route 89 South.

This historic monument at the graveyard honors the soldiers of Arkansas and Texas who served in the Confederacy and Camp Nelson.

Camden

53 Confederate Cemetery (site)
North Adams Avenue.

A tall marble shaft surrounded by seven rows of simple graves honors Confederate soldiers from the Battles of Poison Spring and Jenkins' Ferry. Most of the headstones are simply inscribed: "Unknown Confederate Soldier." Other graves scattered throughout the cemetery are marked with little iron stars; these are graves of Confederate veterans.

54 Fort Lookout (site)
North end of Monroe Street.

Camden, on the Ouachita River, was a key port for the shipping of cotton, which became scarce in the North immediately after the outbreak of the war. To protect the river town nine earthen forts were arranged in a semicircle around town, beginning and ending at the river. When Camden finally fell into Union hands, the forts were abandoned rather than defended.

On a bluff overlooking the river, Fort Lookout is the only fort to remain. The rifle trenches and cannon pits remain much as they were constructed, unmarred by plow and asphalt.

55 McCollum-Chidester House (site)
926 Washington Street; 501-836-9243; Apr–Oct: Wed–Sat, 9–4. Admission charged.

Once a stagecoach stop, this 1847 house was built by Peter McCollum and sold to Colonel John T. Chidester a decade later. During the Civil War the house was occupied by Union general Frederick Steele. Bullet scars from Confederate snipers are still visible. Now the building is the home of the

Ouachita County Historical Society; mementos from the war are on display.

56 Poison Spring Battlefield State Park
(site)
Route 76, west of town; 501-685-2748.

With his men on half-rations going on three weeks in the Red River Campaign, Union general Frederick Steele sent a foraging train of 198 wagons down the Upper Washington Road to collect corn and foodstuffs. The Confederates, learning of the movement, gathered some 3,100 cavalry and eight cannon under brigadier generals Samuel B. Maxey and John S. Marmaduke. They swept down on the front and south flank of the unwieldy train about 14 miles west of Camden on April 18, 1864. The Federal force of less than 1,200 men was routed and all 198 wagons lost. The loss of these supplies helped to hasten Steele's retreat back to his base in Little Rock.

Reenactment: Now a historic state park, the battlefield area features interpretive markers and trails. In early spring the Battle of Poison Spring is reenacted on a weekend. Artifacts and camp life are demonstrated.

57 White Oak Lake State Park (site)
Route 24; 501-685-2748.

Here, west of town, Union troops camped prior to occupying Camden.

Fayetteville

58 Confederate Memorial (mem)
Confederate Cemetery; Rock Street.

The monument was dedicated on June 10, 1897. The sculpture is a bronze Confederate soldier at rest; the stone base pays tribute to action in four states: Arkansas, Missouri, Louisiana and Texas.

59 Headquarters House (site)
118 East Dickson Street; 501-521-2970; Apr–Dec: Tues–Sat, 1–4; other times: Tues–Fri, 1–4. Free.

Built in 1853 by Jonas Tebbetts, this house served as a command center for both sides during the Civil War and was dubbed "Headquarters House" when the Washington County Historical Society acquired it in 1967. Tebbetts was an Arkansas judge, originally from New Hampshire, who maintained his Union sympathies. Arrested as a spy, he was awaiting court-martial in Fort Smith when friends engineered his release. He returned to Fayetteville, then under Union control, and was spirited away to Missouri in a Union ambulance. He was not destined to ever live in his Arkansas home again.

Much of the action in the Battle of Fayetteville took place across the street. Two exterior doors in the Tebbetts' home were damaged by stray musket balls, and the damage is still visible in the interior woodwork.

Fordyce

60 Marks' Mills Battlefield (site)
Routes 97 and 8.

On April 25, 1864, the Confederates here intercepted a Federal supply wagon train, the second within a week during the Red River Campaign. As at Poison Springs, the Union advance was blocked and ambushed by General James F. Fagan, who captured the 240-wagon supply train and many prisoners. Included in the bounty were 1,500 horses and mules, ambulances, and valuable official reports concerning the Union army, which now had to abandon its plans to attack Shreveport, Louisiana.

Reenactment: Trails with interpretive markers wind through this state historic park, telling the tale of the five-hour Confederate victory. A commemorative reenactment of the Battle of Marks' Mills is staged on the weekend closest to the anniversary date in late April. Guest speakers explain why the battle happened, who fought, and what the outcome was. Reenactors fight the skirmish.

Fort Smith

61 Confederate Monument (mem)
Sebastian County Courthouse; East Side of 6th Street between Parker and Rogers avenues.

A tall granite shaft, topped by a bronze statue of an infantryman, was placed on the courthouse lawn in Fort Smith in memory of the Confederacy. The War Department officials originally objected to its installation at the national cemetery because it did not have any Federal names inscribed on it.

62 Fort Smith National Cemetery (site)
522 Garland and South 6th streets; 501-783-5345.

Overlooking the Poteau River, this burial ground was set aside in 1832 for soldiers at Fort Smith. It became a national cemetery in 1867. Both Confederate and Union dead are buried here.

63 Fort Smith National Historic Site
(site)
Rogers Avenue at 3rd Street; 501-783-3961; Daily, 9–5. Admission charged.

Fort Smith was established in 1817 to maintain peace between settlers and native tribes in the Arkansas wilderness. The first fort was abandoned in 1824, but by the time of the Civil War it was in use again as a supply depot, garrisoned first by

Confederate and then by Union troops. By 1871 it could no longer effectively supply the expanding frontier and the Federal Court for the Western District of Arkansas moved in, presided over by Judge Isaac Parker. From 1875 to 1896 "Hanging Judge" Parker presided over 13,000 cases and sentenced 160 felons to be hanged. Of those sentenced, 79 men died on the gallows.

The original foundations of the 1817 fort remain; in the northern section of the site is the commissary storehouse from which supplies were dispensed during the war. "Hanging Judge" Parker's courtroom and the gallows are reproduced.

Gillett

64 Arkansas Post National Memorial (site)

Route 169 off Route 165, south of town.

Here was the first permanent French settlement on the lower Mississippi, established by de Tonti in 1686. The Confederates erected Fort Hindman here in 1862. General John McClernand massed 29,000 Union soldiers, and David Dixon Porter led Union gunboats against the fort in early 1863. After three-and-a-half hours on January 11, Fort Hindman, with less than 5,000 guardians, displayed the white flag.

The assault was unauthorized and did little to aid Grant's campaign at Vicksburg, but the community was destroyed. The battlefield is gone, but a few scruffy rifle pits have remained.

Helena

65 Confederate Military Cemetery (site)

1801 Holly Street; 501-338-8327.

Helena was occupied by Federal general Samuel Curtis and on July 4, 1862, the Confederates under generals T. H. Holmes, J. S. Marmaduke, and L. M. Walker vainly attacked Curtis in an effort to divert forces from the siege of Vicksburg. Ill feeling arose between Marmaduke and Walker after the Battle of Helena, resulting in a duel two months later in Little Rock. Walker was killed. The cemetery on Crowley's Ridge at the northern boundary of town provides a panoramic view of the Mississippi River.

66 Philips County Library and Museum (col)

Porter and Pecan streets; 501-338-7790; Mon–Fri 1:30–4:30, Sat 10–12 and 1–4. Free.

The town gave seven generals to the Confederacy, most prominent among them Thomas C. Hindman and Patrick R. Cleburne. The two met as nurses in 1855, battling a yellow fever epidemic that was gripping Helena, and became fast friends.

Both led colorful lives and died violently. Hindman refused to surrender his army at Bentonville, North Carolina, in 1862 and fled to Mexico for a year. In 1868 an unknown assailant shot him as he bent over his mother's bed.

Cleburne enlisted as a private in the Yell Rifles and was quickly breveted to general. His death at Franklin, Tennessee, was described in the *Tennessee Historical Magazine* in January of 1931: "Pat Cleburne died on one of the bloodiest battlefields of Christendom in his stocking feet because as he rode into battle that morning he saw one of his Irish boys from Little Rock tramping barefooted over the frozen furrows of a wintry cornfield and leaving tracks of blood behind him. So he drew off his boots and bade the soldier put them on, and fifteen minutes later he went to his God in his stocking feet."

The museum contains relics of Helena's colorful Civil War past as well as an artwork collection.

Hot Springs

67 Confederate Memorial (mem)

Landmark Plaza; Market and Ouachita streets and Central Avenue.

The marble statue of the Confederate soldier at rest was erected by the Hot Springs chapter of the United Daughters of the Confederacy on June 2, 1934.

Reenactment: At Hot Springs National Park, off Route 7, a Civil War weekend is held during July, commemorating the period when Hot Springs was briefly the state capital. The program features reenactors and discussions.

Jacksonport

68 Jacksonport State Park (site)

Route 67; 501-523-2143; Park: daily; Museum: Wed–Sat, 9–5, Sun, 1–5. Admission charged for museum.

Jacksonport sits strategically near both the Mississippi and Arkansas rivers and was occupied by both Confederate and Union troops during the Civil War. Five generals set up headquarters in town at one time or another. The Jacksonport courthouse features a War Memorial Room.

Leola

69 Jenkins' Ferry State Park (site)

Route 46.

When his Red River expedition was doomed by inadequate supplies and facing starvation, General Frederick Steele turned his command north of Camden and back to his base in Little Rock. He chose the Camden Trail, which crossed the Saline

River at Jenkins' Ferry. He used an India rubber pontoon bridge to transport his supplies through the swampy terrain. The heavy wagons bogged down, and others had difficulty traversing the poor roads, making the retreat a perfect target for Confederate ambush.

The attack came on April 29, 1864. Steele managed to maneuver most of his army away from the sea of mud caused by three days of rain, but he was forced to abandon his supply train, leaving burning wagons along the road. He arrived back in Little Rock on May 3. His Red River fiasco had cost him 635 wagons, 2,500 mules and horses, and 2,750 casualties. The southwestern region of Arkansas remained in Confederate hands until the end of the war.

The state park recounts the events of the final days of the Red River Campaign; nearby in Sheridan the Grant County Museum describes the swampy battle in more detail.

Little Rock

70 Lady Baxter (mem)
War Memorial Building; Markham Street facing Center Street.

This imposing iron cannon was brought from New Orleans in 1861 to defend Little Rock against a Union attack that was not made until 1863.

71 Monument to Confederate Women (mem)
Arkansas State Capitol; West 7th and Marshall streets.

The Confederate women of Arkansas received this memorial on April 30, 1913. J. Otto Schweizer designed the bronze sculpture of a family of four. The mother is seated and clutching the uniformed father's hand; the little boy looks on, and the daughter is crying. The third floor of the capitol is the Arkansas State History Museum, displaying flags and relics.

72 Mount Holly Cemetery (site)
14th and Broadway streets.

David Owen Dodd was buried here after being hanged on January 8, 1864. Dodd, a 17-year-old Confederate dispatcher who was captured as a spy, was offered his freedom in exchange for revealing his contact. He refused and was executed. Many other Arkansas notables rest here, under ponderous tall columns and monuments. The graveyard is known as the "Westminster of Arkansas."

73 Museum of Science and History (col)
MacArthur Park; 501-324-9231; Mon–Sat 9–4:30, Sun 1–4:30. Admission charged.

The building dates back to 1836, the year Arkansas became a state. In 1842 the Tower Building was completed, and today it is all that remains of the structure used originally as an arsenal. In the days before the Civil War, Federal troops from Kansas were sent to garrison the arsenal. Rumors flew wildly that the guns of the arsenal were fixed on the town in an effort to intimidate the secessionist sympathizers.

Finally, when bands of armed citizens began organizing to take the arsenal, the governor demanded its surrender; and the Federal troops left on February 12, 1861. Two years later General Frederick Steele marched into Little Rock and took the arsenal for the United States again.

74 National Cemetery (site)
2523 Confederate Boulevard; 501-324-6401.

Established in 1866, this graveyard holds the remains of 22,000 United States veterans, beginning with those who fell in the Civil War.

75 Old State House (site)
300 West Markham Street; 501-324-9685; Mon–Sat 9–5, Sun 1–5. Free.

The Old State House now serves as an Arkansas history museum but was once the original capitol from 1836 until 1911. Union general Frederick Steele quartered his army in the State House during the Federal occupation of the city.

76 Albert Pike Home (site)
411 East 7th Street.

Albert Pike built this home in 1840. His diverse career ranged from exploration, journalism, and poetry, to the military. During the Civil War he served as Indian commissioner for the Confederacy and led troops from the Five Nations into the Battle of Pea Ridge. Pike quarreled with his superiors and condemned them in a letter of resignation to the Confederate Congress. What happened to him after that is not known, but he is believed to have settled along the Little Missouri River where the Albert Pike Recreational Area is today. His original home is now a retirement village.

Lonoke

77 Camp Nelson Confederate Cemetery (site)
Cherry Road; 501-676-6403.

A measles epidemic swept through a camp of Texas Confederates near Old Austin, Arkansas, causing the deaths of several hundred men. The soldiers were buried near the encampment, but in 1907 funds were appropriated to move the remains into the area that became the cemetery. A monument at the cemetery tells their story.

Monticello

78 Confederate Monument (mem)

Oakland Cemetery; Hyatt and West Oakland streets.

This marble sculpture, dedicated in 1914, commemorates the service of Drew County soldiers to the Confederate States of America.

North Little Rock

79 The Old Mill (site)

Lakeshore and Fairway streets; 800-643-4690.

This grist mill was filmed in the opening scenes of the beloved Civil War–era movie, *Gone with the Wind*, released in 1939. Also the site of the unveiling of the *Gone with the Wind* commemorative stamp, it is believed to be the only remaining structure from the movie.

Prairie Grove

80 Prairie Grove Battlefield State Park (site)

Route 62, east of town; 501-846-2990; Park: daily, 8–10 P.M.; Museum: daily, 8–5. Admission charged.

In late 1862 both armies vied for control of northwestern Arkansas. Confederate general Thomas Hindman engaged Union general James F. Blount in a brief skirmish at Cane Hill on November 28. Blount called for reinforcements and General Francis J. Herron marched down from Springfield, only to be met here on December 7 by Hindman, who had led a march over the mountains to annihilate the reinforcements before they could reach the main army.

Both sides claimed victory as more than 2,500 troops fell during the fighting. Hindman saw triumph because the enemy fled beyond the prairie, leaving the colors of several regiments in his hands. After lack of food and ammunition forced the Confederates to retreat four days later, Herron was able to say, "The victory is more complete and decisive than I imagined."

About 130 acres of the battlefield have been preserved, including a 55-foot battle monument and the Borden House, the scene of the heaviest fighting. The Hindman Hall Museum houses the visitor center. Prairie Grove also offers a recreated village depicting the hill country heritage of the area in the mid-nineteenth century.

Reenactment: The pivotal battle is reenacted every other year in December.

Rogers

81 Pea Ridge National Military Park (site)

Route 62, ten miles northeast of town; 501-451-8122; Daily, 8–5. Admission charged.

On March 7, 1862, snow still covered the frozen ground when the Union Army of the Southwest, 10,500 troops under Brigadier General Samuel R. Curtis, clashed with 16,000 Confederates commanded by Major General Earl Van Dorn. The battle occurred on two separate battlefields: Leetown and Elkhorn Tavern.

The Union, most of whom were German and spoke no English, prevailed at Leetown, killing two Confederate generals, Ben McCullough and James I. McIntosh. The outcome at Elkhorn Tavern was less decisive, although the Southerners left the field under heavy Union artillery bombardment. When the Battle of Pea Ridge ended the next day, the state of Missouri was secure for the Union.

Van Dorn was to die a year later on May 8, 1863, killed by "a resident of Spring Hill, Dr. Peters, who stated in justification that Van Dorn had violated the sanctity of his home." Friends said that Van Dorn was shot in the back for political reasons.

Pea Ridge was the first battlefield west of the Mississippi River to be declared a national military park. It is also the largest. A self-guided seven-mile battlefield loop of the 4,300 acres begins at the visitor center, which also features a slide presentation and battle relics.

Rondo

82 Rondo Cemetery (site)

Route 237.

When the Federals threatened the temporary state capitol at Washington, the state records were moved to Rondo. The cemetery contains the graves of 85 unidentified Confederates belonging to a regiment decimated by disease while stationed at Rondo.

St. Francis

83 Chalk Bluff Park (site)

Route 62 north of town.

Skirmishing took place in this area during 1863 at the Missouri border. The park along the St. Francis River is listed on the National Register in remembrance of the fighting here.

Washington

84 Old Washington Historic State Park (site)

Route 4; 501-983-2684; Daily, 9–5. Admission charged.

Governor Harris Flanigin chose the Old Hempstead County Courthouse, built in 1836, as the Confederate capitol of Arkansas following the capture of Little Rock in 1863. This simple, two-story building on Franklin Street was restored by the United Daughters of the Confederacy in 1929. Established in 1973, Old Washington Historic State Park interprets the town's history from 1824 to 1875.

California

Civil War Status: Union
1860 Population: 379,994
Troops Provided: Negligible outside the state
Known Scenes of Action: 88

Lebec

85 Fort Tejon State Historic Park (site)

I-5, 3½ miles north of town; 805-248-6692; Daily, 10–4:30. Admission charged.

Fort Tejon is a restored U.S. Army dragoon post that was in use from 1854 to 1864. It was established to guard the pass through the Tehachapi Mountains. This was the terminus for the U.S. Camel Corps, an experimental group of 25 camels used to haul supplies from San Antonio. Of the 15 officers who served at the garrison, eight became Union generals and seven Confederate generals. There is a museum on the grounds.

Reenactment: Civil War battles are reenacted on the third Sunday of every month; military demonstrations are given the day before.

Sacramento

86 State Capitol (mem)

Between 10th and 15th, L and N streets; 916-324-0333; Daily, 9–5. Free.

It is estimated that 88 military engagements took place in California, mainly against Indians. Capitol Park has a collection of trees from around the world, including some transplanted from Civil War battlefields. A memorial marker in the park honors Californians who served in both armies.

San Francisco

87 Fort Point National Historic Site (site)

South end of Golden Gate Bridge, off Lincoln Boulevard; 415-556-1693; Wed–Sun, 10–5. Free.

The fort was completed by the United States

Army in 1861 and was reinforced after the bombing of Fort Sumter, from whose design it heavily borrowed. It was once the largest defensive installation on the Pacific Coast.

88 Lincoln Statue (mem)

City Hall; Grove Street and Van Ness Avenue.

Haig Patigan's reflective statue of a grave Lincoln was presented to the city on February 12, 1913, to replace a previous monument destroyed in the great earthquake and fire of 1906.

89 Union Square (site)

Post and Leavenworth streets.

The main commercial district is so named for the series of spirited pro–Union demonstrations staged here on eve of the Civil War.

Colorado

Civil War Status: Colorado Territory established February 28, 1861
1860 Population: 34,277
Troops Provided: Negligible outside territory
Known Scenes of Action: fewer than 50

Chivington

90 Sand Creek Massacre (site)

Off Route 96, north of town.

With many of the Federal soldiers withdrawn from the frontier to fight the Civil War, the Plains tribes seized the opportunity to attack settlers and wagon trains. Sporadic forays continued despite the signing of a treaty with the Cheyenne and Arapaho at Fort Lyon, in which the two tribes agreed to cede all lands east of the mountains between Arkansas and the Platee in return for $450,000 to be paid in five yearly installments. The United States government failed to fulfill the treaty obligations, which resulted in starvation among the Indians and led to even more attacks.

Conditions grew steadily worse until the summer of 1864 when Territorial Governor John Evans called a grand council of Indian chiefs to settle the difficulties. Black Kettle, chief of the Cheyenne, insisted the raiding was being done by the Sioux and Comanche, together with a few irresponsible members of his tribe, and asserted there was no offensive alliance between his people and the Arapaho. While admitting that most of the raiding was done by Sioux, the white leaders blamed the two tribes that had signed the peace treaty. A deadlock resulted and Evans turned the matter over to the military.

Colonel John Chivington ordered all Plains tribes to report to the nearest garrison to surrender. According to one account, Black Kettle and his Cheyenne soon appeared at the post to surrender under Chivington's terms. Others have questioned Black Kettle's good faith, asserting that he was in constant contact with the rampaging tribes and had merely adopted the oft-practiced Indian strategy of surrendering during the cold season while preparing to take to the war trail in the spring. In any event, Major Scott J. Anthony ordered the band away from the fort saying that he could no longer feed them.

Meanwhile, the 100-day recruits of the Third Regiment in Denver had grown bored with camp life. They hungered for action on the Plains and got it when Chivington suddenly and secretly marched them south in a blizzard. On the way they were joined by 125 men of the First Colorado Cavalry. On November 28, 1864, they reached Fort Lyon. Chivington threw a cordon around the post so word of their arrival would not leak out. Anthony told Chivington that hostile Arapaho were in a village on Sand Creek.

His force was augmented by 125 more First Colorado Cavalrymen and a howitzer battery, bringing the total number of soldiers to 900. Chivington marched north that same evening, and at dawn his troops closed in upon the sleeping village and opened fire. Chivington had given orders that no prisoners were to be taken, and his orders were obeyed. An Indian interpreter, who was in the camp at the time, later testified that of the 650 Indians in the encampment, 450 were women and children. The exact number of Indians killed has never been determined — estimates range from 150 to 500, but the losses were unquestionably heavy. The majority of the victims were old men, women, and children who were shot down indiscriminately. Black Kettle was killed. Left Hand, a head chief of the Arapaho, was slain in front of his tent as he stood with folded arms defying his foes. By midafternoon the troopers, suffering ten killed and 38 wounded, had broken all resistance, and that night they burned the village.

The Sand Creek massacre aroused such a countrywide storm of protest that a Senatorial investigation began in January 1865. Chivington was cited for court-martial but was never brought to trial. Testimony before the committee revealed that the bodies of slain Indians, women and men alike, had been horribly mutilated by the soldiers. For his part Chivington, a former minister, stated in an official report that he had attacked because he believed the Indians in the camp were hostile. He added that in

his opinion most of the women and children escaped.

Far from subduing the Indians, the massacre at Sand Creek incited frenzied retaliation. Eventually the government condemned the army action and paid retribution to the survivors. But Sand Creek remained one of the gravest results of the drain of Federal troops from the Indian territories. A marker on the ridge overlooks the site of the Indian encampment.

Denver

91 Colorado State Capitol (mem)

East 14th and East Colfax streets.

The Colorado Territory was established on February 28, 1861, and was only six weeks old when the war started. It was not even known that the United States was splintered until May, and the first legislature convened in Denver in August, naming Colorado City as its capital. The legislature convened once in 1862 and went back to Denver; statehood was not achieved for the Centennial State until 1876.

The cornerstone of this building was laid on July 4, 1890, and the structure was completed in 1907. Two years later the bronze soldier by Jack Howland was dedicated to the Colorado soldiers from both sides who died in the Civil War. Two Civil War cannons flank the statue. Also on the lawn are 50 varieties of trees, including two black walnuts that came from the home of Abraham Lincoln.

The west steps of the capitol are exactly 5,280 feet above sea level in the Mile High City.

Las Animas

92 Boggsville (site)

Route 101, two miles south of town.

Colonel Kit Carson died here on May 23, 1868, at the age of 58; his third wife, Maria Josefa Jaramillo, had died a month earlier after giving birth to a daughter. Carson was buried here, but later his remains were removed to Taos, New Mexico, as he had requested. The building he died in at Boggsville, the first nonfortified settlement in southeastern Colorado, is now a museum.

Connecticut

Civil War Status: Union
1860 Population: 460,147
Troops Provided: 50,000

Ansonia

93 Soldiers' Monument (mem)

Pine Grove Cemetery; 71 Howard Avenue.
Ansonia's tribute to her sons in the Civil War was sculpted by M. J. Walsh and dedicated on May 30, 1876. A bronze artilleryman surveys the field from a granite base.

Berlin

94 Soldiers' Monument (mem)

Kensington Congregational Church; 312 Percival Avenue.
The inscription on a bronze plaque reads: "First monument in the United States to be dedicated to the soldiers of the Civil War." The memorial was conceived by Reverend Charles Hilliard, minister of Kensington, and the stone was quarried in March of 1863 — four months before Gettysburg. Nelson Augustus Moore sculpted the obelisk of Portland brownstone, which was dedicated on July 28, 1863. Names were added later.

95 War Memorial (mem)

Worthington Ridge and Farmington Avenue.
The south side of this 40-foot tall granite obelisk is devoted to the Civil War. A bronze eagle surmounting the shaft is believed to have been sculpted by Charles Henry Niehaus. It was unveiled on Armistice Day, November 11, 1920.

Bristol

96 Soldiers' Monument (mem)

West Cemetery; 49 Pound Street.
Bristol was the first town in Connecticut to erect a Civil War monument. The column crowned by an eagle in flight was dedicated on January 20, 1866, with detailed descriptions of the Bristol Civil War dead. Subscriptions as small as $1.00 built the $1,500 memorial.

Colchester

97 Soldiers' Monument (mem)

Village Green.
Unique among the legion of Civil War memorials that dot the New England landscape, this rendering of a Union soldier depicts an older man.

Cornwall

98 Sedgwick Monument (mem)

Route 43, Cornwall Hollow Road.
Native son Major General John Sedgwick was born in 1813. An able leader during the Union's Peninsular Campaign, Sedgwick was wounded at Antietam. He served under Ulysses S. Grant in the push toward Richmond in 1864 and was killed by a sniper at Spotsylvania on May 9. Grant called his loss "greater than a whole division."

Danbury

99 Civil War Monument (mem)

Main Street and West.
This memorial was erected in memory of the men from Danbury who served the Union cause.

100 Soldiers' and Sailors' Monument (mem)

Wooster Cemetery; Ellsworth Avenue.
Created from a design by Solon Borglum, this monument was dedicated to the unknown soldiers who fell in the Civil War.

Derby

101 Civil War Monument (mem)

Derby Green; 5th and Elizabeth streets.
This design by M. J. Walsh was executed and dedicated on July 4, 1877. It features a high granite pedestal with a life-size bronze soldier on it. When additional moneys were raised, the monument was remodeled and rededicated on July 4, 1883, in front of 8,000 people.

Hartford

102 Andersonville Boy (mem)

Bushnell Park.
Bela Lyon Pratt's bronze, a copy of which is also at the national cemetery in Andersonville, was dedicated in 1907. The inscription reads: "In memory of the men of Connecticut who suffered in Southern military prisons, 1861–1865." Two Farragut cannons, the Dahlgren guns, from the flagship *Hartford* are also in the park.

103 Soldiers' and Sailors' Memorial Arch (mem)

Trinity Street.
The arch was dedicated on September 17, 1886, to the memory of the men of Hartford who fell in the Civil War. Casper Buberl was the sculptor.

104 State Capitol (col)

Capitol Avenue and Trinity Street; 203-240-0222; Mon–Fri, 8–5. Free.
Inside the capitol are Civil War battle flags and historical relics, including the figurehead of Admiral

Farragut's flagship *Hartford*. On the grounds is the "Petersburg Express," a mortar used by the 1st Connecticut Heavy Artillery during the siege of Petersburg.

105 Harriet Beecher Stowe House (site)

73 Forest Street; 203-525-9317; June–Columbus Day and Dec: Mon–Sat 9:30–4, Sun 12–4; other times: closed Monday. Admission charged.

The author of the influential *Uncle Tom's Cabin* lived the last 23 years of her life in this Victorian cottage. *Uncle Tom's Cabin; or, Life Among the Lowly*, written between 1851 and 1855, fanned abolitionist sympathy. The restored home contains items that belonged to Stowe.

Litchfield

106 Mustered Out (mem)

West Cemetery; White's Woods Road and South Lake Street.

In 1894 the town of Litchfield set aside Soldiers' Lot in West Cemetery for the burial of soldiers not having lots of their own. This stone monument was erected the same year. The sculpture highlights a drum of the type used in military bands.

107 Stowe Birthplace (site)

Forman School.

Harriet Beecher Stowe, whose writings inflamed the nation's antislavery feelings, was born in this house on June 14, 1811. *Uncle Tom's Cabin* sold 300,000 copies in its first year.

Madison

108 Civil War Battles and Reenactment (mem)

Hammonasset Beach State Park; Route 1, two miles east of town.

Reenactment: Union and Confederate military and civilian camps, circa 1862, are established at Connecticut's largest waterfront park in remembrance of the Civil War. Music is provided by fife and drum corps.

Meridien

109 Meridien Soldiers' Monument (mem)

City Hall; 148 East Main Street.

More than 20,000 people attended the dedication of the 38-foot granite monument on June 18, 1873. The names of Meridien's soldiers who fell in some of the Civil War's greatest battles are inscribed. A Union soldier at rest surmounts the shaft.

Middletown

110 24th Regiment C. V. Monument (mem)

Washington Green.

Dedicated on October 20, 1904, by the members of the 24th Regiment, this monument lists the names of the unit. A bronze eagle is perched on a granite sphere at the top of a pedestal, sculpted by H. Hillard Smith.

New Haven

111 Broadway Civil War Monument (mem)

Christ Church Episcopal; 318 Elm Street.

A cylindrical shaft topped by an eagle is flanked by an infantryman readying his musket and by an artilleryman. Dedicated to Connecticut service in the Civil War, it was erected on June 16, 1905.

112 Cornelius Scranton Bushnell (mem)

Monitor Square.; Chapel Street, Derby and Winthrop avenues.

Following plans drawn up by John Ericsson, the memorial was erected to honor Bushnell, who led the efforts to build the Union ironclad warship *Monitor*.

113 Civil War Soldiers' and Sailors' Monument (mem)

East Rock Park; Davis Road.

East Rock Park covers 647 acres. The namesake rock is 359 feet high and more than a mile long. It affords a panoramic view of the park and of the Civil War Soldiers' and Sailors' Monument, dedicated in 1887.

114 Grove Street Cemetery (site)

Grove Street between Prospect and Ashmun streets.

Theodore Winthrop, one of the first officers killed in the Civil War, is buried here. Eli Whitney, whose invention of the cotton gin helped develop the industry in the South and whose work on the repeating rifle helped bring about its downfall, is also interred here.

115 Knight Hospital Monument (mem)

Evergreen Cemetery; 92 Winthrop Avenue.

The state of Connecticut dedicated this 26-foot stone monument in 1870 to the soldiers who died at Knight Hospital in memory of some of the major battles of the Civil War. The obelisk with crowning soldier is surrounded by 120 Civil War headstones.

116 Soldiers' Monument (mem)

St. Bernard Cemetery; St. Patrick's Avenue, Ella Grasso Boulevard, and Columbus Avenue.

This gray granite monument was erected by the state of Connecticut in honor of "her sons who offered their lives that the Union should not perish." Executed by Edward Pausch, it was purchased in 1889.

New London

117 21st Regiment Connecticut Volunteers (mem)

Williams Park; Hempstead Street.

Apparently intended for nearby Willimantic, this granite obelisk was instead dedicated here on September 5, 1898, to Connecticut's 21st Regiment.

Prospect

118 Civil War Monument (mem)

Village Green.

This memorial was dedicated by the state of Connecticut in recognition of Prospect's sacrifices during the Civil War. As in many Southern states, the number of Prospect men serving in the Union army was actually greater than that of the registered voters in town.

Seymour

119 Soldiers' Monument (mem)

French Memorial Park; Spruce Street.

This monument, dedicated on June 11, 1904, features a granite soldier at parade rest on a cylindrical base. Three of the four corner positions are occupied by cannons; the fourth is a triangular pile of cannonballs.

Southington

120 Soldiers' Monument (mem)

The Green; Main Street.

Carl Conrads created this figure of a Union soldier at parade rest from tan Westerly granite. It rests on a blue granite pedestal with four small columns at the corners. A crowd of 3,000, the largest assembly ever in Southington, gathered for the dedication on August 18, 1880.

Wallingford

121 Soldiers' Monument (mem)

Dutton Park; North Main Street.

A cylindrical base supporting a standing Union soldier was dedicated in October 1902 in memory of "the brave men who died that their country might live."

Waterbury

122 Soldiers' Monument (mem)

The Green; West Main Street.

The *Soldiers' Monument* was erected by George E. Bissell. Also on the Green of this onetime major brass center is a Civil War memorial with a statue of Liberty.

Westbrook

123 Military Historian's Headquarters-Museum (col)

North Main Street; 860-399-9460; Tues–Fri, 8–3:30. Free.

This museum contains one of America's largest collections of military uniforms, many from the Civil War. A research and video library is available.

Delaware

Civil War Status: Slave state remaining with the Union
1860 Population: 112,216
Troops Provided: Union — 10,000
Confederacy — none organized, but estimated at 1,000

Delaware City

124 Fort Delaware State Park (site)

Pea Patch Island; 302-834-7941; Summer: Wed–Fri 11–4, Sat–Sun 11–6; May and Sept: Sat–Sun 11–6. Admission charged.

The fort was constructed in 1859 to protect the entrance to the Delaware River. During the Civil War it became an overcrowded Federal prison. Its secure position in the center of the river was fortified by 131 guns.

Pea Patch Island is reached by a ten-minute boat ride in the warm months. Boats leave Delaware City, off Route 9. Trails wind through the old fort, which was garrisoned in the Spanish-American War in 1898. There is also an observation tower. A museum and audiovisual program detail the history of Fort Delaware.

Wilmington

125 Admiral Samuel Francis du Pont
(mem)

Rockford Park; Tower Road and West 19th Street.

Samuel Francis du Pont (1803–1865) rose to the rank of rear admiral, a rank created especially for him. Du Pont commanded the South Atlantic Blockading Squadron in September 1861 as the Union attempted to isolate the Confederacy from foreign trade. Later that year du Pont led a fleet of 77 vessels and 12,000 men, the largest naval expedition ever assembled in the United States, against the Confederacy in South Carolina. The Union victory achieved by du Pont in the Battle of Port Royal Sound established a menacing Union beachhead between Savannah and Charleston.

Samuel Francis du Pont was relieved of active duty at his own request on July 6, 1863, after failing to break through Confederate defenses at Charleston while following orders with which he did not agree. He served on military boards and commissions in Washington until his sudden death in Philadelphia on June 23, 1865.

The statue of Admiral du Pont was originally located in the du Pont Circle in Washington, D.C. when it was dedicated on December 20, 1884. The rendering by Launt Thompson of DuPont with binoculars at the ready was moved to Wilmington by the family, and a fountain was put in its place in Washington.

126 Hagley Museum (site)

Route 141; 302-658-2400; Mar 15–Dec 31: daily, 9:30–4:30; other times: Sat–Sun 9:30–4:30, Mon–Fri 1:30. Admission charged.

The museum preserves the original E. I. DuPont de Nemours & Co. mills, the largest supplier of military powder to the Union during the Civil War. More than four million pounds of powder were mixed along the Brandywine River, including DuPont Mammoth Powder, which gave Union guns the greatest range in history.

Shortly after the Southern secession, Henry du Pont, a West point graduate, canceled all orders from the state of Virginia and wrote a letter to President Lincoln affirming his support of the Union, although Delaware was a slave state. When the Confederacy sent representatives to the state capital in Dover, Governor Gove Saulsbury told them that, "Delaware was the first state to join the Union and it will be the last state to leave the Union." Delaware and the DuPont powder mills remained on the side of the Union.

The library at Hagley Museum includes the papers of Samuel Francis du Pont and Henry du Pont, who became major general in command of Delaware's volunteers but saw no action in the Civil War. An operating black powder mill has been restored.

127 Soldiers' and Sailors' Monument
(mem)

In triangle bounded by Delaware Avenue, West 14th Street, and North Broom Street.

The tall marble column was erected in memory of Delaware's dead during the Civil War. The monument was threatened by a sheriff's sale for an unpaid construction debt after it had been unveiled in 1871. The shaft, from one of the columns of the Pennsylvania Bank Building that was razed in Philadelphia in 1868, was saved by a local newspaper writer who raised enough money to release the monument. Harry Lowe sculpted the eagle group atop the monument, which remains the highest in Delaware.

District of Columbia

Civil War Status: Union capitol
1860 Population: 75,080
Troops Provided: estimated 5,000

Civil War Timeline
March 4, 1861: Abraham Lincoln is inaugurated 16th president of the United States
April 15, 1861: President Lincoln calls for 75,000 volunteers
July 12, 1864: Battle of Fort Stevens
November 8, 1864: Lincoln reelected president of the United States
April 14, 1865: Lincoln is shot by John Wilkes Booth at Ford's Theatre and dies the next day
May 23–24, 1865: Grand review of Federal armies

128 The Arts of Peace (mem)

West Potomac Park; Lincoln Memorial Circle, S.W.

At the entrance to Rock Creek Parkway stand two 17-foot heroic bronze statues on square pedestals, each decorated with 36 stars to represent the number of states at the close of the Civil War. Designed in 1925 by James Earle Fraser, the monuments were not executed until 1951.

129 Blair House (site)

1651 Pennsylvania Avenue, N.W.

Across the street from the White House is the

home of Missouri statesman Francis Blair, who served as postmaster general in President Lincoln's administration. The president offered Virginian Robert E. Lee command of the Union army in this house.

130 Capitol Prison (site)
1st and A Street, S.E.

This is the site of the Old Brick Capitol, used by Congress after the British burned the Capitol in 1814; during the Civil War it was known as Capitol Prison. Confederate spies Rose O'Neal Greenhow and Belle Boyd were imprisoned here. The controversial commandant of the Andersonville prison camp, Henry Wirz, was hanged in the courtyard, having been tried and sentenced for his maltreatment of prisoners.

131 Samuel P. Carter Monument (mem)
Oak Hill Cemetery; R and 30th streets, N.W.

This mortuary art done by stonecarvers marks the grave of Samuel P. Carter, a native of Carter County, Tennessee, who reportedly is the only American military officer ever to hold the highest ranks in both the United States Army and the United States Navy. During the Civil War he served simultaneously as a lieutenant commander in the navy and as a brevet major general in the army. Carter and a select group of other officers were known as "horse marines" for their dual duties.

132 Congressional Cemetery (site)
1801 E Street, S.E.; 202-543-0539.

The oldest national cemetery in the United States was established on 4½ acres in 1807. A self-guided walking tour brings into view some of the most historic funereal sculpture in Washington. Among those buried here are celebrated Civil War photographer Mathew B. Brady (in 1895), Lincoln assassination conspirators, and military officers.

The *Arsenal Monument* was funded by donations from citizens. The statue of a woman atop a 20-foot high rectangular shaft is dedicated to the memory of 21 women buried in a mass grave. An explosion of the Washington arsenal on June 18, 1864, obliterated the 100-foot long wooden shed where 108 women were working. This was the worst civil disaster in the city during the Civil War. The coroner found the factory superintendent culpable of negligence. President Lincoln was in the funeral procession of 150 carriages. The marble statue erected in 1867 is by Lot Flannery.

133 Frederick Douglass National Historic Site (site)
1411 W Street, S.E.; 202-426-5961; Summer: daily, 9–5; Winter: daily, 9–4. Free.

Frederick Douglass was born into slavery in 1818 and sent to Baltimore at the age of eight to be a house servant. As it was illegal to educate slaves, he stealthily learned how to read through a tedious series of clandestine acts. After escaping to freedom in 1838, he became America's leading black spokesman against slavery. This was his home in the final two decades of his life, until his death in 1895.

134 Fort De Russy (site)
Rock Creek Park; Oregon Avenue and Military Road.

Fort De Russy was a link in the chain of forts that defended the capital city during the Civil War. The remains can be reached by a foot trail.

135 Rear Admiral Samuel Francis du Pont Memorial Fountain
DuPont Circle; Massachusetts and Connecticut avenues, N.W.

Five important streets converge at what was originally called Pacific Circle. The name was changed in 1884 when Launt Thompson's bronze statue of Rear Admiral Samuel F. du Pont, the first Union naval hero for his daring capture of Fort Royal, South Carolina, was erected by Congress at the center of circle. The statue was replaced in 1921 by a stone fountain, a gift of the du Pont family. In the niches on the three sides of the marble shaft, supporting a shallow upper bowl, are sculptured seminude figures symbolizing sea, stars, and wind — the work of Daniel Chester French.

136 Emancipation Monument (mem)
Lincoln Park; East Capitol Street between 11th and 13th streets, N.E.

This life-size bronze shows Lincoln holding in his right hand the Emancipation Proclamation, his left hand raised over the shoulder of a crouching slave whose shackles have been broken. The $18,000 statue, executed by Thomas Ball, was paid for entirely by voluntary subscriptions of emancipated slaves. It was dedicated on April 14, 1876, the eleventh anniversary of Lincoln's assassination. Frederick Douglass was the main speaker at the occasion, and he described Lincoln as the only white man with whom he could speak for more than a few minutes and not draw attention to the fact that he was black. The statue was so popular that a duplicate was ordered for Boston within a year.

137 John Ericsson Monument (mem)
West Potomac Park; Independence Avenue and Ohio Drive, S.W.

This work by James Earle Fraser, a sculptured group carved from pink Milford granite, honors the Swedish-American builder of the Civil War ironclad *Monitor*. The seated figure of the designer is backed by a shaft of granite on which are sculpted three allegorical figures — the nude woman Vision, the Norse seaman Adventure, and the iron molder, Workmanship — grouped around the gnarled trunk of the Norse Tree of Life. The memorial, dedicated in 1926, is a gift of Scandinavian-American citizens. Contrary to the inscription, however, Ericsson can be credited with perfecting the screw propeller rather than with its invention.

138 Admiral David G. Farragut (mem)

Farragut Square; K Street between 16th and 17th streets, N.W.

The first monument in Washington to be dedicated to a naval war hero was executed by a celebrated woman sculptor, Vinnie Ream Hoxie. She worked for six years after Farragut's widow commissioned a bust of her late husband. The heroic bronze shows Farragut standing on a ship's deck, telescope at the ready. Unveiled on April 25, 1881, the monument faces south toward the admiral's birthplace in the East Tennessee Valley.

139 Ford's Theatre (site)

511 10th Street, N.W.; 202-347-4833; Daily, 9–5. Free.

After a harried day of post–Civil War meetings, including a cabinet meeting with General Grant in attendance, Abraham Lincoln left the White House to attend a light comedy, *Our American Cousin*, at Ford's Theatre. The president arrived in the middle of the play, and his appearance generated spontaneous cheering, which halted the performance. Shortly thereafter actor John Wilkes Booth entered the presidential box and fatally shot Abraham Lincoln in the head. Booth vaulted down from the box overlooking the right side of the stage, brandishing a knife to effect his escape. Booth hobbled into the night after injuring his leg in the leap.

Ford's Theatre has been restored to its 1860s appearance and is still an active theater. The basement features a museum containing cases chronicling Lincoln's life and detailing the events before and after the assassination. Among the artifacts is the single-shot derringer used by Booth.

140 Fort Stevens (site)

Piney Branch Road, N.W.

Originally named Fort Massachusetts, this garrison defended the north entrance to the capital. It was enlarged in 1862 and renamed in memory of Brigadier General Isaac Ingalls Stevens, who fell at Chantilly. The Union defenders repulsed a Confederate attack from General Jubal Early on July 11–12, 1864. Lincoln stood on a parapet watching the battle; this was the only time in American history an American president was under fire by enemy guns while in office. Fort Stevens was the site of the only battle within the limits of the District of Columbia. Beyond the remains are the graves of 41 Union soldiers who fell during the defense of the capital — the smallest national cemetery.

141 President James Abraham Garfield Memorial (mem)

1st Street and Maryland Avenue, S.W.

Like Lincoln, Garfield was born in a rural midwestern log cabin. He rapidly advanced to the rank of major general in the Civil War and was appointed chief of staff of the Army of the Cumberland. This nine-foot statue by John Quincy Adams Ward was erected by Garfield's former army in 1887, six years after President Garfield died of an assassin's bullet, having been in office for not even a year.

142 General Ulysses S. Grant Memorial (mem)

Union Square, east end of the Mall.

This is one of largest equestrian statues in the world and one of the most important in Washington. A relatively unknown sculptor, the self-taught Henry Merwin Shrady, was chosen from among 23 artists to honor the Civil War leader and eighteenth president. Shrady labored for 22 years to complete the final memorial, which has 12 horses, 11 soldiers, 4 lions and soldier groups from the artillery, infantry and cavalry. The Grant Memorial was dedicated on April 27, 1922, the hundredth anniversary of Grant's birth. Shrady was not among the dignitaries on hand for the unveiling — he had died two weeks earlier from strain and overwork.

143 Major General Winfield Scott Hancock (mem)

7th Street and Pennsylvania Avenue, N.W.

This massive equestrian statue of General Winfield Scott Hancock was executed by Henry Jackson Ellicott. It was dedicated in 1896 in a ceremony attended by every major official in Washington, honoring one of 15 officers who received the thanks of Congress for his service at Gettysburg. Hancock defused a Confederate assault on Union lines in Pennsylvania, despite being shot from his horse. His try for the presidency in 1880 fell short by only 10,000 votes.

144 Library of Congress (col)

Independence Avenue, S.E.; 202-707-5458; Mon–Fri, 8:30–5. Free.

The three-building complex, built in 1897, features more than 100 million items in its collection. Among the notable artifacts are the first and second drafts of Lincoln's Gettysburg Address.

145 Abraham Lincoln (mem)

D Street between 4th and 5th streets.

Immediately after the assassination of the president an emotional campaign raised funds for a monument. Lot Flannery, a Washington stonecarver who knew Lincoln, received the commission and created a simple, spontaneous expression of sorrow, which was dedicated on April 15, 1868, the third anniversary of Lincoln's death. It was the first public monument to Abraham Lincoln.

Its subsequent history was stormy. Originally in front of city hall, now the U.S. Courthouse, it was removed and stored when the courthouse was expanded. When the Lincoln Memorial was being created, officials did not want to display Flannery's rendering, protesting that it was the work of a "gravestone maker." But public outcry caused the first Lincoln memorial to be reerected.

146 Abe Lincoln, Rail Joiner
Negro Mother and Child (mem)

Department of the Interior Building; C Street between 18th and 19th streets, N.W.

In the interior courtyard are two bronzes from the Civil War era. In this least known of the four Lincoln statues in Washington, Louis Slobodkin portrayed the sixteenth president as a tall, lanky farmhand. Maurice Glickman created *Negro Mother and Child* in 1934; it is one of the few monuments to American blacks in the nation's capital.

147 Lincoln Memorial (mem)

The Mall; West Potomac Park at 23rd Street, N.W.; 202-619-7222; Daily, 8 A.M.–midnight. Free.

Daniel French Chester's seated portrait of Abraham Lincoln is possibly the most famous sculpture by any American artist. The sculpture of crystalline Georgia marble is constructed of 28 identical blocks so perfectly interlocked that the statue seems to be one huge monolith; stone cutters under Ernest C. Bairstow took four years to execute the memorial. It is 19 feet high and the 12½-foot armchair is mounted on a high pedestal. Plans for the memorial were started as early as 1867, but political scuffling delayed groundbreaking for almost 50 years. The dedication was on Memorial Day 1922.

148 Major General John A. Logan (mem)

Logan Circle; Vermont Avenue at 13th and P streets.

This equestrian statue of Logan sits atop a base with reliefs on four sides. Allegorical figures to the north and south represent war and peace; the other two depict scenes from Logan's career. This bronze sculpture by Franklin Simmons was dedicated on April 9, 1901.

149 Major General George B. McClellan (mem)

Connecticut Avenue and Columbia Road, N.W.

Sculptor Frederick MacMonnies won the commission for this nine-foot bronze of the Union general, regarded as a brilliant but hesitant leader, whom Lee identified as the best commander he ever faced. After being relieved of his command by Lincoln, he challenged him unsuccessfully for the presidency in 1864. This equestrian statue of McClellan, unveiled in 1907, occupies a commanding position in this open triangle.

150 Brigadier General James B. McPherson (mem)

McPherson Square; 15th between K and I streets, N.W.

When James Birdseye McPherson, commander of the Army of Tennessee, was killed in the Battle of Atlanta, Grant reportedly said, "The country has lost one of its best soldiers and I have lost my best friend." This 12-foot equestrian statue, cast from a Confederate cannon captured at Atlanta, portrays an alert general surveying a field of battle. Sculpted by Louis T. Rebiso, it was dedicated in 1876.

151 Meade Memorial (mem)

North side of Mall; Union Square and 1st Street.

General George Gordon Meade was born in Spain to American parents. Wounded at White Oak Swamp near Richmond in 1862, he never fully recovered. Meade commanded the Army of the Potomac at Gettysburg and this monument, executed by Charles A. Grafly, was presented by the Commonwealth of Pennsylvania after his death in 1872.

152 National Archives (col)

Constitution Avenue between 7th and 9th streets, N.W.; 202-501-5205; Apr–Labor Day: daily, 10–9; other times: 10–5:30. Free.

The National Archives preserve Federal government records, including Civil War memorabilia. Exhibition Hall displays famous American documents, and research rooms are available with extensive military service records.

153 National Museum of American History (col)

Constitution Avenue between 12th and 14th streets, N.W.; 202-357-1729; Daily, 10–5:30. Free.

Included in the exhaustive collection of "America's Attic" are exhibits devoted to the history of the armed forces and the Civil War.

154 National Museum of Health and Medicine (col)

6825 16th Street, N.W.; 202-576-2348; daily, 10–5:30. Free.

The museum on the Walter Reed Army Medical Center campus is located in Building 54. The exhibits depict the treatment of wounded soldiers from the Civil War to the present. On display are diagnostic and surgical tools from the middle of the nineteenth century.

155 National Portrait Gallery (col)

8th and G streets, N.W.; 202-357-2700; Daily, 10–5:30. Free.

The collection features Civil War personalities and the photographs of Mathew Brady. A gallery is devoted to the Civil War and includes one of the last photographs ever snapped of Abraham Lincoln. The building itself, formerly the Patent Office, served as a Civil War hospital and was the setting for Lincoln's second inaugural ball.

156 The Navy Museum (col)

Washington Navy Yard; 9th and M streets, S.E., Building 76; 202-433-2651; Summer: Mon–Fri, 9–5, Sat–Sun, 10–5; other times: Mon–Fri, 9–4, Sat–Sun, 9–4. Free.

The museum, with more than 5,000 objects on display, interprets the history of the United States Navy from 1775 on. Exhibits depict important Civil War heroes and battles.

157 New York Avenue Presbyterian Church (site)

New York Avenue and H Street.

This church was organized in 1803 by the Scottish stonemasons who built the White House. Abraham Lincoln worshiped at this church. The Lincoln pew and hitching post have been preserved; the tower chimes were a gift of Robert Todd Lincoln. On display is the original manuscript of the president's proposal to abolish slavery.

158 Nuns of the Battlefield (mem)

Rhode Island Avenue and M Street, N.W.

The inscription on this large bronze panel, erected in 1924, reads: "To the memory and in honor of the various orders of sisters who gave their services as nurses on battlefields and in hospitals during the Civil War." The design was sculpted by Jerome Connor, who later filed a $45,000 suit against the Ancient Order of the Hibernians for alleged nonpayment.

159 Peace Monument (mem)

Pennsylvania Avenue and 1st Street, N.W.

Originally known as the *Navy Monument,* it was created by Franklin Simmons in 1877 to honor the Union navy. The two allegorical female figures at the top of the 40-foot high memorial represent America weeping on the shoulders of History over the loss of her naval defenders during the Civil War.

160 Petersen House (site)

516 10th Street, N.W.; 202-426-6924; Daily, 9–5. Free.

Located across the street from Ford's Theatre, this is the house where Abraham Lincoln, clinging to life, was carried after being shot. He died the next morning on April 15, 1865. The Petersen House, built in 1849, is more commonly known as "The House Where Lincoln Died."

The front parlor has been restored to its appearance in 1865, although nothing is original; in this room Captain Robert Todd Lincoln attempted to comfort his mother. In the tiny back bedroom the original bed was not long enough for Lincoln, who had to be laid diagonally across this deathbed. In this house Secretary of War Edwin Stanton announced, "Now he belongs to the ages."

161 Pike Monument (mem)

Indiana Avenue and 3rd Street, N.W.

This statue honors General Albert Pike of Arkansas, who helped enlist the Five Nations of the Indian Territory for the Confederate cause.

162 Major General John A. Rawlins (mem)

Rawlins Park; 18th and E streets, N.W.

Major General John Aaron Rawlins began a long association with Ulysses Grant as a neighbor in Galena, Illinois. Despite not having any military training, he became Grant's aide-de-camp during the Civil War and was credited with keeping the general from abusing drink. Every time Grant was promoted, he made certain that Rawlins was too. Rawlins became secretary of war in the Grant cabinet but died five months into his tenure from tuberculosis. The bronze statue of Rawlins by Joseph A. Bailey is one of the few Washington statues erected with funds provided by Congress. It was unveiled in 1874.

163 Red Cross Museum (col)

East Building; American Red Cross; 17th and D street N.W.

In the museum is material pertaining to women in the Civil War. The inscription over the portico reads: "In memory of the Heroic Women of the Civil War." The library features the Clara Barton Memorial Collection, and exhibits contain such artifacts as the trunk-bed used by Barton during the war.

164 Lieutenant General Winfield Scott
(mem)

Scott Circle; Massachusetts and Rhode Island avenues and 16th Street N.W.

The bronze equestrian statue of General Winfield Scott by Henry Kirke Brown appropriately faces toward the White House — he served every president from Jefferson to Lincoln. The 1874 statue was made from a cast iron cannon captured by Scott during the Mexican War when he was commanding general of the American army. Scott was commander in chief of the army when the Civil War began.

165 Lieutenant General Winfield Scott
(mem)

United States Soldiers' Home; 2nd and Upshur streets, N.W.

Scott founded this organization in 1851 with tribute money that the United States received from General Santa Anna at the conclusion of the Mexican War. This heroic bronze by Launt Thompson was sculpted in 1873.

166 General Philip H. Sheridan (mem)

Sheridan Circle; Massachusetts Avenue and 23rd Street, N.W.

This dashing equestrian statue is as much a tribute to Rienzi — the horse that carried Sheridan through 85 battles and who, on October 19, 1864, spirited his master into a fight near Winchester, Virginia after a furious 20-mile ride — as it is to the popular leader himself. Gutzon Borglum executed this 11-foot depiction of Sheridan in 1908.

167 General William Tecumseh Sherman (mem)

15th Street and Pennsylvania Avenue, N.W.

One of the most elaborate memorials in Washington. On the main pedestal alone are a series of inscriptions, eight bas-reliefs, and two groups representing War and Peace. This 14-foot equestrian statue of General Sherman in President's Park is primarily by Carl Rohl-Smith. It was dedicated in 1903.

168 Dr. Benjamin F. Stephenson (mem)

7th and C streets, N.W.

Stephenson first served in the Civil War at the age of 38 as surgeon of the 14th Illinois Infantry Regiment. By the time of his discharge in 1864, he had achieved the rank of brigade surgeon. Upon the conclusion of the war, he formed the Grand Army of the Republic, a national honorary society of discharged Union veterans, in Decatur, Illinois.

This 25-foot monument to his Grand Army of the Republic is a granite shaft with bronze figures on three of the faces and with a bust of Dr. Stephenson. John Massey Rhind was the sculptor; the monument was dedicated in 1909. The Grand Army of the Republic passed out of existence in 1959, when Albert Woolson, the last remaining Union veteran, died at the age of 109.

169 Major General George H. Thomas
(mem)

Thomas Circle; Massachusetts Avenue and 14th Street, N.W.

Although a Virginian, Thomas chose to remain with the Union army. His gallantry in the western theater earned him the sobriquet, "Rock of Chickamauga." John Quincy Adams Ward's spirited equestrian statue was erected in 1879 by the Society of the Army of the Cumberland and is considered one of Washington's best.

170 United States Capitol (site)

Constitution Avenue and Independence Avenue.

The Capitol building was used as a barracks during the early days of war. Brick ovens in the basement cranked out bread for the forts around town, and foodstuffs were packed into vaults in preparation for a possible siege of the city. Among the statues in the Capitol Rotunda are those of Lincoln, Grant, and Edward D. Baker, killed at Balls Bluff, Virginia.

171 United States Soldiers and Sailors of the Civil War (mem)

Pension Building; between 4th and 5th, F, and G streets, N.W.

Lincoln's quartermaster general during the Civil War, Major General Montgomery C. Meigs, built this Roman-inspired structure in 1882 to disburse pensions to Civil War veterans. He embellished the exterior with a 1,200-foot terra-cotta frieze celebrating the deeds of the Union army. Meigs had served brilliantly as a quartermaster but received mixed reviews as an architect. When General Philip Sheridan was proudly escorted through the Pension Building by Meigs, he was asked what he thought. "I have one fault to find with it," said Sheridan, "it's fireproof."

172 White House (site)

1600 Pennsylvania Avenue, N.W.; 202-456-7041; Tues–Sat, 10–12. Free.

The White House served as barracks shortly after the Civil War erupted. Abraham Lincoln signed the Emancipation Proclamation in what is today Lincoln's Bedroom but which was originally his cabinet room. One of five copies of the Gettysburg

Address in Lincoln's handwriting is in the Lincoln Sitting Room in the corner of the second floor; Harry S Truman gathered pieces from Lincoln's life to turn this room into a shrine.

Florida

Civil War Status: Confederacy; seceded from the Union on March 10, 1861
1860 Population: 140,424
Troops Provided: 15,000
Known Scenes of Action: 168

Civil War Timeline

February 20, 1864: Battle of Olustee (Ocean Pond)

Apalachicola

173 Fort Gadsden State Historic Site (site)

Route 65, 24 miles north of town.

The fort built here in 1814 was originally a British post. The Confederates occupied the fort on the Apalachicola River from 1862 until July 1863 when malaria drove them out of the lowlands along the river. Four field pieces and a detachment of infantry and cavalry were removed to a healthier position. With the war's end, Fort Gadsden receded into oblivion. Only an outline of the foundation remains.

Bradenton

174 South Florida Museum (col)

201 10th Street West; 941-746-4131; Jan–Apr: Mon–Sat 10–5, Sun 12–5; other times: Tues–Sat 10–5, Sun 12–5. Admission charged.

The extensive treatment of South Florida history includes Civil War memorabilia. The fighting seldom spilled into this region of Florida.

DeFuniak Springs

175 Confederate Monument (mem)

Courthouse Grounds.

This white marble shaft with a hand and index finger thrust skyward was Florida's first memorial to the Confederacy and was erected in 1871.

Dry Tortugas

176 Fort Jefferson (site)

Dry Tortugas Key; 305-247-6211.

About 70 miles west of Key West lies a cluster of seven islands, composed of coral reefs and sand. In 1846 construction of a fortress began on this atoll, known as the key to the Gulf of Mexico. Although never completely finished, Fort Jefferson was the largest nineteenth-century coastal defense fort in America. During the Civil War the fort hampered Confederate blockade runners, but its primary use was as a Union military prison for captured deserters.

Dr. Samuel Mudd, who set John Wilkes Booth's leg, was held here with three others convicted of complicity. In return for fighting a yellow fever epidemic that killed 38 prisoners and guards in 1869, Mudd was pardoned from his sentence of life imprisonment. The government abandoned Fort Jefferson in 1874 after a severe hurricane and another outbreak of yellow fever.

Although most visitors come to this remote outpost for its natural splendor, those who arrive by boat or seaplane are given a slide orientation and self-guided tour that includes Mudd's cell. The parade ground contains ghostly remains of two huge buildings, the officers' quarters, soldiers' barracks, two magazines, and a water cistern.

Ellenton

177 Gamble Mansion and Judah P. Benjamin Confederate Memorial Historic Site (site)

3708 Patten Avenue; 941-723-4536; Thurs–Mon 9:30, 10:30, 1, 2, 3. Admission charged.

John Gratton Gamble took over a sugarcane farm begun by his father in 1845 and, far from any civilization, built it into a massive 3,450-acre plantation. Plagued by financial reverses of this tenuous empire, Gamble sold the operation for $190,000 in 1856 and returned to Tallahassee. During the war a Federal raiding party from the *James L. Davis* destroyed the sugar mill in 1864 but did not harm the mansion, except for some looting.

In May 1865 Judah P. Benjamin, Confederate secretary of state, took refuge here, hiding in a palmetto grove to evade bounty-hunting Federal soldiers. He escaped to England via a hazardous route and became a leading member of the English bar. Today, only 16 acres of the original plantation and mansion remain, making the location the only antebellum plantation house surviving in southern Florida. It stands as a memorial to Benjamin's daring escape.

Fernandina Beach

178 Fort Clinch State Park (site)

Amelia Island; 2601 Atlantic Avenue; 904-277-7274; Daily, 9–5. Admission charged.

Facing Georgia across the Cumberland Sound on the Atlantic Ocean, Fort Clinch was started in 1847 and named for General Duncan Lamont Clinch, an important figure in Florida's Seminole Wars. The Confederates seized the unfinished fort at the beginning of the war, and the 3rd Regiment of Florida Volunteers was stationed here. Lee ordered it evacuated in March 1862, and the Federals moved in and began attempting to finish construction. The 1st New York Volunteer Engineers labored on with the masonry construction although the rifled barrel used at Fort Pulaski had made brick and stone fortifications obsolete. In the end, although the fort was of strategic importance, neither side ever engaged its guns in battle.

Converted into a state park in 1935, Fort Clinch is in a remarkable state of preservation. All told, the state park encompasses 1,153 acres at the end of Amelia Island. Park rangers dressed in Union uniforms carry out the daily chores of the 1864 garrison soldier.

Homasassa Springs

179 Yulee Sugar Mill State Historic Site (site)

Route 490, Fish Bowl Drive; 904-795-3817.

Florida senator David Levy Yulee built a thriving sugar plantation here in 1851. At its height the Yulee Mill operated on 5,100 acres, utilized 1,000 slaves, and was a major supplier of sugar products for Southern troops during the Civil War. In 1864 Yulee Mill was destroyed by marauding Federal troops, but ruins, including boiler, engine parts, cog wheels, pressing rolls, and kettles, remain.

Jacksonville

180 Confederate Memorial (site)

Hemming Park; Hogan Street between West Duval and West Monroe streets.

The monument in the central plaza here was donated to Jacksonville in 1898 by Charles G. Hemming, for whom the park was named. Hemming was a member of the Jacksonville Light Infantry and Third Regiment that encamped in the city during the Civil War.

181 Florida's Tribute to the Women of the Confederacy (mem)

Confederate Park; Main and Hubbard streets.

This site was the eastern end of the Confederate trenches that extended to Union Terminal. About 14,000 soldiers camped here. The monument by Allan George Newman consists of a large temple with a standing female atop the roof and a seated female figure inside the structure. It was dedicated to "those noble women who sacrificed their all" on October 26, 1915.

182 Museum of Science and History (col)

1025 Museum Circle; 904-396-7061; Mon–Fri 10–5, Sat 10–6, Sun 1–6. Admission charged.

Among the exhibits here is a permanent display of the Civil War on the St. John's River. Federal troops occupied and evacuated Jacksonville several times during the war, seldom with much bloodshed.

183 Museum of Southern History (col)

4304 Herschel Street; 904-388-3574; Tues–Sat, 10–5. Admission charged.

The museum presents American history in the ante-bellum and Civil War periods. There are displays of camp and civilian life and period artifacts.

Jupiter

184 Jupiter Inlet Lighthouse (col)

805 North Route 1; 407-747-6639; Sun–Wed, 10–5. Admission charged.

The lighthouse was designed by Lieutenant General George Meade and was completed in 1860. Meade later commanded the Federal defense of Gettysburg. Early in the Civil War, Confederate sympathizers disabled the lighthouse and buried the illuminating devices in the sand. After the hostilities had concluded, the keeper dug up the mechanism, and the house was relit in 1866. The Jupiter Lighthouse is now home to the Florida History Center and Museum.

Key West

185 Fort Zachary Taylor (site)

Southard Street; 305-292-6713; Daily, 8–dusk. Admission charged.

Construction of this remote outpost began in 1845, shortly after Florida became a state. In 1850 it was named for President Zachary Taylor, who had died in office earlier that year. When the Civil War broke out, Captain John Brannon occupied the fort, placing it in Union hands — and so it remained for the duration of the war. Fort Taylor's cannons had a range of three miles, which proved an impressive deterrent to the Confederate navy.

A museum is located at the fort site with a display of artifacts and models of the original guns and facilities. Several original Civil War cannons are still here. Guided tours are available.

Marianna

186 Battle of Marianna Memorial (mem)
Confederate Park.

Federal troops operating in the area annihilated a ragtag home guard of boys and elderly known as the "Cradle of the Grave" detachment here on October 2, 1864. About 60 were killed or wounded and another 100 taken prisoner.

Natural Bridge

187 Natural Bridge State Historic Site
(site)
Route 363; 904-922-6007.

Between March 1 and 3, 1865, a Union flotilla arrived in Apalachicola Bay to begin an assault on Tallahassee. Navy gunboats ran aground in the shallow waters of the St. Mark's River, giving a Confederate messenger time to travel to the capitol and warn of the impending attack. The defensive group assembled was hardly imposing: wounded soldiers home to recuperate, men as old as 70, and cadets as young as 14 from West Florida Seminary (now Florida State University).

The irregulars joined the Confederate Fifth Cavalry in pushing Union general John Newton into taking a roundabout route over Natural Bridge. After a series of skirmishes on March 6, Newton decided the bridge was impassable and, having not been supported by his navy, withdrew to Key West. Union losses totaled 21 killed, 89 wounded, and 38 captured. The defenders' losses numbered three killed and 22 wounded. Tallahassee was the only Confederate capital east of the Mississippi never to fall into Union hands.

Reenactment: The St. Mark's River disappears underground here and rises to the surface a short distance to the south, thus forming the natural bridge. Battle markers and earthen breastworks are on the field of battle, as is a monument to the Confederate effort. The Battle of Natural Bridge is reenacted every year in March on a weekend near the anniversary of the actual battle.

Olustee

188 Olustee Battlefield State Historic Site (site)
Route 90, two miles east of town; 904-758-0400; Daily, 8–5. Free.

Union general Truman A. Seymour left Hilton Head, South Carolina, in February 1864 on a mission to cut the Confederate supply line from central Florida and, not secondarily, to induce Unionists in east Florida to organize a loyal state government. The landing on February 7 at Jacksonville was met with no resistance.

The defense of Florida was placed in the hands of General Joseph Finegan who prepared to stop the Union's westward movement at Olustee, where advancing troops were confronted with only a narrow passage between a lake, Ocean Pond, and an impassable swamp. The Union force of 5,500 men and 16 cannon was cut off here by an equal number of Confederate forces in the largest Civil War battle in Florida.

Musket fire rang out over a forest floor of virgin pines, free of underbrush, on February 20. Finegan's defenders inflicted heavy losses in driving back the United States army as fighting raged into the darkness. Seymour retreated with 1,861 casualties; the Confederates lost 946 soldiers. Union forces remained in Jacksonville for the final year of the war but did not venture out into Florida in significant force again.

An interpretive center offers exhibits interpreting this Confederate victory. The battlefield is marked by a trail and by signs along the battle lines. A monument to the fighting was dedicated in 1913.

Pensacola

189 Civil War Soldiers' Museum (col)
108 South Palafox Place; 904-469-1900; Mon–Sat, 10–4:30. Admission charged.

Over 80 separate exhibits include some less well-known topics: musical instruments, black soldiers, women during the war, and military medicine. A 23-minute video tells the story of Confederate and Union Pensacola during the Civil War.

190 Fort Barrancas (site)
1801 Gulf Breeze Parkway; 904-934-2600; Apr–Oct: daily, 9:30–5; Nov–Mar: daily, 10:30–4. Free.

The Confederate forces occupied this fort early in 1861, and from here they exchanged artillery fire with Fort Pickens in the harbor.

Pensacola Beach

191 Fort Pickens (site)
Fort Pickens Road; 904-934-2635; Apr–Oct: daily, 9–5; other times: daily, 8–4. Admission charged.

Fort Pickens occupies the western tip of Santa Rosa Island and commanded the eastern entrance to Pensacola Harbor during the Civil War. Completed in 1834, this fort, shaped like a pentagon, saw much action early in the war. The United States artillery under Lieutenant Adam J. Slemmer refused to surrender as Florida seceded. The Federal naval yard in Pensacola, lightly fortified, was given over to the Rebels, but Fort Pickens could be supplied from the sea and so the company held out.

Artillery battles occurred several times between Fort Pickens and Confederate batteries on shore. On November 22 and 23, 1861, two warships drove the Confederates from two sister forts on the barrier islands, Fort Barrancas and Fort McRee.

On May 9, 1862, the Confederates abandoned Pensacola, and Fort Pickens, once a linchpin in the Union blockade, became a prison. Now restored, the fort features a museum with Civil War exhibits. Guided tours are offered.

St. Augustine

192 Castillo de San Marcos (The Fort) (site)

One Castillo Drive; 904-829-6506; Daily, 8:45–4:45. Admission charged.

The oldest city in America has been fortified since 1565. The Americans moved in during 1821. Just after Lincoln was elected, Florida militia troops took over the fort from a single federal caretaker without a struggle. Cannon were hauled away to defend Jacksonville from Union gunboats. There was no fighting here during the Civil War, even though both sides used the fortress.

193 Museum of Weapons and Early American History (col)

81C King Street; 904-829-3727; Daily, 10–6. Admission charged.

The collection ranges back to the 1500s; the Civil War collection is elaborate and wide-ranging.

St. Marks

194 Fort Ward (site)

San Marcos de Apalache State Historic Site; 1022 DeSoto Park Drive; 904-925-6216; Daily, 9–5. Admission charged.

Fortifications have been on this site for most of the last 320 years. The Confederates took the fort at the confluence of the St. Marks and Wakulla rivers in 1861 and named it Fort Ward. A Union squadron subsequently blockaded the mouth of the St. Marks River until 1865. Confederate earthworks are still visible, and a military cemetery is on the grounds.

195 St. Marks Lighthouse (site)

Route 59; 904-925-6121.

The lighthouse, now part of the St. Marks National Wildlife Refuge, witnessed several military operations during the Civil War. In June 1862 Union shelling destroyed a nearby Confederate fortress and the lighthouse was vandalized a year later in an attempt to disable it.

St. Petersburg

196 Fort De Soto (site)

Pinellas Bayway; 813-866-2484; Daily, dawn to dusk. Free.

The fort on the southern end of Mullet Key was designed by Robert E. Lee while he served as a lieutenant colonel in the United States Army. The guns were set up to guard the entrance to Tampa Bay but were never needed.

Tallahassee

197 Museum of Florida History (col)

500 South Bronough Street; 904-488-1484; Mon–Fri 9–4:30, Sat 10–4:30, Sun 12–4:30. Free.

Although the capitol was never captured, Confederate major general Samuel Jones surrendered forces under his command here on May 10, 1865. The Old Capitol, completed in Florida's birth year of 1845, has been restored to its 1902 appearance, complete with red candy-striped awnings. It is administered by the museum, which preserves Florida's Civil War history with military arms, battle flags, and other memorabilia.

Georgia

Civil War Status: Confederacy; seceded from the Union on January 19, 1861
1860 Population: 1,057,286
Troops Provided: 112,000
Known Scenes of Action: 549

Civil War Timeline

April 10, 1862: Bombardment and capture of Fort Pulaski
September 18–20, 1863: Battle of Chickamauga
May 13–15, 1864: Battle of Resaca
May 25–28, 1864: Battles of New Hope Church, Pickett's Mill, and Dallas
June 27, 1864: Battle of Kennesaw Mountain
July 20, 1864: Battle of Peachtree Creek
July 22, 1864: Battle of Atlanta
July 28, 1864: Battle of Ezra Church
August 31–September 1, 1864: Battle of Jonesboro

September 2, 1864: Federal troops occupy At-
lanta
November 22, 1864: Engagement at Gris-
woldville
December 13, 1864: Capture of Fort McAllister
December 21, 1864: Savannah occupied

Abbeville

198 Confederate Memorial (mem)

Wilcox County Library Square.
This monument of Georgia marble to the Confederate dead was erected in 1909.

Adairsville

199 Adairsville Depot (site)

Off Route 140 in business district.
The railroad station was the point of departure
for the "Great Locomotive Chase." It was here that
Captain Fuller commandeered the locomotive *Texas*
and charged after James Andrews on the *General*—
in reverse. This was also the site of the Georgia State
Arsenal, which was destroyed by Sherman's troops
on May 18, 1864.
Reenactment: The Great Locomotive Chase Festival is held here annually on the first weekend in
October.

200 Barnsley Gardens (col)

597 Barnsley Gardens Road; 770-773-7480;
Feb–Dec: Tues–Sat, 10–6, Sun 12–6. Admission
charged.
This brick manor house was started in 1859 by
Sir Godfrey Barnsley from Derbyshire, England,
who built a fortune exporting cotton from Savannah. Barnsley bought 10,000 acres on this site in
northwestern Georgia to build his plantation but
came to financial ruin because of the war. He in-
vested all of his available funds in Confederate war
bonds and donated his fleet of 12 ships to the Confederate navy. Situated directly in the path of General William Sherman's advance through Georgia,
the estate was irreparably damaged by a cavalry battle on May 18, 1864, and subsequent Federal occupation. General James McPherson, who occupied
the house, called it one of the most beautiful spots
on earth.
Reenactment: The grounds still include 30 acres
of wild and manicured gardens, and the house tour
includes Civil War memorabilia. Confederate
colonel R. G. Earle, who was killed on his way to
warn townspeople of the coming invasion, is buried
on the property. In mid–July a Civil War battle is
reenacted on the grounds.

Albany

201 Bridge House (site)

Front Street and Pine River.
This house at the Flint River was commissioned
by the founder of Albany and designed by noted
black architect Horace King. During the Civil War
the bridge was burned and the building used as
meatpacking house for the Confederacy. Later, this
welcoming point to Albany was converted to a theater.

Americus

202 Confederate Monument (mem)

Rees Park.
This marble monument honors "those who
fought in their ragged old suits of gray." It is dedicated to the memory of the soldiers of Sumter
County.

Andersonville

203 Andersonville National Historic Site (site)

Route 49; 912-924-0343; Daily, 8–5. Free.
A Confederate prison camp called Fort Sumter
opened here on February 27, 1864. The area behind the 15-foot stockade walls of pine logs was intended to hold 10,000 men — but there were as
many as 33,000 here at times. Andersonville, as it
was called in the North, became the largest and
most notorious of the Confederate prisons.
Sentries stood in boxes called "pigeon roosts" and
a "deadline" was drawn 19 feet from the walls. There
were some escape tunnels dug, but nearly all who
escaped were recaptured. Thirteen months before
the end of the war, nearly 13,000 men died in Andersonville.
The former prison was restored in 1970 "to provide an understanding of the overall prisoner-of-
war story of the Civil War, to interpret the role of
prisoner-of-war camps in history, and to commemorate the sacrifice of Americans who lost their
lives in such prison camps." There is a 12-minute
slide presentation in the visitor center.
On the grounds is a stone pavilion erected in 1901
at the Providence Spring — so-called because a sudden downpour opened a clogged spring on the
property, releasing fresh water to dying Union soldiers in the oppressive summer heat.

204 Civil War Drummer Boy Museum (col)

109 Church Street; 912-924-2558; Jan 2–
Thanksgiving: weekends, 10–4. Admission
charged.

Historic mannequins from the North and South accent the collection, which features an Andersonville Prison diorama.

205 Henry Wirz Monument (mem)

Church Street.

Henry Wirz was the Confederate commandant at Andersonville who was hanged by the Federal government on November 10, 1865, despite pleas from both sides that he had tried to ease the putrid conditions in the camp. The monument was erected in the center of town as a protest against the execution. The inscription reads: "When time shall have softened passion and prejudice, when reason shall have stripped the mask of representation, then justice holding evenly her scales will require much of past censure and praise to change places."

Athens

206 Double Barreled Cannon (mem)

City Hall; College and Hancock streets.

This unique artifact of the Civil War was designed locally in 1863 to protect Athens from Sherman's rampaging army. The cannon, however, failed to fire two cannon balls simultaneously.

Atlanta

207 Atlanta Cyclorama (col)

Grant Park; 800 Cherokee Avenue S.E.; 404-624-1071; Summer: daily, 9:30–5:30; other times: daily, 9:30–4:30. Admission charged.

This three-dimensional, 360-degree panorama with music and narration tells the tale of the Battle of Atlanta on July 22, 1864. The cyclorama was completed in 1886 by German artists from Milwaukee. Its circumference is 358 feet and its height is 42 feet. The figures are 22 inches to four feet high, all placed to appear life-size. The steam locomotive *Texas*, which Captain Fuller used to chase Andrews' Raiders, is in the exhibit hall.

208 Atlanta Heritage Row (col)

55 Upper Alabama Street; 404-584-7879; Tues–Sat, 10–5; Sun, 1–5. Admission charged.

The Museum at Underground is an interactive history of Atlanta that recreates the drama of Civil War Georgia in a bomb shelter replica.

209 Atlanta History Center (col)

130 West Paces Ferry Road; 404-814-4000; Daily, Mon–Sat 10–5:30, Sun 12–5:30. Admission charged

In the history complex are 83,000 square feet of museum space and many references to Atlanta and the Civil War, including a permanent exhibition.

210 Ben W. Fortson, Jr., State Archives and Records Building (col)

330 Capitol Avenue S.E.; 404-656-2393; Mon–Fri 8–4:15, Sat 9:30–3:15. Free.

The official state records include many pertaining to the Civil War. The building features three panels of stained glass depicting the rise and fall of the Confederacy: (1) Davis takes the oath of office, (2) Jackson at first Manassas, (3) Lee and Traveller bid farewell to men.

211 Georgia State Capitol (site)

431 State Capitol; 404-651-6996; Mon–Fri 8–5:30, Sat 10–4, Sun 12–4; Free.

At one time Union troops camped on the grounds of this building, then Atlanta City Hall. The Georgia capitol building rose on this site and today is decorated with statues of Civil War governors and other historic figures. The collection includes battle flags and portraits.

212 McPherson Monument (mem)

McPherson and Monument avenues.

On this spot Union general James Birdseye McPherson was killed on July 22, 1864. He had planned to return to Ohio to be married, but Sherman wanted him for the Atlanta campaign. His fiancée went into seclusion for more than a year after his death.

213 Oakland Cemetery (site)

248 Oakland Avenue; 404-658-6019.

Atlanta's most significant burial ground has more than 2,000 Civil War dead, including five generals, among the imposing oak and magnolia trees. The author of *Gone with the Wind*, Margaret Mitchell, is buried here. The *Lion of Atlanta* is a carved block of Atlanta marble dedicated to the unknown Confederate dead on April 16, 1894.

214 Peace Monument (mem)

Piedmont Park; Piedmont Avenue, north of 10th Street, near the 14th Street entrance.

The figure of Peace, in bronze, commands a kneeling Southern soldier to lower his weapon. The sculptor was Allen Newman of New York; both Federal and Confederate soldiers attended the unveiling on October 19, 1911.

215 The Road to Tara Museum (col)

Georgian Terrace Hotel; 659 Peachtree Street; Suite 600; 404-897-1939; Daily, Mon–Sat 10–6, Sun 1–5. Admission charged.

The largest public exhibit of *Gone with the Wind* memorabilia is on the concourse level of the Georgia Terrace Hotel. Also available is a 22-minute documentary on the life of author Margaret Mitchell.

Augusta

216 Confederate Monument (mem)

Broad Street between 7th and 8th streets.

Dedicated on October 31, 1878, this 72-foot marble shaft cost $17,000. It was carved in Italy from Arrera marble. Atop the center shaft is a Confederate private based on Berry Greenwood Benson, a Georgia scout and sharpshooter who lived until New Year's Day, 1923, and never surrendered his rifle. Life-size figures of Lee; Jackson; Thomas Reade Rootes Cobb, secession leader in Georgia; and General William Henry Talbot Walker of Richmond County, who was killed in Atlanta in 1864; are prominent. The design was by Van Gunden & Young of Philadelphia.

217 Confederate Powder Mill (site)

1717 Goodrich Street.

A 176-foot obelisk-shaped chimney in front of Sibley Manufacturing Company is the only thing left of the Confederate Powder Works, the only one in the South. From 1862 until 1865 the mills, stretching two miles along the river, produced 2,750,000 pounds of gunpowder; under strict guard the powder mill was dismantled in 1871.

218 United States Arsenal (site)

2500 Walton Way.

This Federal armory was seized by state troops only days after Georgia seceded. Today it is an administration building of Augusta College. The facility manufactured 75,000 rifle cartridges daily.

Blakely

219 Confederate Flag Pole (mem)

Courthouse Square, Route 27.

Erected in 1861, this is the last wooden pole remaining that flew the Stars and Bars of the Confederate States of America.

Cartersville

220 Battle of Allatoona Pass (site)

Old Allatoona Road.

C.S.A. general Samuel French massed 2,000 troops for an assault on Sherman's supply line at the strategic Western and Atlantic Railroad pass at Allatoona. Defense of the garrison was in the hands of Brigadier General John M. Corse. Three hours of gruesome fighting on October 5, 1864, left nearly 40 percent casualties on both sides. Sherman, 18 miles away at Kennesaw Mountain, signaled, "Hold the fort; for we are coming." But he never did. French, however, received the same information and withdrew. P. P. Bliss, an evangelist, immortalized Corse's spirited defense in a hymn, "Hold the Fort, for We Are Coming," which inspired recruits long after Sherman had evacuated the area.

Much of the battleground has been left undisturbed, and interpretive trails along the trenches lead to two earthen forts. Across the street is the Clayton House, which was used as a field hospital during the conflict. At a nearby railroad crossing is a grave of the Unknown Soldier, unknown even as to the side on which he fought.

221 Cartersville Depot (site)

Route 113.

General Johnston's rear guard, pulling back from Cassville, encountered Union troops near the depot on May 20, 1864. The Confederates barricaded themselves inside the depot and scraped out blocks for gunports during the skirmish. Much of the original structure has survived.

222 Cooper's Iron Works (site)

River Road.

Mark A. Cooper's Iron Empire was a major supplier of Confederate iron. In 1863 he conveyed his Etowah Mining and Manufacturing Company to the Confederate States of America. Sherman destroyed the iron works and the town of Etowah during occupation in May 1864. Cooper is buried in the town's Oak Hill Cemetery along with C.S.A. general P. M. B. Young, a West Point roommate of General George Armstrong Custer.

All that remains of this important Confederate manufacturing site is a single cold-blast furnace at the foot of Allatoona Dam. Nearby, in the Etowah River, are stone pillars, the only remnants of a railroad bridge destroyed by retreating Confederate troops on May 20, 1864.

223 Lake Allatoona Visitors Center (col)

Spur 20 off Route 20; 770-382-4700; April–Sept: daily, 8–6; Oct–Mar: daily, 8–4:30. Free.

Maintained by the U.S. Army Corps of Engineers, the visitor center atop a dam on this 12,000-acre lake features Civil War relics, photographs, and other memorabilia of the period.

224 Roselawn Museum (col)

224 West Cherokee Avenue; 770-387-5162; Mon–Fri, 10–12 and 1–5. Free.

This immaculately restored Victorian mansion of evangelist Samuel Porter Jones houses a small Civil War collection of the United Daughters of the Confederacy.

Cassville

225 Atlanta Campaign Relief Map at Cassville (site)

Route 41 at Cassville Road.

Describes the Battle of Cassville on May 18, 1864, which resulted in the burning of the town. Only three houses and three churches were spared. A monument on the town square recounts Cassville's ante-bellum past.

226 Cassville Confederate Cemetery (site)

Cass-White Road.

Here are nearly 300 unknown Confederate grave sites, as well as the final resting place for Brigadier General William T. Wofford (1824–1884).

Columbus

227 Columbus Iron Works (site)

801 Front Avenue.

Known as the Confederate Naval Iron Works during the war, in 1863 it produced a breechloading cannon made from the wheel shaft of a sunken river steamer.

228 Confederate Naval Museum (col)

202 4th-Victory Drive; 706-327-9798; Daily, Tues–Fri 10–5, Sat–Sun 1–5. Free.

The new nation of the Confederate States of America struggled to build a powerful navy from scratch; that history is related here. In addition to naval artifacts and ship models, the remains of the ironclad C.S.S. *Muscogee*, raised from the Chattahoochie River, and the gunboat C.S.S. *Chattahoochie* are displayed here.

229 National Infantry Museum (col)

Fort Benning; Baltzell Avenue; 706-545-2958; Mon–Fri 8:30–4:30; Sat–Sun 12:30–4:30. Free.

This military museum traces the evolution of the foot soldier in America, including period exhibits on the Civil War.

Crawfordville

230 A. H. Stephens State Historic Park (site)

Route 22; 706-456-2602; Tues–Sat 9–5, Sun 2–5:30. Admission charged.

Alexander Hamilton Stephens, the vice president of the Confederacy, was arrested here at his home and imprisoned in Boston's Fort Wayne for several months. "Little Aleck" never weighed more than 100 pounds and served Georgia in virtually every elected office: U.S. Congressman in 1843, elected to the U.S. Senate in 1866 but disqualified because of his service in the Confederacy, and finally governor of Georgia in 1882. He died in office a year later.

Liberty Hall, Stephens's two-story white frame house, is in the park; in front is a white marble monument of Alexander Stephens. Stephens wrote *A Constitutional View of the Late War Between the States*. His grave is in a stone wall. A Confederate museum is adjacent to the 1875 home.

Culloden

231 Confederate Museum (col)

Main Street; 912-994-9239; by appointment.

On April 19, 1865, only 200 men of the Worrill Grays held off Union troops here. The collection consists of Confederate memorabilia.

Dallas

232 Atlanta Campaign Relief Map at New Hope Church Monument and Battle Site (site)

Route 381, four miles north of town.

Beginning on May 25, 1864, savage fighting continued in the Dallas area for ten days with the Confederates suffering particularly heavy losses.

233 Pickett's Mill Historic Site (site)

2640 Mt. Tabor Road; 770-443-7850; Tues–Sat 9–5, Sun 12–5. Admission charged.

On May 27, 1864, Union troops advancing toward Atlanta were repulsed in heavily wooded terrain. It was one of the few setbacks for Sherman's army during the Atlanta campaign.

Reenactment: Walking trails with interpretive signs cross the battlefield; the site itself covers 765 acres. The visitor center offers audiovisual programs describing the battle. Some battlefield artifacts are on display. A Living History Program is presented every first and third weekend of each month.

Dalton

234 Atlanta Campaign Relief Map at Rocky Face Ridge (site)

Route 41.

The marker describes the parrying movements of Sherman and Johnston between May 7 and 13, 1864.

235 Confederate Cemetery and Monument (site)

Emory Street.

This cemetery has the graves of 421 Confederate and four unknown Union soldiers. The monument pays tributes to Confederates killed in battles in Dalton, Rocky Face, Chickamauga, and Resaca.

236 Dug Gap Battle Park (site)
Dug Gap Battle Road; 706-278-0217.
Confederates made a successful stand here against invading Union troops on May 8, 1864, although outnumbered ten to one. The small park covers only 2½ acres but contains 1,237 feet of Confederate breastworks.

237 General Joseph Johnston (mem)
Hamilton and Crawford streets.
This is the only statue of Confederate general Johnston. He commanded the Army of Tennessee during the Atlanta Campaign.

Douglas

238 Confederate Soldier (mem)
Ashley and Peterson avenues.
Commemorating Confederate soldiers, this stone monument of a soldier at parade rest was dedicated on October 14, 1911.

Fayetteville

239 Fayette County Historical Society
     (col)
195 Lee Street; 770-461-7152; Tues 6–9, Thurs 10–1, Sat 9–1. Free.
The former Margaret Mitchell Library has a noted Civil War collection; the county courthouse is the oldest in Georgia, predating the Civil war by 35 years.

Fitzgerald

240 Blue and Gray Museum (col)
Municipal Building; Johnson Street; 912-423-5375; Apr–Sept: Mon–Fri, 2–5. Admission charged.
Fitzgerald was founded after an 1894 drought in the Midwest when governor William Northern of Georgia organized relief efforts for the devastated farmers. This friendly gesture appealed to a number of Union veterans looking to move south. In 1895 they formed the American Soldiers Colony Association and bought 50,000 acres of pine and wire grass where they could find warm winters and had abundant rainfall. Families came down, and contrary to expectations, the local people greeted them enthusiastically. The town was plotted in dual symmetry with streets named for Union and Confederate generals. The hotel was the Lee-Grant House and the recreation area the Blue-Gray Park.
Appropriately, this museum in "Yank-Reb City" chronicles the Civil War experiences of both sides.

Forsyth

241 Confederate Cemetery (site)
Newton Memorial Road.
The Confederate Cemetery is a special section located in the Forsyth Cemetery.

242 The Marching Confederate Soldier
     (mem)
Monroe County Courthouse Square; Corner of North Lee and East Johnson streets.
This monument to the soldiers of Monroe County shows a young Confederate infantryman surging forward. Frederick Cleveland Hibbard created this bronze, which was dedicated on June 20, 1908.

243 Chickamauga and Chattanooga National Military Park (site)
Route 27, south of town; 706-866-9241; Summer: daily, 8–5:45; other times: daily, 8–4:45; Grounds free, some fees for attractions.
Two desperate battles were fought in this area in the fall of 1863. Twenty-five years after the war had ended, President Benjamin Harrison signed a bill on August 19, 1890, establishing this park as America's first national military park. And today it remains the nation's largest, and is located mostly in Georgia and partly in Tennessee.
Early in September 1863, Union General William Rosecrans and 58,000 men crossed the Tennessee River southwest of Chattanooga, forcing the Confederate forces of General Braxton Bragg to abandon the city and move south to protect supply lines in Atlanta. Once he had gained reinforcements, Bragg turned back, hoping to retake Chattanooga, and the two armies clashed on the Georgia-Tennessee line at Chickamauga Creek.
It was a new type of battle — fought in the woods and heavy underbrush and not in open fields. The Confederates maneuvered brilliantly but their victory came at a terrible cost. Of the 66,000 Southern forces more than 18,000 became casualties; the casualty total for the Union was over 16,000.
The Union forces withdrew to Chattanooga where the Confederate siege almost subdued the Federal army. But on November 23 Ulysses S. Grant directed an all-day attack at Missionary Ridge and won control of the steep slopes above the city. Further attacks at Lookout Mountain and Orchard Knob forced the Confederates to withdraw. Their defeat opened the way to Atlanta and the heart of the Confederacy.
More than 1,600 markers, monuments, cannons, and tablets document the fighting in the 5,400-acre park. The Chickamauga visitor center features the Fuller collection of American military shoulder

arms, totaling more than 385 weapons. On the former parade field is the 6th Cavalry Museum. The battle grounds can be explored with a 7-mile self-guided driving tour where the metal markers (blue and red) are positioned so the field appears as it did to the generals trying to direct their scattered troops in the woods.

Fort Oglethorpe

244 River of Death (col)

Stuart Crossing; 706-866-5771; Summer: daily 9:30–8; Winter: daily 9:30–5:30. Admission charged.

An audiovisual show featuring musket sounds and cannons plays as an electronic map lights up troop movements and battle lines to explain the Battle of Chickamauga, the bloodiest two-day campaign of the war. Casualties were 28 percent of the more than 120,000 men. The name Chickamauga is Cherokee for, appropriately, "River of Death."

Fort Pulaski

245 Fort Pulaski National Monument (site)

Route 80; 15 miles east of Savannah; 912-786-5787; Summer: daily, 8:30–6:45; other times: daily, 8:30–5:15. Admission charged.

This is the third fortification on Cockspur Island; the first in 1761 was Fort George, dismantled by the Americans in 1776, and the second was Fort Greene, built in 1794 but swept away by a hurricane in 1804. Brigadier General Simon Bernard, Napoleon's chief engineer, began work on this structure in 1829. Robert E. Lee's first assignment after graduation was here at Cockspur Island where he assisted with the completion of the fort in 1833. Except for Bernard, every army engineer who worked on the construction of the fort became either a Union or a Confederate general. It was named for Count Casimir Pulaski, who served the American cause in the Revolution and died in the siege of Savannah.

With an estimated 25 million bricks and seven-and-a-half-foot thick walls, Fort Pulaski, facing seaward and protecting the entrance to the Savannah River, was considered impregnable. Georgia occupied the fort, manned only by an ordnance sergeant and a civilian, without resistance before the Civil War on January 3, 1861. Federal troops stationed on Tybee Island began bombardment on April 10, 1862, and after 30 hours of sustained bombardment breached the southeastern angle of the wall with new rifled cannons. Over 5,000 shot and shell were fired, with the loss of only one Union sailor. For the Confederacy 385 men and 48 cannons were lost

as the Union sealed off the port of Savannah and much of the South to foreign trade. The new rifled cannon changed defense strategy worldwide.

Fort Pulaski is one of the best-preserved fortresses constructed in the early 1800s. It was established as a national monument on October 15, 1924, after having been abandoned since the Spanish-American War. The grounds cover 5,365 acres on McQueen and Cockspur Island on the Georgia coast. The self-guided tour of the fort covers breastworks made of half-moon shaped earthen mounds overgrown with sweet myrtles. Two moats spanned by draw bridges encircle the fort; inside, massive brick walls as high as 32 feet enclose a parade ground. Numbered markers are at significant points. A 17-minute film, *The Battle for Fort Pulaski*, is offered in the visitor center. Encampments of troops and demonstrations are offered periodically during the year.

Gainesville

246 Alta Vista Cemetery (site)

Jesse Jewell Park.

A large granite monument and American flag mark the gravesite of Confederate lieutenant general James Longstreet, Lee's second in command during the Civil War.

247 Georgia Mountains Museum (col)

311 Green Street S.E.; 770-536-0889; Tues–Fri 10–5; Sat 10–3:30. Free.

Among the exhibits is the James Longstreet Room, which contains Confederate memorabilia.

Guyton

248 Guyton Cemetery (site)

Cemetery Road.

A section of the graveyard is devoted to Confederate soldiers who died of wounds and disease in a hospital in town.

Irwinville

249 Jefferson Davis Memorial State Park (site)

Route 32; 912-831-2335.

Confederate president Jefferson Davis and his family were taken prisoner here on May 10, 1865 — in disguise, according to some reports. He was detained in Macon and sent to Fort Monroe outside Washington. With his capture the Confederacy ceased to exist.

Michigan and Wisconsin cavalry overtook one another on the same mission and actually fired upon each other in the darkness. A marker identifies this spot; a stone marker is on the exact spot of the capture. The Davis Monument is a granite shaft with a bronze bust and bas-relief panel depicting the final act of the Confederacy. Included in the 12-acre park is a Confederate museum.

Jonesboro

250 Patrick Cleburne Memorial Cemetery (site)

McDonough and Johnson streets.

Jonesboro was visited frequently by Union raiders during 1864; early that fall Hugh Kilpatrick's cavalry ended the Atlanta Campaign. Between 600 and 1,000 unknown Confederate soldiers were buried here in two mass graves by victorious Federal troops. The unmarked headstones are laid out in the pattern of the Confederate Battle Flag.

Kennesaw

251 Kennesaw Civil War Museum (col)

2829 Cherokee Street; 800-742-6897; Daily: Mon–Sat 9:30–5:30, Sun 12:00–5:30. Admission charged.

Housed in an authentic cotton gin, this museum contains *The General*, the locomotive stolen within 100 yards of the museum by James Andrews and 21 Union volunteers on April 12, 1862. A videotape and art displays describe the daring escapade intended to tear up track, cut telegraph wires, and destroy the main supply line to Confederate armies. Only the stubborn persistence of *The General's* conductor, Captain William Fuller, who engaged in the "Great Locomotive Chase," sabotaged the plot. Andrews and his men abandoned the locomotive near the Tennessee-Georgia border and were all captured. Eight, including Andrews, were hanged, six were exchanged, and eight escaped. These soldiers, except for Andrews who was a civilian spy, became the first recipients of the Congressional Medal of Honor.

Kingston

252 Kingston Confederate Cemetery (site)

Johnson Street.

The makeshift hospitals in Kingston served more than 10,000 Confederate soldiers. The cemetery contains the graves of 250 unknown Confederate and 4 Union soldiers. The citizens of Kingston began decorating these burial sites in April 1864 and have continued to do so to this day. Here was the site of the first Confederate Memorial Day observation called Decoration Day, now celebrated as a Georgia holiday.

253 Kingston Confederate Memorial Museum (site)

13 East Main Street; 770-387-1357. By appointment.

The last surrender of Confederate troops in Georgia, some 4,000 men, was executed here by Brigadier General William T. Wofford on May 12, 1865. Sherman's infamous "March to the Sea" had begun in Kingston six months earlier. This private residence is identified by a historical marker.

254 Kingston Depot (site)

Railroad Street.

Andrews' Raiders were delayed 45 minutes here on the "Great Locomotive Chase," dooming their Union espionage mission. Chasing them down, Confederate pursuers Fuller, Cain, and Murphy exchanged their small engine *Yonah* for the locomotive *William R. Smith*. Historic marker only.

LaGrange

255 Bellvue (site)

204 Ben Hill Street; 706-884-1832; Tues–Sat 10–12, 2–5. Admission charged.

Confederate navy secretary Stephen Mallory and Confederate senator Benjamin Hill were arrested here by Federal soldiers. The town of LaGrange was so feverishly loyal to the Confederate cause that every man enlisted. To defend the town the only female military company in the Confederacy was formed — named for Revolutionary War heroine Nancy Hart. Threatened by Wilson's Raiders, the Nancy Harts marched out to do battle but were met by a sympathetic Colonel LaGrange, ironically named the same as the town, who moved on down the road.

Lithia Springs

256 Sweetwater Creek State Conservation Park (site)

Mt. Vernon Road; 770-732-5871.

At the park are the ruins of the New Manchester Manufacturing Company, a textile mill burned by General Sherman's pillaging troops in 1864. Many of the factory's female workers were deported to the North.

Macon

257 Old Cannonball House and Confederate Museum (site)

856 Mulberry Street; 912-745-5982; Mon–Sat 10–1, 2–4; Sun 1–4:30. Admission charged.

Built in 1853, the house was struck by a Union cannonball during an attack on July 30, 1864. Today it is a United Daughters of the Confederacy museum.

258 Rose Hill Cemetery (site)

Riverside Drive at Spring Street; 912-751-9119.

These terraced hills are the burial site of 600 Confederate officers and enlisted men, many of whom died in the fiasco at Griswoldville. General P. J. Phillips, boasting little military experience, was placed in charge of the local militia defending Macon. When he discovered that his force, comprised mostly of old men and boys not even 14 years old, outnumbered a nearby Union detachment, he decided to leave the safety of the woods and charge across open fields at the Union position.

The Federal troops were not expecting an attack, but they quickly reversed the advantage of surprise held by the Confederates. The green recruits were mowed down in waves during the suicidal assault. The sight of the field strewn with unwilling recruits who had no training in fighting was one of the most terrible of the war.

Marietta

259 Gilgal Church Battle Site (site)

Kennesaw Due West Road and Acworth Due West Road.

Scuffling took place here on June 15 and 16, 1864. This 20-acre historical park preserves trenches that were left undisturbed, although the church here was destroyed and never rebuilt.

260 Kennesaw Mountain National Battlefield Park (site)

Route 41, 2½ miles northwest of town; 770-427-4686; Summer: daily, Mon–Fri 8:30–5, Sat–Sun 8:30–6; other times: 8:30–5. Free.

The most severe fighting of Sherman's march through Georgia to this point cost him over 3,000 men on June 27, 1864. It was a severe defeat for Sherman and delayed his advance for two weeks, but it did not in any way affect his ultimate goal: the capture of Atlanta.

The earthworks are well-preserved, and important military positions are marked with monuments and exhibits. The visitor center is at the foot of the mountain; at the peak is a panoramic observation platform and a memorial to 14 Confederate generals. Cheatham Hill, called by Union soldiers the "Dead Angle," was the site of the heaviest fighting and losses. The Illinois Memorial to the unit that bore the brunt of the attack is here.

261 Marietta Confederate Cemetery (site)

Powder Springs Street.

This cemetery was originally established in 1863 for soldiers killed in a train wreck at Allatoona Pass. More than 3,000 Confederate soldiers are buried here.

262 Marietta National Cemetery (site)

500 Washington Street, five blocks left of Public Square.

In 1866 Henry Cole, a local businessman, donated land for a cemetery to be used by both sides. But his gesture of conciliation went unheeded and the Confederate dead continued to be buried in the cemetery half a block away. Inside the 24 acres, behind a high stone wall, are 10,158 Union dead with state markers.

263 Old Courthouse (col)

101 Court Square; 404-373-1088; Mon–Fri, 9–4. Free.

The 1898 Old Courthouse contains a three-room museum with many Civil War artifacts, including naval relics. A Confederate memorial is on the grounds.

264 Western and Atlantic Passenger Depot (site)

No. 4 Depot Street; 770-429-1115; Mon–Fri 9–4, Sat 11–4, Sun 1–4. Free.

At the passenger depot on this site, James Andrews' Raiders boarded *The General* and began the "Great Locomotive Chase." The depot was burned by Sherman in 1864. Rebuilt as a Victorian brick depot in 1898, it now serves as a visitor center. Next door is the Kennesaw House, built in 1855 as a summer resort called the Fletcher House. James Andrews and his band of Union spies met here the night before they stole *The General* in April 1862. Sherman made this building his headquarters. It is a restaurant today.

Midway

265 Midway Church (site)

Route 17.

This clapboard church was built in 1729. Two colonial members of the congregation signed the Declaration of Independence. During the Civil War it was a temporary headquarters for Union general Hugh Judson Kilpatrick's raiding troops.

Milledgeville

266 Old Governor's Mansion (site)

120 South Clark Street; 912-453-4545; Hourly tours: Tues–Sat 10–4, Sun 2–4. Admission charged.

This 1838 Greek Revival home was built for Georgia's governors. General Sherman, who burnt government buildings during his occupation in November 1864 but spared most of the residences, stayed here.

267 Old State Capitol (site)

George Military College; 201 East Greene Street.

Built in 1807, the Old Capitol is one of the oldest Gothic-style public buildings in America. It served as the seat of the Georgia government from 1804 until the capital moved to Atlanta in 1868 and housed the Secession Convention in 1861. Later, during the occupation by Union troops, a mock session of the legislature was held repealing the ordinance of secession and burning Confederate money. Today the restored Capitol provides classrooms for the Georgia Military College.

268 St. Stephen's Episcopal Church (site)

220 South Wayne Street.

Sherman's troops stabled horses in this 1841 church during the two-day occupation; the roof was damaged when a nearby arsenal was disintegrated. Union soldiers poured syrup into the organ to prevent its use as a signal to sympathizers and burned the pews. More than forty years later, when New Yorker George Perkins heard about the damage he presented the parish with a new organ.

Millen

269 Magnolia Springs State Park (site)

Route 121/Route 25, south of town.

A Confederate prison here, one of three built to handle the overflow from Andersonville, housed 10,000 men. Known as Camp Lawton, it was destroyed by Sherman's men, but the earthworks, where artillery was placed to prevent escapes, are clearly visible.

Newnan

270 Male Academy Museum (col)

30 Temple Avenue; 770-251-0207. Admission charged.

Civil War weapons and other memorabilia are on display here. Buildings in town from the Civil War era were used as hospitals.

Resaca

271 Atlanta Campaign Relief Map (site)

Route 41.

Confederate general Joseph Johnston fortified Resaca to such a degree that Sherman was reduced to sniping at his flanks. He sent General Hooker against Confederate general Hood's reinforced troops to some success on May 15, 1864. Fearing being trapped against the Oostenaula River, Johnston withdrew during the night, burning a railroad bridge behind him.

Reenactment: The Battle of Resaca is described in this small park. A reenactment takes place each May on the third weekend.

272 Resaca Confederate Cemetery (site)

Route 41, two miles north of town.

The cemetery was dedicated to Mary Green, a young girl who with her sister, Pyatt, and two former slaves buried two fallen soldiers in their flower garden. Their father, Colonel John Green, donated the land for the burial of 450 Confederates who lay in shallow graves around the family plantation.

Richmond Hill

273 Fort McAllister State Historic Park (site)

3894 Ft. McAllister Road; 912-727-2339; Tues–Sat 9–5, Sun 2–5:30. Admission charged.

These massive earthworks on the Ogeechee River opposite Genesis Point were the principal defense of Savannah and withstood three significant bombardments in 1862 and 1863 with little adverse effect, although the garrison's mascot, Tom Cat, was killed. At one point the U.S.S. *Montauk* rained the heaviest shells ever launched from a naval vessel onto the fort. Finally on December 13, 1864, the fort was taken by William B. Hazen after Major George W. Anderson had made a gallant effort to defend it with 200 men. After this defeat General Hardee withdrew his Confederate forces from Savannah. Sherman called the capture "the handsomest thing I have seen in this war" and offered the prize as a Christmas present to Lincoln.

The visitor center features an exhibit on artillery, and the walking trails provide an explanation of defensive fortifications.

Ringgold

274 Atlanta Campaign Relief Map (site)

Route 41.

This is one of five roadside parks built in the 1930s by the United States government to graphically describe the Atlanta Campaign from May 7 to September 2, 1864.

275 Western and Atlantic Railroad Depot (site)

Off Route 41.

During the Battle of Ringgold Gap in 1863,

Confederate forces surrounding the old depot managed to keep Union forces at bay long enough for the main army to establish a defense line around Dalton. Two miles north of the depot on the Ooltewah-Ringgold Road is the site where Andrews' Raiders abandoned *The General* and fled on foot during the "Great Locomotive Chase."

Rome

276 Fort Norton (site)

Civic Center Hill.

The trenches visible here were part of a chain of earthworks located atop the seven hills around Rome. Constructed in 1863 by the Confederate army, Fort Norton is the only surviving inland fortification in Georgia.

277 Myrtle Hill Cemetery (site)

Broad Street and Myrtle Street.

Interred here are 377 Confederate and 2 Union soldiers. Included in the mortuary art is the first monument of its type dedicated to the Confederate women who cared for the wounded soldiers of both sides, and a statue of Lieutenant General Nathan B. Forrest, who saved Rome with a force of 425 soldiers.

278 Noble Brothers Foundry (site)

Broad Street and 1st Avenue.

A marker shows the grounds of the Noble Brothers Foundry and Machine Shop, where cannon barrels for the Confederacy were rifled. General Sherman destroyed the foundry and all factories in town.

Reenactment: During the third weekend in October the Rome Heritage Days feature a Civil War Reenactment of the Siege of Rome.

279 Oak Hill (site)

Berry College Campus; Veteran's Memorial Highway at Route 27N; 706-291-1883; Tues–Sat 10–5, Sun 1–5. Admission charged.

Home of Martha Berry, the founder of Berry College in 1902, this ante-bellum home was built in 1847. Union troops camped on the grounds during the battles in Rome.

280 St. Paul African-Methodist-Episcopal Church (site)

6th Avenue and West 2nd Street.

Union troops quartered their horses inside this building during the war. It was built in 1847 as the sanctuary of the original Methodist-Episcopal Church.

Roswell

281 Bulloch Hall (col)

180 Bulloch Avenue; 404-992-1731; Mon–Sat 10–3, Sun 1–3. Free.

Once the childhood home of Mittie Bulloch, the mother of President Theodore Roosevelt, the building is today a house museum with a Civil War artifact room. This milling town manufactured gray cloth for Confederate uniforms, and when General Sherman marched through town, he destroyed only the mill. Ante-bellum owner James Bulloch was a Confederate naval agent.

Sandersville

282 Old City Cemetery (site)

Virginia Avenue and West Church Street.

On November 25, 1863, Union cavalry met unexpected resistance here and was driven out of town. Eleven men were captured. While they were incarcerated in a town store, a band of vigilantes overpowered the guards, dragged the captives to a nearby field, and shot them. There was no doubt about what Sherman would do next. The attack came early in the morning and crushed Fighting Joe Wheeler's defense. Incensed by the murders, Sherman declared his intentions to burn the town to the ground but was dissuaded by a townswoman. Like most of his raids, the torching was confined to government and business buildings.

In the cemetery are graves of several Confederates killed defending the town, and in an unmarked, raised brick crypt, the murdered Union soldiers are believed to rest.

283 Washington County Museum (col)

129 Jones Street; 706-552-6965; Tues and Thurs, 2–5. Free.

The collection highlights the fighting around Sandersville and includes a couch General Sherman slept on during his one-night stay.

Savannah

284 Confederate Monument (mem)

Forsyth Park; Gaston Street to Park Avenue.

The sandstone pyramid stands with a bronze Confederate on its top. Surrounding the base are memorial busts of General Lafayette McLaws and Brigadier General Francis S. Bartow, both from Savannah.

285 Fort Jackson (site)

One Fort Jackson Road, two miles east of town; 912-232-3945; Daily, 9–5; Admission charged.

This is the oldest standing fort in Georgia and

was the headquarters for the Confederate River defenses. It is surrounded by a nine-foot deep tidal moat, which is crossed by a single drawbridge. Two small cannon could sweep the entrance. Inside the fort, behind thick brick walls, are several gallery exhibits. A 32-pounder cannon, the largest black powder cannon still fired in America, is ignited on special occasions.

286 Fort Wimberly (site)

Wormsloe Plantation Historic Site; 7601 Skidaway Road; 912-351-3023; Tues–Sat 9–5, Sun 2–5. Admission charged.

The Confederates built these earthworks to protect an inland approach to the city. The fort was rarely garrisoned and never used in combat. A walking tour explores the earthworks.

287 Great Savannah Exposition (col)

303 Martin Luther King Jr. Boulevard; 912-238-1779; Daily, 8:30–5. Admission charged.

The Central of Georgia Railroad Station, constructed in 1860, has been converted into a grand museum hall of Savannah history. Among the Civil War exhibits is an animated Sherman writing his famous letter to Lincoln, presenting Savannah as a Christmas gift.

288 Green-Meldrim House at St. John's Church (site)

One West Macon Street; 912-232-1251; Tues, Thurs–Sat, 10–4. Admission charged.

This Gothic Revival home, built in 1856, was Sherman's headquarters in 1864. Here he learned that his seventh child, whom he had never seen, had died of pneumonia. Across the street, the parish house of St. John's Episcopal Church features tall, wooden steeple chimes, which were spared due to a special plea to President Lincoln.

289 Second African Baptist Church (site)

123 Houston Street; 912-233-6163; Mon–Fri, 10:10–5. Free; tours by appointment only.

On the steps of the church, formed in 1802 by Andrew Bryan, General William Tecumseh Sherman read the Emancipation Proclamation to Savannah's citizens and promised newly freed slaves 40 acres and a mule.

290 Skidaway Island State Park (site)

52 Diamond Causeway, six miles southeast of town; 912-589-2300.

Visible on the nature trail are earthworks erected for the defense of Savannah.

Stone Mountain

291 Confederate Memorial (mem)

Route 78; 770-498-5702; Daily, 6–midnight. Admission charged.

Rising 400 feet above the ground is the world's largest bas-relief sculpture depicting three Southern heroes of the Civil War: Confederate president Jefferson Davis, General Robert E. Lee, and General Thomas J. "Stonewall" Jackson. The carving is 90 feet tall and 100 feet wide, standing out eleven feet from the mountain.

The idea for the memorial originated in 1909 with Mrs. Helen Plane, a charter member of the United Daughters of the Confederacy. A deed was obtained for the mountain in 1916 with a 12-year provision to complete a Civil War monument. Funding problems delayed carving until 1923, and then sculptor Gutzon Borglum, who later was to gain fame as the creator of Mount Rushmore, quit after only two years because of a dispute with management. Augustus Lukeman took over the project and, starting from scratch, was able to complete the faces of Lee and Davis before the 1928 deadline, but the owners reclaimed the property.

Work was halted for 36 years until the state of Georgia purchased the land to develop the site. Lukeman's master model of the three leaders on horseback was realized, although a trailing army rising out of the granite was omitted. The Confederate Memorial Carving was dedicated in a ceremony on May 9, 1970. The proportions of the carving are so enormous that workers could stand inside a horse's mouth to escape a rain shower.

Facing the structure is Memorial Hall, which features Confederate artifacts, maps, and audiovisual programs on significant Civil War events in Georgia.

Tunnel Hill

292 Railroad Tunnel (site)

Off Route 201S.

This engineering marvel is the oldest tunnel in the Southeast, completed in 1850. In 1862 *The General* steamed through here, with James Andrews' Raiders at the controls. Many skirmishes took place at the tunnel during the Atlanta Campaign in 1864, and when Sherman occupied the area, he made his headquarters in the nearby Clisby Austin House.

Varnell

293 Prater's Mill (site)

Route 2.

This 1855, three-story grist mill was a Union campsite for 600 troops under Colonel Eli Long in

February 1864. Two months later Confederate General Joseph Wheeler used the mill as a base for 2,500 soldiers.

Washington

294 Robert Toombs House (site)

215 E. Robert Toombs Avenue; 706-678-2226; Tues–Sat, 9–5 Sun 2–5:30. Admission charged.

Toombs, an ardent secessionist and Confederate diplomat, served as the rebel nation's first secretary of state. The home, built in 1797, is restored to its appearance at Toombs' death in 1885.

295 Washington Historical Museum (col)

308 E. Robert Toombs Avenue; 706-678-2105; Tues–Sat 10–5, Sun 2–5. Admission charged.

Confederate relics include Jefferson Davis's camp chest, as this town was along his escape route. Also in the collection is an assortment of Civil War guns.

Waynesboro

296 Burke County Museum (col)

536 Liberty Street; 706-554-4889; Mon–Fri and first Sat, 10–5. Admission charged.

As part of the plan to divert attention from his true mission, Sherman sent Hugh Judson Kilpatrick's cavalry in a feint attack on Augusta. Waynesboro was the site of one of several clashes between Kilpatrick — nicknamed "Kill-Cav" for his sometimes foolhardy attacks against Confederate troopers and for long marches that needlessly fatigued both soldier and steed — and his West Point classmate, Joe Wheeler. On December 4, 1864, the Federals subdued Waynesboro after heavy fighting in Brier Creek, continuing the ruse of an advance on Augusta. The bluff worked — General Braxton Bragg reinforced Augusta with 10,000 men who could have been deployed against Sherman's true attack.

A monument to Confederate soldiers in the Waynesboro cemetery on Jones Street is surrounded by the graves of unknown soldiers, mostly cavalrymen who died in the battle for Waynesboro. Nearby is the Burke County Courthouse, built in 1857 and partially destroyed by Kilpatrick's raiders. Two Civil War cannon guard the entrance; across the street is the Carter-Munnerlyn House with a collection of Civil War artifacts.

West Point

297 Fort Tyler (site)

Off 6th Avenue.

The day after Lincoln died, James Harrison Wilson's Federal cavalry captured Fort Tyler in the Battle of West Point, ending the fighting in Georgia.

Illinois

Civil War Status: Union
1860 Population: 1,711,951
Troops Provided: 257,000

Alton

298 Confederate Monument (site)

Confederate Soldiers Cemetery; Rozier and State streets in North Alton.

The monument commemorates 1,354 Confederate soldiers who died in the reviled prison camp established during the war in Illinois State Prison, the first state prison in Illinois.

299 Confederate Prison Site (site)

Broadway and William streets.

Only some foundations remain of the notorious prison that opened here on February 1, 1861. By February 12 it was reported to be overcrowded. Worse, built too close to the Mississippi River, its poor drainage created instant unsanitary conditions, and smallpox soon raced through the detention camp. Prison reformer Dorothea Dix led the outcry that caused all stricken prisoners to be removed to an island in the river. Although no records were kept, there were no reports of any victims who ever returned alive; it is estimated that several thousand prisoners were buried on the island. A portion of the prison is still standing.

300 Lincoln-Douglas Debate Site (site)

Broadway at the foot of Market Street.

The last of the great senatorial debates between Stephen A. Douglas and Abraham Lincoln took place on a temporary platform in front of city hall on October 15, 1858. An estimated crowd of 6,000 heard Douglas again voice the opinion that each state should have the right to decide its own policy on slavery and Lincoln again emphasize that a nation divided against itself cannot stand. A plaque designates the spot.

301 Elijah Lovejoy Monument (mem)

Alton City Cemetery; North end of Monument Avenue at entrance.

Locals like to claim the first battle of the Civil War was fought in Alton on November 7, 1837. Abolitionist publisher Elijah P. Lovejoy was a pastor and writer of the *Alton Observer*, whose presses were destroyed and thrown into the Mississippi River three times by proslavery groups.

A fourth press was being readied for installation on November 7, guarded by Lovejoy and 20 of his supporters at the Godfrey & Gilman warehouse. The proslavery party gathered outside, lobbing rocks through the windows. The defenders retaliated by bombing the crowd with earthenware pots, and the exchange escalated to gunfire. Five bullets tore into Lovejoy's chest as he assisted in putting out a fire on the roof. He was buried on his thirty-fifth birthday two days later, in an unmarked grave.

In 1897 a slim, 91-foot-high granite column was erected in the memory of the antislavery editor. Atop the shaft is a 17-foot bronze figure *Victory*, flanked by two shorter columns, each bearing an eagle with outstretched wings.

Batavia

302 Newton War Memorial (mem)
Batavia West Side Cemetery; Route 31.
Dedicated in 1918, this bronze soldier was "erected in honor and in commemoration of the loyal patriotic men who enlisted from the township of Batavia in the War for the Preservation of the Union."

Beardstown

303 Lincoln Courthouse Museum (site)
On the square; 217-323-3261; Mon–Fri, 9–5. Free.

In this courtroom Abraham Lincoln defended William Duff Armstrong, the son of a friend, against the charge of murder. Young Armstrong had allegedly beaten an acquaintance, James Preston Marker, to death one night. Lincoln was able to cast doubt on eyewitness testimony that Armstrong had delivered the fatal blows by producing an almanac showing that the night of the murder had been moonless. Armstrong was acquitted in the "Almanac Trial."

The courthouse was built in 1844 for Cass County and has been kept in its original state. It is the only courtroom still in use where Abraham Lincoln practiced law. On the square are granite memorials marking the sites where Lincoln and Douglas spoke during the 1858 senatorial campaign.

Belvidere

304 Soldiers' & Sailors' Monument (mem)
Big Thunder Park; Menomonie and Main streets.
The granite standing figure honoring the soldiers and sailors of Boone County was installed in 1910.

Bement

305 Bryant Cottage State Historic Site (site)
146 East Wilson Street; 217-678-8184; Apr–Sept: daily, 8–4; Oct–Mar: 9–5. Free.
This four-room cottage is where Stephen Douglas and Abraham Lincoln are said to have met on July 29, 1858, to plan the series of debates that would decide their senatorial race, ultimately won by Douglas.

Berwyn

306 Lincoln the Friendly Neighbor (mem)
6655 Cermak Road.
This memorial, created by Avard Fairbanks in 1959, depicts a young, beardless Lincoln informally posed with two children and a dog.

Bloomington

307 Lincoln's Lost Speech (site)
Southwest corner of East and Front streets.
In 1856 the first Republican state convention met here and on May 29 heard candidate Abraham Lincoln deliver such a spellbinding speech against secession that, legend has it, reporters forgot to take notes. As a result, this is the Lost Speech. The site of the speech, the former Major's Hall, built in 1852, was taken down in 1959, and a tablet marks the location.

308 McLean County Historical Society Museum (col)
200 North Main Street; 309-827-0428; Mon–Sat 10–5, Tues 10–9. Admission charged.
More than 3,000 maps, manuscripts, photographs and books trace the hisstory of the Illinois military. This building formerly was the county courthouse.

309 Soldiers' Monument (mem)
Miller Park; Morris Avenue at Wood Street.
Around the historic Miller Park Pavilion are monuments to McLean County's war dead. This

one, dedicated in 1913, is an ornamental arch with a shaft rising from the roof. The arch has two doorways with a walk-through tunnel, and above one doorway is a Civil War soldier. The bronze was sculpted by Frederick Cleveland Hibbard from a design by Dwight Earl Frink.

Bunker Hill

310 Lincoln Statue (mem)
Main Street.

Captain Charles Clinton of Cincinnati raised a battle group of men known as Company B of the First Missouri Cavalry in Bunker Hill. In 1904 Clinton, an enthusiastic admirer of Lincoln, presented duplicate statues of the president to his home town and Bunker Hill.

Byron

311 Soldiers' Monument (mem)
Chestnut and 2nd streets.

Erected in 1866, this was the first memorial to Civil War soldiers in the state of Illinois.

Cairo

312 The Custom House (mem)
14th and Washington streets.

This government building, currently being restored, is graced on the southwest lawn by "Duncan Cannon," an artillery piece captured by Grant's forces at Columbus, Kentucky. Inside the Custom House is the flagpole recovered from the river packet *Tigress*, which was commandeered by the Union army and carried General Grant up the Tennessee River to Shiloh on April 6, 1862. The *Tigress* was sunk a year later while running batteries at Vicksburg. The crew survived and returned the flagpole to Cairo.

313 Fort Defiance (site)
Route 51, south of town.

At the confluence of two of America's great rivers, the Ohio and Mississippi, there is no more unique and strategic port city than Cairo. Three thousand miles of navigable waterways radiate out from Cairo, and it is the nation's farthest inland port having yearlong navigation — the Ohio River has frozen over only once in recorded history. Due to its strategic location, Cairo was fortified immediately at the outbreak of the Civil War.

General Ulysses S. Grant was placed in charge of Fort Defiance, and all the major campaigns of the Mississippi River were launched from Cairo's riverbanks. Once called "probably the ugliest park in America," the area has been revitalized by Cairo's

citizens. Although the churning rivers have caused the point of confluence to move more than a mile south from the fort's original site, the military value of the area can still be seen clearly.

314 Safford Memorial Library Building (col)
1609 Washington Street.

In 1883 Mrs. Alfred B. Safford presented this Queen Anne–style library to Cairo. Included among its museum-quality collections are Civil War relics and documents. *Fighting Boys*, an original bronze by Janet Scudder, stands at the entrance.

Carbondale

315 Woodlawn Cemetery (site)
405 East Main Street.

This town is one of the many claimants to the first Memorial Day; a Civil War general organized the service here in 1866. Listed on the National Register of Historic Places, this cemetery contains over 60 graves of Civil War soldiers.

Carlinville

316 Lincoln Memorial Boulder (site)
South Broad and East 1st South Street.

Abraham Lincoln spoke to a crowd of unenthusiastic listeners in Carlinville on August 31, 1858 — Southern Illinois did not cotton to the new Republican party. A three-ton boulder sporting a bronze memorial plaque is on the exact spot of the address.

Champaign

317 County Court House (site)
Corner of Main Street and Broadway.

Dedicated in 1901, this is the fourth courthouse to stand on this site. A memorial at the north entrance attests to the fact that Abraham Lincoln rode this way as an eighth judicial circuit judge. He also spoke against Stephen Douglas here.

Charleston

318 Lincoln-Douglas Debate Site (site)
Coles County Fairgrounds.

On September 8, 1858, Lincoln and Douglas held their fourth debate. In front of a crowd of 12,000 on the western side of town, Lincoln answered the charge that he advocated intermarriage between whites and blacks. He began his rebuttal with the words, "I am not in favor of Negro citizenship."

319 Moore Home State Historical Site
(site)
4th Street, eight miles south of town; 217-345-6489; Tues–Sat, 10–4. Free.

Before leaving for his inauguration as the sixteenth president of the United States, Abraham Lincoln ate his last meal here with his stepmother and her daughter, Mrs. Matilda Moore.

320 Shiloh Cemetery (site)
Lincoln Highway Road, south of town.

The graveyard is the final resting place for many Civil War veterans and for Thomas and Sarah Lincoln, Abraham Lincoln's father and stepmother.

Chicago

321 Chicago Historical Society (col)
Clark Street and North Avenue; 312-642-4600; Mon–Sat 9:30–4:30, Sun 12–5. Admission charged.

The collection in the oldest museum and library in the city includes Lincoln's deathbed. The Lincoln collection is part of an exhibition called *A House Divided: America in the Age of Lincoln.*

322 The Chicago Lincoln (mem)
Lincoln Square; intersection of Lincoln, Lawrence, and Western avenues.

This monument by Avard Fairbanks was unveiled in 1956 on the centennial of a speech delivered by Lincoln in Chicago. Striding, holding his books and stovepipe hat, the Lincoln sculpture bears the words he spoke on that occasion: "Free society is not, and shall not be, a failure."

323 Chicago Public Library (col)
78 East Washington Street.

There are many items of Civil War interest in the collection including uniforms, rare antislavery pamphlets, and the Confederate battle plan for the Battle of Shiloh.

324 Douglas Monument (mem)
East end of 35th Street.

Leonard Wells Volk created the 12-foot bronze figure atop a 100-foot shaft in 1881. Stephen A. Douglas is buried underneath the circular base. Efforts to erect the monument began two decades earlier in 1861, but the senator's popularity was greatly overestimated, and supporters had to sell off some of his land to raise money for the memorial. A Confederate prison rose on part of that land.

325 Ulysses S. Grant Memorial (mem)
Lincoln Park; Ridge and Lake Shore drives.

This heroic equestrian bronze of General Grant was considered too expensive to move and rests in Lincoln Park and not his own park. The monument stands 18 feet above a rugged stone base. It is the work of Louis T. Rebisso and was unveiled on October 7, 1891.

326 Lincoln the Orator (mem)
Oakwoods Cemetery; 1035 East 67th Street.

This monument of Abraham Lincoln, 11 feet high, was sculpted by Charles Mulligan in 1905. More than 4,000 Confederates rest in the graveyard, most of whom perished as prisoners of war at Camp Douglas. A 40-foot shaft of Georgia granite is surmounted by an appropriate Confederate soldier in an attitude of mourning.

327 Lincoln the Railsplitter (mem)
Garfield Park; Northwest corner of Washington and Central Park boulevards.

A famous bronze by Charles Mulligan, this smooth-faced, rawboned Lincoln was unveiled in 1911. The statue stresses the president's humble beginnings.

328 General John Logan Memorial
(mem)
Grant Park; Michigan Avenue at 9th Street.

General John Logan is depicted astride a splendid horse and hoisting an American flag. Logan served with distinction under Grant and Sherman and died in his third term as a United States senator. Saint-Gaudens created Logan, and Alexander Proctor, a specialist in animals, sculpted his horse. The statue was dedicated on July 22, 1897.

329 Newberry Library (col)
60 West Walton Street.

Augmenting the extensive Civil War collection are portraits of many Union leaders. Parts of the collection that are not on display can be made available upon request.

330 Our Heroes: Civil War Monument
(mem)
Rosehill Cemetery; 5800 North Ravenswood Avenue.

Erected in 1869–1870 and based on a design by Leonard Wells Volk, this 30-foot monument was dedicated to the Union dead. The limestone base is topped with a Union standard-bearer. There are 230 Union army soldiers, many of them members of the Eighth Illinois Cavalry, which fired the first shots at Gettysburg, buried in two large plots to the east of the monument. Rosehill Cemetery contains the graves of 14 Union generals. Also of note is the grave of the Chicago mayor who was acquitted of charges that he assisted Confederate prisoners in escaping from Camp Douglas.

331 The Seated Lincoln (mem)

Grant Park; North of Congress Parkway.

While critics prefer Augustus Saint-Gaudens's *Standing Lincoln*, the sculptor favored this work 12 years in the rendering. It was cast a year after his death in 1908 and was displayed elsewhere until funds brought the bronze to Grant Park in 1928.

332 General Philip Henry Sheridan (mem)

Lincoln Park; Sheridan Road, Belmont Avenue and Lake Shore Drive.

This bronze designed by Gutzon Borglum represents Sheridan mounted on his favorite horse, Rienzi. Sheridan was commander of the Northern Illinois military area after the war. The monument, which cost $50,000, was dedicated on May 30, 1923.

333 The Standing Lincoln (mem)

Lincoln Park; Clark Street at North Avenue.

Considered by many the masterpiece of Saint-Gaudens, this 11½-foot likeness portrays Lincoln with head bowed and clutching his lapel. It was unveiled at the Dearborn Parkway entrance on October 22, 1887. Larger than life, it portrays Lincoln in a reflective attitude in the mood of the Gettysburg Address. The simple base and the spacious exedra are the work of Stanford White.

Clinton

334 Abraham Lincoln Statue (mem)

Courthouse Lawn.

This life-size standing Lincoln by Belgian artist Van den Bergen marks the site of the speech in which Lincoln supposedly remarked, "You can fool all of the people part of the time and part of the people all of the time, but you cannot fool all of the people all of the time." Historians do not agree that Lincoln actually ever made the remark at all, let alone here in Clinton. Nevertheless, the bronze was paid for by private citizens and was dedicated on November 11, 1931.

Danville

335 Civil War Monument (mem)

Soldiers' Circle; 301 East Voorhees Street.

The soldiers of Vermilion County are commemorated by a 50-foot granite shaft with a bronze soldier at the top, dedicated in 1900. The founders of

Danville and friends of Abraham Lincoln are buried here.

336 Civil War Soldier (mem)

Veterans Affairs Medical Center National Cemetery; 1900 East Main Street.

This standing bronze by W. Clark Noble was offered in memory of "the men who offered their lives in defense of their country." The Civil War soldier holds his rifle across his chest, his hat between his feet.

337 Vermilion County Museum (site)

116 North Gilbert Street; 217-442-2922; Tues–Sat 10–5, Sun 1–5. Admission charged.

Lincoln practiced law in Danville and often stayed at this home, now the county museum, then owned by his close friend and Civil War surgeon, William Fithian. The bedroom he used on his many visits remains as it was, as does the south balcony, from where he spoke in 1858. Lincoln sites around town are marked with plaques.

Decatur

338 The Defense of the Flag (mem)

Central Park; Water & North streets.

Sigvald Asbjornsen sculpted three bronze soldiers and a tattered flag honoring the Civil War soldiers of Macon County. The sculpture was unveiled on April 6, 1905.

339 First National Bank (site)

130 North Water Street.

On this site stood the Wigwam, a giant structure of wood and canvas where on May 9, 1860 the Republican party of Illinois held its state convention. During the opening session, two men entered carrying a banner stretched between fence rails. It read: "Abraham Lincoln The Rail Candidate. Two rails from a lot of 3,000 made in 1830 by Thos, Hanks and Abe Lincoln, whose father was the first pioneer of Macon County." Pandemonium broke out, and the local favorite easily won the convention's endorsement for president — as Lincoln the Rail Splitter. A plaque marks the spot.

340 Greenwood Cemetery (site)

West Decatur and Greenwood streets.

This final resting place for many Civil War veterans contains several monuments to local heroes and pioneers.

341 Lincoln as a Young Man (mem)

Millikin University; 1184 West Main Street.

The seated statue of Lincoln as a young man of 21 was executed by Fred Torrey. The inscription on the Millikin University campus reads: "At twenty-one, I came to Illinois."

342 Lincoln Homestead State Park (site)

Route 36.

This is the site of the first Lincoln homestead in Illinois. It is located at a bend of the Sangamon River. Lincoln lived here a year, splitting rails for fences, building a cabin, and working a farm.

343 Lincoln the Lawyer (mem)

Entrance to Macon County Building; 253 East Woods Street.

This bronze statue, privately funded, is the work of sculptor Boris Lovet-Lorsky.

344 Macon County Museum Complex (site)

5580 North Fork Road; 217-422-4919; Tues–Sun, 1–4. Free.

The Macon County Historical Society Museum has gathered historical buildings into the Prairie Village, which contains the 1830 log courthouse where Abraham Lincoln once practiced. Also in the society's collection is a rare life mask made two months before Lincoln's death and casts of his hands.

345 Red Granite Bullet Monument (mem)

Fairview Park.

This monument is "in memory of Soldiers and Sailors of Union Veterans of the Civil War who defended the Union 1861–1865." Also in the park is a large bronze monument sculpted by G. Lorenze Miller of Decatur and cast by the Fairies Manufacturing Company in town. The tablet on the monument, erected in 1927, bears the names of 2,085 Macon County Civil War veterans.

346 "Stump Speaker" Lincoln (site)

Lincoln Square.

This statue, marking Lincoln's first political oratory, was sculpted by Anthony Vestuto and erected on October 12, 1968. A bronze plaque recalls the moment: "Lincoln mounted a stump by Harrell's Tavern facing this square and defended the Illinois Whig party candidates near this spot at age 21 in the summer of 1830." Other markers on the square designate the spot where Lincoln practiced law until 1838, and a bronze tablet on the building at the southeast corner commemorates the arrival of the Lincoln family by covered wagon in mid–March 1830. The Lincolns set up camp in a muddy clearing amid a smattering of log houses. The next day the family moved on.

Dixon

347 The Captain (mem)

Lincoln Statue Drive between the Abraham Lincoln Bridge and Ronald Reagan Bridge.

On the west bank of the Rock River, Jefferson Davis, Zachary Taylor, and Abraham Lincoln met during the Black Hawk War in 1832. The bronze statue, by Leonard Crunelle, depicts a 23-year-old Lincoln as a young captain of volunteers. The larger-than-life bronze is ten feet tall.

It was placed near the site of the old Fort Dixon blockhouse when dedicated on August 23, 1930. A small granite block behind the statue pays tribute to Lincoln's service here. Dixon is one of only two towns on the famous coast-to-coast Lincoln Highway, today Route 30, that Abraham Lincoln personally visited. The other is Gettysburg.

Elizabethtown

348 Illinois Iron Furnace (site)

Route 146.

During the Civil War this furnace was used for smelting iron ore. The restored structure features interpretive information.

Freeport

349 Civil War Monument (mem)

Stephenson County Courthouse; Galena and Stephenson streets.

Marble from Joliet, Illinois, was used for the square base of this 83-foot-high memorial, which was dedicated in 1871. The four bronze figures represent the arms of the nineteenth-century military service: infantry, cavalry, artillery, and navy. Names of all the men from Stephenson County who lost their lives are recorded on bronze plaques inscribed on the four sides.

350 Lincoln-Douglas Debate Site (site)

North State Avenue and East Douglas Street.

This town of 5,000 swelled to four times its size when Abraham Lincoln and Stephen Douglas engaged in their second debate here on August 27, 1858. Lincoln said, "this government cannot endure permanently half slave and half free." Douglas replied that "the people have the lawful means to introduce it or exclude it as they please." His "Freeport Doctrine" would aid him in winning the Illinois senatorial race but helped Lincoln secure the presidency in 1860 and helped precipitate the Civil War.

The site was marked by a boulder here in 1902 and dedicated by President Theodore Roosevelt the next year. As the twentieth century slipped into its last decade, the boulder was left incongruously in the middle of a city parking lot. The town restored the parklike setting, and in 1992 the statue *Lincoln and Douglas in Debate* was unveiled. Crafted by Lily Tolpo, it is the only known statue to depict Lincoln, seated in a chair on the speaker's platform, and Douglas, standing, together in debate.

351 Lincoln the Debater (mem)

Taylor Park; East Stephenson Street.

This bronze statue by Leonard Crunelle of Chicago was unveiled in this former private racetrack on August 27, 1929, on the 71st anniversary of the Freeport debate.

Galena

352 Galena/Jo Davies County History Museum (col)

211 S. Bench Street; 815-777-9129; Daily, 9–4:30. Admission charged.

Thomas Nast's life-size painting *Peace in Union*, depicting the surrender at Appomattox, is part of the permanent Civil War display here. The extensive collection of artifacts from Ulysses S. Grant and others include Civil War flags and a muzzle-loader that belonged to Confederate raider James Quantrill.

353 Ulysses S. Grant Home State Historic Site (site)

500 Bouthillier Street; 815-777-0248; Apr–Dec: daily, 9–5; other times: Thurs–Mon, 9–5. Free.

Galena in northwest Illinois was home to nine Union generals, including Ulysses S. Grant. Many homes in the historic district are connected to these leaders. This two-story Italianate brick house was presented to Grant at the end of the Civil War. He lived here until 1867, when Andrew Johnson named him secretary of war and he moved to Washington. Grant was to return in 1879 before moving to New York for his final days. Much of the furniture in the house is from the White House and other stages of Grant's life here.

354 Soldiers' Monument (mem)

Grant Park; Park Avenue and Jackson Street.

On July 4, 1883, this monument was dedicated to all the Jo Davies County soldiers who served in the Civil War. Their names are inscribed around the 33-foot high granite obelisk. On each face is a high relief depicting General Grant, General Rawlins, the American shield, and a soldier's cap on a pair of crossed bayonets. *Grant— Our Citizen* by Johannes Gelert is a bronze portrait of Grant, standing and dressed as a civilian. On the pedestal is a relief of Grant and Lee meeting at Appomattox.

Galesburg

355 Mother Bickerdyke Memorial (mem)

Courthouse Park; 200 South Cherry Street.

At the age of 45 Mary Ann Ball Bickerdyke left Galesburg to volunteer as a Union army nurse. At Cairo she provided dressings for the wounded, made soup for soldiers, and traveled on a mule with supplies. She collected 200 cows and 1,000 hens and had them conveyed on flatboats to Memphis; General Grant gave her the use of President's Island for the livestock. One of America's first war nurses, she is credited with serving in 19 battles and setting up 300 hospitals. The Mother Bickerdyke Historical Collection is in the Galesburg Public Library.

This bronze of Mother Bickerdyke giving aid to a wounded soldier was created by Theo Alice Ruggles Kitson. Eight thousand people attended the dedication ceremony on May 22, 1906. The base bears the inscription from General Sherman: "She outranks me."

356 Civil War Soldiers' Monument (mem)

Hope Cemetery; Academy and Main streets.

Gray Vermont granite was used to sculpt this Civil War soldier, in full uniform, at parade rest. The statue was dedicated on the October 7, 1896, the 38th anniversary of the fifth Abraham Lincoln-Stephen Douglas debate, which was staged in Galesburg at Knox College. More than 15,000 people attended the ceremony, including Robert Lincoln, son of the president.

357 "Old Main" Knox College (site)

South Street; 309-343-0112; Sept–May: Mon–Fri, 8–4:30. Free.

This is the only site of a Lincoln-Douglas debate that retains the original setting. Debate number five was staged against the east wall of Old Main on October 7, 1858. Two large bronze likenesses of Abraham Lincoln and Stephen Douglas stand on the wall.

Geneseo

358 Geneseo Civil War Monument (mem)

City Park; State Street.

The stone monument to the Union dead was erected in 1893 at the cost of $1,500. It features a figure of a soldier standing at parade rest.

Geneva

359 Soldiers' and Sailors' Monument (mem)

Kane County Courthouse; 100 South 3rd Street.

Twenty-two plaques with names grace this monument erected in 1915 to the memory of Kane County's soldiers and sailors.

Havana

360 Civil War Soldier (site)

West Main Street, 100 block.

Lincoln returned to Havana as a soldier, surveyor, lawyer, and political candidate in his Illinois days. During his senatorial campaign he arrived in Havana on August 13, 1858, and listened to Douglas speak. Then he delivered his own speech the next day. The tribute to Mason County's Civil War soldiers is a granite soldier in full dress uniform.

Heyworth

361 Simpkins War Museum (col)

Route 51; 309-473-3989; May–Sept, Sat–Sun, 1–4. Free.

Gary Simpkins began his Civil War collection when he was 12 years old. That hobby has mushroomed into a permanent exhibition that includes nearly 1,000 American shoulder patches, over 130 pieces of military headgear, 100 uniforms, and 50 rifles from the Civil War and recent conflicts.

Hillsboro

362 Soldiers' and Sailors' Monument (mem)

Oak Grove Cemetery; 904 South Main Street.

Dedicated on November 7, 1902, this granite Civil War soldier at rest with long coat and buttoned cape commemorates the fallen heroes of Hillsboro.

Homer

363 Civil War Monument (mem)

Grand Army of the Republic Cemetery; Route 512.

This granite figure of a soldier standing at parade rest was dedicated to the memory of Union soldiers on August 20, 1901.

Jacksonville

364 Jacksonville's Civil War Monument (mem)

Jacksonville Square.

Abraham Lincoln frequented this town and spoke here on February 11, 1859. This work by Leonard Crunelle is said to be inspired by his "Noble Women of the North." It features a standing bronze female figure atop a pedestal and is inscribed to the deeds of men and women in the Civil War. The monument was erected by Morgan County in 1920.

Joliet

365 Civil War Bench (mem)

Ottawa and Clinton streets.

A bronze plaque in the center of this ornate stone bench dedicates this resting area to "our fathers in the Grand Army of the Republic."

366 Will County Memorial (mem)

Will County Courthouse; Chicago and Jefferson streets.

Michael Muldoon was the artist for this monument to Will County's participation in the Civil War. A granite Union army officer stands atop a concrete obelisk, upon which are inscribed the major battles of the war. It was dedicated on October 10, 1889.

Jonesboro

367 Lincoln-Douglas Debate Site (site)

Fairgrounds; North Main Street.

The marker in the town square commemorates the third Lincoln-Douglas engagement, where Lincoln was on enemy ground. In this strong Democratic seat Lincoln went unrecognized by many in the town before the event on September 15, 1858.

Kankakee

368 Civil War Soldiers' Statue (mem)

North lawn of courthouse.

This memorial was erected by the Grand Army of the Republic in 1887.

369 Kankakee County Historical Society Museum (col)

8th Avenue and Water Street; 815-932-5279; Mon–Sat, 12–4. Admission charged.

The extensive collection in this Chicago-area

museum features vintage firearms and Civil War documents.

Lawrenceville

370 Lincoln Land State Park (mem)

Lincoln Memorial Bridge; Route 250.

In March 1830 the Lincoln family ferried here across the Wabash River from Indiana. The Lincoln Memorial Bridge was constructed in 1931. At the bridge approach on the Illinois side, in a small park, is the work of Nellie Walker, a Chicago sculptor, whose monument depicts the Lincoln family entering Illinois on foot with their belongings hauled by oxcart.

Lerna

371 Lincoln Log Cabin State Historic Site (site)

4th Street; 217-345-6489; Summer: daily, 9–5; other times: Sat–Sun, 9–5. Free.

This site in eastern Illinois was the home of Thomas and Sarah Bush Lincoln, Abraham's father and stepmother, in the 1840s. The 86-acre site contains a replica of their home and farm.

Lincoln

372 Civil War Monument (mem)

Logan County Courthouse; South Kickapoo and Broadway streets.

This standing figure of a soldier by F. C. Bushway was dedicated on June 9, 1869. The names inscribed on the middle tier of the stone base are now barely visible; the bronze plaque near the bottom lists the names of 326 war dead. The courthouse dates back to 1905.

373 Stephen A. Douglas Site (site)

Corner of Logan and 4th streets.

On this site during the senatorial campaign of 1858, Stephen A. Douglas spoke to a Democratic political rally in a circus tent. Lincoln, his opponent, was also on the train. He exited the train from the rear car, following at a distance the retinue accompanying his opponent and listened to his speech later from the rear of the tent.

374 Lincoln Museum (col)

Lincoln College; 300 Keokuk Street; 217-732-3155; Mon–Fri 10–4, Sat–Sun 1–4, closed Dec–Jan. Free.

The college was founded in 1865 and was the first and only college named for Lincoln in his lifetime. Lincoln College maintains two museums in

the McKinstry Library and includes the Abraham Lincoln Collection, with over 2,000 volumes and related items of historical interest. *Lincoln, The Student* is a statue on campus.

375 Postville Courthouse State Historic Site (site)

914 5th Street; 217-732-8930; Fri–Sat, 12–5. Free.

This is a reproduction of the first Logan County Courthouse, in use from 1840 to 1847. Abraham Lincoln served here while riding on the eighth judicial circuit.

376 Town of Lincoln Christening Scene (site)

Broadway and Chicago streets.

On August 27, 1853, the first lots were sold in the new town of Lincoln. After the lots had been sold, the crowd urged Abraham Lincoln to christen the new town, which had been named in his honor. Lincoln took a watermelon, broke it open, and with its juice christened the new village. The original settlement was Postville, a short distance to the west. Lincoln had visited here often on business as a lawyer.

Litchfield

377 Civil War Soldier (mem)

Elmwood Cemetery; Tremont Street.

The limestone mustachioed soldier was dedicated on July 4, 1868, to the town's dead soldiers. The figure stands in front of a tree stump; on the front of the shaft is a patriotic relief.

Macomb

378 Civil War Monument (mem)

Chandler Park.

This monument to the "men of McDonough County who voluntarily offered and freely gave their lives" in the Civil War was dedicated on August 3, 1899. The stone Civil War soldier stands at parade rest.

Metamora

379 Metamora Courthouse State Historic Site (site)

113 East Partridge; 309-367-4470; Mon, Wed, Fri, Sat, 1–5. Free.

This courthouse, built in 1845, is one of two remaining courthouses where Abraham Lincoln practiced law while traveling the eighth judicial circuit. The courtroom has been completely restored and contains a museum. The bricks used to build the courthouse were fired in Metamora.

Morris

380 Civil War Monument (mem)
Grundy County Courthouse; 111 East Washington.

The memory of the soldiers and sailors of Grundy County is honored by a granite Civil War soldier at parade rest on a 40-foot-tall granite shaft. This sculpture by Lorado Zadoc Taft was dedicated on May 30, 1890.

Mound City

381 Mound City National Cemetery (site)
Routes 51 and 37.

In this cemetery are the graves of 5,686 soldiers from the Civil War and other later wars. Nearby was Mound City Marine Hospital, where wounded were brought following the battle of Shiloh; a marker at the Ohio levee indicates the site where soldiers were brought into the southern portion of the brick building. The 75-foot *Civil War Monument* was installed in 1874.

Mt. Pulaski

382 Mt. Pulaski Courthouse (site)
Route 121 in downtown area.

Mt. Pulaski Courthouse, a two-story red brick building, served as the Logan County Courthouse from 1847 to 1853. One of two remaining courthouses on Abraham Lincoln's eighth judicial circuit, it is on the National Register of Historic Places.

Mount Vernon

383 Appellate Courthouse (site)
Main and 14th streets.

Abraham Lincoln successfully argued one of his biggest corporate tax cases in this building, erected in 1857, and won in litigation for the Illinois Central Gulf Railroad in 1859. Guided tours are available.

Murphysboro

384 General John A. Logan Museum (col)
1613 Edith Street; 618-684-3455; Jun–Aug: Mon, Wed, Fri–Sun 1–4; Apr–May and Sept–Oct: Sat–Sun 1–4. Admission charged.

This museum is devoted to "Blackjack" John Logan, a ferocious and controversial Union general who served under Sherman in the Atlanta campaign. The site also features an extensive collection on black Civil War history.

Naperville

385 Civil War Monument (mem)
Washington Street, east of library.

Naperville, west of Chicago, was founded in 1831. A nineteenth-century living history museum maintains 25 historic buildings from that time. The statue was erected in 1870 by the Grand Army of the Republic.

Ottawa

386 Civil War Monument (mem)
301 West Madison Street.

This 40-foot-tall, hexagonal stone shaft, conceived by Edward McInhill, is inscribed with the names of Civil War soldiers. The shaft is surmounted by a female figure. It was unveiled on September 21, 1873.

387 Lincoln-Douglas Debate Site (site)
Washington Park.

The site of the first Lincoln-Douglas debate on August 21, 1858, is marked by a monstrous boulder. There was a total of seven debates, and Douglas eventually defeated Lincoln for the Senate seat.

Pana

388 Lincoln Statue (mem)
Rosamond Grove Cemetery; Route 16, five miles west of town.

This work of Charles J. Mulligan was dedicated in 1903 to Union soldiers and sailors.

Peoria

389 The Civil War Memorial (mem)
Courthouse Square; Main and Adams streets.

On the southeast corner of the square is a 65-foot column with a bronze eagle perched atop. The base of the memorial depicts the defense of the flag with two battle groups of five men and one female figure representing History. The memorial, sculpted by Frederick Triebel, was dedicated in 1899. The courthouse is the site where Lincoln is said to have denounced slavery in a speech on October 16, 1854.

390 Civil War Monument (mem)
Arcadia and Prospect streets.

This stone monument was erected in 1907 in memory of the Civil War soldiers stationed at Camp Lyon in Peoria.

Peru

391 Civil War Monument (mem)

City Park; Second, Pine and Schuyler streets.

The standing figure of a Civil War soldier was dedicated by the citizens of Peru to its soldiers on June 25, 1902. Inscribed are significant battles of the war.

Petersburg

392 Abraham Lincoln's New Salem Historic Site (site)

Route 97, two miles south of town; 217-632-7953; Apr–Oct: daily, 9–5, other times: 8–4. Free.

Calling himself an "aimless piece of driftwood" after moving to Illinois, Lincoln decided to settle in this growing village after stopping during an expedition copiloting a flatboat. He became a captain in the local militia and undertook the study of law in New Salem.

The village has been restored to its appearance at the time Lincoln lived here from 1831 to 1837. A heroic statue, *The Lincoln from New Salem*, by Avard Fairbanks, sits atop a hill. Ann Rutledge, Lincoln's first sweetheart, is buried in the town's Oakland Cemetery. The *Great American People Show* stages performances based on history nightly in the summer, except Mondays.

393 Menard County Court House (col)

Jackson Street.

Lincoln completed the survey for the town of Petersburg on February 17, 1836. A display of his documents is on the second floor of this 1897 Renaissance Revival building of rose granite and red sandstone.

Princeton

394 Bureau County Historical Society Museum (col)

109 Park Avenue West; 815-875-2184; Mon, Wed–Sun, 1–5. Admission charged.

The museum features one of the finest regimental histories extant, the 93rd Illinois Infantry, which was mustered from Bureau County into the Union army.

Quincy

395 All Wars Museum (col)

1707 North 12th Street; 217-222-8641; Wed–Thurs 1–4, Sat–Sun 9–12 and 1–4. Free.

Located on the grounds of one of America's oldest and largest veteran's homes, the museum contains relics from the Civil War in its collection. On the grounds, a French bronze figure of a soldier standing at parade rest honors Union veterans. A wooden rifle replaces the original metal weapon, which was stolen.

396 Lincoln and Douglas (site)

Washington Park.

This memorial is at the site of debate number six between senatorial candidates Lincoln and Douglas. The large plaque explaining the events of October 13, 1858, is by Lorado Taft.

Rock Island

397 Rock Island Arsenal (site)

Arsenal Island; 309-782-5021; Daily, 10–4. Free.

Part of an active U.S. Army ordnance factory, the museum in building 60 was established in 1905; only West Point has an older United States Army museum. Fort Armstrong was built on the island in 1816 during the Black Hawk War, and in 1863 it was converted into one of the largest Civil War northern prisons. Nearly 2,000 prisoners died in the prison camp, notorious for its harsh conditions. In addition to interpreting the history of Rock Island Arsenal, the museum has a scale model of Fort Armstrong and displays over 1,100 military firearms. Confederate and Union cemeteries are off Rodman Avenue near the eastern end of the island.

398 Rock Island County Civil War Soldiers' Monument (mem)

Rock Island Courthouse; 1504 3rd Avenue.

The names carved on this marble column, dedicated on April 9, 1869, have long since eroded. A Civil War soldier by Leonard Volk surmounts the decorated column.

399 Soldiers' and Sailors' Monument (mem)

Chippiannock Cemetery; 2901 12th Street.

On each side of the granite base is a six-foot soldier standing at parade rest; the one on the left is the Civil War infantryman. Dedication took place on September 25, 1915.

Sidney

400 Civil War Soldier (mem)

Mt. Hope Cemetery.

A granite Civil War soldier stands atop a 20-foot limestone base, which is inscribed with the names of 37 Sidney Union veterans.

Springfield

401 Camp Butler National Cemetery (site)

5063 Camp Butler Road, Route 36 East.

Once the site of a Union Civil War training camp and a Confederate prison, it is now a graveyard for veterans.

402 Daughters of Union Veterans of the Civil War Museum (col)

503 South Walnut Street; 217-544-0616; Mon–Fri 9–12, 1–4. Free.

In addition to the requisite medals and guns and uniforms, the museum maintains a complete set of the "War of Rebellion: Official Records of the Union and Confederate Armies," an indispensable genealogical research aid.

403 Grand Army of the Republic Memorial Museum (col)

629 South 7th; 217-522-4373; Tues–Sat, 10–4. Free.

The Grand Army of the Republic was founded in Springfield, and this museum has a wide variety of Civil War relics, including tintypes by Civil War photographic chronicler Mathew Brady.

404 Lincoln Depot Museum (site)

10th and Monroe streets; 217-544-8695; Apr–Aug: daily, 10–4. Free.

Abraham Lincoln left his comfortable security in Springfield for the caldron of uncertainty in Washington when he departed from this Great Western Railroad Depot in 1861. His farewell address before leaving to assume the presidency is considered one of his most eloquent. The museum contains exhibits of people and places close to Lincoln and offers a slide show recreating the 12-day journey to his inauguration.

405 Lincoln-Herndon Law Offices (site)

Sixth and Adams streets; 217-785-7289; Mar–Oct: daily, 9–5; Nov–Feb: daily, 9–4. Free.

A trio of young lawyers practiced in the offices above Seth Tinsley's store from 1843 until 1853. Lincoln's partners during this time were Stephen Logan (1843–1844) and William Herndon (1844–1865). This is the only surviving structure in which Lincoln maintained working law offices. A ten-minute slide show highlights Lincoln's legal career.

406 Lincoln Home National Historic Site (site)

8th and Jackson streets; 217-492-4150; May–Aug: daily, 8–8; other times: 8:30–5. Free.

The only home that Abraham Lincoln ever owned was built in 1839 and purchased by him in 1844. The Lincolns lived here until they moved to Washington in 1861. Free tickets to tour the Quaker-brown residence are required; they can be picked up in the Lincoln visitor center at 426 South 7th Street.

407 Lincoln Ledger (col)

Bank One; 6th and Washington streets; 217-525-9600; Mon–Fri 9–5, Sat 9–12. Free.

Abraham Lincoln's original account ledger with the Springfield Marine and Fire Insurance Company is on display during bank hours.

408 Lincoln Memorial Garden and Nature Center (site)

2301 East Lake Drive; 217-529-1111.

A "living memorial" to Abraham Lincoln comprised of plants native to Illinois, Indiana, and Kentucky. Designed by Jens Jensen, it is on the shores of Lake Springfield.

409 Lincoln's Family Pew (site)

First Presbyterian Church; 7th and Capitol streets; 217-528-4311; Jun–Sept: Mon–Fri, 10–4. Free.

Abraham and Mary Lincoln maintained a family pew in their place of worship. There are also copies of original letters and baptismal certificates. Seven Tiffany windows illuminate the sanctuary.

410 Lincoln's Tomb Historic Site (site)

Oak Ridge Cemetery; 217-782-2717; Mar–Oct: daily, 9–5; Nov–Feb: daily, 9–4. Free.

Abraham Lincoln was buried in Oak Ridge Cemetery at the request of Mrs. Lincoln. The imposing tomb was sculpted by Larkin Mead and is the final resting place for Mary Todd, Tad, Eddie, and Willie Lincoln. Their oldest son, Robert, is buried in Arlington National Cemetery. Bronze tablets bear the text of the Gettysburg Address, Lincoln's farewell address in Springfield, and his second inaugural address.

The monument to Lincoln was dedicated on October 15, 1874, on six acres of ground. Larkin Goldsmith Mead won the commission, a contract worth $206,000, the largest commission ever received by an American sculptor up to that time.

Reenactment: The 114th Infantry Regiment demonstrates drill movements during a Civil War retreat ceremony held each Tuesday evening in the summer.

411 Old State Capitol (site)

6th and Adams Street; 217-785-7961; Mar–Oct: daily, 9–5; Nov–Feb: daily, 9–4. Free.

Abraham Lincoln borrowed books from the state library here and tried several hundred cases in the Illinois Supreme Court between 1837 and 1858. It was in the Hall of Representatives that he spoke the immortal words, "A house divided against itself cannot stand." The library's holdings include the largest collection devoted to the prepresidential career of Lincoln.

412 The President Elect (mem)

Illinois State Capitol; 425 South College Avenue.

Andrew O'Connor portrayed Lincoln with downcast eyes as he leaves Springfield for Washington. His farewell address is carved on a huge granite slab. The statue was dedicated on October 5, 1918.

Stockton

413 The Old Sentry (mem)

Stockton Memorial Park; Pearl Street at Summit.

Originally dedicated to the sacrifice for the Union in 1908, this stone Civil War soldier had brass plaques added in 1974 to honor soldiers from other wars as well.

Summer Hill

414 Major Sam Hayes (mem)

Route 54.

Slightly less than life-size, this monument was dedicated to the members of the Major Sam Hayes Post 477 of Illinois. The figure is a Civil War soldier standing at parade rest.

Sycamore

415 Civil War Monument (mem)

Dekalb County Courthouse; 133 State Street.

Both a Confederate and a Union soldier grace the base of this monument, dedicated on May 30, 1897, to the Dekalb County Civil War effort. Highlights of the war are inscribed.

Taylorville

416 Soldiers and Sailors of Christian County (mem)

Oak Hill Cemetery; Cherokee Street.

A bronze Civil War soldier, facing west, was erected to the memory of Christian County soldiers on May 30, 1895. The multitiered base sports relief carvings near the bottom.

Tolono

417 Civil War Memorial (mem)

Bailey Memorial Cemetery; County Road 800 North.

The figure of a Civil War soldier standing at parade rest on a low granite shaft was installed in 1895.

Urbana

418 The Circuit Rider (mem)

Carle Park.

This privately funded statue of Abraham Lincoln was provided by a judge who knew Lincoln from his days on the court circuit. The monument was sculpted by Lorado Taft, who created a young, vigorous lawyer.

Utica

419 Civil War Monument (mem)

Oak Hill Cemetery; Route 178.

The inscription reads: "In memory of our soldiers who fought in the Rebellion." The monument is a granite Civil War soldier standing at parade rest.

Vandalia

420 Vandalia Statehouse State Historic Site (site)

315 West Gallatin Street; 618-283-1161; Daily, 9–5. Free.

Vandalia was Illinois' second state capital, the seat of government from 1820 until 1839. The Statehouse, where Abraham Lincoln served in the legislature, was the first to be built specifically for that purpose and is the oldest still standing in Illinois.

Woodhull

421 Max Nordeen's Wheels Museum (col)

Route 17, two miles north of town; 309-334-2589; Summer: Tues–Sun, 9–4; other times: Sat–Sun, 9–4. Admission charged.

This wide-ranging collection of more than 2,500 items includes Civil War relics.

Indiana

Civil War Status: Union
1860 Population: 1,350,428
Troops Provided: 200,000

Bloomington

422 Lilly Library (col)

Fine Arts Plaza; Indiana University; 812-855-2452; Mon–Fri 8–6, Sat 9–1. Free.

This internationally recognized rare book library contains more than 400,000 books, 100,000 pieces of sheet music, and 6 million documents. Occasional Civil War exhibits complement a strong collection.

Brookville

423 Hackleman Monument (mem)

Southwest courthouse lawn facing Main Street.

This statue honors Indiana's only general to die in the Civil War, Pleasant A. Hackleman, who fell at Corinth on October 3, 1862, at the age of 37. The monument, erected by the Grand Army of the Republic, bears the inscription, "I am dying but I die for my country."

Butler

424 Soldiers' and Sailors' Monument (mem)

Butler Cemetery; County Road 28.

Dedicated on August 5, 1908, this granite monument of a standing infantryman honors Union defenders.

Columbia City

425 Civil War Monument (mem)

Courthouse Square; Van Buren Street.

More than 300 names of Civil War soldiers who died are listed on the main base, which supports a Union soldier at parade rest. The monument was dedicated on May 30, 1897.

Corydon

426 Corydon Capitol State Historic Site (col)

202 East Walnut Street; 812-738-4890; mid-Mar–mid-Dec: Tues–Sat 9–5, Sun 1–5. Free.

On July 9, 1863, General John Hunt Morgan and Confederate raiders crossed the Ohio River from Brandenburg, Kentucky, on commandeered steamboats. They were met by 400 Corydon home guards in this onetime state capital. Three of the defenders were killed and two wounded while eight invaders lost their lives. The home guards surrendered and were held prisoner for the few hours the raiders remained. The Corydon Battlefield south of town is a park that looks much as it did in 1863.

Crawfordsville

427 Henry S. Lane Home (col)

212 South Water Street; 317-362-3416; Apr–Oct: Tues–Sun, 1–4. Admission charged.

Henry Lane was governor of Indiana and a United States senator during the Civil War, but his greatest contribution was his direct involvement with securing the nomination of Abraham Lincoln for the presidency of the United States. Lane later served as a pallbearer at Lincoln's funeral, and a lock of the president's hair is on display at the Lane Mansion.

428 General Lew Wallace Study (col)

East Pike Street and Wallace Avenue; 317-362-5769; Apr–Oct: Wed–Sat 10–4:30, Tues and Sun 1–4:30. Admission charged.

In downtown Crawfordsville Union general Lew Wallace crafted "a pleasure house for my soul" in 1896. Wallace served in the Mexican and Civil Wars and was president of the Andersonville trial, but today he is best remembered as the author of *Ben-Hur*, published in 1880. This unusual cubic-style house now contains personal memorabilia of Wallace the general, Wallace the diplomat, Wallace the author, and Wallace the artist. He is buried at Oak Hill Cemetery on the north edge of town, across Sugar Creek, where his grave is marked by a 35-foot obelisk.

Fort Wayne

429 Lincoln Museum (col)

200 East Berry Street; 219-455-3864; Mon–Sat 10–5, Sun 1–5. Admission charged.

The Lincoln Museum evolved out of a letter written by Arthur Hall to Robert Todd Lincoln in 1895 asking for permission to use his father's name on a new insurance company. Created in 1928, the

Lincoln Museum today holds the largest privately owned Lincoln collection in the world. Eleven permanent galleries and four theaters spread across 3,000 square feet. The exhibit *Years of War 1861–1865* features three seven-minute videos and interactive computer stations. Paul Manship sculpted the statue of Lincoln as a youth in Indiana for the Lincoln National Life Insurance Company.

Fountain City

430 Levi Coffin State Historic Site (site)

North Main Street; 317-847-2432; Jun–Aug: Tues–Sat, 1–4; Sept–Oct: Sat, 1–4. Admission charged.

Levi Coffin and his wife, Aunt Katie, were Quakers who moved from Guilford County, North Carolina, to Indiana because of their opposition to slavery. They soon let it be known that their eight-room Federal-style brick house could be used by any fugitive slave reaching them. Frustrated slave hunters could track runaway slaves as far as Newport (Fountain City) where the trail always dried up. One frustrated slave hunter from Kentucky remarked that the slaves must have "an underground railroad running from Newport to Canada with the Coffin house Grand Central Station and Levi the president." More than 2,000 fugitives were helped to safety during the 20 years the Coffins lived here. Although their leadership was quite open, the home was never searched.

Gentryville

431 Colonel William Jones State Historic Site (site)

Old Booneville-Corydon Road, one mile west of Route 231; 812-937-2802; Mid-Mar–mid-Dec: Tues–Sat 9–5, Sun 12–5. Free.

This early nineteenth-century home belonged to the Indiana politician and Union army soldier who once employed Abraham Lincoln in his store. Jones was probably one of Lincoln's earliest political influences.

Indianapolis

432 Lincoln Monument (mem)

University Park; Pennsylvania and Vermont streets.

This sculpted bronze of Lincoln, by Henry Hering, sits in a memorial park that is also home to the American Legion. Other notables, including Civil War veteran General Benjamin Harrison, are honored in the park.

433 Soldiers' and Sailors' Monument: War and Peace (mem)

Monument Circle.

From the center of a plaza 342 feet in diameter this limestone monument rises to a height of 284 feet. It is said to be the first monument ever erected to the private soldier. On the north and south sides, standing guard at the entrance doors, are figures representing the four branches of service during the Civil War: the scout, the cavalry, the sailor, the infantry. Rudolf Schwarz completed this memorial in 1902, although the $600,000 work had been dedicated a year earlier.

Lincoln City

434 Lincoln Boyhood National Memorial (site)

Route 162; 812-937-4541; Daily, 8–5. Admission charged.

Thomas Lincoln moved his family into this rugged wilderness of southern Indiana in December of 1816. Abraham grew up here, attending his first school at age 11, clerking at James Gentry's store in his first job, and working the farm until leaving the state at the age of 21.

In 1863 a group of John Hunt Morgan's raiders passed through this area, hotly pursued by Union forces trying to retrieve stolen horses. Barely gaining the river, the Rebel cavalrymen swam their horses to a small island that lay about one mile upstream from town and were stranded when the river became too deep to make it back to Kentucky. Some made it, the rest drowned. The remaining Confederates, about 80 of them, were forced to surrender.

The visitor center features a museum and film on Lincoln's life. The working farm is typical of an early nineteenth-century midwest homestead. A trail of 12 stones, each taken from a structure of importance in Lincoln's life, leads to the grave of his mother, Nancy Hanks Lincoln, who died here on October 5, 1818. The Lincoln Amphitheater in the park offers musical dramas such as *Young Abe Lincoln* during the summer.

Linton

435 Levi Price Monument (mem)

Fairview Cemetery; Fairview Road and 4th Street.

The monument honors Levi Price of the 59th Indiana Regiment of Volunteers, Company E. The figure of a Union soldier standing at parade rest was sculpted by Wilbur Wright Marbler.

Madison

436 Lanier Mansion State Historic Site
(site)

511 West 1st Street; 812-265-3526; Mar–Dec: Tues–Sat 9–5, Sun 1–5. Admission charged.

This 1844 Greek Revival structure was the home of James F. D. Lanier, a wealthy pioneer banker who presented Indiana with an unsecured $1,000,000 loan to equip troops for the Civil War.

437 Soldiers' and Sailors' Monument
(mem)

Town Square.

This work by Sigvald Asbjornsen was dedicated on May 30, 1908. The privately funded monument features a group of four servicemen atop a granite pedestal.

Mt. Vernon

438 Soldiers' and Sailors' Monument
(mem)

Main Street at courthouse.

This monument pays tribute to war heroes of Posey County. It was created by Rudolph Schwartz, who also sculpted the Indianapolis Civil War memorial, which this monument resembles.

New Carlisle

439 Civil War Memorial (mem)

New Carlisle Cemetery; northeast corner of Route 20 and County Line Road.

This figure of a Union soldier standing at parade rest was installed in 1909 "in memory of the unknown dead soldiers, sailors and marines of the War of the Rebellion."

Newburgh

440 Historic Newburgh (site)

State and Jennings streets; 800-636-9489.

On July 18, 1862, Confederate General Adam Rankin "Stovepipe" Johnson of Henderson, Kentucky, fashioned a couple of "cannons" of charred wood and aimed them across the river at Newburgh, Indiana. Properly intimidated, the town of 2,900 surrendered without firing a shot. Newburgh was the first town north of the Mason-Dixon Line to be captured by Confederate forces during the Civil War. This ignominious history is recounted in guided and self-guided tours of this scenic town about 15 miles upriver from Evansville.

Rising Sun

441 Soldiers' and Sailors' Monument
(mem)

Union Cemetery; Downey Street.

This marble figure of a Union soldier at parade rest was dedicated on May 13, 1891, in tribute to "the Union soldiers and sailors who enlisted in Ohio Co."

Rockville

442 Civil War Days (mem)

317-569-3430; Second weekend in June.

Reenactment: Over 2,000 people march, battle, mourn, and celebrate the Civil War in Indiana's largest reenactment. The celebration began during America's bicentennial.

Saint Joe

443 Civil War Monument (mem)

Cemetery, southeast side of town, along St. Joseph River.

The granite figure of an infantryman on a tall, multitiered pedestal was dedicated to the Civil War soldiers of Saint Joe on May 30, 1912. The base on the west side contains a list of 144 names.

Salem

444 John Hay Center and Birthplace
(site)

307 East Market Street; 812-883-6495; Tues–Sun, 1–5. Admission charged.

The home of John Milton Hay, who served as private secretary to President Lincoln and in other capacities in further administrations, is preserved as a museum. Hay, born on October 8, 1838, was a biographer of Lincoln.

Vincennes

445 Soldiers' and Sailors' Monument
(mem)

North Seventh and Broadway streets.

Rudolf Schwarz honored the Civil War veterans of Vincennes with this bronze figure group representing the four branches of military service. It was dedicated on October 8, 1914.

Wabash

446 Lincoln of the People (mem)

Courthouse Square.

In the northeast corner of the square is a 35-ton statue of Abraham Lincoln by Charles Keck. It was a gift to the city by Alexander New of New York, a native of Wabash. In the city park is the Lincoln Memorial Cabin.

447 Wabash County Historical Museum (col)

89 West Hill Street; 219-563-0661; Tues–Sat, 9–1. Free.

The building was dedicated on November 2, 1899, to the Union soldiers of Wabash County. Two standing figures, a Union soldier and a Union sailor, flank the entrance to the former Memorial Hall.

Washington

448 Soldiers' Monument (mem)

Daviess County Courthouse.

John Walsh sculpted this granite monument consisting of a large granite pedestal with a standing Union soldier at the top and two soldiers on the lower pedestals. It was dedicated on October 8, 1913, to the "brave soldiers who endured the hardships and fought the battles 1861 to 1865 that the Union might be preserved."

Winchester

449 The James Moorman Monument (mem)

Randolph County Courthouse Square; northeast corner on Main Street.

This cenotaph to the Civil War dead was bequeathed by James Moorman. Dedicated on July 21, 1892, it was the first of its kind erected in Indiana. Created by Lorado Zadoc Taft, the memorial contains bronze figures of the branches of the military, and a bronze relief on the bottom segment depicts the Battle of the Wilderness. At a height of 67 feet it is the second highest in Indiana, after the Soldiers' and Sailors' Monument in Indianapolis.

Iowa

Civil War Status: Union
1860 Population: 674,913
Troops Provided: 75,000

Council Bluffs

450 Historic General Dodge House (site)

605 3rd Street; 712-322-2406; Feb–Dec: Tues–Sat 10–5, Sun 1–5. Admission charged.

This 14-room Victorian mansion was built by Civil War general Grenville M. Dodge, who was a colonel of the 4th Iowa and was wounded at Pea Ridge and Atlanta. Dodge was a banker and railroad builder; he is buried in Fairview Cemetery off Lafayette Avenue.

451 Lincoln Monument (mem)

Oakland Drive and Lafayette Avenue.

Abraham Lincoln visited Council Bluffs in August of 1859. Later he selected the city as the eastern terminus of the Union Pacific Railroad. The statue honors his visit and relationship with Council Bluffs.

Davenport

452 Civil War Muster and Mercantile Exposition (mem)

Scott County Park; 319-285-9656.

Camp McClellan was established in the village of East Davenport to train Iowa and Illinois Civil War recruits; today it is Lindsay Park on the Mississippi River and affords spectacular views of the Rock Island Arsenal.

Reenactment: On a mid–September weekend musket fire rocks the park during a Civil War reenactment. The festivities are highlighted by a costume ball in the encampment.

Des Moines

453 Jordan House Museum (col)

2001 Fuller Road, in West Des Moines; 515-225-1286; May–Oct: Wed and Sat 1–4, Sun 2–5. Free.

This stately 1848 Victorian home was built by James C. Jordan, the first white settler in West Des Moines. Once part of the Underground Railroad, this refurbished mansion now houses 16 period rooms, a railroad museum, and a museum dedicated to the Underground Railroad in Iowa.

454 Soldiers' and Sailors' Monument (mem)

Capitol Park.

This 145-foot granite shaft towers in memory to Iowa Civil War heroes. It was designed by Harriet A. Ketcham of nearby Mount Pleasant.

455 State Capitol (col)

East 9th Street and Grand Avenue; 515-281-5591; Daily, 8–4. Free.

The Iowa State Capitol, constructed with 29 different types of marble, is dominated by a 275-foot gold-leafed dome and flanked by four smaller domes. Battle flags of Iowa Civil War regiments are on display. One, the 37th Infantry, was known as the Graybeards — they were all over 45 years old.

456 State of Iowa Historical Building (col)

600 East Locust Street; 515-281-5111; Tues–Sat 9–4:30, Sun 12–4:30. Free.

Among the relics of Iowa's past are a Civil War cannon, weapons, photos, war records, and journals.

Keokuk

457 Keokuk National Cemetery (site)

1701 J Street; 319-524-1304.

Keokuk was designated in 1861 as one of the original 12 national cemeteries. The town was an important port for Union troop movements, and many hospitals were established here during the Civil War. Some 750 Union soldiers and 8 Confederate prisoners are buried here.

Reenactment: In Rand Park the Battle of Pea Ridge is recreated in April (800-383-1219).

Sibley

458 McCallum Museum & Brunson Heritage House (col)

Sibley Park, Fifth Street and Eighth Avenue; 712-754-2416; Summer: Sun, 1–4:30. Free.

A permanent Civil War display is a highlight in this historical museum.

Tabor

459 Todd House (site)

705 Park Street; 712-629-2675; open by appointment.

Built in 1853 of native oak, black walnut, and cottonwood on an adobe foundation, the Todd House was a station on the Underground Railroad and was often visited by John Brown, Jim Lane, and others. Two thousand rifles for Kansas' free state fight were stored here. It was the home of the Reverend John Todd, pastor of Tabor Congregational Church for 30 years.

Kansas

Civil War Status: Union
1860 Population: 107,206
Troops Provided: 20,000
Known Scenes of Action: Fewer than 100, involving Southern sympathizers

Atchison

460 Atchison County Courthouse (site)

Southwest corner of North 5th and Parallel streets.

A marker on the lawn commemorates a speech made by Abraham Lincoln on December 2, 1859, although the address was actually delivered in a nearby Methodist Church. The speech gave Lincoln national recognition and catapulted him to the presidential nomination. He later gave the speech to the Cooper Union in New York City.

Baxter Springs

461 Baxter Springs Historical Museum (col)

8th Street and East Avenue; 316-856-2385; Apr–Oct: Tues–Sat 10:30–4:30, Sun 1–4:30. Free.

Baxter Springs was garrisoned by a small Federal force during the Civil War. On the morning of October 6, 1863, Confederate raider James Quantrill attacked while part of the defending force was away on a foraging expedition. After 20 minutes of disjointed fighting, the invaders withdrew. They had lost two men and killed nine Federals.

Union major general James Blunt and his staff, on their way to a new command, mistook the departing raiders for a welcoming escort and were quickly surrounded. Quantrill killed all but seven or eight men, among them escapee Blunt who reported: "I soon discovered that every man who had fallen, except three, who escaped by feigning death, had been murdered, all shot through the head." Eighty-seven were killed.

The museum preserves the town's Civil War history. A walking tour around town visits 19 Civil War sites, including the national cemetery where most of the victims of the Baxter Springs Massacre are interred.

Dodge City

462 Fort Dodge (site)

Route 154, five miles east of town; 316-227-

2121; Summer: Mon–Sat 10–4, Sun 1–4; other times: daily, 1–4. Free.

Fort Dodge, once a camping ground for wagon trains, was established in 1865 by General Grenville Dodge to protect the Santa Fe Trail against warring Plains Indians. The first buildings were made of sod and adobe, and some troops lived in dugouts until stone buildings began appearing in 1867. Custer, Sheridan, and Hancock are among the Union generals associated with the fort. A museum houses historical military artifacts. The fort was abandoned in 1882.

Fort Riley

463 Custer House (site)

Sheridan Avenue, Building 24; 913-238-2743; Memorial Day–Labor Day: Mon–Sat 10–4, Sun 1–4. Free.

Although George Armstrong Custer did not live in the house, it is named for him. Fort Riley was the headquarters for Custer's 7th Cavalry. A guided tour of the 1855 limestone house depicts military life on the western frontier.

464 United States Cavalry Museum (col)

Sheridan and Custer avenues, Building 205; 913-239-2737; Mon–Sat 9–4:30, Sun 12–4:30. Free.

Fort Riley was established in 1853 to protect the expanding frontier. The museum tells the history of America's mounted soldier from 1776 to 1950, including his pivotal role in the Civil War. On the parade ground near the museum is the *Old Trooper* statue, depicting a horse and its soldier rider. Chief, the last cavalry horse, died in 1968 and is buried in front of the memorial.

Fort Scott

465 Lunette Blair (mem)

Old Fort Boulevard.

This is a replica of a Civil War blockhouse that was part of the fortifications surrounding Fort Scott between 1863 and 1865. The original blockhouse was sold for $50 and used as a carpenter shop and stable. Nearby is the Twin Trees Monument, dedicated to the civil and military conflicts in Kansas before and during the Civil War.

466 Fort Scott National Cemetery (site)

East National Avenue.

On July 17, 1862, President Lincoln signed an act authorizing the purchase of land to establish national cemeteries to bury the Union dead. Fort Scott was one of the first established. Among the straight rows of white headstones are 13 grave markers, set at an angle. The bodies of Confederate soldiers, who were at cross-purposes with Union troops, are buried there.

One of the more unusual Civil War profiteers was Charles W. Goodlander. He arrived in Fort Scott in 1858 with 25 cents and began hammering together coffins. He was able to parlay his earnings from coffin-making into one of Fort Scott's first fortunes.

467 Fort Scott National Historic Site (site)

Wall Street; 316-223-0310; Summer: daily, 8–6; other times: daily, 8–5. Admission charged.

In 1842 dragoon soldiers established a fort in Indian territory on a bluff overlooking the Marmaton River Valley. Named after General Winfield Scott, the fort's mission was to police the Indian frontier. The U.S. Army formally abandoned Fort Scott in 1853 but returned several times to restore order in the Kansas border wars.

During the Civil War the fort served as the headquarters of the Army of the Frontier, a supply depot, a refugee center for displaced Indians, and a base for one of the first black regiments, the 1st Kansas Colored Infantry, raised during the war. By 1863 the post quartermaster employed 350 wagons, 400 horses, 2,200 mules, and 460 men.

Reenactment: The restored frontier military fort features 20 historic structures and 33 historically furnished rooms. The infantry barracks houses a museum with an extensive Bleeding Kansas interpretive exhibit. On January 29, 1861, Kansas entered the Union as a free state, but the turmoil of the prairies continued unabated throughout the war. Each April, Civil War soldiers drill, perform inspections, and demonstrate weapons at a Civil War encampment reenactment.

Lane

468 Pottawatomie Massacre (site)

Dutch Henrys Crossing, one mile north.

On May 24, 1856, a small party, consisting mainly of John Brown and his sons, raided the cabins of two proslavery families and killed five men. Those murdered were not even slave owners, but poor white farmers. Up to that time, there had been little bloodshed between free-state and proslavery groups, but now retaliation was swift and the range wars began. For his part, Brown blamed his actions on a raid of Lawrence three days earlier. "God is my judge. We were justified under the circumstances," he said.

Larned

469 Fort Larned National Historic Site
(site)

Route 156, six miles west of town; 316-285-6911; Daily, 8:30–5:30. Free.

Fort Larned was built to protect travelers along the nearby Santa Fe Trail and today has nine restored sandstone buildings as they appeared in Civil War times. The restored fort is regarded as one of the best preserved of the old frontier forts.

Lawrence

470 Lawrence Massacre (site)
Downtown area.

On August 21, 1863, William Clarke Quantrill and some of his most notorious raiders, the James and Younger brothers among them, shot their way through Lawrence, a town of 2,000. It was said that they carried lists of men to kill. After shooting down the Reverend S. S. Snyder in his barnyard southeast of town, the heavily armed guerrillas, 300 in all, galloped toward the city. Snyder, a Lieutenant in the 2nd Colored Regiment, had been milking a cow when he was shot. Reaching Lawrence, the raiders were opposed by only a few unarmed recruits, mostly boys, twenty of whom were mowed down on New Hampshire Street.

On Massachusetts Avenue, the main thoroughfare through Lawrence, Quantrill stopped at the Eldridge Hotel. The guests pleaded for mercy and were spared after being robbed; the hotel was plundered and burned. Quantrill's men scattered in small groups throughout town, slaying and burning. After four hours they withdrew, leaving 150 dead and the town in ruins. Only the women had been spared.

Quantrill lost only one raider. In front of the Speer House on Maryland Avenue, Larkin M. Skaggs was slain by White Turkey, a Delaware Indian. Many of the victims are buried in Oak Hill Cemetery on 15th Street. A series of simple granite markers recall the events of that day.

Leavenworth

471 Fort Leavenworth (site)
Route 73 and 7th Street; 913-684-1719; Mon–Fri 9–4, Sat 10–4, Sun 12–4. Free.

The post was established in 1827 by Colonel Henry Leavenworth as protection along the Santa Fe and Oregon trails; it is one of the oldest army posts in the country. During the Civil War volunteers were trained and mustered here. Important ordnances were cached here, but the expected Southern attack never came. In 1881 General William Tecumseh Sherman established a college here; today it is considered the finest senior tactical school for advanced military education in the world.

The imposing Buffalo Soldier Monument on the grounds, erected in 1992, is dedicated to the black troopers of the 9th and 10th Cavalry who helped protect the trails. The Frontier Army Museum in Building 80 at 100 Reynolds Avenue boasts the largest collection of horse-drawn vehicles in the country, including a carriage that Lincoln used while campaigning for the presidency. The national cemetery on Biddle Boulevard was one of the first 12 of such graveyards established by Lincoln in 1862; many Civil War veterans, including officers of the 7th Cavalry, are buried here. A memorial to Ulysses S. Grant, sculpted by Lorado Taft in 1889, stands at Grant and Scott avenues.

Lecompton

472 Constitution Hall State Historic Site (site)
315 Elmore Street; 913-887-6520; Wed–Sat 10–5, Sun 1–5. Free.

From within these walls the Lecompton Constitution fanned the flames that became the Civil War.

Mound City

473 Mound City Cemetery (site)
5th and Elm streets.

In 1865 a plot for Union soldiers was set aside in the Mound City Cemetery, located on a bend in the Little Sugar Creek. Antislave crusader James Montgomery is buried here, as is William Stillwell, a victim of the Marais des Cygnes Massacre. The courthouse in town is the second oldest in Kansas and still in use. Here, the only man held accountable for his actions in the massacre was tried, found guilty, and hanged on October 23, 1863.

Osawatomie

474 Samuel Adair (John Brown) Cabin State Historic Site (site)
10th and Main streets; 913-755-4384; Wed–Sat 10–5, Sun 1–5. Free.

Originally located one mile west of Osawatomie, the cabin was purchased by Reverend Adair and his wife Florella — John Brown's stepsister — in March of 1854 for $200. Within six months Brown and five of his sons had moved in. He promptly built an addition to the rear of the 18 × 20 foot cabin — an area used for free-state meetings. A concealed trap door hid a crawl space for runaway slaves.

On the morning of August 30, Frederick Brown, John's son, was killed en route to the Adair cabin, probably in retaliation for the Pottawatomie Massacre. Brown gathered 40 men and fought the Battle of Osawatomie against a band of proslavers.

In 1912 the cabin was dismantled, moved from its original site, and reconstructed in what is now the John Brown Memorial Park. The interior of the cabin is much as it was when it was the Adair home and a stopping place for John Brown. Many pieces of furniture are original to the cabin, and the melodeon played at Brown's funeral is on display. A statue of Brown is in the park.

475 Soldiers' Monument (mem)

9th and Main streets.

This monument was erected to honor five free-staters, including Frederick Brown, son of John Brown, who died in the battle of Osawatomie.

Pleasanton

476 Linn County Historical Museum (col)

107 West Park Street; 913-352-8739; Summer: Fri–Mon and Wed 1–5, Tues and Thurs 9–4; other times: Tues–Thurs 9–5, Sat–Sun 1–5. Free.

Included in the period rooms are displays about the area's border conflicts. The raids of William Quantrill, James Montgomery, and Doc Jennison are chronicled. So many stark chimneys, jutting out of the smoldering ashes of proslaver cabins dotted the region that they were known as Jennison's Monument. Battle relics from the Battle of Mine Creek are also exhibited.

477 Mine Creek Battlefield Park (site)

County Road 1103, 1½ miles south of Route 52.

After his defeat at the Battle of Westport in Missouri, General Sterling Price began a 100-mile Confederate retreat with wagon trains loaded with loot from his raids. On October 25, 1864, the wagon train became bogged down in Mine Creek. Rather than abandon the booty, Price decided to fight a rearguard action, jeopardizing his men and position.

On Round Mound, Union general Alfred Pleasonton stationed a battery of seven howitzers that shelled the Confederate battle line. Price was forced to burn about a third of his train and hurry south with the remnant of his command. In the final tally 2,500 Union troops had scattered 6,500 Confederates.

The only major battlefield in Kansas is undeveloped, although a visitor center is under construction. The town of Pleasanton is named after the Union general, albeit misspelled.

Topeka

478 The Man of Sorrows (mem)

State House Grounds, between the State House and the Memorial Building; 10th and Jackson streets.

Robert Merrill Gage's conception of Abraham Lincoln was financed through the combined efforts of women's clubs and schools. The president is seated in this portrayal.

Trading Post

479 Trading Post Museum (col)

Route 69; 913-352-6441; Mar–Oct: Mon–Sat 9–5, Sun 11:15–5. Free.

In the spring of 1858, James Montgomery raided Trading Post, located along the Military Road between Fort Leavenworth and Fort Gibson. He struck a popular proslavery watering hole, dumping barrel upon barrel of sod-corn whiskey into the dusty soil. Soon after that, a band of border ruffians, led by Charles Hamilton, traveled the surrounding area, rounding up their neighbors and acquaintances. The proslavers marched their hostages to a ravine one mile from the Missouri line. Still seated on their horses, the proslavers mowed down their neighbors, although amazingly, six survived the slaughter.

The Trading Post museum complex tells the story of the border wars that raged before and during the Civil War. It is located beside the cemetery where four of the victims of the Marais des Cygnes Massacre are interred. The site is marked 1½ miles north and 1½ miles east of Trading Post. A monument honoring the victims was erected in town in 1888.

Kentucky

Civil War Status: Border state that stayed with the Union, although a Confederate capital was established
1860 Population: 1,155,684
Troops Provided: 75,000 — Union
45,000 — Confederacy
Known Scenes of Action: 453

Civil War Timeline
January 10, 1862: Battle of Middle Creek
January 19, 1862: Battle of Mill Springs
August 29–30, 1862: Battle of Richmond
September 14–17, 1862: Battle of Munfordville
October 8, 1862: Battle of Perryville

Augusta

480 Civil War Skirmishing (site)

Route 8.

Fighting broke out along the Ohio River when Confederate general Basil Duke skirmished with sharpshooting Federal Home Guards under Colonel Joshua T. Branford on September 27, 1862. The Augusta men fired at the invading horsemen from positions inside the town's buildings. A marker recounts the action, which took 21 lives.

Barbourville

481 Battle Marker (site)

Cumberland Avenue and Daniel Boone Drive.

The Civil War in Kentucky began about 1½ miles north of Barbourville on September 19, 1861, at the Barbourville Bridge. A recruiting camp called Andy Johnson, for Abraham Lincoln's eventual vice president, was set up in Barbourville to enlist men into the Union army in the early days of the war. When General Felix Zollicoffer brought his Confederate troops through the Cumberland Gap to secure eastern Kentucky, he dispatched troops under Colonel Joel Battle to break up Camp Andy Johnson. Battle's force encountered a detachment of Union home guards foraging in a cornfield, and hotly contested fighting broke out where a bridge crossed an unnamed stream. The home guards were driven off and Camp Andy Johnson burned. Exhibits and information regarding the battle are located in the Knox County Historical Museum in the Barbourville Municipal Building.

Bardstown

482 My Old Kentucky Home State Park (site)

Route 150; 502-348-3502; Mar–Dec: daily, except Mondays. Admission charged.

Many of the songs associated with the Old South were written by Stephen Foster, who visited his cousin Judge John Rowan here at Federal Hill, said to be the inspiration for "My Old Kentucky Home."

483 Spalding Hall (col)

114 North 5th Street; 502-348-2999; May–Oct: Tues–Sat 9–5, Sun 1–5; other times: Mon–Sat 10–4, Sun 1–4. Free.

Built in 1826 for use as a college and seminary, the building was a hospital during the Civil War. The Hall now houses the Bardstown Historical Museum, with Civil War weapons, and the Oscar Getz Museum of Whiskey History, which displays a copy of Abraham Lincoln's liquor license, purchased while he was running a tavern in New Salem, Illinois, in 1833. During their debates Douglas once referred to Lincoln's having sold liquor, and Lincoln in turn recalled that Douglas had been one of his best customers.

A Confederate recruiting camp, Camp Charity, was located down Route 62.

Beech Grove

484 Confederate Camp (site)

Moulden's Hill; Old Mill Spring Road.

The old chimney in the field on this high ground is all that remains of General Felix Zollicoffer's headquarters. The Confederate camp during 1861 and 1862 covered the entire area on this narrow neck of land between the Cumberland River and White Oak Creek. South of here, at the edge of Lake Cumberland, was the spot where the Confederate retreat from the Battle of Mill Springs ended when troops ferried across the Cumberland to Mill Springs.

Bowling Green

485 Visitor Center (site)

352 Three Springs Road; 502-782-0800; Mon–Fri, 8–5; Summer: Mon–Fri 8–5, Sat–Sun 9–5. Free.

In 1861 the heart of the Confederate defensive line in Kentucky was Bowling Green, which was selected as Confederate capital of Kentucky. Here, initially under General Simon B. Buckner and later under General Albert S. Johnston, the Confederates began construction of fortifications to secure their southern foothold in the border state. The Confederate forces evacuated Bowling Green following the fall of key forts Henry and Donelson in the winter of 1862.

Walking tours of the town's six historic districts are available from the visitor center. There are three forts left in Bowling Green — Lytle, C. F. Smith, and Webb. All of them were originally begun by the Confederate forces in 1861 and subsequently finished by the occupying Union army. Forts Lytle and C. F. Smith are located on the campus of Western Kentucky University, where many trenches were converted into student walking paths, and the third is located in Fort Webb Park.

Campbellsville

486 Atkinson-Griffin Log House (site)

Route 55 at dam at Green River, eight miles south of town; 502-465-4463; Summer: daily, 8–6; other times: Mon–Fri, 8–4. Free.

On July 4, 1863, 260 Union soldiers from the 25th Michigan Volunteer Infantry defended the river crossing here against the invading troops of Confederate general John Hunt Morgan, some 2,500 strong. The Federals, under Colonel O. H. Moore, successfully repulsed the attackers and killed some of Morgan's top officers. It was, however, only a momentary setback for Morgan's raiders.

The 1840 log structure served as a Confederate hospital after the Battle of Tebbs Bend, as the engagement came to be called. The museum features a diorama of the battle. A driving tour of the battle site begins here. A Confederate marker was erected decades ago near the steps leading to a monument that honors both troops. The Union marker was not dedicated until Independence Day in 1988, on the 125th anniversary of the battle, when a group from Michigan raised money to honor the gallant defensive stand by the Michigan volunteers.

487 Clay Hill (site)

Route 68, north of town.

This modified Georgian house was built by slaves, the bricks having been fired on the site. It was used as Confederate General John Hunt Morgan's headquarters at various times; Morgan disguised himself as a Union soldier in this hideaway. A hole due to the Union gunfire is still in the plaster of one wall and is exposed.

Carrollton

488 General Butler State Resort Park (site)

Route 227; 502-732-4384; Daily, 24 hours. Park: free; admission charged for house.

Reenactment: The restored home of Kentucky's Butler family, which included generals William Orlando and Thomas Butler, hosts a timeline event that features a military encampment of the Civil War, among other things.

Caseyville

489 Union Raid (site)

Route 130.

Nathan Bedford Forrest was an unknown Confederate cavalryman when he rode against this Ohio River town on October 24, 1861. A marker tells that a Union gunboat shelled Caseyville on July 26, 1862, and took everyone prisoner. Most were detained only briefly, but 19 hostages were taken to Evansville, Indiana.

Columbus

490 Columbus-Belmont State Park (site)

Route 58; 502-677-2327; Apr–Oct: 7–10 P.M.; other times: 9–5, museum 9–5. Park: free; admission charged for museum.

Here, on the bluffs above the Mississippi River, Kentucky neutrality during the war came to an end. In September 1861 General Leonidas Polk marched his Confederate army into Columbus and began fortifying the position. So successful were his engineers that Columbus became known as the "Gibraltar of the West." On November 7, 1861, General Ulysses S. Grant fought his first battle here, launching the Union army's Western Campaign at a river landing in Belmont, Missouri. As part of their defenses the Confederates stretched a massive chain across the river to keep Union gunboats from moving south. Grant's attack was little more than a reconnaissance mission to test the strength of the Confederate fortifications, and he was quickly driven back.

On the Kentucky side of the river the six-ton anchor that held the chain remains. The earthwork fortifications are still visible. A building used as a Civil War infirmary houses a museum. An audiovisual program describes the battle.

Covington

491 Behringer-Crawford Museum (col)

Devou Park; 606-491-4003; Tues–Fri 10–5, Sat–Sun 1–5. Admission charged.

During the Civil War, Covington was connected to Cincinnati only by a military pontoon bridge comprised of coal barges. The bridge was just east of the present Roebling Suspension Bridge, designed by Brooklyn Bridge architect John Roebling and under construction during the war. It did not, however, provide permanent transportation across the Ohio River until 1866.

Following the Confederate invasion of Kentucky in the summer of 1862, Federal troops set about fortifying Covington, now Ohio's fourth largest city. The city was once ringed with more than 20 guardian forts and batteries designed to protect Cincinnati. Remains of batteries Bates, Holt, Larz Anderson, McLean, and Shaler can be found in and around Covington. The towns of Fort Mitchell — which saw skirmishing when the Confederates advanced to within three miles of the city on September 10, 1862 — and Fort Wright are named for Civil War forts.

Information on these forts and the Civil War in northern Kentucky can be found in the museum, which has a display of artifacts.

Cumberland Gap

492 Cumberland Gap National Historical Park (site)

Route 25E; 606-248-2817.

This strategic mountain pass changed hands four times in the course of the war. Union troops captured the gap on June 17, 1862, but had to evacuate three months later. It was recaptured on September 9, 1863, and held by the U.S. Army for the remainder of the war. The numerous captures and recaptures spawned the legend of Long Tom.

Long Tom was the largest gun in use when the Confederates hauled it up the mountainside to command the valley below. When threatened by General George Morgan's Union army, the Confederates pitched the gun over the side of a cliff. Morgan ordered it dragged back up the mountain and installed against its former owners. Upon reaching the top, the Union troops discovered that they had no suitable ammunition to arm the behemoth. Before they evacuated in 1862, the cannon was spiked—a rat-tail file was driven into the touchhole and broken off—to make the gun useless, and again pushed over the edge. Long Tom was not heard from again. Although it most likely was melted down in a foundry, a local legend insists that the cannon buried itself in the earth and is waiting to be found.

The park covers 32 miles in three states. The visitor center has historical exhibits, an observation deck, and interpretive displays on the region's strategic importance. In the park are numerous earthenwork forts used by both sides.

Cynthiana

493 Battle at Keller's Bridge (site)

Battle Grove Cemetery; Millersburg Pike, east of town.

In separate fighting at Keller's Bridge during the second Battle of Cynthiana, the Confederates achieved victory on June 11, 1864. The area now contained in the Battle Grove Cemetery, established in 1868, has long been described as being the main site of the battle. Buried at the Confederate monument, erected in 1869, are soldiers from Morgan's two raids.

494 Battles of Cynthiana (site)

Cynthiana Public Library.

Confederate General John Hunt Morgan twice targeted Cynthiana for attack, each time to appear as a threat to Cincinnati, 60 miles to the north. On July 17, 1862, Morgan's raiders decimated a force of 500 Federal home guards and a handful of Union regulars. The railroad depot, a bridge, and a recruiting camp were burned.

The second battle occurred in three engagements over two days, June 11–12, 1864. Morgan's forces, numbering 1,200, again overpowered the Union garrison in Cynthiana only to be scattered by reinforcements under Union General Stephen Burbridge the next day. This ended Morgan's last raid into Kentucky. A self-guided tour of the town and the battles is available at the library.

Elizabethtown

495 Brown-Pusey House (site)

128 North Main Street; 502-765-2515; Mon–Sat, 10–4. Free.

Elizabethtown was shelled by Morgan on December 27, 1862, as he sacked the town. This stately Georgian Colonial building housed General George Armstrong Custer and his wife in the 1870s. Walking tours are available at the visitor center on 24 Public Square; the town's history includes ties to Abraham Lincoln's family.

Fairview

496 Jefferson Davis Monument State Historic Site (mem)

Route 68; 502-886-1765; May–Oct: daily, 9–5. Free.

The birthplace of Confederate president Davis has been marked by a 351-foot obelisk, the fourth-highest cast-concrete obelisk in the country. A museum is at the top of the monument. On the grounds of the 22-acre park is a replica of the cabin where Davis was born on June 3, 1808. The memorial was dedicated in 1924 after funding by public subscription raised $200,000.

Reenactment: A Civil War reenactment on the first Saturday in June is part of the Davis Birthday Celebration.

Fort Knox

497 Patton Museum of Cavalry and Armor (col)

4554 Fayette Avenue; 502-624-3812; May–Sept: Mon–Fri 9–4:30, Sat–Sun 10–6; Oct–Apr: Sat–Sun 10–4:30. Free.

Famous as the United States gold depository, the Patton Museum at Fort Knox is one of the largest museums in the U.S. Army system. Although the emphasis is on armored fighting vehicles and George Patton, there is also cavalry material from the Civil War on exhibit.

Frankfort

498 Frankfort Cemetery (site)

215 East Main Street; 502-227-2403; Summer: daily, 7–8:30; Winter: 8–5:30. Free.

A Confederate memorial honors soldiers from the Civil War; notables buried here include Daniel Boone and seventeen Kentucky governors. In fact, so many historic figures are interred here that the burial ground is called "Kentucky's Westminster."

499 Green Hill Cemetery (site)

Main Street.

This graveyard contains the remains of several black soldiers who fought in the Civil War. There is a monument to 154 blacks from Franklin County who fought in the war.

500 Kentucky Military History Museum (col)

Main Street and Capitol Avenue; 502-564-3265; Mon–Sat 9–4, Sun 12–4. Free.

The Old State Arsenal, built in 1850, now exhibits the state's history during our nation's wars. The arsenal was a cartridge factory for the Union army as well as a supply center for Northern troops from the Midwest. The collection emphasizes the service of Kentucky Militia, State Guard, and other volunteer military organizations.

501 Old State Capitol (site)

Broadway and Lewis streets; 502-564-3016; Mon–Fri 9–4, Sat 12–5, Sun 1–5. Free.

This 1829 Greek Revival building was the only non–Confederate capitol captured by Southern troops. Although the state of Kentucky remained officially neutral during the Civil War, the people became so bitterly divisive from harsh Union treatment that it was observed, "Kentucky seceded after the war!"

502 State Capitol Rotunda (mem)

Capitol Avenue; 502-564-3449; Mon–Fri 8:30–4:30, Sat 8:30–4:30, Sun 1–4:30. Free.

Considered one of the most beautiful capitols in America, the rotunda features statues of Kentucky natives Jefferson Davis and Abraham Lincoln. Murals and paintings depict Kentucky history.

Franklin

503 Simpson County Archives and Museum (col)

206 North College Street; 502-586-4228; Mon–Fri, 9–4. Free.

The walls of the old jail and jailer's residence are speckled with drawings left by Civil War soldiers

held prisoner here. Nearby is a marker for the grave of Franklin County outlaw Marcellus Jerome Clarke, one of Kentucky's best known Civil War guerrillas, who fought under the nom de guerre "Sue Mundy." He was captured with two companions at Webster on May 12, had one of the briefest trials in Kentucky history, and was hanged at Broadway and 18th streets in Louisville on May 16, 1865.

Georgetown

504 Confederate Monument (mem)

Georgetown Cemetery; Hamilton Street.

In June of 1888 the Confederate Monument was dedicated after a parade the likes of which had never been seen in Georgetown before. Thousands came from throughout Kentucky for the reinterment of 18 bodies, two of whom had been ordered shot by the military commander of Kentucky, General Stephen Burbridge. Also buried in this graveyard is Confederate governor George Johnson, who was killed at Shiloh.

505 Georgetown and Scott County Museum (mem)

Cardome Centre; 800 Cincinnati Road; 502-863-1575; Mon–Fri, 10–5. Admission charged.

Reenactment: Confederate general John Hunt Morgan capped a day of raiding during which he plundered 7,000 horses from Lexington with a stop at Georgetown on June 10, 1864. A living history camp features artillery and night firings and a Civil War ball in the memory of the Confederate raider in early June.

Glasgow

506 Fort Williams (site)

Route 68.

The Confederates made Glasgow their first site of occupation in Kentucky. When General Braxton Bragg arrived on September 18, 1862, he proclaimed that the Confederate army had come to Kentucky to free the people from tyranny and not to conquer them.

Fort Williams was built by the Union army in 1863 to protect the surrounding area from Confederate infantry raiders. The city renovated the earthwork fort in the early 1980s.

Harrodsburg

507 Old Fort Harrod State Park (col)

Lexington and College streets; 606-734-3314; Mar–Oct, daily, 8:30–5; rest of the year: 8–4:30. Admission charged.

The first permanent settlement west of the Alleghenies contains the brick Lincoln Marriage Temple, a log cabin in which Thomas Lincoln and Nancy Hanks are thought to have been wed on June 12, 1806. The cabin was removed from its original site in neighboring Washington County. Another house in the park, the Matheny-Taylor House, features the Union Room with a life-size portrait of President Lincoln and an autographed law book from his collection.

Reenactment: At Shaker Hill, in September, the town reverts to its Civil War appearance during an encampment. The Shakers were staunchly pro–Union and antiabolitionist, but as pacifists they stayed out of the war, extending generosity to both armies as they passed the Shaker village of Pleasant Hill.

Hawesville

508 Pate House (site)

Route 334, four miles east of town; 502-295-6637; Apr–Oct: Sun, 2–4. Free.

In 1827 in this Ohio River town, the 18-year-old Abraham Lincoln defended himself for operating a ferry without a license. Judge Pate was so impressed by Lincoln that he encouraged him to study law.

Henderson

509 Rankin-Royer House (site)

616 North Main Street.

Henderson was the site of several skirmishes during the war. The owner of an older structure on this site, James E. Rankin, also owned a business downtown and was murdered there during the Civil War by a band of outlaws, associated with neither the North nor the South. Two Confederate soldiers, however, were executed for the crime, though Union sympathizers pleaded for their release.

Hodgenville

510 Abraham Lincoln Birthplace National Historic Site (site)

Route 31 East and Route 61; 502-358-3137; Summer: daily, 8–6:45; other times: 8–5:45. Free.

An impressive memorial building rises from the site of the birth of America's sixteenth president. He was born here on February 12, 1809, to Thomas and Nancy Hanks Lincoln. Each of the 56 steps leading up the granite and marble memorial represents one year in Lincoln's life. The log cabin housed inside was once believed to be the actual cabin of Lincoln's birth, but further research has indicated otherwise. The Memorial Building was built in 1911, financed by contributions from more than 100,000 people.

Lincoln lived the first two-and-a-half years of his life on the 110-acre Sinking Spring farm, which is included in the historic site. A visitor center focuses on Lincoln's earliest days with dioramas and a movie about the family.

511 Lincoln Boyhood Home (site)

Knob Creek; Route 31 East; Summer: daily, 9–7; Apr–May and Sept–Oct: daily, 9–5. Admission charged.

The Lincoln family moved about six miles north of Hodgenville in 1811. Lincoln later wrote that his earliest memories were of the five years he spent at Knob Creek. Here he attended school for the first time and watched slaves being marched to auction for the first time. In December 1816, due to faulty land titles and subsequent squabbling, the Lincolns left Kentucky for Indiana.

A log cabin made of material of the time, erected in 1800 and moved from an adjacent farm in 1931, is on the site. The construction is typical of the Lincoln era, with a prominent chimney made of logs and mud.

512 The Lincoln Museum (col)

66 Lincoln Square; 502-358-3163; Mon–Sat 8:30–5, Sun 12:30–5. Admission charged.

Wax figures depict 12 significant episodes in Lincoln's life. Also included is an art collection, a short film, and Lincoln and Civil War memorabilia.

513 Lincoln Statue (mem)

Hodgenville Public Square.

This bronze statue is the work of Adolph A. Weinman, a pupil of the American sculptor Augustus Saint-Gaudens. Lincoln is depicted seated, with his head bowed in pensive concentration. The six-foot-high figure, mounted on a 12-foot pedestal, was dedicated in 1909, on the centennial anniversary of Lincoln's birth in this town. The town's courthouse was burned by Quantrill on February 22, 1865.

Hopkinsville

514 Pennyroyal Area Museum (col)

217 East 9th Street; 502-887-4270; Mon–Fri 8:30–4:30, Sat 10–3. Admission charged.

The museum features exhibits on the city, which was burned by occupying forces in wartime. Artifacts relating to the career of Jefferson Davis are also on display. The town's Riverside Cemetery has an impressive Confederate memorial.

Lexington

515 Ashland (site)

120 Sycamore Road; 606-266-8581; Feb–
Dec: Tues–Sat 10–4:30, Sun 1–4:30. Admission
charged.

Ashland was the home of Henry Clay, "the Great
Compromiser," from 1811 until his death in 1852.
Clay was devoted to the Union and fought tirelessly
to prevent a civil war in America. A Civil War skirmish took place near the estate, and the home was
used as a hospital for the wounded.

516 Breckinridge Statue (mem)

Cheapside Park.

John Cabell Breckinridge, vice president under
James Buchanan, left Kentucky in 1861 to avoid ar-
rest as a traitor. He served under Johnston at Shiloh
and was an advisor during the surrender in North
Carolina. The family home was at 429 West 2nd
Street, and he is buried in Lexington Cemetery.

517 Hunt-Morgan House (site)

201 North Mill Street; 606-253-0362; Mar–
Dec: Tues–Sat 10–4, Sun 2–5. Admission
charged.

John Wesley Hunt, the first millionaire west of
the Alleghenies, built Hopemont in 1814. A small
Civil War museum, including memorabilia of his
grandson, John Hunt Morgan, "the Thunderbolt
of the Confederacy," is on the first floor.

518 Lexington Cemetery (site)

833 W. Main Street; 606-255-5522; Daily,
8–5. Free.

The Lexington National Cemetery contains the
graves of 1,100 soldiers; more than 500 Confederate soldiers are buried here. Also interred here are
members of Mary Todd Lincoln's family, Henry
Clay, General John Hunt Morgan, Colonel W. C. P.
Breckinridge, John Cabell Breckinridge, and Union
general Gordon Granger.

519 Mary Todd Lincoln House (site)

578 West Main Street; 606-233-9999; Apr–
Dec: Tues–Sat, 10–4. Admission charged.

In 1832 Robert Todd, a prominent Lexington attorney, renovated an 1803 brick tavern into a proper
Georgian-style home for his family. Mary Todd
lived fourteen years here, attending two fashion-
able Lexington private schools. Abraham Lincoln
visited his wife's family on three occasions here; the
tour includes personal articles from the Todd and
Lincoln families.

520 Morgan Statue (mem)

Fayette County Courthouse; Main Street.

This equestrian monument to General John
Hunt Morgan was unveiled amid great controversy
in 1911. The Confederate raider is shown astride a
mount that is clearly a stallion — in real life he always rode a mare, Black Bess.

521 London (mem)

Battle of Camp Wildcat; Camp Wildcat Mountain; I-75, Exit 49; 800-348-0095; April. Free.

This is the site of one of the earliest Union victories of the Civil War. On October 21, 1861, Union
troops numbering 5,400, under the command of
General Albin Schoepf and entrenched on Wildcat
Mountain, were engaged by a much larger force of
7,500 Confederates under the command of General Felix Zollicoffer. Due to the rugged terrain, the
casualties were low despite fierce fighting. The Federals carried the day.

Reenactment: The reenactment by the Laurel
home guard takes place on private property near
the original battlefield. This annual reenactment
and encampment in April commemorate the pre-
vention of Southern troops storming into Kentucky.

Louisville

522 The Candidate (mem)

West lawn of Louisville Public Library; 4th
Street.

This heroic statue is a replica of the controversial work of George Grey Barnard in Lytle Park in
Cincinnati. People originally objected to such a "realistic" Lincoln.

523 Confederate Monument (mem)

3rd and Avery streets.

Erected by the Kentucky Women's Confederate
Monument Association, this 70-foot-high bronze
on a granite base was installed in 1895. The male
figure was created by Ferdinand von Miller II.

524 Eastern Cemetery (site)

641 Baxter Avenue.

The Taylor Barracks at Third and Oak streets
was the Civil War induction point for black recruits, 438 of whom entered the Union army from
Kentucky. Many of those who died in battle are
buried here.

525 The Filson Club (col)

1310 South Third Street; 502-635-5083;
Mon–Fri 9–5, Sat 9–12. Admission charged.

Founded in 1884 and named for John Filson,
who published the first history of Kentucky, the library now contains more than one million items
and is especially strong on the history of the ante-
bellum and Civil War periods.

526 Louisville Defense Forts (site)

Around city.

A ring of forts was built in August 1864 to protect the city from an invasion which never came. The city contributed $12,000 of the cost and provided labor in the form of vagrants who were arrested and sentenced to work on the fortifications. None of these forts, named for Union officers killed in battle, survive. The sites, however, can be visited and give an idea of how the Union sought to protect this key Ohio River city.

From the north, clockwise, they are: Fort Elster, between Frankfort Avenue and Brownsboro Road; Fort Engle, near Spring Street and Arlington Avenue; Fort Saunders, in Cave Hill Cemetery; Fort Hill, between Goddard Avenue and St. Louis Cemetery; Fort Horton, at the junction of Shelby and Merriwether streets; Fort McPherson, the largest and linchpin of the defenses, in the Preston Street area; Fort Philpot, in the vicinity of Seventh Street Road and Algonquin Parkway; Fort Saint Clair Morton, at 16th and Hill; Fort Karnash, on Wilson Avenue between 26th and 28th streets; Fort Clark, at 36th and Magnolia; and Fort Southworth, the westernmost, on Paddys Run.

Mayfield

527 Confederate Memorial Fountain
(mem)

Courthouse Square.

One of the most outstanding Confederate memorials in Kentucky is the Confederate Memorial Fountain, designed to serve as a drinking fountain, making it the only utilitarian Civil War monument in the state. The Memorial Gates at the entrance to Maplewood Cemetery were placed there by the United Daughters of the Confederacy.

Maysville

528 National Underground Railroad Museum (col)

115 East 3rd Street; 606-564-6986; Daily, 10–4. Free.

A Union training facility, Camp Kenton was established in Maysville in the fall of 1861. The museum in the visitor center highlights the area's role as an escape route for thousands of slaves. It is also the departure point for self-guided walking tours.

Munfordville

529 Hart County Museum (col)

109 Main Street; 502-524-0101; Mon–Fri, 10–2. Free.

There were two battles in the Munfordville area, considered one of the keys in the Federal supply network. The first, the Battle of Rowletts, exploded on December 17, 1861, south of the Green River. The Siege of Munfordville was fought September 14–17, 1862, between 4,000 Union troops and a Confederate force of 35,000—the second largest engagement in Kentucky. The Rebels, under General Braxton Bragg, forced the capitulation of the Union garrison.

Several of the forts remain, as does the strategic railroad bridge over the Green River. A walking tour brochure is available at the museum and historical society.

Nancy

530 Mill Springs National Cemetery (site)

Route 80, east of town.

The Battle of Mill Springs was one of the two principal battles of the war in Kentucky. The Confederates under General Felix Zollicoffer seized the early advantage, but Zollicoffer, nearsighted and wearing a white raincoat obscuring his uniform, was shot and killed when he became confused on the field of battle as to who was friend and who was foe. Federal troops under George H. Thomas eventually broke through the demoralized Confederate line and sent the Southerners into retreat. It was the first break in the Confederate Kentucky defense line, which stretched from the Cumberland Gap to the Mississippi River.

The small yet strategic conflict on January 19, 1862, left 39 Federals killed from a force of 4,000. They are buried here; the Confederates lost 125 and are buried in Zollicoffer Park, south on KY 235, in a mass grave with a monument.

Nicholasville

531 Camp Nelson Federal Cemetery (site)

Route 27.

This fortified supply depot and training camp was named for Union major general William Bull Nelson. When the Union began to draft blacks into the service in 1863, Camp Nelson became the most important mustering site in the state for black regiments, including the 5th and 6th U.S. Colored Cavalry and the 114th and 116th U.S. Colored Heavy Artillery. A national cemetery with the graves of 3,000 Union soldiers is now on the site.

Paducah

532 Fort Anderson (site)

Trimble Street between 4th and 5th streets.

Occupying Federal troops built a fortification on the northern boundary of town at the Paducah Marine Hospital. On March 25, 1864, Confederate general Nathan Forrest attacked Fort Anderson and was repelled. Colonel A. P. Thompson, a Paducah resident, was given the honor of leading the Rebel attack but was killed by a cannonball. After the Battle of Paducah, Union commander Stephen Hicks ordered the burning of all the surrounding houses so that they could not provide shelter in the event of another attack.

533 Grant's Landing (site)

1st and Broadway streets on the wharf.

Ulysses S. Grant arrived at the Paducah riverfront on September 6, 1861. Leaving his headquarters in Cairo, Illinois, the general arrived with 5,000 soldiers after crossing the Ohio River on a pontoon bridge with 123 barges bound together. Spurred on by the Confederate capture of Columbus and Hickman the day before, Grant moved to secure the river town. He issued a proclamation to the citizens of Paducah and returned to Cairo. Paducah remained under Union control throughout the war.

534 Tilghman Statue (mem)

Lang Park; 17th and Madison streets.

This monument honors Confederate Brigadier General Lloyd Tilghman, who organized the 3rd Kentucky Regiment. Commander of Fort Henry on the Tennessee River, he was killed during the Battle of Champion's Hill near Vicksburg on May 16, 1863. A graduate of West Point, Tilghman came to Paducah in the 1850s as the chief engineer and surveyor for the New Orleans and Jackson Railroad. Tilghman's home at 7th Street and Kentucky Avenue is being renovated to house a military museum.

Perryville

535 Perryville Battlefield State Historic Site (site)

Route 1920; 606-332-8631; Apr–Oct: 9–9; museum: daily, 9–5. Park: free; admission charged for museum.

A major Confederate offensive begun in 1862 culminated at Perryville in the largest battle fought in Kentucky. Throughout the summer Confederate forces under General Braxton Bragg had hoped that a string of Southern victories in the state would pull Kentuckians into the Confederacy. The hopes were false, however, and as the invasion dragged into the autumn, Bragg poised his force of 16,000 to attack what he believed to be the smallest Union force at Perryville. Instead, he encountered the main Union army of 22,000 men under General Don Carlos Buell.

A summer-long drought had left both armies constantly on the prowl for fresh water. On October 8 thirsty soldiers from both sides stumbled upon Doctors Fork Creek — and each other. Buell, having been thrown from a horse and back at headquarters, did not hear the battle sounds because of the way the wind was blowing until four in the afternoon and arrived at the fray hours after hostilities had begun. This was just one of many confusing events on a day that left both leaders criticized: Bragg for losing Kentucky and Buell for allowing the Southerners to withdraw safely. He was relieved of his command after the battle.

The Southern troops carried the day on the field but they were forced to retreat, abandoning Kentucky to the Union for the last time. The Battle of Perryville was the battle for Kentucky, and Kentucky remained in the Union. Casualties for the Union were 4,211; the Confederates lost 3,396.

The self-guided tour of the park grounds includes burial sites and monuments. Authentic weapons and equipment used in the battle are on display in the museum where exhibits trace troop movements. Crawford House, which was Bragg's headquarters, and the Squire Bottom House, still standing, were at the center of the action.

Reenactment: The entire town of Perryville is on the National Register. Each October, on the weekend closest to the actual battle date, the Battle of Perryville can be seen again in a full-scale reenactment.

Prestonburg

536 Battle of Middle Creek (site)

Route 114.

On the high ridges of this mountain valley east of town, the largest battle in eastern Kentucky was fought. Colonel James A. Garfield commanded a brigade of Ohio and Kentucky troops, some 3,000 strong, against a like number led by a prominent Kentucky politician, General Humphrey Marshall. Garfield swept down the valley on January 10, 1862, attacking Confederate artillery entrenchments on the bluffs. Although the fighting was technically a draw, Marshall's troops retreated, leaving the Union in control of the Big Sandy Valley. Garfield, a future United States president, was promoted to brigadier general for his efforts at Middle Creek.

Richmond

537 Battle of Richmond (site)

City Hall; 800-866-3705; Mon–Fri, 8–5. Free.

The Battle of Richmond was a part of the 1862 Perryville campaign. To begin this offensive, the Confederate army invaded Kentucky from two points. The Richmond prong of the invasion produced one of the Confederacy's greatest victories and its first in Kentucky. Between August 29 and 30, 1862, a Union force of some 6,500 men suffered 5,353 casualties at the hands of 9,000 Southerners. The armies clashed in three separate engagements, the first beginning south of Richmond at Big Hill and the second near Berea.

The fighting finished in the Richmond Cemetery. Retreating Union forces were nearing this point when they were overtaken by the Union commander, Major General William Nelson, who began berating them as cowards. The 300-pound Nelson attempted to form a defensive line, riding back and forth along the line and shouting, "Boys, if they can't hit anything as big as I am, they can't hit anything." He was hit almost immediately in the thigh and carried from the field.

A self-guided driving tour, including tapes and maps, is available for retracing this complete tactical Confederate victory.

Somerset

538 Zollicoffer Memorial Park (mem)

Route 235.

The surrounding area was the scene for much of the heaviest fighting during the Battle of Mill Springs. It was here that General Felix Zollicoffer rode forward to speak with what he mistakenly thought were his own troops and was killed. The main sites in the park are the monument to Zollicoffer and his men, the Confederate grave, and the "Zollie Tree," the large oak near the park entrance where Zollicoffer's body was placed.

Springfield

539 Lincoln Homestead State Park (site)

Route 528; 606-336-7461; May–Sept: daily, 8–6; Oct: Sat–Sun, 8–6; park: open daily, 24 hours. Admission charged.

The park contains three buildings associated with Abraham Lincoln's ancestry. The Lincoln Cabin is a 1782 replica where President Lincoln's grandmother, Bersheba, raised five children after her husband, Captain Abraham Lincoln, was murdered by an Indian in Jefferson County. Thomas Lincoln, the president's father, lived here until he was 25.

The Francis Berry House is a two-story log dwelling, built around 1785, where Lincoln's mother Nancy Hanks lived with her cousin while being courted by Thomas Lincoln. The house was moved to the site from its original location a mile away. The blacksmith shop is a replica of the one in which Thomas Lincoln learned his smithing trade.

Across the street is the Mordecai Lincoln House, reputedly the only property associated with Abraham Lincoln in Kentucky still standing on its original foundations. Mordecai Lincoln, an uncle of Abraham, married Mary Mudd, a first cousin twice removed of Dr. Samuel Mudd, who would be tried as a conspirator in the assassination of the president decades later.

540 Washington County Courthouse (site)

Mon–Fri 8:30–4:30; Sat 9–12. Free.

Built in 1792, the year Kentucky achieved statehood, the courthouse retains the marriage documents of Nancy Hanks and Thomas Lincoln. A facsimile is on permanent display.

Versailles

541 Woodford County Historical Society Museum and Genealogical Library (col)

121 Rose Hill; 606-873-6786; Tues–Sat, 9–4. Free.

Morgan passed through the town during his raids. Civil War items from the collection, which includes many rare books on Kentucky history, are displayed.

Washington

542 Old Washington (site)

2215 Old Main Street; 606-759-7411; Apr–Dec: Mon–Sat 10–4:30, Sun 1–4:30. Admission charged.

Harriet Beecher Stowe visited this outpost for pioneer travelers in 1833 and witnessed a slave auction, which influenced the writing of *Uncle Tom's Cabin*. Also on the site is a documented Underground Railroad station, Paxton Inn, and the ancestral home of Confederate general Albert Sidney Johnston.

Water Valley

543 Camp Beauregard (site)

Route 45.

This secluded region near the Tennessee line was

the site of Camp Beauregard, a Confederate recruiting and training camp. Union general C. F. Smith captured the camp on January 7, 1862. A monument sits on a hill marking the spot of the camp; Confederate soldiers who died here are buried nearby.

West Point

544 Fort Duffield (site)

16706 Abbotts Beach Road.

On Muldraugh Heights a Union Civil War fort still towers over the beautiful Ohio and Salt River Valley at West Point. Work was begun at Fort Duffield in November, 1861, by the 9th Michigan Infantry Regiment, commanded by William W. Duffield, and by the 37th Indiana Infantry Regiment, commanded by Colonel George W. Hazzard. The bulk of the work and garrison duty fell to the 9th Michigan; completion of the massive earthworks, trenches, and log cabins took 45 days. Up to ten cannons, mounted on pedestals for easy turning, protected the fort — not in the direction of the rivers, but in the direction of the many back roads that converged here from the south.

Although no soldiers were killed in battle at Fort Duffield, death due to disease was widespread. At one point 300 of the 1000 troops garrisoned here were stricken with dysentery, pneumonia, or smallpox. All told, 61 soldiers died from disease. Of those 61 soldiers, 36 were not claimed by family and were buried at the fort.

The fort has recently been partially restored. Visible are original earthen walls and trenches, old campsites, stone chimney ruins, and a spectacular vista of the Ohio River. On an adjoining hillcrest is a memorial cemetery, honoring those who died at Fort Duffield in defense of the Union.

Reenactment: Civil War reenactments are scheduled the first weekend of every month. The Civil War Days celebration is staged on Memorial Day weekend. Included in the festivities are fort tours, a bank robbery, and a period ball.

Louisiana

Civil War Status: Confederacy; seceded from the Union on January 26, 1861
1860 Population: 708,002
Troops Provided: 65,000
Known Scenes of Action: 566

Civil War Timeline

April 18–24, 1862: Battle of Forts Jackson and St. Philip

August 5, 1862: Battle of Baton Rouge
May 21–July 9, 1863: Siege and surrender of Port Hudson
June 7, 1863: Battle of Milliken's Bend
April 8, 1864: Battle of Mansfield
April 9, 1864: Battle of Pleasant Hill
May 26, 1865: Surrender of Lieutenant General E. Kirby Smith's Confederate forces in New Orleans

Alexandria

545 Bailey's Dam (site)

O. K. Allen Bridge over Red River.

A marker indicates that Union troops constructed this dam to deepen the river channel to move Federal gunboats over the rapids.

546 Kent House (site)

3601 Bayou Rapides Road; 318-487-5998; Mon–Sat 9–5, Sun 1–5. Admission charged.

Kent House is the oldest remaining structure in central Louisiana. During the Civil War, its owner, Robert Hynson, stubbornly refused to leave his home in the face of retreating Union troops from the Battle of Mansfield and so it was not burned. The complex includes many replicas of outbuildings.

547 Louisiana Seminary Site (site)

Route 165, three miles north of town.

The first home of Louisiana State University was opened on this site, now a picnic area, in 1860 under headmaster William Tecumseh Sherman. Closed during the Civil War, the school was opened in 1865 but burned four years later and was moved to its present location in Baton Rouge.

548 St. Francis Xavier Cathedral (site)

4th and Beauregard streets.

The church has been erected on the site of a mutiny of troops under the command of General George Armstrong Custer.

Bastrop

549 Snyder Museum (col)

1620 East Madison Street; 318-281-8760; Tues–Sun, 10–3. Free.

There is a special display on the Civil War in this local history museum.

Baton Rouge

550 Battle of Baton Rouge State Monument (mem)

North Boulevard and Riverside Street.

On August 5, 1862, the Confederates under General John Breckinridge attacked the Union forces from the north in an attempt to control the Mississippi River. Brigadier General Thomas Williams had been expecting the attack, but a thick fog covered troop movements. Williams, a former mathematics professor at West Point and veteran of the Seminole and Mexican Wars, was killed almost immediately. Each side mounted a force of about 2,500 men, but heavy artillery from Federal gunboats forced Breckinridge to retreat and fortify Port Hudson.

551 Magnolia Cemetery (site)

Bounded by Florida Boulevard, Main Street, North 22nd, and North 19th boulevards.

Site of the fiercest fighting of the Battle of Baton Rouge; Confederates hid behind tombs and trees while launching attacks on Federal positions. A mass grave holds the Confederates who died here.

552 Old Arsenal Powder Magazine Museum (site)

State Capitol grounds, between capitol building and governor's mansion; 504-342-0401; Mon–Fri 9–4, Sat 10–4, Sun 1–4. Admission charged.

The Federal arsenal in Baton Rouge was seized on January 26, 1861, as Louisiana left the Union. By the time the Union army reoccupied the town in May 1862, the weapons and ammunition had been rushed to desperate Southern armies.

553 Old State Capitol (site)

100 North Boulevard; 504-342-0500; Tues–Sat 10–4, Sun 12–4. Admission charged.

The Gothic Revival castle was burned by the Union Army and finally repaired in 1882. It remained the capitol until 1932. To the west of the entrance gate is the grave of Brigadier General Henry Watkins Allen, the Confederate governor of Louisiana from 1864 to 1865. Allen died in Mexico City in 1866 and was buried in his Confederate uniform that had been pierced by Federal ordnance in the Battle of Baton Rouge. A tablet at Dufrocq and Spain streets in City Park marks the spot where he was hit on August 5, 1862.

554 Pentagon Barracks (site)

959 3rd Street; 504-342-1866; Tues–Sat 10–4, Sun 1–4. Free.

The two-story brick garrison was active from its building, between 1819 and 1829, until it closed in 1877. Many famous soldiers served here, including Robert E. Lee, Thomas Jackson, and Wade Hampton. The barracks were briefly under Confederate control during the Civil War.

Buras

555 Fort Jackson (site)

Route 23; 504-657-7083; Daily, 7–6. Free.

The original structure to guard the mouth of the Mississippi River was built in 1815 and named for General Andrew Jackson. The Confederates refortified the position in 1861. Fort Jackson and its sister, Fort St. Philip, across the river, were entrusted with the protection of New Orleans during the war.

It was considered impossible for wooden ships to oppose any shore defense, regardless of strength, so very little attention was paid to defending the city elsewhere. On the morning of April 18, 1862, Admiral David Farragut brought a Federal fleet of 24 wooden gunboats and 19 mortar schooners within striking distance of the forts, camouflaging the masts of his vessels with willow boughs. All that night and for four successive days the two forts were subjected to a hailstorm of bombs while the Rebels counterattacked fiercely but with inferior powder, which caused little damage.

On the fifth day Farragut ran past the forts with 17 war vessels under continuous fire from the forts and harassment from Confederate gunboats. His ship *Hartford* burst into flames, but the fire was brought under control and the Federals continued into New Orleans and took the city bloodlessly.

Chalmette

556 Chalmette Monument and National Cemetery (site)

8606 West St. Bernard Highway.

On the site of the 1815 Battle of New Orleans, Confederate guns attempted to stop Farragut's advance in 1862. The site was named a national cemetery in 1864 and holds the remains of 15,000 veterans, 6,700 of them unidentified. It was closed for burials in 1945. In 1874 members of the Grand Army of the Republic erected a monument in the center of the cemetery.

Cheyneyville

557 Loyd Hall Plantation (site)

292 Loyd Bridge Road. Open for tours daily.

Now a bed-and-breakfast, this 1820 plantation south of Alexandria is still riddled with bullet holes. Its Civil War owner was hanged as a Confederate spy.

Franklin

558 Battle of Franklin (site)
Route 90.

The town was settled in 1800 by a Pennsylvanian who named it for Ben Franklin, and it maintained strong Union sympathies throughout the war. Federal troops occupied Franklin on April 15, 1863, at the spot identified by a marker. All the sugarcane grown here during the Civil War was appropriated by the North.

Lafayette

559 Louisiana Museum of Military History (col)
3000 Northeast Evangeline Thruway; 318-235-4322; Tues–Sun, 9–4. Admission charged.

This hands-on history museum features exhibits on the military heritage in Louisiana, including Civil War exhibits.

560 Mouton Statue (mem)
Lee and Jefferson avenues.

The monument honors Brigadier General Jean Jacques Alfred Mouton (1829–1864) who captained the Acadian Guards, organized in 1861. Mouton was wounded at Shiloh, and he died in the Battle of Mansfield in 1864.

Lake Providence

561 Grant's Canal (site)
600 Lake Street.

In a scheme to break the siege at Vicksburg, Ulysses S. Grant attempted to change the course of the Mississippi River here to enable him to slip troops past the Rebel batteries. His plan to connect the Mississippi with Lake Providence through a 1,000-foot canal was unsuccessful. Federal government funds converted the site into a park in 1936.

Mansfield

562 Mansfield Commemorative Area (site)
Route 175; 318-872-1474; Daily, 9–5. Admission charged.

As Union general Nathaniel Banks, with an army of 25,000, marched on Shreveport, his lines became stretched and vulnerable. Confederate general Richard Taylor formed a defensive line at Mansfield, or Sabine Crossroads, with a force of 12,000. Outflanked on both sides, the Federals gave way, and their retreat was hindered by supply wagons, which had been interspersed with the marching troops along the road. Finally, at Pleasant Grove the Union troops of William H. Emory stemmed the Confederate assault. The defeat resulted in the collapse of the Federal Red River campaign, the object of which had been to gain control of the river ports, including Shreveport. The Federal troops retreated to Pleasant Hill, twenty miles to the south, and fought again the following day and won a minor Northern tactical victory. The Battle of Sabine Crossroads on April 8, 1864, proved to be the last major fighting on Louisiana soil during the war.

The Mansfield Commemorative Area Museum has exhibits, an electrical map, a slide show, and battle relics. Outside, a self-guided walking tour covers the 44-acre battlefield.

Mansura

563 Battle of Mansura (site)
Route 1.

On May 16, 1864, the Confederates attempted to prevent the Union forces from retreating from Mansfield. A marker is on the spot.

Many

564 Battle of Pleasant Hill (mem)
Sabine Parish Tourist Commission; 800-358-7802; March. Free.

Reenactment: General Nathaniel Banks's attempt to march his Union forces into Texas ended with the engagement at Pleasant Hill on April 9, 1864. No battlefield exists, but a three-day event each March commemorates the fighting.

Merryville

565 Battle of Bear Head Creek (mem)
Beauregard Tourist Commission; Route 190; 800-738-5534; Last weekend in February. Free.

Reenactment: Although no actual battles were fought in Merryville, there were guerrillas called jayhawkers who often attacked either Confederate or Union forces to steal goods and weapons. The Living History Presentation with uniforms and weapons is held annually on the last weekend in February. Camp life and living conditions are on display before the battle reenactment.

New Iberia

566 Shadows-on-the-Teche (site)
317 East Main Street; 318-369-6446; Daily, 9–4:30. Admission charged.

The plantation was built in 1834 by sugar baron

David Weeks and occupied by the Union during the Civil War. It has been authentically restored to its opulent nineteenth-century appearance.

New Orleans

567 General Pierre G. Beauregard Statue (mem)

City Park; Esplanade Avenue.

The elegant equestrian statue at the park entrance was unveiled in 1915. The great Confederate commander died in 1893.

568 Confederate Museum (col)

929 Camp Street; 504-523-4522; Mon–Sat, 10–4. Admission charged.

This is the oldest museum in Louisiana and contains memorabilia of the Civil War, including uniforms, weapons, the battle flag of the Louisiana Tigers, war art, and personal effects of Jefferson Davis and General Pierre Beauregard. In the collection is the sword carried by General Albert Sidney Johnston when he was killed at Shiloh.

569 Davis Monument (mem)

Jefferson Davis Parkway.

The Confederate president died here in 1889, and his body lay in state in the city hall. The monument, designed by Edward Valentine, was unveiled on February 22, 1911.

570 Dreux Monument (mem)

Canal Street at Jefferson Davis Parkway,

The granite monument by Victor Holm honors Charles Didier Dreux, the first New Orleans officer to be killed in action in the Civil War. It stands opposite the memorial to Jefferson Davis.

571 Fort Pike State Commemorative Area (site)

Route 90; 504-662-5703; Daily, 9–5. Admission charged.

Fort Pike was named for explorer and soldier General Zebulon Montgomery Pike, who died in 1813 at the age of 34. Pikes Peak in Colorado also bears his name. The fort was built after the War of 1812 as part of the country's increased perimeter defenses; it guarded the entrance to Lake Pontchartrain. The Louisiana militia took control of the fort before the Civil War in 1861 but abandoned the area when Federal forces seized New Orleans in 1862. No Civil War cannon ball was ever fired from Fort Pike.

A self-guided tour explores the citadel, surrounded by two moats. Historical exhibits are displayed.

572 Jackson Barracks Military Museum (col)

6400 St. Claude Avenue; 504-278-6242; Mon–Fri, 7:30–4. Free.

The barracks were seized by the Confederates when Louisiana joined the Confederate States of America and were later retaken by Union troops. Weapons and military memorabilia from all wars are on display.

573 Jackson Statue (mem)

Jackson Square; Decatur Street.

Federal general Benjamin Butler had an inscription cut on the base of the Andrew Jackson statue when he occupied the city in 1862: "The Union Must and Shall be Preserved."

574 Lee Monument (mem)

Lee Circle, St. Charles Street, and Howard Avenue.

The monument to Robert E. Lee was planned in 1870 when he died but was not unveiled for the public until February 22, 1884. It was sculpted by Alexander Doyle.

575 U.S. Mint (site)

400 Esplanade Avenue; 504-568-6968; Tues–Sun, 9–5. Admission charged.

Built in 1836 at a cost of $182,000, this was for a few months the only mint in the Confederacy. It was here that William Mumford and others tore down the American flag and dragged it through the muddy street after Admiral David Farragut had occupied New Orleans. General Butler had Mumford arrested, tried, and court-martialed. He was hanged just below the flagstaff. Today, as part of the extensive Louisiana State Museum complex, it is a museum to New Orleans jazz.

Newellton

576 Winter Quarters State Commemorative Area (site)

Route 1, six miles east of town; 318-467-5439; Daily, 9–5. Admission charged.

General Grant's troops occupied this home during the Civil War, but it was saved from conflagration by its owner, Julia Nutt.

Pineville

577 Alexandria National Cemetery (site)

Shamrock Street.

The Confederates were headquartered here for part of the war. The national cemetery, one of four in Louisiana, was established in 1867. The gray granite monument marks a trench containing the remains of 1,537 unknown Federal soldiers moved here from Brownsville, Texas in 1911.

Sunset

578 Chretien Point Plantation (site)

Route 1; 318-233-7050; Daily, 10–5. Admission charged.

This is the site of a Civil War skirmish; the tour features Civil War artifacts. The stairway was reproduced for Tara in *Gone with the Wind*.

Tangipahoa

579 Camp Moore Confederate Cemetery and Museum (site)

Route 51; 504-229-2438; Tues–Sat, 1–4. Free.

After Louisiana's secession from the Union, a training and recruiting camp was established at mosquito-infested Camp Walker. Shortly, a new training site sprouted along the rail line at Tangipahoa, 78 miles north of New Orleans. At Camp Moore, named for Confederate Governor Thomas Overton Moore, there was an abundance of clean, fresh drinking water, plenty of shade—and no mosquitoes.

As Confederate defenses in Louisiana crumbled, the training camp waned. Camp Moore was first raided by Federal cavalry in April 1863 and again in October 1864, at which time large stores of clothing were destroyed and cattle dispersed. In the next month a force of 5,000 Union troops marched through Tangipahoa and burned Camp Moore. The wooden headboards that marked the graves of recruits who had died of disease were also destroyed. This final raid ended Camp Moore as a military camp.

The site is operated as a private, nonprofit entity. A small museum is open, and the cemetery, graced by a 1907 monument, can be visited.

Vinton

580 Niblett's Bluff (site)

Off Route 109; 319-589-7117.

Confederate breastworks are still visible in this campground overlooking the Old Sabine River.

Zachary

581 Port Hudson State Commemorative Area (site)

756 West Plains-Port Hudson Road; 504-654-3775.

Perched on high bluffs overlooking a substantial bend in the Mississippi River, Port Hudson was recognized for its strategic importance long before the Civil War. With the fall of New Orleans, the Confederates quickly took pains to make the area impregnable. Port Hudson was the southern stronghold of Confederate defenses along the Mississippi all the way to Vicksburg, 150 miles further north. If the river fell into Union hands, the military forces of the Confederate States of America would be divided—vital supplies such as salt, cattle, and horses would not be able to move east, and arms and munitions would not be able to be shipped out west.

Union Major General Nathaniel P. Banks brought 30,000 Union troops to bear on Port Hudson on May 23, 1863. Major General Franklin Gardner and 6,800 Confederate soldiers manned the defensive position. Ferocious fighting ensued along almost five miles of fortifications on the Mississippi over the next few weeks as the Union attack dissolved into a siege.

In July Grant broke through the southern defenses at Vicksburg, and when word of this reached Gardner, he realized that his situation was hopeless and negotiated the surrender of the last Confederate stronghold on the Mississippi River on July 9, 1863. The 48-day siege had exhausted the defenders' ammunition supply and reduced them to eating mules, horses, and rats.

An interpretive center includes a museum with displays of original Civil War artifacts and an audiovisual program explaining the siege of Port Hudson. Six miles of trails wind through the commemorative area, and original breastworks at such defensive strongholds as Fort Desperate can still be seen.

Maine

Civil War Status: Union
1860 Population: 628,279
Troops Provided: 72,000

Augusta

582 Monument Park (site)

Capitol and State streets.

Known as Augusta Mall during the Civil War, these 20 acres were the mustering point for the Kennebec Valley troops. After the war the site was conveyed to the city of Augusta in trust for a Civil War monument. Since that time other war memorials have been added to the landscaped grounds.

583 State House (col)

State and Capitol streets; 207-287-1400; Mon–Fri, 8–5. Free.

Built of native Hallowell granite, the original building was constructed in 1829, two years after Augusta became the state capital. The Hall of Flags features Maine's battle flags.

Bangor

584 Bangor Historical Society Museum (col)

159 Union Street; 207-942-5766; Mar–Dec: Tues–Fri, 12–4. Admission charged.

In the collection housed in an 1836 Greek Revival home are numerous Civil War items.

Brewer

585 Chamberlain House (site)

80 Chamberlain Street.

General Joshua Chamberlain received the Congressional Medal of Honor for his defense of Little Round Top at the Battle of Gettysburg. With Confederate troops storming the hill, Chamberlain led a saber charge that sealed the critical defensive position. He later served as governor of Maine and president of Bowdoin College.

Portland

586 Civil War Memorial (mem)

Market Square.

At the center is a memorial to the Portland men who served in the Civil War. The bronze group of three soldiers was completed in 1890 by Franklin Simmons.

Prospect

587 Fort Knox State Historic Site (site)

Route 1; 207-469-7719; Summer: daily, 9–dusk; May and October: 9–5. Free.

This pentagon-shaped fort overlooking the Penobscot River was built in the 1840s. The granite fort was outfitted with mounts for 64 cannons but was never threatened in the Civil War when troops trained here.

Rockland

588 Shore Village Museum (col)

104 Limerick Street; 207-594-0311; June–Oct 15: daily, 10–4. Free.

Maine's lighthouse museum has one of the largest collections of lighthouse and Coast Guard artifacts in the country. There is also a permanent exhibition of Civil War memorabilia including uniforms, weapons, medals, photographs, and correspondence.

Maryland

Civil War Status: Slave state that remained with the Union
1860 Population: 687,049
Troops Provided: 50,000 — Union
10,000 — Confederacy
Known Scenes of Action: 203

Civil War Timeline
September 14–17, 1862: Battles of South Mountain and Antietam
July 9, 1864: Battle of Monocacy

Annapolis

589 U.S. Naval Academy (col)

Gate 1; 52 King George Street; 410-263-6933; Mar–Nov: daily, 9–5; Dec–Feb: daily, 9–4. Free.

The U.S.S. *Constitution* sailed from Newport, Rhode Island, to protect the academy, and arrived on May 9, 1861. The faculty and administration were transferred to Newport, and the academy closed at Annapolis until 1865. The museum includes the sword of Franklin Buchanan, the first superintendent of the Naval Academy, who became a Confederate admiral.

Baltimore

590 Federal Hill (site)

Warren Avenue and Key Highway.

On May 13, 1861, shortly after an unsuccessful attempt by Southern sympathizers to raise a Confederate flag on the hill, Brigadier General Benjamin Butler moved 3,000 troops from Relay Station, Maryland, into Baltimore and took possession of Federal Hill. He manned it with 50 guns, which he trained on the city. Butler had no authority for such an action, which roused considerable resentment.

591 Fort McHenry National Monument (site)

East end of Fort Avenue; 410-962-4290; Daily, 8–5. Admission charged.

The setting for the creation of *The Star Spangled Banner* was built in 1794 and was an infantry post during the Civil War. Forty-seven years to the day after Francis Scott Key penned the future national anthem, his grandson, Francis Key Howard, was arrested as a secessionist sympathizer and brought to the fort, where he joined his father in captivity as political prisoner with, among others, the mayor of Baltimore.

592 Great Blacks In Wax Museum (col)

1601-03 East North Avenue; 410-563-3404; Tues–Sat 10–6, Sun 12–6. Admission charged.

The black experience in America is captured in more than 100 life-size, lifelike wax figures. Among the exhibits is a model slave ship depicting the 400-year history of the Atlantic slave trade.

593 Greenmount Cemetery (site)

Greenmount Avenue and Oliver Street.

Lincoln's assassin, John Wilkes Booth, is buried here. Also interred are many generals from both sides. Confederates include Joseph Eggleston Johnston, Arnold Elzey, Benjamin Huger, Isaac Ridgeway Trimble, Joseph Lancaster Brent, Lewis Henry Little, and John Henry Winder. Union commanders in the graveyard are John Reese Kenly and Richard Neville Bowerman.

594 Lee and Jackson's Final Meeting (mem)

Wyman Park; Howard Street and Wyman Park Drive.

The memorial depicting the final meeting of the Confederate leaders at Chancellorsville is said to be the only double equestrian statue in the world. Dedicated on May 1, 1948, the statue was funded through a bequest of $100,000 from the will of Henry Ferguson.

595 Maryland Historical Society Museum and Library (col)

201 West Monument Street; 410-685-3750; Mon–Fri: 10–4; Sun: tours at noon. Admission charged.

The owners of the original *Star Spangled Banner* manuscript and the country's largest collection of nineteenth-century silver also maintain a permanent Civil War gallery.

596 Monument to Confederate Women in Maryland (mem)

University Parkway and North Charles Street.

Joseph Maxwell Miller created three figures to honor the caring women of Maryland. The male bronze represents the Fallen Fighter, clutching a tattered banner as a nurse supports him, and a girl, her fists clenched, represents the Spirit of Rebellion. Erected in 1913, the sculpture rests on an inscribed red granite base.

597 The Shot Tower (site)

801 East Fayette Street; 410-396-3523; Wed–Sun, 10–4. Free.

Built in 1828 for the production of lead shot, this 234-foot "factory in a smokestack" contains one million wood-fired bricks.

598 Spirit of the Confederacy (mem)

Mount Royal Avenue between Lafayette and Mosher streets.

Frederic Wellington Ruckstull was commissioned by the United Daughters of the Confederacy to complete this monument to the Confederate sailors and soldiers of Maryland. The bronze sculpture is composed of two standing figures — the allegorical Winged Glory holds aloft the laurel of History as she supports a dying standard-bearer, in whose hand the flag droops in defeat but does not fall. The dedication was in 1903.

599 Union Soldiers' and Sailors' Monument (mem)

Druid Hill Park; Druid Park Lake Drive.

The park dates to 1688; the central bronze figure is a soldier turning from the plow and anvil to the sword. It was unveiled in 1909 and is the work of A. A. Weinman.

Big Pool

600 Fort Frederick State Park (site)

11100 Fort Frederick Road; 301-842-2155; Apr–Dec: daily, 8–dusk; other times: Wed–Sun, 8–4. Free.

This ancient stone fort was built in 1756 and held by Union troops in 1861 and 1862. Maryland's first skirmish took place here at the site of McCoy's Ferry when a party of Confederates tried to take a ferryboat in May 1861.

Boonsboro

601 Boonsboro Museum of History (col)

113 North Main Street; 301-432-6969; May–Sept: Sun, 1–5. Admission charged.

The varied collection of objects from Boonsboro and Washington County includes Civil War relics.

Burkittsville

602 War Correspondents Memorial Arch (mem)

Gathland State Park; Route 17, one mile west of town.

This memorial is located at Crampton's Gap, an

important site during the Battle of South Mountain. George Alfred Townsend, Civil War correspondent and novelist, decided to honor his fellow newspapermen who covered the Civil War. This strange structure, 50 feet high and 40 feet broad, was designed by Townsend to include the bizarre features of a Moorish arch topped by three Roman arches. It was dedicated on October 16, 1896. The arch is of local stone trimmed with brown sandstone, blue limestone, and brick. In a niche near the top of the arch is the six-foot figure of Orpheus sheathing a sword and playing a pipe. Tablets on one side of the arch bear the names of 157 correspondents and artists of the war, and other tablets include a description of the skirmish that occurred in the mountain pass. Despite Townsend's earnest intentions, the *War Correspondents Memorial Arch* is considered by many to be the worst looking memorial of the era.

Also on the grounds of Townsend's former estate is a museum housing Civil War era firearms and other relics. A self-guided walking tour traverses the quartzite ridge of South Mountain, where the Confederate forces fought a successful delaying action as part of their invasion of Northern territory in the fall of 1862.

Cambridge

603 The Underground Railroad: Harriet Tubman Museum (col)

424 Race Street; 410-228-0401; Tues–Fri 1–5, Sat 12–4. Free.

Harriet Tubman, whose birthplace marker is one-and-a-half miles down Green Briar Road, was raised in Dorchester County. She came back to the area 19 times to rescue slaves. The collection describes the resources at her disposal on the Underground Railroad.

Chestertown

604 Civil War Monument (mem)

Kent County Courthouse.

The memorial was erected in 1917 by Judge James Alfred Pearce to honor the soldiers of Kent County who fought for either side during the Civil War; the Federal inscription faces north, the Confederate inscription south.

Clinton

605 Surratt House and Tavern (site)

9110 Brandywine Road; 301-868-1121; Mar–Dec: Thurs–Fri 11–3, Sat–Sun 12–4. Admission charged.

In 1852 John Surratt purchased 287 acres of farmland in Prince George's County, obtained a tavern license, and opened a public house and hotel for traveling gentlemen. Two nighttime travelers 13 years later would make the Surratt House and Tavern famous nationwide.

After John died in 1862, life became a struggle for his wife Mary. Her two sons were serving in the Confederacy, and she decided to lease the tavern and move to Washington to run a boardinghouse. One of her frequent guests was John Wilkes Booth, who was friendly with her son. Following his murder of Abraham Lincoln on the night of April 14, 1865, Booth and an accomplice, David E. Herold, stopped at the Surratt Tavern to pick up field glasses and carbines.

In the aftermath of the tragedy anyone suspected of having been involved in the assassination plot in any way was apprehended. Among them was Mary Surratt. A tenant, John Lloyd, testified that she had delivered field glasses to him for safekeeping on the morning of April 14. This thin strand of evidence sent Mary Surratt, a gentle and deeply religious woman, to the gallows on July 7, 1865.

Reenactment: Guided tours of the historic house museum, opened in 1976, are conducted by costumed docents. In the spring and fall popular 12-hour bus tours of John Wilkes Booth's escape route are offered. A Civil War wedding reenactment takes place in the summer.

Cumberland

606 Turkey Flight Manor (site)

Route 2; 301-777-3553.

On the night of February 21, 1865, Union generals Benjamin Franklin Kelley and George Crook were captured in Cumberland, despite the presence of 6,000 Federal troops in town. This building, originally a tavern, still has interior woodwork held in place with hand-forged nails. Hit by a cannonball during the Civil War, the manor was used as a hospital for sick and wounded soldiers, who scribbled reminders on the attic walls.

Easton

607 Talbot Monument (mem)

Opposite courthouse on South Washington Street.

The memorial honors the Confederate soldiers of Talbot County. The name of Admiral Franklin Buchanan, whose home was here and who is buried in the town's Wye Cemetery, heads the list. Buchanan commanded the Southern ironclad C.S.S. *Virginia* before being wounded.

Elkridge

608 Thomas Viaduct (site)

Levering Avenue, west of Route 1.

Built in 1835, this is the oldest curved railroad bridge with multiple arches in the world. This bridge was part of the main railroad between Baltimore and Washington, which allowed boat and rail transport to move troops and supplies during the Civil War.

Elkton

609 Sheriff John F. Dewitt Museum (col)

135 East Main Street; 410-398-1790; Mon 12–4, Tues 6–8:30 P.M., Thurs 10–4, fourth Sat of month 10–2. Free.

The military memorabilia collection in this private museum showcases artifacts dating back to the Civil War.

Frederick

610 Evangelical Reformed Church (site)

9-13 West Church Street.

In this church, built in 1848, Stonewall Jackson learned that pastor Reverend Daniel Zacharias was planning to pray for the success of Union troops in September 1862 and fearing trouble from his men, he came to the service to ward off any such action. The minister indeed prayed for the Union triumph, but there was no trouble to awaken Jackson, who slept through the sermon. Several of the buildings in this downtown area served as hospitals during the Civil War.

611 Barbara Fritchie House and Museum (site)

154 West Patrick Street; 301-698-0630; Apr–Sept: Mon, Thurs–Sat 10–4, Sun 1–4; Oct–Nov: Sat–Sun 1–4. Admission charged.

Supposedly, fiery Barbara Fritchie, then in her nineties, confronted Stonewall Jackson and his "Rebel hordes" by waving the American flag as the Confederates marched past her house in 1862. Although some think another woman was involved in the exchange, it was Fritchie's name that was passed to abolitionist John Greenleaf Whittier, who immortalized the incident in a poem for the October 1863 *Atlantic Magazine* when he wrote, "'Shoot if you must, this gray old head, but spare your country's flag,' she said." The museum is an exact replica of the Fritchie home, which was ruined by a flood.

612 Monocacy National Battlefield (site)

4801 Urbana Pike; 301-662-3515; Summer: daily, 8–4:30; other times: Wed–Sun 8–4:30. Free.

On July 7, 1864, Union general Lew Wallace, with 2,700 men, took up a defensive position at Monocacy Junction, planning to check the advance of General Jubal Early and his 18,000 Confederates. On July 8 Wallace was joined by 3,350 men from General Rickett's force. The bloody battle fought the next day ended in a decisive defeat for the outnumbered Federals, but the delay it caused Early probably kept Washington from falling into Confederate hands.

The farm land is virtually unchanged since the battle. An electronic map in the visitor center, opened in 1991, presents details of the "Battle That Saved Washington." Artifacts are displayed and monuments dot the field. Walking tours are available.

613 Mount Olivet Cemetery (site)

515 South Market Street.

Established in 1852, Mount Olivet is the final resting place for 800 Union and Confederate soldiers killed at South Mountain, Monocacy, and Antietam, buried along the western edge of the graveyard. Barbara Fritchie and Francis Scott Key are also buried here. The Confederate monument, with infantryman and flag, was erected in 1880.

614 National Museum of Civil War Medicine (col)

48 E. Patrick Street; 301-695-1864; due to open in 1997.

This unique collection will look at the Civil War from the perspective of the wounded and the caregivers. More than 3,000 items will include medical instruments and books that will demonstrate the state of medicine in the 1860s.

Glen Echo

615 Clara Barton National Historic Site (site)

5801 Oxford Road; 301-492-6245; Daily, 10–5. Free.

The 1891 house was the final home of the Civil War nurse and Red Cross founder Clara Barton. The house also served as headquarters and warehouse space for the American Red Cross from 1897 to 1904. Now restored, it contains relics from Barton's career.

Hagerstown

616 Mt. Prospect (site)

201 West Washington Street.

The building was constructed in 1789 by a Virginian, Nathaniel Rochester, a Revolutionary War colonel. Rochester operated a nail factory here and was the town's first banker before moving to upstate New York to found the town that bears his name. Three days after the Battle of Antietam, Mrs. Howard Kennedy, a resident in the house since 1850, and her small daughter Annie were watching a dreary procession of wounded pass by the house when a badly wounded Union officer collapsed before their door. Mrs. Kennedy nursed the young man brought into her house. The officer was Oliver Wendell Holmes, Jr., later a Justice of the United States Supreme Court. His father, after a frantic search of the battlefield, had given him up for dead. He later wrote about the incident in the poem *My Search for the Captain.*

617 Rose Hill Cemetery (site)

600 South Potomac Street.

The statue of *Hope* marks the burial place of more than 2,000 Confederate soldiers who died in the Civil War battles of Antietam and South Mountain. The Confederate monument was erected in 1877.

La Plata

618 The Dr. Samuel A. Mudd House Museum (site)

Dr. Samuel A. Mudd Road; 3½ miles east of Routes 5 and 205; 301-645-6870; Apr–Nov: Wed 11–3, Sun 12–4. Admission charged.

Dr. Samuel Mudd set the broken leg of John Wilkes Booth, assassin of President Lincoln, during his escape past this plantation on April 14, 1865. For this, Dr. Mudd was sentenced to life in prison and sent to Dry Tortugas Prison, off the coast of Florida, where he aided many yellow fever victims as he had aided his unknown caller in the night. President Andrew Johnson pardoned Dr. Mudd in 1869.

Oxon Hill

619 Fort Foote Park (site)

Route 210, 1½ miles west of town.

The crude concrete and stone gun emplacements and earthworks of the fort, built in 1863 to protect Washington, remain on the site. Fort Foote was garrisoned throughout the war.

Scotland

620 Point Lookout State Park and Civil War Museum (site)

Route 5, 3½ miles south of town; 301-872-5688; Summer: daily, 10–5; other times: Sat–Sun, 10–5. Admission charged.

Two forts were built here to defend the mouth of the Potomac River on the Chesapeake Bay. The site originally functioned as a Civil War Union hospital and then as a prison camp. More than 20,000 Confederates were detained here, and almost 5,000 died from exposure, starvation, and disease. The park's museum has what little remains from the darker side of the site's history; it has returned to the resort area it was before the Civil War.

Reenactment: Living history at Point Lookout is offered each June during the Blue and Gray Days. There are demonstrations of battles and a Civil War hospital.

Sharpsburg

621 Antietam National Battlefield (site)

Route 34/65, north and east of town; 301-432-5124; Summer: daily, 8:30–6; other times: 8–5. Admission charged.

On September 17, 1862, Robert E. Lee's first attempt to invade the North came to a climax. After his smashing victory at the First Battle of Manassas in August, Lee marched his army into Maryland, hoping to find vitally needed men and supplies. George McClellan followed with his Union troops, and after being joined by Stonewall Jackson's troops the armies clashed at Antietam Creek.

Some 41,000 Southerners were pitted against the 87,000-man Army of the Potomac of the Union when the fighting began. When silence again fell across the field, it had become "The Bloodiest Day of the Civil War." Federal losses were 12,410, Confederate losses 10,700. An old sunken road separating area farms came to be known as "Bloody Lane"—the dead and wounded were piled two to five deep in its dirt.

The fighting was indecisive, but Lee's initial foray into the North was over. Great Britain now hesitated to recognize the new Confederate government, and President Lincoln had the opportunity he needed to issue the Emancipation Proclamation, freeing all slaves in the states in rebellion.

The tour of the 12 square mile battlefield breaks the fighting into three phases: morning, midday, and afternoon. An audiovisual program and exhibits in the visitor center provide an introduction to Antietam, also known as Sharpsburg, for the nearest town. Interpretive markers also explain the preliminary skirmishing on South Mountain in the days before Antietam.

Reenactment: The battle is commemorated during the Sharpsburg Heritage Festival on the September weekend closest to the Antietam anniversary. In December 23,110 candles in bags are set out along the driving route of the battlefield to honor the soldiers who fell here.

622 Kennedy Farmhouse (site)

2406 Chestnut Grove Road; 301-432-2666; May–Oct: Sat–Sun, 9–5. Free.

This farm in the hills was the staging area where John Brown and his Provincial Army of the United States planned and prepared for their Harpers Ferry raid during the summer of 1859.

Thurmont

623 Catoctin Furnace (site)

Route 806 South, off Route 15.

Constructed in 1774, this foundry produced iron for the Revolutionary War and the Civil War.

Massachusetts

Civil War Status: Union
1860 Population: 1,231,066
Troops Provided: 160,000

Boston

624 Cass Statue (mem)

Boston Public Garden; Boylston Street Mall.

A native of Ireland, Colonel Thomas Cass commanded the Fighting Ninth Massachusetts Regiment and was killed at Malvern Hill, Virginia. The original statue was considered so poor that the monument was redone and rededicated in front of his family here in 1899.

625 Devens Statue (mem)

Charles River Esplanade.

Worcester lawyer Charles Devens was commissioned a major in the Union Army in 1861 and was breveted to a major general by the end of the Civil War. This bronze was sculpted by Olin Warner.

626 Emancipation Statue (mem)

Park Square.

The duplicate casting of Thomas Ball's Emancipation Group was given to Boston in 1877, commemorating Lincoln's freeing of the slaves.

627 Farragut Statue (mem)

Marine Park.

This monument to Admiral David Glasgow Farragut by Henry Hudson Kitson was dedicated on June 28, 1893, with a parade.

628 Fort Warren (site)

Boston Harbor Islands State Park; 617-727-5250; July 1–Columbus Day: daily, 10–5; May: Wed–Sun, 10–5. Free.

The fort on George Island became a prison for Confederates for the duration of the war. It gained renown in late 1861 as the detention center for two Confederate diplomats taken from the British packet *Trent*, a nonbelligerent ship. Until the two diplomats were released, the *Trent* affair threatened to entangle foreign influence in the Civil War.

629 Phillips Monument (mem)

Boylston Street.

The memorial honors Wendell Phillips (1811–1884), "Champion of the Slave." Daniel Chester French sculpted the president of the American Anti-Slavery Society who spoke extensively around the country — many times to audiences who did not care to hear what he had to say.

630 Colonel Robert Gould Shaw Memorial (mem)

Beacon Street, across from State House at entrance to Common.

This finest of all Boston monuments is a high bronze relief memorial to the 26-year-old Shaw and the famous 54th Regiment of Massachusetts Volunteer Infantry, by sculptor Augustus Saint-Gaudens. The 54th, the first black regiment recruited in the North to serve in the Civil War, distinguished itself in leading a frontal assault on Battery Wagner, South Carolina, on July 18, 1863. Colonel Shaw, a member of a prominent white Boston family, died along with large numbers of his men. The surviving veterans of the 54th and 55th regiments were among those present for the memorial's dedication in 1897, at which Booker T. Washington was one of many speakers.

631 Soldiers' Monument (mem)

Forest Hills Cemetery.

This was the first of Martin Milmore's numerous Civil War monuments throughout New England. As one of the early bronze sentinels with a standing soldier leaning on a rifle, erected in 1867, it influenced hundreds that followed.

632 Soldiers' Monument (mem)

South and Centre streets.

This granite figure by W. W. Lummus to commemorate the service of Union men in the Civil War was installed here in 1871.

633 Soldiers' and Sailors' Monument (mem)

Boston Common.

On the highest point in America's oldest public park is a memorial honoring the Civil War dead. Martin Milmore sculpted four bronze statues at the base, representing Peace, the Sailor, the Muse of History, and the Soldier. The Genius of the American stands at the top of the 70-foot-high monument, erected in 1877.

634 State House (mem)

Beacon Street; 617-727-3676; Mon–Fri, 9–5. Free.

Distinguished by the familiar gold dome, the State House, designed by Charles Bullfinch, was built in 1798. The second floor has Civil War battle flags, including the rescued flag of the 54th Regiment of Massachusetts, saved during the assault on Fort Morgan by Sergeant William Carney of New Bedford, who became the first black American to receive the Congressional Medal of Honor.

Doric Hall has busts and statues of Civil War leaders, including John Albion Andrew, the Civil War governor of Massachusetts. Andrew was an effective supporter of the Union. The design by Thomas Ball, unveiled in 1871, features a voluminous cloak that fails to obscure a pair of decidedly rumpled trousers. A statue of William Francis Bartlett, by Daniel Chester French, honors the Massachusetts soldier who made major general at the age of 24.

On the lawn is an equestrian statue of General Joseph Hooker, tabbed "Fighting Joe" by the press, much to his consternation. This design, unveiled on June 25, 1903, includes a figure by French and a horse by Edward Putter. Hooker was defeated by Lee at Chancellorsville, despite a two-to-one advantage in troop strength. Of this statue Charles Francis Adams, a Civil War brevet brigadier general, once said: "Never since it has been placed there have I passed in front of the State House without feeling a sense of wrong and insult at the presence, opposite the head of Park Street, of the equestrian statue of Hooker. That statue I look upon as an opprobrium cast on every genuine Massachusetts man who served in the Civil War. Hooker in no way and in no degree represents the typical soldiership of the Commonwealth."

Foxborough

635 Civil War Memorial (mem)

Foxborough Library; South and Central streets.

The town's monument to the Civil War was sculpted by Charles Pizanno.

Framingham

636 Civil War Statue (mem)

Framingham Center; Oak Street.

Typical of the numerous Civil War monuments by Martin Milmore in New England, this bronze is a simple rendering of a soldier leaning on a rifle. It was erected in 1872.

Haverhill

637 Civil War Monument (mem)

Route 110.

This bronze monument to Union soldiers, sculpted by Calvin Weeks, was erected in 1869.

Lawrence

638 Civil War Monument (mem)

Lawrence Common.

Erected in 1881, this Civil War bronze by William Rudolph O'Donovan features a military group representing the four branches of nineteenth-century service.

Newburyport

639 Civil War Memorial: The Volunteer (mem)

Atkinson Common; High Street and Mosely Avenue.

Theo Alice Ruggles Kitson crafted this bronze monument to Massachusetts volunteers.

Peabody

640 Soldiers' and Sailors' Monument (mem)

Peabody Square.

The 50-foot granite and bronze monument to Union soldiers was created by Thomas Crawford and dedicated in 1881.

Randolph

641 Civil War Memorial (mem)

Stetson Hall; North Main and Union streets.

The bronze by F. Kohlhagen honors Union soldiers.

Revere

642 Civil War Memorial (mem)

Broadway and Hyde streets.

A monument was placed here in 1931 by the city of Revere to honor Union soldiers.

Saugus

643 Civil War Memorial (mem)
Main and Central streets.

This private gift to the town in honor of the Union struggle is a monument of stone and bronze by Melzar Hunt Mosman and was installed in 1875.

Somerville

644 American Valor (mem)
Somerville Public Library.

This bronze by Edward McCartan features a man wearing a long coat and marching with a gun over his shoulder. Behind him is a winged figure holding a large flag.

Springfield

645 Springfield Armory National Historic Site (site)
Federal Street; 413-734-8551; Summer: daily, 10–5; Tues–Sun, 10–5. Free.

Production at the first of two Federal armories commissioned by George Washington was spurred by the Civil War — 3,000 men turned out 1,000 Springfield rifles a day. On display are a collection of small arms and Civil War muskets; the surrounding fence is made of recast cannons.

Wakefield

646 Civil War Memorial (mem)
Main and Salem streets.

This soldier group in a 30-foot monument was erected in 1902; it is attributed to Melzar Mosman.

Woburn

647 Civil War Memorial (mem)
Main and Pleasant streets.

In 1869 this bronze honoring the recently completed Civil War was concluded by Martin Milmore.

Worcester

648 Soldiers' Memorial (mem)
Worcester Common.

Randolph Rogers created a Corinthian granite column resting on a three-level pedestal, dedicated to the soldiers of Worcester in 1874. The bronze figure of Athena stands at the top of the column, with a sailor, soldier, infantryman, and artilleryman at the corners.

Michigan

Civil War Status: Union
1860 Population: 749,113
Troops Provided: 45,000

Ann Arbor

649 William L. Clements Library (col)
University of Michigan; 313-764-2347; Mon–Fri, 10:30–12 and 1–5. Free.

Among the notable collections in this vast repository are original photos of Michigan Civil War soldiers.

Battle Creek

650 Oak Hill Cemetery (site)
South Avenue and Oak Hill Drive.

Battle Creek was an abolitionist stronghold in the years prior to the Civil War. Sojourner Truth, an impressive six-foot former slave, traveled throughout New England and the West speaking against slavery. She died in 1883 and is buried at Oak Hill. Her grave is marked with a simple square monument.

Dearborn

651 Henry Ford Museum and Greenfield Village (col)
Village Road and Oakwood Boulevard; 800-TELL-A-FRIEND; Daily, 9–5. Admission charged.

Several areas of this cornucopia of artifacts of American life touch on the Civil War. The Hermitage Slave Houses are humble dwellings from the times of enslavement; the exhibit *Battle Scenes of the Rebellion* is a panorama of 15 oils by Indiana folk artist Thomas Clarkson Gordon, and a Civil War Remembrance is staged on Memorial Day weekend. Also in the eclectic collection is the Victorian rocking chair Abraham Lincoln was sitting in at Ford's Theatre when he was murdered.

Detroit

652 Soldiers' and Sailors' Monument (mem)
Cadillac Square.

Designed by Randolph Rogers as a memorial to the Northern forces, the 50-foot-tall granite shaft is ornamented with bronze figures on four levels and surmounted by a symbolic figure of Michigan, ten feet high, armed with shield and sword. It was dedicated in 1872.

Grand Rapids

653 Soldiers' Monument (mem)

Monroe Center; Fulton and Division streets.

This 34-foot white bronze is topped by an individual soldier and includes portraits of Union heroes Lincoln, Grant, Farragut, and Garfield. The names and dates of the engagements in which Kent County soldiers fought are engraved on this monument dating from the 1880s.

Hastings

654 Charlton Park Village and Museum (col)

Route 79; 616-945-3775; Summer: daily, 9–5. Admission charged.

Civil War artifacts are an attraction of this 300-acre museum. In the collection are clothing, weapons, and documents.

Kalamazoo

655 Soldiers' Monument (mem)

Riverside Cemetery; 1015 Gull Road.

The lone soldier at ease honors the private soldier who fought in the Civil War. It was dedicated on September 26, 1901.

Lansing

656 First Michigan Sharpshooters (mem)

Michigan State Capitol; Allegan Street and Capitol Avenue.

Frank Black crafted this memorial to the survivors of the First Regiment of the Michigan Sharpshooters. The granite soldier is leaning against a rock structure with his gun aimed.

Mackinac Island

657 Fort Mackinac (site)

906-847-3328; Summer: daily, 9–6. Admission charged.

The fort was constructed in 1780 and was used as a prison camp for Confederate prisoners in the Civil War. The history is interpreted through rooms in period settings.

Manistee

658 Lyman Building (col)

425 River Street; 616-723-5531; Jun–Sept, Mon–Sat, 10–5. Admission charged.

In the permanent Civil War display is Confederate money, documents, clothing items, equipment, and weapons.

Monroe

659 Custer Sighting the Enemy (mem)

North Monroe Street and West Elm Avenue.

George Armstrong Custer met his future wife, Elizabeth Bacon, while visiting a married sister here. Elizabeth first spurned his proposal but later relented and married him on February 28, 1864. The equestrian statue was designed by Edward C. Potter.

660 Monroe County Historical Museum (col)

126 South Monroe Street; 313-243-7137; May–Sept: daily, 10–5; other times: Wed–Sun, 10–5. Free.

There are Civil War items such as weapons, flags, and medical items here, but the focus of the collection is Custer, who not only married into the prominent family of Judge Bacon but moved his parents from Ohio to Monroe during the war. Museum exhibits trace General Custer through West Point and focus on his career in the Civil War.

Reenactment: Civil War battles, featuring cavalry, infantry, and artillery are presented in authentic uniforms and costumes each May in Nike County Park (313-654-8265).

Muskegon

661 Soldiers' and Sailors' Monument (mem)

Hackley Park; West Clay Avenue between 3rd and 4th streets.

The tall granite shaft by Joseph Carabelli features a Union hero at each of its four corners: Lincoln and Farragut, by Charles Niehaus, and Grant and Sherman, by J. Massey Rhind.

Niles

662 Fort St. Joseph Museum (col)

5th and Main streets; 616-683-4702; Wed–Sat 10–4, Sun 1–4. Free.

The museum contains more than 10,000 historical items, including Civil War weapons and flags.

Port Huron

663 Soldiers' Monument (mem)

Pine Grove Park; 1104 Grove Avenue.

In the southeast corner of the park is a memorial to commemorate those who died in the Civil War. At the base of the central shaft are two large cannon that were used in the siege of Vicksburg. This monument was dedicated in 1893.

Minnesota

Civil War Status: Union
1860 Population: 172,023
Troops Provided: 20,000

Cannon Falls

664 City Cemetery (mem)

Routes 52 and 19.

In the graveyard is a granite shaft with a statue of William Colvill, who led the 1st Minnesota Regiment at Gettysburg in 1863.

Fairfax

665 Fort Ridgely State Park (site)

Route 4, six miles south of town; 507-426-7840.

When Minnesota entered the Union as the thirty-second state in 1858, this outpost was fully manned by regular army troops. Four years later the Civil War rapidly siphoned off the manpower at Fort Ridgely, leaving it garrisoned by volunteers from local towns. On August 17, 1862, the Lakotah Sioux, facing semistarvation on their enforced reservations, revolted in southern Minnesota and murdered settlers near Acton, Minnesota. Fort Ridgely was successfully defended over the next week as the surrounding villages were aflame. The uprising lasted for another month.

Reenactment: Fort Ridgely became a training ground for Union soldiers and was once again an active army post after the war. The Fort Ridgely Historical Festival every June features uniformed soldiers conducting live Civil War era drills, music, and demonstrations.

Hutchinson

666 Chief Little Crow Statue (mem)

Eheim Park; Crow River Dam at Main Street. Little Crow, the reluctant leader of the Sioux up-

rising, attacked the stockade in the Hutchinson Public Square on September 4, 1862. After escaping the Federal capture, Little Crow was ambushed near town on July 2, 1863, and killed while picking berries. The body was taken into Hutchinson on July 4, scalped and mutilated, and buried ignominiously in a pile of offal. His killer, a local farmer named Nathan Lamson, received a $500 bounty, and his son Chauncey was given $75 for the Sioux chief's scalp.

A 550-pound concrete statue was created by the 20-year-old aspiring wildlife artist Les Kouba in 1937, depicting the Sioux leader in full headdress. A new bronze statue honoring Little Crow was placed on this spot in 1982.

667 McLeod County Heritage and Cultural Center (col)

Highway 7 and School Road; 612-587-2109; Mon–Fri 10–4:30, Sat–Sun 1–4. Admission charged.

The original concrete casting of Little Crow is located here, as well as information on the Sioux uprisings during the Civil War.

Le Sueur

668 Dr. W.W. Mayo House (site)

118 North Main Street; 612-665-3250; Summer: Tues–Sun, 12–4:30; May, Sept, Oct: Sat–Sun, 12–4:30. Admission charged.

Dr. William Mayo worked from his office on the second floor of this 1859 dwelling, caring for the sick and wounded who survived the Sioux uprising of 1862. Later he served as examining surgeon of the 1st Minnesota district examining board, testing prospective Civil War soldiers. In 1864 he moved to Rochester, founding the world famous Mayo Clinic with his sons.

Litchfield

669 G. A. R. Hall (col)

308 North Marshall Avenue; 612-693-8911; Tues–Sun, 12–4. Admission charged.

The hall was built in 1885 by Union veterans to display Civil War relics. Two rooms remain in the original condition. Civil War research material is available.

Little Falls

670 Minnesota Military Museum (col)

Camp Ripley; Route 115 off Route 371, seven miles north of town; 612-632-6631; May–Sept: Wed–Sun, 10–5. Free.

Exhibits include weapons, uniforms, equipment, memorabilia, and more than 1,000 photographs depicting Minnesota military history from 1819 to the present. Camp Ripley is a former regimental headquarters.

Mankato

671 Sioux Execution Site (site)

North Front and East Main streets.

A military tribunal sentenced 303 Sioux warriors to death for their part in the slaughter of more than 500 Minnesota settlers, but Lincoln communed the sentence of all but 38, who were put to death in a mass public execution here on December 26, 1862. A marker identifies the site.

Minneapolis

672 The Congressman (mem)

Grand Army Circle; Victory Memorial Drive.

Partially funded by the pennies of schoolchildren, this rendering of Abraham Lincoln by Max Bachman borrows heavily from Saint-Gaudens' classic Standing Lincoln. The dedication was held on Memorial Day, 1930.

Morton

673 Lower Sioux Agency History Center (site)

Route 2, off Route 19, south of town; 507-697-6321; May–Aug: Mon–Sat 10–5, Sun 12–5; Sept–Oct: daily, 1–5. Free.

The Sioux uprising of 1862 ended on the Wood Lake Battlefield when troops under the first Minnesota governor, Henry Hastings Sibley, repulsed the attackers under Little Crow on September 23. More than 1,000 Sioux were captured and 38 were later executed in Mankato. The uprising took as many as 500 lives among the settlers.

This historic site contains an interpretive center with displays commemorating the war. Historical markers along a trail system recount the first organized attack by the Sioux on a white settlement.

New Ulm

674 Sioux Uprising Monument (mem)

Center Street.

During the Sioux uprising of 1862 the town was almost completely destroyed, but home guards safely evacuated 2,000 refugees out of town. Many were wounded and two score killed, but the town was rebuilt. The bronze monument next to the courthouse square commemorates the heroism of New Ulm's defenders.

Mississippi

Civil War Status: Confederacy; seceded from the Union on January 9, 1861
1860 Population: 791,305
Troops Provided: 80,000
Known Scenes of Action: 772

Civil War Timeline

April 29–May 30, 1862: Siege of Corinth
September 19, 1862: Battle of Iuka
October 3–4, 1862: Battle of Corinth
December 17–28, 1862: Van Dorn's Holly Springs Raid
December 27–29, 1862: Battle of Chickasaw Bayou
April 16–22, 1863: Union fleet passes Vicksburg river batteries
April 29, 1863: Battle of Grand Gulf
May 1, 1863: Battle of Port Gibson
May 12, 1863: Battle of Raymond
May 14, 1863: Battle of Jackson
May 16, 1863: Battle of Champion Hill
May 17, 1863: Battle of Big Black River Bridge
May 19–July 4, 1863: Siege and surrender of Vicksburg
July 10–16, 1863: Siege of Jackson
February 22, 1864: Battle of Okolona
June 10, 1864: Battle of Brice's Cross Roads
July 14, 1864: Battle of Tupelo

Aberdeen

675 Monument to the Confederate Dead (mem)

Route 45.

Names of Monroe County soldiers are inscribed on the sandstone base of this 1901 monument.

Baldwyn

676 Brice's Cross Roads National Battlefield Site (site)

Route 370 and Bethany Road; six miles west of town; 601-680-4025.

Here on June 10, 1864, Nathan Bedford Forrest won his most smashing tactical victory against much larger — and wearier — Union forces under General Samuel D. Sturgis, forcing them to withdraw to Memphis. Forrest deployed his cavalry force of 3,500 against 8,100 Federal soldiers across marshy terrain around Tishomingo Creek. It was a signal victory to Forrest's peculiar way of fighting.

The muddy ground was to his advantage as he charged the Union troops before they could emerge from the woods. At one time he was in the front rank, pistol in hand, his courage and aggressiveness carrying the day.

The Union retreat stalled at a bridge crossing the treacherous Tishomingo Creek, and the battle turned into a Confederate rout. Forrest captured 14 pieces of artillery, 5,000 stand of fire arms, 500,000 rounds of ammunition and 176 wagons. The Federal casualties were 223 killed, 394 wounded and 1,623 missing or captured, as against Forrest's 96 killed and 396 wounded.

An interpretive center is in the works, but for now this tiny national battlefield is only a small one-acre piece of land, unmanned and with no facilities. It is only a small part of the field, but from it most of the scene of battle action is visible. There are a few cannons and several monuments. A small cemetery is nearby with Civil War graves. Plaques placed at Brice's Cross Roads detail troop movements during the battle. Granite markers along Route 370 also show the progress of the battle.

Biloxi

677 Beauvoir (site)

2244 Beach Boulevard; 601-388-1313; Daily, 9–5. Admission charged.

Beauvoir became the last home of Jefferson Davis, who first rented East Cottage here in 1877. He spent three years writing *The Rise and Fall of the Confederate Government* in longhand and received a parade of former soldiers and well-wishers. Following his death in 1889, his widow rejected an offer of $100,000 and instead sold the mansion for $10,000 to serve as a Confederate Veterans Home. In a shaded cemetery are more than 700 of their graves as well as the Tomb of the Unknown Soldier of the Confederacy. Davis family memorabilia is in the house museum.

Reenactment: A Confederate Day celebration and mock battle is staged at Beauvoir in April, and the largest Civil War reenactment in Mississippi is the Fall Muster in October.

678 Biloxi Lighthouse (site)

Route 90, West Beach Boulevard at foot of Porter Avenue.

When Biloxi was threatened by Union ships, a townsman climbed the 65-foot lighthouse tower, removed the lens, and buried it. The lighthouse was painted black after Lincoln's assassination.

Booneville

679 Cavalry skirmish (site)

Route 45.

This town near the pivotal railroads at Corinth was the site of skirmishing and maneuvering during 1862. On July 1, Union general Philip Sheridan's forces prevailed in an all-day fight with Confederate cavalry. Historical markers are in the area.

Bruinsburg

680 Union March (site)

Claiborne County.

Ulysses S. Grant landed 40,000 forces here, across Bayou Pierre on April 30, 1863, as he prepared to move on the Confederate stronghold at Vicksburg. The county erected a series of markers that tell the story of the long column as it passed through rural Mississippi, many times led by escaped slaves.

Canton

681 Harvey Scouts Monument (site)

Canton Cemetery.

The town was under the control of both the Union and Confederacy during the Civil War and much of it was burned, but the courthouse remains one of only seven unaltered pre–Civil War government seats in Mississippi.

The cemetery contains the graves of 350 soldiers, mostly from the Army of Tennessee, who fell at Corinth or Shiloh. The monument was erected in September 1894 to Addison Harvey, captain of the Harvey Scouts, by the surviving members of his band of men who fought over 100 battles.

The Harvey Scouts were 100 volunteers commissioned by Jefferson Davis. Their forays caused Sherman's army as much trouble as an entire regiment. On the west side of the monument is a list of those Scouts killed in battle.

Clinton

682 Clinton Cemetery (site)

College Street.

Graves in this burial ground date back to 1800 and include many Civil War veterans.

683 Provine Chapel (site)

Mississippi College.

During a minor skirmish in 1864 the chapel's first floor was used as a hospital and its basement as a stable for Union horses during the war.

Columbus

684 Blewett-Harrison-Lee House (site)

316 7th Street North; 601-327-8888.

This was the home of Lieutenant General Stephen D. Lee, legislator, historian, and first president of Agricultural and Mechanical College, now Mississippi State University. Lee was born in Charleston, South Carolina, and graduated from West Point in 1854 before resigning his commission to join the Confederacy. He was one of two officers sent by General Beauregard to demand the surrender of Fort Sumter. Lee distinguished himself in battle on several occasions and was described by Jefferson Davis as "one of the best all-round soldiers the war has produced." He died in 1908 as national commander of the United Confederate Veterans of America. The house contains Lee's personal effects.

685 Confederate Soldier (site)

Friendship Cemetery; 4th South Street.

Columbus was never a military target and is one of the few Mississippi towns never invaded. It served as a medical center and arsenal and briefly as the state capital after the fall of Jackson. Several houses in town have a connection to the short stay there of the Confederate Mississippi legislature. The grounds here were purchased by the Odd Fellows for recreational purposes in 1849 but were converted to a cemetery during the war; the first burials came from Shiloh. Under spreading magnolias rest 100 Federal and 1,500 Confederate soldiers, whose names were recorded in a book, which has since been lost.

On April 25, 1866, a group of widows visiting the graveyard decided to decorate not only the graves of their husbands and fathers but those of the Union soldiers interred there as well. Their Decoration Day, it is said, evolved into America's national Memorial Day, and the cemetery was renamed "Friendship." The limestone carving of a soldier was dedicated in 1894.

686 Lowndes County Confederate Monument (mem)

Lowndes County Courthouse; 5th Street South.

Dedicated on August 12, 1912, this classical marble temple honors the soldiers of Lowndes County. The monument includes three separate soldier statues imported from Italy.

Corinth

687 Battery F (site)

Davis Street.

West of town is Corinth's finest original piece of earthworks. This perfectly formed and preserved lunette is a four-gun position of the embrasure type.

688 Battery Robinette (site)

Confederate Park; Linden Street.

The heaviest fighting of the Battle of Corinth on October 3 and 4, 1862, took place at Battery Robinette. The Union forces withstood the Confederate onslaught, counterattacked, and kept control of Corinth. This battery was the northernmost of the College Hill Line constructed by the Federals during the summer of 1862 as their inner line of defense. When the fighting ended, nearly 2,000 lay dead and 7,500 were wounded.

Although there were six batteries and many rifle pits built around Corinth, Battery Robinette, reconstructed in 1976, is the only public property accessible to visitors. To maintain the integrity of the site, the annual reenactment of the Battle of Corinth takes place on the outer edge of the city.

A shaft marks the spot where Colonel William P. Rogers was fatally wounded by a Union bullet. As Rogers was leading the 2nd Texas Regiment, his horse was shot from under him. He grabbed the regimental battle flag from a wounded color-bearer, led the assault on foot, reached the scarp of Battery Robinett, planted the colors, and was shot. United States general Rosecrans ordered that Rogers be buried where he fell.

689 Corinth Battlefield and National Cemetery (site)

Horton Street; 901-386-8311.

Twenty acres were set aside by Congress in 1866 as a resting place for Union soldiers from northern Mississippi battle fields. More than 6,000 Union soldiers from 273 regiments of the 15 states are buried here. Three Confederate soldiers are buried near the flag pole.

690 Curlee House (site)

301 Childs Street; 601-287-9501; Fri–Wed, 1–4. Admission charged.

Known as the Verandah House for its encircling porches, this 1857 house for years was the showplace of Corinth. It attracted the attention of occupying troops as well, and generals from each side made their headquarters at Curlee House. Several houses in the immediate vicinity, although not open to the public, played lesser roles in the Civil War during army occupations and are marked.

691 Northeast Mississippi Museum (col)

Washington Street and 4th Street; 601-287-3120; Mar–Oct: Mon–Sat 10–5, Sun 2–5; Nov–Feb: Mon–Sat 10:30–4:30, Sun 2:00–4:30. Free.

The main room of this three-room museum, opened in 1986, is devoted to Civil War artifacts. The role of Corinth in the war is the common theme of all exhibits. A file of letters and diaries written by Civil War soldiers is preserved here.

692 Railroad Intersection (site)

Off Fillmore Street.

This railroad crossing made Corinth, a tiny hamlet of 1,200, one of the key strategic sites in the Civil War. At this spot the Confederacy's only east-west link, the Memphis and Charleston Railroad, crossed the vital Mobile and Ohio rail line. These were the two longest railroads in the western Confederacy. The village came to be known as the Crossroads of the Confederacy. With Corinth in Union hands, two avenues of conquest were open to the Federal armies: one led to Vicksburg, which would bisect the Confederacy, and the other led to Atlanta.

693 Rogers Monument (mem)

Courthouse; Waldron Street.

In front of the third courthouse to occupy this square is a statue of Colonel William P. Rogers at rest.

Edwards

694 Battle of Champion Hill Site (site)

I-20, Exit 19; 601-373-7144.

"The drums of Champion's Hill sounded the doom of Richmond." Such was the importance of the battle on the crest of this hill on May 18, 1863, that led to the fall of Vicksburg. Confederate general John C. Pemberton and 30,000 troops were entrenched at Vicksburg and trying desperately to unite with General Joseph E. Johnston and his 20,000 men moving toward Jackson. Ulysses S. Grant was in possession of Jackson and moving toward Vicksburg and moved in between the Confederate armies.

South of Champion Hill Pemberton's army stretched three miles, and it was for the hill that Grant and Pemberton fought. The crest of the hill changed hands three times before Grant turned Pemberton back across the Big Black River. Federal losses were 410 killed and 2,031 wounded; the Confederates suffered 324 killed and 3,269 wounded. Grant's victory was a decisive stroke of the campaign, scattering the Confederates. That evening Grant received Henry Wager Halleck's order, sent five days before, telling him on no account whatever to undertake such a campaign.

The undeveloped battlefield site, so crucial to the outcome of the war in the West, is marked only by a plaque. The Henry Coker House, used by both sides as a hospital and artillery site, is being re-

stored. On the next ridge to the west is the Tilghman Monument, reached by footpath. The inscription reads: "Lloyd Tilghman, Brigadier General C.S.A., Commander First Brigade, Loring's Division. Killed here on the afternoon of May 18, 1863, near the close of the battle of Champion's Hill." Tilghman died defending the ford across Baker's Creek while the Confederates retreated. The story is that he was shot by a sniper from the Coker house on the next hill.

Reenactment: The Battle of Champion Hill is reenacted in May.

Greenwood

695 Confederate Cemetery (site)

Strong Avenue.

This small graveyard contains the graves of soldiers who fell during the action in central Mississippi.

696 Cottonlandia Museum (col)

Route 49, Route 82 Bypass West; 601-453-0925; Mon–Fri: 9–5; Sat–Sun: 2–5. Admission charged.

This museum of Mississippi Delta history displays artifacts from Fort Pemberton, including souvenirs from the ironclad *Star of the West*, a Union gunboat captured by the Confederacy that was stripped and sunk to obstruct the river channel and delay advancing Federal navies. The bulk of the warship still rests in the river channel, buried beneath layers of mud. A rare Blakely 12-pound rifle gun cannon was restored here for display. During rehabilitation it was found to have stood loaded with powder, primer, and shell ready to fire for at least 128 years.

697 Fort Pemberton Park (site)

Route 82 Bypass West.

A marker identifies the site of Fort Pemberton, a hastily constructed fortification that consisted mainly of cotton bales and timbers. Confederate soldiers, not knowing that the war was over, manned the fort for two months after the peace was signed. Civil War Live Shoot competitions are held in Greenwood.

698 Leflore County Confederate Monument (mem)

Leflore County Courthouse; Fulton Street.

This tribute to Leflore County's sons and daughters of the Confederacy surmounts two time capsules. The stepped marble monument depicts a woman caring for a fallen soldier. Among the inscriptions is: "to the Confederate woman, none has told the story of her, whose heart and life were a sacrifice. Offered as valiantly and unselfishly upon the altar of her Southland, as was any warrior's life upon the battlefield." The dedication took place on October 9, 1913.

Grenada

699 Confederate Cemetery (site)

Cemetery Street, behind Odd Fellows' Cemetery; 606-226-2571.

Federal plans to attack here were abandoned; all of the 180 graves in the cemetery are marked "Unknown Soldier."

700 Confederate Earthworks (site)

Grenada Lake Visitor Center Museum; 601-226-1679; Route 51 at Grenada Dam.

After Grant broke through at Vicksburg, his next objective was the interior of Mississippi, and the railroad stock at Grenada made a tempting prize. The Confederate cavalry withdrew from the town before the Union forces arrived. Unopposed, the Union forces destroyed 51 engines and nearly 500 railroad cars. The main defensive positions on the Yalobusha River line have been protected on the National Register of Historic Places. The Civil War exhibit in the museum describes the successful raid by Confederate general John Pemberton on Grant's supply depot in Holly Springs, which was planned by the Southern leaders at Grenada.

Hattiesburg

701 Armed Forces Museum at Camp Shelby (col)

Route 49, 12 miles south of town; 601-558-2757; Tues–Sat 9–4, Sun 1–5. Free.

Over 6,000 items are in the collection, including many from the Civil War. The museum also features a research library.

702 McCain Library (col)

University of Southern Mississippi; 601-266-4345. Hours vary.

Extensive genealogical material is available, as well as the Ernest A. Walen Collection on the history of the Confederate States of America.

Holly Springs

703 First Presbyterian Church (site)

Gholson and Memphis streets.

Construction of this Romanesque Revival church, begun in 1860, was stopped during the Civil War, and Federal troops occupying the town used the basement as a stable for their horses.

704 Hillcrest Cemetery (site)

Elder Avenue at Center Street; 601-252-3757.

This is the final resting place for the fallen of both the Civil War and the deadly 1878 yellow fever epidemic in Holly Springs. The Marshall County Confederate Memorial — two marble sculptures of Confederate soldiers standing on either side of a tall, draped shaft — was dedicated here in 1876.

705 Marshall County Historical Museum (col)

220 East College Avenue; 601-252-3669; Mon–Sat, 10–5. Admission charged.

Ulysses S. Grant set up a supply depot in Holly Springs before moving to Vicksburg. The town was recaptured by Confederate general Earl Van Dorn, who imprisoned more than 1,000 Union soldiers and destroyed Grant's supplies. By the end of the war Holly Springs had suffered 60 raids. Citizens made it a practice to check each day which flag was flying as they went about their business. The Memorial Civil War Exhibit recalls this past.

706 Walter Place (site)

330 W. Chulahoma Avenue. Open during Holly Springs Pilgrimage.

General and Mrs. Grant lived in the home of Harvey W. Walter, built on the eve of the hostilities in 1862. Mrs. Grant speaks in her memoirs of the sea of army tents outside of Walter Place. It is said that General Grant's papers were spared through an appeal to General Van Dorn's chivalry.

Iuka

707 Shady Grove Cemetery (site)

Indian Street; 601-423-9933.

With Grant marching to reinforce Buell in Kentucky, the Confederates, under Colonel Sterling Price, sought to intervene on September 19, 1862. Union general William Rosecrans carried most of the battle against Price in the Battle of Iuka on the eastern slopes of Woodall Mountain. Price held his ground, but knowing that Grant was nearby, withdrew in the night. All the homes in town were converted into makeshift hospitals and the dead separated by uniform color and buried in trenches.

Jackson

708 Battlefield Park (site)

Porter Street.

Confederate fortifications have remained in this naturally wooded area. Some trenches can be seen and cannon are on the grounds.

709 City Hall and Gardens (site)

219 South President Street; 601-960-1084; Daily, private tours available on request. Free.

Union troops under Sherman twice occupied the capital city in 1863 and burned so much of Jackson that it came to be called "Chimneyville." The city hall served as a hospital and was one of only a handful of structures to survive the conflagration.

710 Governor's Mansion (site)

300 East Capitol Street; 601-359-6421; Tues–Fri, 9:30–11. Free.

General Sherman celebrated the fall of Vicksburg with a victory dinner in this mansion, the home of Mississippi's governors since 1842. During the war, wounded soldiers were treated here.

711 Greenwood Cemetery (site)

West Street at Lamar Street.

This Confederate burial ground has the graves of more than 100 soldiers, including several officers.

712 Manship House (site)

420 East Fortification Street; 601-961-4724; Tues–Fri 9–4, Sat 1–4. Free.

As the street name implies, Confederate earthworks extended across the lawn of the Charles Henry Manship House, the home of Jackson's Civil War mayor, who surrendered the city to Sherman. The silver bell on the front lawn pealed through the streets of Jackson to proclaim the news that Mississippi had seceded from the United States in 1861.

713 The Oaks House Museum (site)

823 North Jefferson Street; 601-353-9339; Tues–Sat 10–4, Sun 1:30–4. Admission charged.

Built in 1846, this is the house where Sherman stayed during his occupation of Jackson. It is one of 11 structures in Jackson predating the Civil War and is the city's oldest house.

714 Old Capitol Museum (site)

100 South State Street; 601-359-6920; Mon–Fri 8–5, Sat 9:30–4:30, Sun 12:30–4:30. Free.

The Old Capitol, completed in 1838, escaped torching and has been restored to house the state's history museum. The Ordinance of Secession was passed in this hall at an emotional meeting on January 9, 1861, by a vote of 84–15. In the collection are Civil War artifacts and animated battle maps. On the grounds is a Confederate monument unveiled by Jefferson Davis's grandson and paid for by the Women of Mississippi.

715 War Memorial Building (col)

120 South State Street; 601-354-7207; Mon–Fri, 8–4. Free.

The War Memorial Building stands as a monument to the Mississippi soldiers who have fallen in America's wars. It features a military museum and unique aluminum elevator doors and panels depicting battle scenes, including some from the Civil War.

Laurel

716 Confederate Monument (mem)

Route 11.

Most of the money for this memorial was provided by a northern-born businessman who remarked slyly at the dedication in the early 1900s: "You see here a handsome monument, erected with Yankee money to the Confederate dead of the Free State of Jones, which seceded from the Confederacy after the Confederacy seceded from the Union."

The Free State of Jones to which he alluded consisted of the citizens from Jones County who resented fighting a "Planters' War" and left the Confederate States of America. They declared nearby Ellisville their capital and Confederate deserter Newt Knight their leader. Much of their activities are shrouded in legend, and the renegades are said to have been so feared in their raids on both Union and Confederate supply bases that Union prisoners of war in Meridian were given arms to protect themselves against Knight and his followers.

Laurerdale

717 Laurerdale Springs Confederate Cemetery (site)

Route 45, north of town; 601-693-1306.

The area's Civil War dead are interred in this graveyard. Many are unknown.

Liberty

718 Amite County Courthouse (col)

Routes 24 and 48; 601-657-8022; Mon–Fri, 9–4. Free.

The oldest operating courthouse in Mississippi, circa 1838, contains original records from 1807 as well as memoirs and mementos of Confederate soldiers. Many buildings in town were destroyed by the invading Union army.

719 Confederate Monument (mem)

North Church Street, one block off Main Street.

Outside Liberty Presbyterian Church stands what is purported to be the first monument to the Confederacy in Mississippi. It was made in New Orleans and hauled the last 30 miles to Liberty in an ox cart and dedicated in 1871. There are four richly carved tablets inscribed with the names of Amite County soldiers who died during the Civil War.

Lorman

720 Rodney skirmish (site)

Route 552, 300 feet west of Highway 61.

The settlement of Rodney was a thriving Mississippi town which saw skirmishing during the Civil War. On September 13, 1863, Southern cavalry seized twenty crewmen of the U.S.S. *Rattler* while they attended church in Rodney. The church has been restored. Rodney became a ghost town when the Mississippi River changed its course in 1876.

Meridian

721 Confederate Monument (mem)

8th Street at 40th Avenue.

The town was a military camp and temporary state capital for one month when state records were brought here for safekeeping. The monument is at Rosehill Cemetery.

722 Marion Confederate Cemetery (site)

Route 45.

Just north of town are the remains of Southern warriors who died in area hospitals and on the battlefields in northern Mississippi.

723 Merrehope and F. W. Williams houses (site)

905 Martin Luther King, Jr., Drive; 601-483-8439; Mar–Oct: Mon–Sat 9–5, Sun 1–5; other times: Mon–Sat 9–4, Sun 1–4. Admission charged.

When General Sherman finished his occupation of the town, he declared, "Meridian no longer exists." However, within two months the townspeople had opened the railroad tracks around which the small community was built. Sherman made his headquarters in the original wing of this house while his troops destroyed the rest of Meridian.

Natchez

724 The Briars (site)

Irving Lane. Open during Natchez Pilgrimage Tours.

This quintessential Southern plantation mansion, built around 1814, was the site of the marriage of Jefferson Davis and Varina Howell.

725 D'Evereux (site)

St. Catherine Street. Open during Natchez Pilgrimage Tours.

Federal troops camped on the lawn, chopping down many of the oaks and magnolias for wood fires. Two Union soldiers were executed under a tree by the front gate following their court-martial for the killing of George Sargent of Gloucester in 1864. This white Greek Revival house was built around 1840.

726 Natchez National Cemetery (site)

Cemetery Road.

Union soldiers who died during the campaign in southern Mississippi are buried in this plot and Confederate remains are in the adjoining graveyard.

727 Rosalie (site)

Canal Street at Broadway; 800-647-6742; Daily, 9–4:30. Admission charged.

When the headquarters of the Union army was here, soldiers camped on the lawn at Rosalie; Grant spent several days here with his family in 1863. Mrs. Andrew Wilson, mistress of Rosalie, and her children remained in residence while Union General Walter Q. Gresham and his family also occupied the house. The two families got on well enough, although Mrs. Wilson proved to be a member of the Confederate secret brigade and was later banished from her house. She became a Confederate nurse when the Greshams moved on. After the war the Greshams were house guests of the Wilsons at Rosalie.

728 Weymouth Hall (site)

One Cemetery Road; 601-445-2304; Daily, 9–4. Admission charged.

Now a bed-and-breakfast, this white Greek Revival mansion built by Judge Reuben Bullock in 1855 survived Union occupation during the war. It commands spectacular views of the Mississippi River.

Newton

729 Doolittle C.S.A. Cemetery (site)

Route 80, east of town.

This family cemetery has the graves of some 100 Confederate soldiers.

Ocean Springs

730 Fort Massachusetts (site)

Ship Island; 601-875-9057.

Twelve miles out into the Gulf of Mexico, on the extreme western tip of the island, is Fort Massachusetts. Used as early as 1847 for military purposes, the Federal garrison was so isolated at the outbreak of the war that it was destroyed to keep it out of Confederate hands. Mississippi troops occupied the fortress on January 20, 1861, and rearmed it with eight small cannon but were eventually driven away on December 3. General Benjamin "Beast" Butler assumed command and renamed it Massachusetts. The fort was used to stage Union naval attacks against the Gulf Coast and, later, as a prison camp for some 4,000 Confederates and civilian military prisoners, including one woman, a New Orleans housewife, charged with enthusiastically celebrating a Union defeat and teaching her children to spit on Federal officers.

An interpretive center is located at Gulf Islands National Seashore visitor center in Ocean Springs. Tides over the years have occasionally exposed skeletons buried in the sand.

Okalona

731 Confederate Cemetery (site)
Church Street.

Union armies burned area cornfields and 100,000 bushels of stored corn here in 1864. Local lore blames the Federals for bringing bitterweed to the prairies, which caused the cows eating the weed to produce bitter milk — a reminder of the Union occupation. Nathan Bedford Forrest recaptured Okalona, but a third Union raid virtually destroyed the town.

In the graveyard are buried more than 1,000 soldiers who perished in the skirmishing in the area. The town's Confederate memorial is a sentry at watch.

Reenactment: A reenactment on an original battle site between Okalona and Pontotoc is staged each February (601-447-5913).

Oxford

732 Confederate Monument (mem)
Lafayette County Courthouse.

The Confederate soldiers of Lafayette County are honored by a standing soldier at parade rest, perched on a stepped marble base. The monument was installed in 1907.

733 University Museums (col)
University Avenue at 5th Street; 601-232-7073; Tues–Sat 10–4:30, Sun 1–4. Free.

Oxford possessed no fortifications nor any military value, yet it suffered frequent raids throughout the war. The final destruction took place on August 22, 1864, with Union general Andrew Jackson Smith superintending the widespread looting. Travelers were said to remark that "Oxford is the most completely demolished town they have ever seen anywhere." Oxford was a curious target for sacking, as it was inhabited only by a few old men and unarmed women. Legend has it that Elliott Jewelers at 118 South Lamar Street is the only building that survived the 1864 burning of the town.

The University of Mississippi, five blocks west of the museums, was founded in 1848 and survived with only a few buildings intact, including the Lyceum and the Barnard Observatory. Ventress Hall features three stained glass windows depicting the mustering of the "University Grays," a company of faculty and students who distinguished themselves at Gettysburg.

Pontotoc

734 Pontotoc Cemetery (site)
Main Street; 601-489-4321.

Soldiers from all wars are interred here, including more than 100 who fell in the Civil War.

Port Gibson

735 Battle of Port Gibson (site)
Market and Carroll streets.

A marker is placed here for the Battle of Port Gibson, where Ulysses S. Grant won a clash in dense forests on his march to Vicksburg. Grant declared Port Gibson "too beautiful to burn," and left the town's picturesque collection of homes and churches unscathed.

736 Claiborne County's Tribute to Her Sons Who Served in the War of 1861–65 (mem)
Market Street across from Claiborne County Courthouse.

This Confederate monument features a standing soldier atop a tall, tiered shaft and base. On the shaft are relief portrait busts of Brigadier General Benjamin Grubb Humphreys and Major General Earl Van Dorn.

737 Grand Gulf Military Park (site)
Grand Gulf Road, seven miles northwest; 601-437-5911; Mon–Sat 8–5, Sun 9–6. Admission charged.

Point of Rock is the highest elevation in the area, situated 75 feet above the Mississippi River. The Confederates fortified this vantage point with Fort Cobun, so heavily armed that it never fell to the Union; Grant's invading force, seeking an indirect route to Vicksburg, was forced to land downriver. Fort Wade, about half a mile from the river, did succumb to two shellings during the war.

The park opened in 1962 with its two well-preserved forts, among the best preserved anywhere. The park also includes the old Grand Gulf Cemetery, where black Union troops who occupied the town are buried. Several restored buildings have been moved here from other sites, and a park museum features hundreds of artifacts, including a rare Civil War ambulance and a small submarine, the only one of its kind remaining today.

738 Ruins of Windsor (site)

Route 552 West, 12 miles west of town; 601-437-4351.

At the end of a dusty road, in a field of eerie quiet, stand 23 towering Corinthian columns. They are all that remain of the largest ante-bellum mansion ever built in Mississippi. The lofty cupola atop Windsor was used as a Confederate observation point, and the Union troops appropriated the building as a hospital. The pleas of its mistress saved the house from destruction on at least three occasions, and Windsor survived the Civil War but burned to the ground in 1890—a victim of careless smoking.

Quitman

739 Texas Hospital Confederate Cemetery (site)

Route 45.

The burial site of soldiers from the battles of Corinth, Iuka, and Shiloh was forgotten for 70 years until it was discovered by a farmer who plowed up a handful of buttons from a Confederate uniform. Now cleared, the graveyard has headstones and a monumental arch. Flags identify states that have soldiers buried here. There is a memorial to Confederate soldiers who died at Texas Field Hospital.

Raymond

740 Hinds County Courthouse (site)

West Main Street.

The Greek Revival building, erected by slave labor between 1854 and 1857, served as a hospital for the Battle of Raymond on May 12, 1863. The Hinds County Courthouse Monument was sculpted by Frederick Cleveland Hibbard and dedicated on April 29, 1908. Grant won the skirmish and decided to take the capital at Jackson rather than assault Vicksburg directly. A marker at mile 78.3 on the Natchez Trace Parkway commemorates the battle.

741 Raymond Cemetery (site)

Old Port Gibson Road.

The dead from the hospital and surrounding battlefields are interred here.

Tupelo

742 Tupelo City Museum (site)

West Main Street; 601-841-6438; Mon–Fri 8–4, Sat–Sun 1–5. Admission charged.

Housed in a renowned area dairy barn, the museum features 2,000 artifacts, among them items recovered from the Battle of Tupelo, Civil War swords, and a diorama of the battlefield.

743 Tupelo National Battlefield (site)

West Main Street; 601-680-4025.

For General Sherman northern Mississippi had to be secured in the summer of 1864 to keep the railroad open and supplies flowing from Louisville to his army. After his troops under Sturgis were routed at Brice's Cross Roads, he ordered his generals to "go out and follow Forrest to the death, if it costs 10,000 lives and breaks the Treasury." Generals Joseph Anthony Mower and Andrew Jackson Smith got the assignment.

The forces clashed at Tupelo, then known as Harrisburg, on July 14, 1864, with the Federals in a fortified position. Wave after wave of Confederates attacked but were forced back. Smith was not able to claim victory, however. With many men wilting in the withering Delta heat and low on supplies, he was compelled to retreat to Memphis, even leaving his wounded behind. The railroad remained open but Forrest also remained free to roam.

This one-acre site where the Confederate line formed to attack the Union position features a large memorial honoring both armies, cannons, an interpretive marker, and a map.

University

744 Confederate Monument (mem)

University of Mississippi Physical Plant.

John Stinson sculpted a uniformed Confederate soldier standing in salute, which honors the Confederate dead.

Vicksburg

745 Balfour House (site)

1002 Crawford Street; 601-638-7113; Mon–Sat, 9–5. Admission charged.

Siege diarist Emma Balfour was hosting a Christmas ball when Union troops broke into her 1835 Greek Revival mansion. The Federals then used the house as their headquarters.

746 Cedar Grove (site)

2200 Oak Street; 800-862-1300; Daily, 10–4. Admission charged.

Hourly tours are conducted through this 1840

Greek Revival mansion, now an elegant inn, overlooking the Mississippi River. Union gunboats shelled the property, and a cannonball remains lodged in the parlor wall.

747 Duff Green Mansion (site)

1114 1st East Street; 800-992-0037; Daily, 2–5. Admission charged.

This three-story mansion was built in 1856 by slave labor for a wealthy merchant, Duff Green; during the Civil War it was used as a hospital. During one of five attacks on the house, Mary Green gave birth to a son in a nearby shelter and named him Siege.

748 Gray and Blue Naval Museum (col)

1102 Washington Street; 601-638-6500; Mon–Sat, 9–5. Admission charged.

An impressive collection of Civil War gunboat models illustrates the vast array of warship designs. Also in the collection are artifacts and Civil War art.

749 McCraven Tour Home (site)

1445 Harrison Street; 601-636-1663; Mar–Nov: Mon–Sat 9–5, Sun 10–5. Admission charged.

Built in three different periods — circa 1797 Frontier, 1836 Empire, and 1849 Greek Revival — the house exhibits visible cannon damage inside and out. There is a large collection of Civil War relics on display, recovered from the three-acre gardens, which were used as a Confederate camp.

750 The Old Court House Museum (site)

1008 Cherry Street; 601-636-0741; Spring/Summer: Mon–Sat 8:30–5, Sun 1:30–5; Fall/Winter: Mon–Sat 8:30–4:30, Sun 1:30–4:30. Admission charged.

Vicksburg's most famous historic building was constructed by slave labor in 1858. Ulysses S. Grant, Jefferson Davis, and John Breckinridge were among the Civil War figures who stood under its porticos. Here the United States flag was raised and the Confederate lowered on July 4, 1863.

751 Southern Cultural Heritage Complex (site)

1021 Crawford Street; 601-631-2997; Mar–Nov: Tues, Thurs, Sat, 9–12. Admission charged.

The original St. Francis Xavier Convent and Academy was a barracks for both armies during the Civil War.

752 *The Vanishing Glory* (col)

717 Clay Street; 601-634-1863; Daily: first show at 9, last show at 5. Admission charged.

The Campaign and Siege of Vicksburg are dramatized in a 30-minute, wide-screen production. *The Vanishing Glory* is told from the diaries and writings of soldiers and citizens who endured the ordeal.

753 Vicksburg Civil War Museum, Inc. (col)

3327 Clay Street; 601-638-4759; Spring/Summer: Mon–Sat 8:30–5, Sun 1:30–5; Fall/Winter: Mon–Sat 8:30–4:30, Sun 1:30–4:30. Admission charged.

Less than 100 yards from the entrance to the Vicksburg National Military Park, the museum displays over 5,000 Civil War items, including artillery shells, bottles, and weapons.

754 Vicksburg National Military Park (site)

Route 80; 601-636-0583; Daily, 8–5. Admission charged.

One of the great military campaigns in history ended when Grant laid siege to Vicksburg on May 18, 1863. The Confederates refused to abandon their immensely strong position on the Mississippi River, crucial to the survival of the Confederacy in the West. General John Clifford Pemberton held the city in hopes that Joseph E. Johnston's Confederate forces could defeat Grant and relieve the pressure on the city. Six weeks later, with food scarce, Vicksburg surrendered on July 4. More than a year of Union military operations ended when this objective was obtained. With Robert E. Lee's troops retreating a thousand miles to the east at Gettysburg at the same time, the Confederacy was doomed.

The final days of the siege and battle are illustrated across the 1,800 acres of the National Military Park where the "Gibraltar of the Confederacy" fell. The Confederate and Union lines are identified, and markers trace the progress of the Union soldiers as they pushed uphill under the blazing Mississippi sun and hotter enemy fire. Cannons positioned in recreated forts guarded the city against a final charge.

Nearly all of the 28 states that sent soldiers to Vicksburg have erected markers, statues, and monuments in the park, the largest of which is the Illinois Memorial, a dome-shaped structure inscribed with the name of every Illinois soldier present at Vicksburg. Of the thousands listed, two are of particular interest: Fred Grant, the general's twelve-year-old son who accompanied him during the campaign, is listed as an aide, and Albert D. Cashire who, when hospitalized at the age of 70, was discovered to be a woman — an immigrant named Jennie Hodgers who had successfully masqueraded as a man for 50 years.

Also displayed is the partially restored U.S.S. *Cairo*, a Union ironclad sunk and raised after 100 years under water. Intact artifacts from the ship are displayed in an adjoining museum.

Reenactment: The Assault on Vicksburg is a weekend of living Civil War history with skirmishing, camp life, fashion shows, and more. The event, including cannon firings over the Mississippi River, takes place on Memorial Day.

Woodville

755 Rosemont Plantation (site)

Route 24; 601-888-6809; Mar–Dec: 10–5. Admission charged.

With the last of their ten children, Jefferson, having been born two years earlier, Samuel and Jane Davis built Rosemont in 1810. It remained the Davis family home until 1895 and is the only home of the president of the Confederacy still in existence.

Yazoo City

756 C.S.A. Navy Yard (site)

Route 49.

A marker identifies the site on the Yazoo River where the ironclad *Arkansas* was built. The ram successfully engaged two Union fleets but suffered mechanical failure, and the Confederates were forced to scuttle the warship rather than let it fall into enemy hands.

757 Glenwood Cemetery (site)

Grady and Lintonia streets.

In the graveyard is the legendary "Witche's Grave" surrounded by link chains and a mass Confederate grave of unidentified soldiers killed in the Battle of Benton Road.

758 Yazoo Historical Museum (col)

Triangle Cultural Center; 332 North Main Street; 601-746-2273. Admission charged.

Civil War artifacts on display include a scale model of the *Arkansas* and war memorabilia. On the grounds is a monument honoring the role of Mississippi's women in the Civil War.

Missouri

Civil War Status: Slave state that stayed with the Union
1860 Population: 1,182,012
Troops Provided: 110,000 — Union
40,000 — Confederacy
Known Scenes of Action: 1,162

Civil War Timeline
July 5, 1861: Engagement at Carthage
August 10, 1861: Battle of Wilson's Creek
September 12–20: Siege and capture of Lexington
November 7, 1861: Battle of Belmont

Carthage

759 Battle of Carthage Civil War Museum (col)

205 Grant Street; 417-358-6643; Daily, hours vary. Free.

Carthage was battered by skirmishing 13 times during the course of the war. Authentic artifacts accent that history in this museum. The focal point of the collection is a 7' × 15'-foot detailed mural painting of the Battle of Carthage. There is also a battle diorama and a video about the Civil War in the Ozark Mountains.

760 Battle of Carthage State Historic Site (site)

East Chestnut Street.

Although several skirmishes had occurred before, the Union and Confederate armies met in full force on land for the first time here on July 5, 1861. On the Confederate side were 6,000 hastily recruited men of the Missouri State Guard, still in civilian clothes, led by Missouri's pro–Southern governor Claiborne Fox Jackson, who was taking his men south where they could be trained and equipped to return and bring Missouri into the Confederacy.

A Union force of 1,100 German-American infantry, with eight pieces of artillery, commanded by Colonel Franz Sigel, was outflanked and retreated orderly, fighting a series of rearguard skirmishes until it reached Carthage. Official records list 48 dead, 35 for the home guards and 13 Union soldiers.

Events of the battle are highlighted in a kiosk with graphics and text describing the fighting. A series of limestone markers have been erected on "Civil War Road" (old County Road 15) north of Carthage. There are statues of Sigel and Jackson in town and a Battle of Carthage Monument on the courthouse lawn in the town square.

Centralia

761 Centralia Historical Society Museum (site)

319 East Sneed Street; 573-682-5711; May–Nov: Wed and Sun. Free.

On the morning of September 27, 1864, 80 Confederate guerrillas led by Bill Anderson entered

Centralia, plundered the two stores and the dozen or so homes for food and supplies and then held up the stagecoach from Columbia, robbing the passengers. The rebels then placed ties across the railroad tracks and opened fire on the St. Louis train, wounding the fireman. Of the 150 people on the train about two dozen were unarmed Union soldiers either discharged or on leave. The bandits robbed the passengers and $3,000 from the baggage car safe and found $10,000 in another piece of baggage. They then stripped the soldiers of their uniforms, evacuated the train, and set fire to it. The engineer was forced to open the throttle, and the train traveled two or three miles before it was completely burned. The soldiers were then lined up, along with a German who protested in his native tongue that he was not a soldier, and shot at 20 paces; those that did not fall with the first volley were shot again and again until they were dead.

Anderson was born in Huntsville and sought revenge for the death of his father in a border skirmish and the death of his sister in the collapse of a Federal prison in Kansas City by killing every Union soldier or sympathizer he could find. Maybe the most infamous guerrilla of the war, he launched his raids with a heart-piercing yell.

That same afternoon a Union force of 175 men under Major A. V. E. Johnson of the 3rd Missouri Infantry arrived in Centralia, which was still reeling from the attack. Believing the band to be but 30 Johnson divided his force in two to pursue the guerrillas, who lured his inexperienced recruits into a trap and fought a furious battle that decimated the Union troops. Only about a dozen survived, and legend has it that Major Johnson was shot dead by 17-year-old Jesse James.

East Prairie

762 Towosahgy State Historic Site (site)
Route 77, 13 miles east of town; 573-649-3149.

On November 6, 1861, the Union launched a flotilla down the Mississippi River from Cairo, Illinois. Ulysses S. Grant did not plan a battle but wanted to test the heavily fortified bluffs of Columbus, Kentucky, with a demonstration by his 3,000 troops. Instead, his men, tired of drilling, landed the next morning on the Missouri shore across from Columbus and captured the tiny hamlet of Belmont. The defenders were reinforced and drove Grant's men back to their boats. Each side lost over 600 men and nothing of strategic value was gained.

Fredericktown

763 Battle of Fredericktown (mem)
Route 67; 573-783-2604.

Reenactment: Federals under Colonel J. B. Plummer flushed Confederates out of the area on October 21, 1861, in moderate skirmishing. The battle featuring the 7th Missouri Cavalry of Confederate forces is restaged each September.

Higginsville

764 Confederate Memorial State Historic Site (site)
Routes 13 and 20; 816-584-2853; Daily, dawn to dusk. Free.

This 115-acre memorial park was established in 1891 by former Confederate soldiers as housing for veterans. Confederate monuments and the cemetery are now state memorials in tribute to the 40,000 Missourians who fought under the Confederate flag.

Independence

765 1859 Jail, Marshal's Home and Museum (col)
217 North Main Street; 816-252-1892; Mar–Dec: Mon–Sat 10–5, Sun 1–4. Admission charged.

The county jail and provost marshal's quarters have been restored to their appearance during the Civil War period. Notorious temporary residents included Frank James, William Quantrill, and the Youngers. The county museum has an extensive collection of Civil War items.

Ironton

766 Fort Davidson State Historic Park (site)
Route 21; 573-546-3454; Mon–Sat 10–4, Sun 12–5. Free.

The fort was erected by the Federals to protect the Pilot Knob and Iron Mountain mineral deposits. In September 1864 Confederate general Sterling Price entered southeastern Missouri with a force of between 12,000 and 20,000 men, intending to capture St. Louis. Only General Thomas Ewing and a Federal force of about 1,000 men at Fort Davidson stood in his way.

On September 27 Price directed a bloody assault but lost 1,500 men in barely 20 minutes of fighting and fell back to regroup. That night Ewing withdrew, spiking his cannon and leaving two soldiers behind to blow up the magazine. The Confederates did not detect the escape until an explosion shook the earth, showering earth and rocks for hundreds of yards. The three days Price wasted in the Battle of Pilot Knob gave the Federals time to fortify St. Louis, and he dared not pursue his attack. Only the earthworks remain of Fort Davidson; the visitor center recounts the battle.

Jefferson City

767 Missouri State Museum (col)
Capitol Building; High Street and Broadway; 314-751-4127; Daily, 8–5. Free.

The state museum features Civil War exhibits including battle flags of Missouri regiments.

768 National Cemetery (site)
1042 East McCarty Street.

The cemetery includes graves of 78 Union soldiers killed in battle near Centralia.

Kahoka

769 Battle of Athens State Historic Site (site)
Off Route 81; 816-877-3871.

Union troops defeated pro–South Missouri state home guards in skirmishing here on August 23, 1861. The site is the northernmost location of a battle fought west of the Mississippi River during the Civil War. It is now a park.

Kansas City

770 Battle of Westport (site)
1130 Westport Road; 816-931-6620.

The greatest number of troops clashing west of the Mississippi met here at the "Gettysburg of the West." The fighting began along the Big Blue River on the morning of October 22, 1864, and by evening Confederate cavalry, although numerically inferior, had succeeded in occupying Union trenches. The major battle started the next morning between 20,000 Federal troops under General Alfred S. Pleasonton and 12,000 Southerners under General Sterling Price, who was invading from Arkansas in an attempt to sever Federal lines. In the midst of desperate fighting on open ground, Confederate general John S. Marmaduke was forced back along the Arkansas River by superior numbers. The last Confederate effort in Missouri, as well as all major fighting west of the Mississippi River, was over.

A self-guided walking tour travels the Big Blue Battlefield, with narratives at the numbered sites along the route. At the final of 14 stops is a Big Blue Battlefield map.

771 Union Cemetery (site)
227 East 28th Street Terrace.

This cemetery was established about 1858. Among the estimated 50,000 graves are those of 15 Southern soldiers who died in Kansas City as prisoners of war. These graves are marked by a ten-foot granite shaft; about 1,200 unknown soldiers are also buried here.

Keytesville

772 General Sterling Price Museum (col)
412 Bridge Street; 816-288-3204; May 15–Oct 15. Free.

Virginia-born Sterling Price moved to Missouri in 1831 and was elected to Congress in 1844. He resigned in 1846 to accept a commission in the Mexican War during which he was promoted to general. Returning to Missouri, he was elected governor in 1852. Although a believer in slavery, he was initially pro–Union but decided to accept a Confederate commission as major general of the state home guards.

During the Civil War Price was often referred to as "knightly" or "courtly," in part for his treatment of Union commander James Mulligan, whom he defeated at Lexington. During the surrender procession he gave the seats in his carriage to Mulligan and his new bride of 19. Defeated at Westport, his final campaign in Missouri, Price was granted land in Mexico by Emperor Maximilian and departed to colonize the region for ex–Confederate soldiers, but he returned to Missouri in 1866.

A bronze statue of the general in Confederate uniform is in Price Park.

La Grange

773 Soldiers' Monument (mem)
Public Square.

This monument was erected in 1864 to honor soldiers of Lewis County who fell in defense of their country. Although the town was never captured during the war, its credit system was undermined, and after the railroads took away its river trade along the Mississippi and Wyaconda, it never recovered.

Lexington

774 Battle of Lexington State Historic Site (site)
Route 13A; 816-259-4654; Apr–Oct: Mon–Sat 8:30–4:30, Sun 12–5:30. Free.

Prior to the battle, Lexington, like other Missouri River ports, was held by the Union to prevent the northern and southern branches of the Confederacy from joining. To break this chain of posts,

General Sterling Price, after the Battle of Wilson's Creek on August 10, 1861, moved toward Lexington. The Union soldiers were engaged in putting up earthworks (still visible today) on September 12 when they learned that Price's troops, 12,000 strong, were upon them.

Placing his troops on three sides of the Union entrenchment, Price demanded surrender. Colonel James A. Mulligan refused, expecting reinforcements to come, and skirmishing continued for the next week. On the evening of September 19 some enterprising invaders hauled huge hemp bales from fields and a nearby warehouse and constructed movable breastworks soaked in water to withstand heated shot. By the next morning a winding line of bales faced the Union fortification, and Price's soldiers began rolling the bales forward. Two or three men would butt the bales forward with their heads while snipers behind them fired on the Union lines. Within hours they had moved under this cover to within 50 yards of the Union position.

Meanwhile, Mulligan reported that his soldiers, dying from thirst, were frenziedly wrestling for water in which the bleeding stumps of mangled limbs had been washed and drinking it with horrid avidity. The Federal troops he had been led to believe were coming never materialized. By midafternoon he raised a white flag, and Price took 3,600 prisoners, stores of supplies, and ammunition. But the Battle of the Hemp Bales proved of little importance. Many of the prosecessionist Missourians returned to their villages and farms as the main army moved into Arkansas.

The 80-acre area was purchased by the county in 1928. A walking tour of the battlefield begins at the restored Anderson House, the center of the battle on North 15th Street. Several buildings still display battle scars. The battlefield is one of the few never cultivated; Union entrenchments and gun positions are still visible, and markers identify the headquarters of Price and Mulligan.

775 Lexington Historical Museum (col)

112 South 13th Street; 816-259-6313; Jun–Oct: daily, 1–4:30. Free.

Built in 1846 originally as the Cumberland Presbyterian Church, the museum now houses a collection that features artifacts from the Battle of Lexington and personal Civil War mementos. A 15-minute slide presentation highlights the battle.

Lone Jack

776 Civil War Museum of Jackson County (col)

Route 150 and Route 50; 816-566-2272; May–Aug: Mon–Sat 9–5, Sun 1–5; other times: Wed–Sat 11–4, Sun 1–5. Admission charged.

Major Emery Foster occupied the town on August 15, 1862, with 985 cavalrymen to prevent nearby Confederate forces from recruiting. Early the next morning a guerrilla attack by those Confederates, supported by Quantrill's irregulars, including the James and Younger brothers, forced the Union out, house by house. In a nearby field stands the single blackjack oak tree for which the surrounding town and the battle are named. The museum stands at the site of the battle, detailing it and other area conflicts.

Next door, Union and Confederate dead were buried in separate trenches. The names of the dead were not obtained, and there are no individual identification marks. The grave of the Confederates is marked by a marble shaft some 26 feet high, erected in 1870. An eight-foot concrete pillar marks the Union grave, from which the bodies were exhumed in 1867 and removed to Leavenworth, Kansas. It was dedicated on the 50th anniversary of the skirmish in 1912.

Nevada

777 Bushwhacker Museum (col)

231 North Main Street; 417-667-5841; May–Oct. Admission charged.

Nevada, headquarters for guerrillas during the Civil War, was known as "Bushwhacker's Capital." It was thus no surprise that Union troops showed the town little mercy during a raid in 1863 and burned it to the ground, after which it was not rebuilt. The old stone jail building housing the museum is original; inside are Civil War artifacts.

Perryville

778 Union Memorial (mem)

Courthouse lawn.

The figure of a Union soldier on a pedestal is of gray Vermont granite and commemorates the 1,800 Union soldiers from Perry County who served during the war.

Republic

779 General Sweeny's: A Museum of Civil War History (col)

5228 South State Highway ZZ; 417-732-1224; Mar–Oct: daily, 10–5; Feb and Nov: Sat–Sun, 10–5. Admission charged.

This private collection is on display to the public in 51 artifact-filled display cases, interpreting the Civil War in the West. In addition to chronicling the major campaigns and battles of the Mississippi River basin, there are stories of the infamous Confederate raiders that operated against Union strongholds.

780 Wilson's Creek National Battlefield (site)

424 West Farm Road 182; 417-732-2662; Summer: daily, 8–9; other times: 8–5. Admission charged.

As the westernmost border state and gateway to the western territories, Missouri was critical to the Union cause early in the war. The loss of Missouri would jeopardize the flow of Western men and resources, build sympathy for the South, and close the Mississippi River to the Union forces. The first major battle for this prize took place along Wilson's Creek, ten miles southwest of Springfield, on August 10, 1861.

The previous night Brigadier General Nathaniel Lyon, with a cadre of 5,000 men, had sent General Franz Sigel to form a semicircle around 12,000 Confederates under the ex-governor of Missouri, Major General Sterling Price. He planned to launch a frontal assault while Sigel took the flank and rear, but at daybreak Sigel's troops were routed and dispersed. Ill-armed and poorly supplied, Price's troops were initially driven back, but in a furious counterattack rallied on Bloody Hill, site of the fiercest fighting of the battle. Alarmed, Lyon rode to the head of his charge and was killed. Lyon was the first Union general to die in the Civil War; a metal flagpole and a limestone slab mark the spot on the rock-strewn clearing where he was killed.

The Federals stemmed a third charge, but Major Samuel Sturgis, lacking leadership, withdrew from the field. The Union army retreated all the way to Rolla, Missouri, outside of St. Louis, leaving all of the state south and west to the prosecessionist Southern Missouri State Guard. All told, the Federals suffered 1,317 casualties; the Southerners 1,230. Missouri did not see so large a fight again.

With the exception of the vegetation, the 1,750 acre battlefield has changed little. A five-mile self-guiding auto tour passes eight wayside exhibits; five walking trails lead to key battle points. The Ray House, which received the body of General Lyon, served as a temporary field hospital for Confederate soldiers. It is open during the summer. In the visitor center is a museum featuring a film and battle map.

St. Joseph

781 National Military Heritage Museum (col)

701 Messanie Street; 816-233-4321; Hours vary. Admission charged.

This historic 1890 building houses exhibits of all armed forces beginning with the Civil War.

St. Louis

782 Edward Bates Statue (mem)

Art Hill.

This statue of Lincoln's attorney general was sculpted by James Wilson Alexander and dedicated in 1876. Medallion reliefs around the red granite pedestal were added later: Captain James Eads, Governor Hamilton R. Gamble, Charles Gibson, and Henry S. Geyer.

783 Bellefontaine Cemetery (site)

4947 West Florissant Street; 314-381-0750.

An eclectic assortment of Civil War personalities are interred here: Edward Bates; Francis P. Blair, Jr., a statesman and Union general; James Eads, a builder of ironclads; Unionist provisional governor Hamilton Gamble; and Confederate major general Sterling Price, among others.

784 Cavalry Cemetery (site)

5239 West Florissant Avenue; 314-381-1313.

North of the entrance is the grave of General William Tecumseh Sherman; also in the cemetery are the graves of General Don Carlos Buell and Thomas Reynolds, Confederate governor-in-exile.

785 Confederate Memorial (mem)

Municipal Opera Theater; Theater Drive at Government Drive.

George Julian Zolnay, a Hungarian professor of sculpture at Washington University, won this commission with his design of a Southern family sending a young man off to war. The figures attached to the granite shaft are in bronze high relief, above which is carved a low relief of an allegorical female Spirit of the South. On the reverse is a quotation from Robert E. Lee, covering most of the monument's height of 30 feet.

786 Freedom's Memorial (mem)

Washington University Gallery of Art.

The best known representation of Lincoln by Thomas Ball, the *Emancipation* in Washington and Boston, was originally a work of small marble, which grew into those famous monuments. This *Freedom's Memorial*, done in 1867, is on display on the campus of Washington University.

787 Ulysses S. Grant National Historic Site (site)

7400 Grant Road; 314-842-3298; Daily, 9–4:30. Free.

Five historic structures remain on a plantation farmed by Ulysses S. Grant in the 1850s. Memorabilia of Grant's personal life are on display as he attempted to make a go of the land known as "Hardscrabble."

788 Ulysses S. Grant Statue (mem)

City Hall; Tucker Boulevard.

This monument to the unsuccessful St. Louis County farmer who went on to lead the Union troops and the country was dedicated in 1888 and sculpted by Robert P. Bringhurst.

789 Jefferson Barracks Historical Park (site)

533 Grant Road; 314-544-5714; Wed–Sat 9–5, Sun 12–5. Free.

Davis, Sherman, and Longstreet, among others, served at this post, established in 1826. Lee was commander in 1855, and Grant met his wife, Julia Dent, while stationed here. In 1861 Jefferson Barracks regulars saved the St. Louis Arsenal from pro-secessionist forces, and the following year the facility was placed under control of the medical department of the U.S. Army. It was to become one of the largest and most important Union hospitals in the country.

In 1866 a national cemetery was established at Jefferson Barracks. The rows of small white marble crosses mark the graves of 16,000 soldiers. A museum is on the grounds.

790 Nathaniel Lyon Statue (mem)

Lyon Park.

The outstanding St. Louis Civil War hero was Union general Nathaniel Lyon, who in 1861 captured Fort Jackson, a secessionist bivouac in the city, and thwarted the Confederate plan to seize the crucial United States arsenal. In 1929 Erdhart Siebert undertook an ambitious project for the former Camp Jackson site on Grand Avenue across from the St. Louis University campus. Its grand scope was to include ornamental walls and a massive monument, but funding disappeared before his vision could be realized. The resulting cramped, unsuccessful monument was placed in Lyon Park, a small green near the site of the original arsenal. Already on the site was a 25-foot obelisk by Adolphus Druiding erected in 1874. Together the three form a memorial to General Lyon, who was killed at Wilson's Creek.

791 General Franz Sigel Monument (mem)

Forest Park; Lindell, Skinker and Kingshighway boulevards and Oakland Avenue.

A bronze equestrian statue by Robert Cauer, executed in 1906, honors the many German-American Union troops during the Civil War. Sigel was a teacher in Missouri after fleeing the German Revolution. He was a popular but undistinguished brigadier general.

Springfield

792 Springfield National Cemetery (site)

1702 Seminole Street; 417-881-9499.

The Springfield National Cemetery was established in 1869 and is the only place in the United States where Union and Confederate cemeteries adjoin each other. Buried here are 2,347 Union soldiers and 569 Confederates. Among the special monuments erected in tribute to Civil War heroes is a distinguished statue of General Sterling Price, dedicated in 1901. The headstones of five Medal of Honor winners are engraved in gold.

Stanton

793 Meramec Caverns (site)

County Road W, three miles south of town; 314-468-3166; May–Aug: daily, 9–7; other times: 9–5. Admission charged.

Discovered in 1716, the cave was outfitted with powder kilns and leaching vats for the Union during the Civil War. In 1864 the outlaw band of Confederate William Quantrill's irregulars, of which Jesse James was a member, seized the mill. James remembered the cave, and later used it as a hideout for his bandit gang.

Nebraska

Civil War Status: Part of the
Nebraska Territory
1860 Population: 28,841
Troops Provided: 3,300

Lincoln

794 The Gettysburg Lincoln (mem)

West entrance to State Capitol; 15th and K streets.

Daniel Chester French created the heroic-sized bronze figure of Lincoln, set at the moment of hush and quiet immediately following the Gettysburg Address. The words of the speech are placed on a high tablet behind the statue.

Omaha

795 Union Pacific Museum (col)

1416 Dodge Street; 402-271-5457; Mon–Fri 9–3, Sat 9–12. Free.

In 1921 officials of the Union Pacific Railroad discovered, locked in a company vault, the silver dinnerware used on Abraham Lincoln's funeral car. The silver was put on display, and today furnishings from the recreated Lincoln funeral car are exhibited.

New Hampshire

Civil War Status: Union
1860 Population: 326,073
Troops Provided: 39,000

Canaan

796 Soldiers' Monument (mem)
Broad Street Park.
The memorial was designed by Martin Milmore; Peterborough has a duplicate on its town common.

Claremont

797 Civil War Monument (mem)
Route 103.
Milmore sculpted this figure of a standing soldier wearing a long coat and holding a rifle. The bronze monument was erected in 1869. Claremont was the home of Salmon P. Chase, Lincoln's secretary of the treasury, whose portrait is on the $10,000 bill.

Concord

798 New Hampshire State House (col)
107 North Main Street; 603-271-2154; Mon–Fri, 8–4:30. Free.
The 1st New Hampshire has been called the first Union regiment to go to the front fully equipped with uniforms, arms, baggage, hospital, and supply train. The Hall of Flags displays battle flags and portraits of New Hampshire officers who served in the Civil War.

Cornish

799 Saint-Gaudens National Historic Site (site)
Route 12A; 603-675-2175; June–Oct: daily, 8:30–4:30. Admission charged.
Augustus Saint-Gaudens, the sculptor who memorialized many noted Civil War heroes including Lincoln, Farragut, and Sherman, worked on this estate from 1885 until 1907. He is said to have been attracted to Cornish because a friend assured him that "there are plenty of Lincoln-shaped men up there." Saint-Gaudens is buried on this estate.

Dover

800 Woodman Institute (site)
182-190 Central Avenue; 603-742-1038; Apr–Jan: Tues–Sat, 2–5. Free.
The three-building complex includes the 1813 Hale Home, which was the house of abolitionist Senator John Parker Hale. So adamant was he on the issue of slavery that he was known as "Hale Storm." Lincoln stayed in Dover in 1860 after making a political address at the old city hall. A war memorial and Civil War rooms are on display.

Lebanon

801 Civil War Private (mem)
Soldiers Memorial Building; North Park Street.
This Civil War private in full uniform and brandishing a rifle was conceived by Hermann Sluettger and dedicated to Lebanon soldiers on May 9, 1891.

Newport

802 Civil War Monument (mem)
Route 10.
Newport native Sarah Josepha Hale successfully lobbied President Lincoln to proclaim Thanksgiving a national holiday. The town's Civil War monument was erected in 1912 in recognition of the services of Newport men in defense of their country.

Peterborough

803 Civil War Monument (mem)
Grand Army of the Republic Hall.
Another Milmore work of a standing soldier that has stood in town since 1869.

Rochester

804 Civil War Memorial (mem)
South Main and Hancock streets.
The bronze memorial is dedicated to soldiers and sailors of the Civil War.

New Jersey

Civil War Status: Union
1860 Population: 672,035
Troops Provided: 88,000

Beverly

805 Beverly National Cemetery (site)
Bridgeboro Road; 609-877-5460.
The burial ground has the graves of many Civil War soldiers.

East Orange

806 Lincoln Statue (mem)
Intersection of North Oraton Parkway and New Street.
The standing Lincoln, dedicated in 1911, is by Francis Edwin Elwell.

Farmingdale

807 Civil War Reenactment (mem)
Allaire State Park; Route 524; 908-938-2371.
Reenactment: This restored nineteenth-century village stages a Great Locomotive Chase and Civil War reenactment on Father's Day each year.

Hackensack

808 War Memorial Monument (mem)
The Green; south end of Main Street.
This bronze statue of an American soldier was dedicated in 1924 in honor of all soldiers who have fought for their country.

Jersey City

809 The Statesman (mem)
The Plaza.
Sculptor James Earle Fraser learned that during the early days of the Civil War, President Lincoln retired each evening to the solitude of an eminence overlooking Washington where, seated on a rock, he contemplated the burdens afflicting the nation. It was this aspect of Lincoln he chose to portray in a sculpture 18 feet high on a base 50 feet wide. The work, which sits at the entrance to the cross-country Lincoln Highway, United States Route 30, was paid for by popular subscription.

Newark

810 Monsignor Doane Statue (mem)
Doane Park.
The small triangular plot is named after Monsignor George Hobart Doane, Civil War chaplain and rector of St. Patrick's Cathedral; his bronze likeness graces this ground.

811 Lincoln Statue (mem)
Essex County Court House Plaza.
The seated image of Lincoln on a bench, in seemingly confidential speech with onlookers, is one of the best known Lincoln monuments in the country. Designed by Gutzon Borglum, it was unveiled in 1911.

812 The Wars of America (mem)
Military Park; Broad Street, Park Place, Rector Street, and Raymond Boulevard.
With a $100,000 bequest Gutzon Borglum created a colossal group of 42 figures and two horses in 1926 to honor all of the wars in America. Among the bronze figures are a Red Cross nurse and a conscientious objector. In the northeast corner of the park is a statue of Major General Philip Kearny, commander of New Jersey volunteers in the Civil War.

Paterson

813 Civil War Monument (mem)
Eastside Park.
Gaetano Frederici crafted the bronze on this site; it was dedicated in 1935.

814 Rogers Mill (Paterson Museum) (col)
2 Market Street; 201-881-3874; Tues–Fri 10–4, Sat–Sun 12:30–4:30. Admission charged.
On exhibit are the hulls of the first two submarines, invented by J. P. Holland and operated on the Passaic River before being introduced into the Civil War.

Salem

815 Finns Point National Cemetery (site)
Fort Mott State Park; 609-935-3218; Summer: daily, 8–7:30; other times: 8–4. Free.
This burial ground was used for Confederate prisoners of war who died in the prison camp at Fort Delaware. The remote site behind high reeds is the only national cemetery in New Jersey with Confederates buried in it. The obelisk marking

where 2,436 Confederate prisoners were buried in six trenches is 85 feet high, with names inscribed on each side of the base. The memorial for the 300 Union soldiers is a circular pavilion.

Woodbury

816 Soldiers' Monument (mem)

Courthouse; Broad and Delaware streets.

Michael Reilly sculpted this marble obelisk with an American eagle at the pinnacle. Names of Gloucester County soldiers are inscribed on the multitiered base. The monument cost $4,000 when dedicated on May 30, 1867.

New Mexico

Civil War Status: Part of the New Mexico Territory; sided mostly with the Union
1860 Population: 964,201
Troops Provided: Negligible outside territory
Known Scenes of Action: 75

Civil War Timeline

February 21, 1862: Engagement at Valverde
March 26–28, 1862: Battle of Glorieta Pass

Albuquerque

817 Old Town (site)

One block north of the 2000 block of Route 66.

The United States established an army post in Albuquerque in 1846, which made it a prize during the Civil War in a territory with strong Southern influences. Most New Mexicans remained loyal to the Union during hostilities, in large part because of an ancient rivalry with Texas. The Confederates held the town for two months, although the battle of Albuquerque in April 1862 was little more than posturing — both sides fired cannons but stopped when townspeople complained.

The Old Town Plaza has been declared a historic zone; both sides were headquartered here. Walking tours of the architecturally rich area are available.

Pecos

818 Glorieta Battlefield (site)

Pecos National Historical Park; Route 63, two miles south of town; 505-757-6032; Daily, 8–5; Summer: 8–6. Admission charged.

Fort Union was once the largest outpost on the Southwestern frontier. Between 1851, when it was established, and 1891, it was the chief quartermaster for more than 50 forts in the region and primary station for troops in charge of protecting settlers along the Santa Fe Trail. The location was perfect for a supply depot — only six miles north of the convergence of two branches of Santa Fe Trail, the Mountain Branch and the Cimarron Cutoff.

The first Fort Union was a stark group of log buildings, but by the Civil War earthwork defenses were in place. It was this garrison the Confederates marched on in March of 1862 as they set their sights on the minerals in Colorado. On March 26 the Confederate tide was momentarily stemmed in minor skirmishing in Apache Canyon at Glorieta Pass, but two days later the main forces collided at Pigeon's Ranch.

The fighting was indecisive, but the Federals, mostly Colorado volunteers, were outnumbered and assumed the defensive position until Major J. M. Chivington led a guerrilla attack over the mountains and swept around the Confederate flank to destroy a supply train. The Southerners were forced to withdraw, and their dream of invading the West was ended forever.

Much of the battle site is in private hands. At the park a self-guided tour along a trail of 1½ miles explores adobe ruins and foundations. The visitor center maintains a museum on Fort Union.

Santa Fe

819 Kit Carson Monument (mem)

South entrance of Federal Building.

The monument honors Carson, a Union colonel and later an Indian scout.

820 Santa Fe National Cemetery (site)

Route 285, north of plaza; 505-988-6400.

Originally the military post cemetery, the graveyard contains the graves of soldiers killed in the Battles of Pigeon's Ranch and Valverde. A nearby monument bears the inscription: "To the heroes of the Federal army, who fell at the battle of Valverde, fought with the rebels, Febuary [sic] 21, 1862."

Socorro

821 Valverde Battlefield (site)

Fort Craig; Route 85.

In February 1862 Texas Confederates began a campaign to capture the goldfields of Colorado. Across the Rio Grande from Fort Craig, on February 21, the Texans under General H. H. Sibley routed the Federals after a two-hour engagement and captured a battery. The Federals withdrew to Fort Craig as Sibley pressed northward to Albuquerque.

The post was abandoned in 1885 after serving during the Apache wars. It is in ruins today and markers interpret the site.

Taos

822 Kit Carson Home and Museum (site)

East Kit Carson Road, ½ block east of historic Taos Plaza; 505-758-4741; June–Oct: daily, 8–6; other times: 9–5. Admission charged.

Colonel Kit Carson and other citizens of this old Spanish town nailed the Union flag to a cottonwood pole in the plaza and stayed in the area to see that it was not removed. Carson gave orders to fly the flag day and night, and today Taos is one of seven places in America where the U.S. flag flies around the clock. The house that was Carson's from 1843 to 1868 has been preserved as a museum. Two blocks north is the Kit Carson Memorial State Park, where the Union officer and frontier fighter is buried.

New York

Civil War Status: Union
1860 Population: 3,880,735
Troops Provided: 500,000

Albany

823 New York State Capitol (col)

Washington Avenue; Swan, State, and Eagle streets; Room 106; 518-474-2418; Mon–Fri 9–4, Sat–Sun 10–4. Free.

Some Civil War artifacts can be seen on the hourly guided tours; on the grounds east of the capitol is a heroic equestrian statue of General Philip Sheridan (1831–1888), an Albany native and cavalry commander under Grant. The bronze monument on polished granite was designed by John Quincy Adams Ward and finished by Daniel Chester French, his pupil. Also in the billion-dollar government center is the New York State Museum, America's oldest and largest state museum, with historical exhibits.

824 Soldiers' and Sailors' Memorial (mem)

Washington Park; State and Willett streets and South Lake and Madison avenues.

Albany's largest park was created in 1865, and at the northern end of the park is a memorial to Albany's Civil War heroes.

Auburn

825 William H. Seward House (site)

33 South Street; 315-252-1283; Apr–Dec: Tues–Sat, 1–4. Admission charged.

William Seward, Lincoln's secretary of state, was born in Orange County in 1801. Seward was included in the plot to assassinate the president; he was attacked in his home that day by a man named Payne who wounded him and his son. Seward survived and eventually served as secretary of state under Johnson until 1872. This house was built in 1816 by his father-in-law and contains many mementos from his career, including letters from Lincoln. Seward often entertained dignitaries here during the Civil War.

William Seward is buried in Auburn's Fort Hill Cemetery at 19 Fort Street, and a statue of Seward stands in a small park adjoining the mansion.

826 Harriet Tubman Home (site)

180 South Street; 315-252-2081; Feb–Oct: Tues–Thurs, 11–4. Admission charged.

This was the last home of abolitionist Harriet Tubman, credited with the rescue of more than 300 slaves. She died here in 1914 at the age of 90.

Buffalo

827 Soldiers' and Sailors' Monument (mem)

Lafayette Square.

The city built this memorial in gratitude to the soldiers and sailors who saved the Union. It is a cylindrical granite shaft surmounted by a female figure representing Buffalo. Scenes at the base include Lincoln announcing the Emancipation Proclamation and civilians answering the call to arms. The monument, now badly worn, was designed in the Victorian Gothic style by George Keller and sculpted by Caspar Buberl. It was dedicated on July 4, 1884.

Corinth

828 Civil War Monument (mem)

Town Hall; Palmer Avenue.

A Civil War soldier stands at parade rest. There is a bas-relief head of President Abraham Lincoln at the top, followed by the text of the Gettysburg Address. The statue was erected in 1908 to Corinth Civil War soldiers, but by 1921 it had become a traffic hazard in its original location at the intersection of Main and Maple streets. A controversy over its placement was allayed when the statue was removed secretly at night to a bathing beach. It has been in its present location since 1990.

Dunkirk

829 Dunkirk Historical Lighthouse (col)

Lighthouse Point Drive; 716-366-5050; Jul–Aug: daily, 10–4; Apr–June and Sept–Dec: daily, 10–2, but closed Sun and Wed. Admission charged.

The lighthouse was built in 1875. Parts of the collection are dedicated to each branch of the service. Civil War cannons are on display.

Elmira

830 Woodlawn National Cemetery (site)

1825 Davis Street; 607-732-5411.

The national cemetery has the graves of 2,963 Confederates who died in the Elmira prison camp. The prison was hastily constructed, unsanitary, and crowded — most of the Southerners brought here in 1864 died within a year. The burial records of the soldiers are maintained by the Chemung County Historical Society at 415 East Water Street (607-734-4167). The Confederate graves, occupying the central ground of the six-acre burial plot, are surrounded by the graves of 322 Union soldiers. Civil War reenactments are held periodically in Elmira throughout the year at Newton Battlefield on Route 17.

Kinderhook

831 Martin Van Buren National Historic Site (col)

Route 9H; 518-758-9689; September. Admission charged.

Reenactment: The Union camp of Instruction Battery "B", 1st Light Artillery and 125th Volunteer Infantry is performed at the estate of the eighth president of the United States.

Lake Placid

832 John Brown Farm State Historic Site (site)

John Brown Road off Route 73; 518-523-3900; May–Oct: Wed–Sat 10–5, Sun 1–5. Free.

Abolitionist John Brown came here in 1849 when Gerrit Smith was offering free land to blacks on his farm. Brown helped them till the land, but the venture failed because the rough terrain did not surrender easily to tilling. Brown continued to make

this his home while making his abolitionist excursions. A bronze memorial on the property dresses him in the rough clothes and cowhide boots of the Adirondack farmer, with his arm draped fatherly around the shoulder of a young black.

After his execution in Virginia, his widow brought Brown's body here, making most of the five-day trip clandestinely with an empty hearse to defuse emotional crowds. The gravesite is fenced and marked by a boulder.

Monroe

833 Museum Village in Orange County (mem)

Route 17, Exit 129; 914-782-8247.

Reenactment: A Civil War weekend every September explores the encampments of Union and Confederate soldiers. Camp life demonstrations, fashion parades, and battles are featured.

New York City

834 Civil War Monument (mem)

Cavalry Cemetery; Laurel Hill Boulevard and Borden Avenue; Queens.

Completed in 1866 by John G. Draddy, this 40-foot granite obelisk supports the symbol of peace. Standing around the monument are four life-size bronzes in different Civil War uniforms. Bronze figures of Civil War soldiers still survey the headstones in the burial ground.

835 Dermody Monument (mem)

48th Avenue and 216th Street; Queens.

Captain William Dermody, a member of the 67th Regiment New York Volunteers, was the first soldier to die from Bayside, killed at Spotsylvania. After the war his sister set aside ground as a memorial that contained a small schoolhouse flanked by two trees. Seventy years later the school building was dilapidated and the trees dying. In 1936 new trees were planted on the site, and a shaped boulder situated in between as a memorial. By 1973 the site was again neglected and the area was again revived and rededicated. The inscription on the boulder reads: "For a better Union 1861–1865."

836 Farragut Statue (mem)

Madison Square Park; West 23rd Street and 5th Avenue; Manhattan.

Augustus Saint-Gaudens was born in Ireland but grew up in New York City. He got his first commission for a depiction of Admiral David Farragut in 1870 because J. Q. A. Ward was too busy. He sculpted a figure and base as a single entity to blend with the backdrop. This work, originally placed at the northwest corner of the park, blended in with the trees and skyline and was considered a nineteenth century masterpiece. Facing 5th Avenue, the Admiral, depicted in his sixties standing on the deck of his flagship *Hartford*, presided over all major city parades. In the 1930s the statue was moved to its present location in the north-central end of the park — ruining the symmetry created by the master artist.

837 Fowler Statue (mem)

Junction of Fulton and Lafayette streets and South Elliott Place; Brooklyn.

The Brooklyn-born Brigadier General Edward Fowler led his "Red-Legged Devils" through 22 major battles of the Civil War. His troops were known for the red puttees strapped to their legs. Fowler died in 1896 although he was reported killed at Bull Run; he was one of the first to note his delight at reading his own obituary. His likeness was created by Henry Baerer in 1902.

838 General Grant National Memorial (site)

Riverside Drive and 122nd Street; 212-666-1640; Daily, 9–5. Free.

General Ulysses S. Grant and his wife are buried in the sarcophagi here. Grant was born Hiram Ulysses Grant but known as U.S. Grant because his name appeared incorrectly on a class roster at West Point and he let it stand.

839 Grant Statue (mem)

Grant Square; Bergen Street and Bedford Avenue; Brooklyn.

William Ordway Partridge's equestrian rendering of General Grant stands across from the former Union League headquarters, which donated the work to the city in 1896. Partridge captured Grant's disheveled look and contemplative posture. In the spandrels of the facade on the Union League building are relief portraits of Lincoln and Grant.

840 Hall of Fame for Great Americans (mem)

Bronx Community College; University Avenue and West 181st Street; Bronx.

The bronze busts around the colonnade include Lincoln, Grant, Farragut, Lee, Sherman, and Jackson.

841 Hancock Statue (mem)

Manhattan Avenue at 123rd Street; Manhattan.

This monument to General Winfield Scott Hancock was executed by James Wilson Alexander McDonald.

842 Lincoln Statue (mem)

Prospect Park; Brooklyn.

This statue by Henry Kirke Brown was one of the first to be erected to the memory of Lincoln and was unveiled on October 21, 1869. It was paid for by 12,959 subscriptions of not more than one dollar.

843 Lincoln's Gettysburg Address (mem)

Bourough Hall; northeast corner of Fulton and Court streets; Brooklyn.

Lincoln's famous speech can be seen on public tablets on many schools around New York; this bronze tablet also has a bas-relief portrait of the sixteenth president.

844 Lone Sentry (mem)

Central Park; West Drive opposite 67th Street; Manhattan.

This Civil War monument, executed by John Quincy Adams Ward in 1869, became the model for hundreds of other memorials around America. It dramatically portrays a lone soldier at rest with the butt of his rifle on the ground. It was commissioned by the Seventh Regiment National Guard to commemorate the 58 men from the unit who died during the Civil War.

845 Madison Square (mem)

Madison Avenue and West 23rd Street; Manhattan.

There are statues of William Seward at 23rd and Broadway and of Admiral Farragut on the 244th Street side. The Seward monument was completed after the founding committee ran out of funds and placed his head on a body of Lincoln that had already been cast.

846 New York Public Library (col)

42nd Street and 5th Avenue; Manhattan; 212-869-8089; Mon–Sat, 10–6. Free.

This is one of the world's great collections and features Civil War items, including the contents of a Confederate mailbag.

847 The Orator (mem)

Union Square; 4th Avenue.

This standing statue of Abraham Lincoln near the 17th Street entrance was executed by Henry Kirke Brown.

848 Sherman Statue (mem)

Central Park; Manhattan.

Near the southeast entrance to the park at Grand Army Plaza and 59th Street is one of the finest equestrian statues ever erected by an American sculptor. This statue by Augustus Saint-Gaudens portrays Sherman on his famous march through Georgia; the front leg of his steed is raised in a symbol of victory. Also in the park is a memorial to the 107th Regiment sculpted by John Quincy Adams Ward.

849 Sigel Statue (mem)

106th Street and Riverside Drive; Manhattan.

This accomplished equestrian statue of General Franz Sigel by Karl Bitter manages to portray the grace of the animal and its rider. It was commissioned in 1902 by members of the German-American community, and is one of many around the country to honor the German-born cavalry general.

850 Soldiers' and Sailors' Monument (mem)

Prospect Park; Riverside Drive and West 89th Street; Brooklyn.

The commission for this monument was won by the brother team of Charles W. and Anthony A. Stoughton who created a permanent memorial to the patriots who died for the Union in the Civil War. The white marble monument is in the form of a circular Greek temple. A bronze plaque on the front lists New York volunteer groups during the war, and the inscription around the top reads: "To the memory of the brave soldiers and sailors who saved the Union." It was dedicated on Memorial Day 1902.

851 Soldiers' and Sailors' Monument (mem)

Hillside Avenue and 173rd Street; Queens.

Designed by Frederic W. Ruckstull in 1896, the *Angel of Peace* is a 10-foot bronze.

852 Warren Statue (mem)

Grand Army Plaza; Brooklyn.

Gouverneur Kemble Warren was a hero at Gettysburg, credited with saving both Round Top and Little Round Top at the height of battle. The pedestal contains stone from Little Round Top, a common practice in Civil War monuments. The statue was created by Henry Baerer and dedicated in 1896.

853 Webb Statue (mem)

City College campus; 138th Street near Convent Avenue; Manhattan.

General Alexander Stewart Webb commanded the Philadelphia Brigade at Chancellorsville and Gettysburg. After the Civil War he was president of City College from 1869 until 1902. When he died in 1911, alumni raised money for this J. Massey Rhind statue, erected in 1917.

Oswego

854 Fort Ontario State Historic Site (site)

East 7th Street; 315-343-4711; May–Oct: Wed–Sat 10–5, Sun 1–5. Admission charged.

The area has been fortified since 1755 and was used through World War II. The pentagon-shaped fort features fronts facing the river, the lake, and the land. It has been restored to its appearance during the period of 1868 to 1873.

Poughkeepsie

855 Soldiers' Fountain (mem)

South Avenue and Montgomery Street.

This ornately figured fountain was unveiled in 1870 in honor of the soldiers of the Civil War.

856 Young-Morse Historic Site (mem)

370 South Road; 914-454-4500.

Reenactment: The Civil War Encampment recreates America's most costly war with demonstrations of the men who fought and the women of the Ladies' Aid who supported them. The event takes place every September.

Rochester

857 Frederick Douglass Monument (mem)

Central Avenue and St. Paul Street.

The bronze statue of Douglass, on a granite pedestal, was dedicated in 1899 by Theodore Roosevelt, then governor of New York. Douglass was born a slave in Easton, Maryland, and ran away from his master in 1838. His home on Alexander Street was a station on the Underground Railroad, and during the war he helped organize troops. His grave is in the Mount Hope Cemetery.

858 Soldiers and Sailors with Abraham Lincoln (mem)

Washington Square.

Lincoln is atop a square pedestal, crafted by Leonard Volk in 1892 as a memorial to soldiers and sailors of Monroe County who fought in Civil War. Four small statues representing the four branches of service surround the 41-foot-high monument. The base is ornamented with four bronze reliefs of important scenes in American history.

Saratoga Springs

859 77th Infantry Regiment Monument (mem)

Congress Park, north of entrance.

The 77th of the New York Volunteers took part in all the campaigns of the Army of the Potomac. Their monument, dedicated on September 21, 1875, depicts a standing bronze soldier holding a rifle in both hands.

Seneca Falls

860 Soldiers' and Sailors' Monument
(mem)
Village Park.
This granite and bronze monument to Union soldiers and sailors was dedicated on May 30, 1889.

Syracuse

861 Root Post Civil War Monument
(mem)
Oakwood Cemetery.
David Richards created this bronze homage to Civil War veteran August Root in 1885. It stands on a pedestal of Rhode Island granite.

862 General Gustavus Sniper (mem)
Schlosser Park; North State and East Laurel streets.
This equestrian statue of General Sniper was sculpted of bronze by Frederick Moynihan and dedicated in 1905.

Tarrytown

863 The Civil War Monument (mem)
Sleepy Hollow Cemetery; Route 9.
This standing soldier at rest was created by Johnson Mundy and is displayed at the Sleepy Hollow Cemetery in honor of the Union dead. The bronze figure was unveiled in 1890.

Watertown

864 Soldiers' and Sailors' Monument
(mem)
228 Washington Street.
At the top of a granite pedestal, a figure of a woman holds a wreath of Victory. Near the stepped base stand bronze figures of a Civil War soldier and sailor. The monument was dedicated in 1890.

West Point

865 United States Military Academy
(site)
Visitor Center; Building 2107; 914-938-2638;

Daily, 9–4:45. Free; fee charged for guided tours.
The information center is inside the south gate. The *Battle Monument*, located at Thayer and Cullum roads, honors 2,240 officers and men of the regular army who were killed in the Civil War. Their names are engraved on the memorial designed by Stanford White. On the Parade Ground is a monument dedicated to the memory of Major General John Sedgwick, USMA, Class of 1837, who was killed by a sharpshooter at the battle of Spotsylvania in 1864; the statue is made from bronze cannon tubes captured by his troops.

Wilton

866 Grant Cottage State Historic Site
(site)
McGregor Mountain Correctional Facility; Exit 16 off I-87; Memorial Day–Labor Day: Wed–Sun, 10–4. Admission charged.
General Ulysses S. Grant spent the last days of his life here completing his memoirs. The former president brought his family here on June 16, 1885, and died five weeks later on July 23, suffering from cancer of the throat. The cottage has been left largely as it was on that day.

North Carolina

Civil War Status: Confederacy; seceded from the Union on May 20, 1861
1860 Population: 992,622
Troops Provided: 125,000
Known Scenes of Action: 313

Civil War Timeline
August 27–29: Battle of Hatteras Inlet
February 8, 1862: Battle of Roanoke Island
February 22, 1865: Capture of Wilmington
January 13–14, 1865: Attack and capture of Fort Fisher
March 8–10, 1865: Battle of Kinston
March 16, 1865: Battle of Averasboro
March 19–21, 1865: Battle of Bentonville
March 23–April 23, 1865: Stoneman's North Carolina raids
April 13, 1865: Raleigh occupied
April 26, 1865: Surrender of General Joseph E. Johnston's Confederate forces near Durham Station

Aberdeen

867 Malcolm Blue Historic Farm (site)

Route 5 South; 910-944-9483; Thurs–Sat,
1–4. Free.

Union general Jordan commandeered the Blue
farm and nearby Bethesda Church for officers' use
in March 1865. The house contains an extensive
exhibit on the battle of Monroe's Crossroads.

Atlantic Beach

868 Fort Macon State Park (site)

Route 58 South; 919-726-3775; Daily, 9–
5:30. Free.

This seacoast brick fort was built between 1826
and 1834 to protect the Beaufort harbor. It was occupied by Confederates during the early part of the
war and held until April 26, 1862, when the garrison surrendered to Generals John C. Parke and Ambrose Burnside after a land and sea bombardment.
Restored rooms and a museum are open to the public.

Beaufort

869 Josiah Bell House (site)

100 block of Turner Street; 919-728-5225;
Mon–Sat, 8:30–4:30. Admission charged.

Tours of this historic district include the home
of Bell, a Civil War spy. Confederate and Union
graves are in the Old Burying Ground.

Brunswick

870 Brunswick Town State Historic Site (site)

Route 133, south of Wilmington; 919-371-
6613; Apr–Oct: Mon–Sat 9–5, Sun 1–5; other
times: Tues–Sat 10–4, Sun 1–4. Free.

Fort Anderson was built diagonally across an old
town which had lain in ruins for nearly a century.
The garrison, part of the Cape Fear defenses, held
out for 20 days after the fall of Fort Fisher.

The earthworks are 90 percent intact; an audiovisual presentation and trails are at the site.

Burgaw

871 Pender Monument (mem)

Courthouse Lawn.

The memorial honors William Dorsey Pender,
youngest major general of the Confederacy. Pender's division led an infantry charge at Gettysburg.

Chapel Hill

872 Silent Sam (mem)

McCorkle Place near Franklin Street.

John Wilson created this bronze statue of a young
Confederate soldier holding a rifle. Inscribed
plaques are on the granite base of the monument,
dedicated on June 2, 1913.

Cherokee

873 Museum of the Cherokee Indian (mem)

Route 441, North Drama Road; Summer:
Mon–Sat 9–8, Sun 9–5; other times: daily, 9–5.
Admission charged.

A special section of the museum is devoted to
Thomas's Legion, a Civil War unit composed of
Cherokee Indians fighting for the Confederacy.
This regiment fired the last shots of the war in
North Carolina.

Creswell

874 Somerset Place State Historic Site (site)

Route 64, seven miles south of town; 919-797-
4560; Apr–Sept: Mon–Sat 9–5, Sun 1–5; Oct–
Mar: Tues–Sat 10–4, Sun 1–4. Free.

This 14-room manor house of a rice plantation
was once home to 300 slaves. Nearby a marker on
the highway denotes the burial site of Confederate general James Johnston Pettigrew, who was
wounded at Gettysburg.

Dunn

875 Battle of Averasboro (site)

Route 82, 3 miles southwest of town.

On March 16, 1865, the Confederates demonstrated that they were still actively opposing the
Northern invasion. William Joseph Hardee's troops
delayed the march of Union troops toward Goldsboro, a strategic move that allowed Confederate
General Johnston more time to mass his men for
the Battle of Bentonville.

Breastworks can still be seen, and Chicora Cemetery has graves of soldiers killed in action. Monuments and plaques are also on the grounds.

Durham

876 Bennett Place State Historic Site (site)

4409 Bennett Memorial Road; 919-383-4345;

Apr–Oct: Mon–Sat 9–5, Sun 1–5, Nov–Mar: Tues–Sat 10–4, Sun 1–4. Free.

Three times Confederate general Joseph E. Johnston and Union general William T. Sherman met here between April 17, 1865, and April 26 to negotiate the terms of surrender. Initially Sherman offered military terms only, but Johnston desired "to arrange the terms of a permanent peace." Sherman returned with lenient terms rather than continue fighting with a strategically nonsignificant foe, but the Union rejected this compromise in light of Lincoln's assassination. Finally a military surrender ended the war in the Carolinas, Georgia, and Florida for 89,270 soldiers. The Bennitt (the correct spelling of family name) home became the site of the largest troop surrender of the Civil War.

Two more surrenders were to follow: Richard Taylor in Alabama on May 4 and E. Kirby Smith in New Orleans on May 26, completely disbanding the Confederacy. In 1889 Johnston served as a pallbearer at Sherman's funeral.

Reenactment: Only a stone chimney remains of the original building, which burned in 1921. The present buildings were reconstructed in the 1960s. A visitor center relates North Carolina's contribution to the war effort and an audiovisual program recounts the events at Bennett Place. The surrender is restaged annually on the weekend closest to April 26.

877 The Boys Who Wore Gray (mem)

Durham County Courthouse; Main and Church streets.

This outdoor sculpture honors the Confederate soldiers from Durham County.

Edenton

878 Confederate Monument (mem)

Village Green.

Federal naval forces captured this town on the Chowan River on February 12, 1862. The monument honors the men of Chowan County who died during the Civil War.

Fayetteville

879 Museum of the Cape Fear (col)

801 Arsenal Avenue; 910-486-1330; Tues–Sat 10–5, Sun 1–5. Free.

In addition to the permanent exhibits on the Civil War, the site contains the remains of a North Carolina arsenal, which produced significant amounts of arms and ammunition for the Confederacy. Nine days after Fort Sumter fell, a contingent of old men and boys under Confederate General Draughon demanded the surrender of the

arsenal where the equipment captured at Harpers Ferry was being stored. When Sherman arrived in 1865, he ordered the arsenal blown up and knocked down with battering rams. The original site is down the street from the Museum.

Franklin

880 Confederate Monument (mem)

Rankin Square.

Between 1,000 and 3,000 Franklin men joined the Confederate cause, despite having few slaves in Macon County. More than half never returned home. At the suggestion of Major N. P. Rankin a memorial was built for those men and placed in the square that bears his name, across from the Old Clock Tower, in 1909. The six-foot statue depicting a Confederate soldier was reportedly made in Italy of Italian marble at the cost of $600. It stands 25 feet above a concrete fountain.

Goldsboro

881 Wayne County Museum (col)

116 North William Street; 919-734-5023; Tues, Thurs, Sun 1–4, Sat 10–1. Free.

On his march through the South, General Sherman passed through Wayne County on his way to Raleigh. The museum commemorates the time with a Civil War display.

Greensboro

882 Greensboro Historical Museum (col)

130 Summit Avenue; 910-373-2043; Tues–Sat 10–5, Sun 2–5; Free.

The highlights of this Civil War exhibit include rare weapons, an 1862 broadside recruiting for the Guilford Grays, everyday items carried in soldiers' haversacks, and a drum left behind by Union soldiers.

Hamilton

883 Fort Branch (site)

Route 1416, Fort Branch Road, 2½ miles east of town; 800-776-8566; Apr–Nov: Sat–Sun, 1:30–5:30. Free.

This Confederate fort was built to guard against Union gunboats sailing up the Roanoke River. In addition, the earthen, star-shaped fort protected "The Lifeline of the Confederacy," a railroad bridge that carried General Lee's troops, and the building site of the ironclad, C.S.S. *Albemarle*. The Union launched an expedition to destroy the fort in July

1862, but the assault was turned away and better fortifications were finished. The Confederacy held the fort throughout the war, finally abandoning Fort Branch on April 10, 1865, the day after Lee's surrender at Appomattox. Before leaving, the Confederates pushed all twelve cannons into the river and destroyed the magazine and commissary.

Reenactment: Fort Branch is a remarkably well-preserved fort. Eight of the original 12 cannons were retrieved from the Roanoke River and are on display, as are many artifacts. A reenactment is held the first weekend of each November.

High Point

884 High Point Museum (col)

1805 E. Lexington Avenue; 910-885-6859; Tues–Sat 10–4:30, Sun 1–4:30. Free.

A significant portion of the display is devoted to the Piedmont area of North Carolina during the war. Relics include original firearms, maps, medals, photographs, and pieces of uniforms.

885 Oakwood Cemetery (site)

North end of Steele Street.

There are graves of Confederate soldiers and the grave of Laura Wesson, called the Florence Nightingale of the Confederacy. Wesson was a nurse at the Wayside Hospital when a smallpox epidemic broke out. She served the quarantined patients until she contracted the disease and died on April 25, 1865.

Hillsborough

886 Alexander Dickson House (site)

150 East King Street; 919-732-7741; Apr–Aug: Mon–Sat 10–4, Sun 12–5; Sept–Mar: Mon- Sat 10–4, Sun 1–4. Free.

A walking tour of Hillsborough includes this 1790 home, used as headquarters for Confederate general Hampton. This was also where General Johnston prepared surrender papers for General Sherman in April 1865.

887 Orange County Historical Museum (site)

201 North Churchton Street; 919-732-2201; Tues–Sun, 1:30–4:30. Free.

The museum chronicles central North Carolina's Civil War history, including information about the Orange Guard Company, through artifacts, letters, and photographs.

Jacksonville

888 Union Raid (site)

Route 17.

On November 23, 1862, Federal naval lieutenant William Cushing guided the steamer *Ellis* up the New River and captured two schooners. On the way back down the river, the *Ellis* ran aground on a shoal but the Federals escaped in one of the stolen vessels. A marker recounts the action.

Jamestown

889 Mendenhall Plantation (site)

Main Street; 910-454-3810; Thurs–Fri 2–4, Sat 1–4. Admission charged.

Richard Mendenhall, a Quaker and active conductor on the Underground Railroad, lived here. Of particular interest is a false-bottom wagon used in these daring escapes; it is one of only two still in existence.

Kinston

890 C.S.S. *Neuse* State Historic Site (site)

Route 70A; 919 522-2091; Apr–Oct: Mon–Sat 9–5, Sun 1–5; Nov–Mar: Tues–Sat 10–4, Sun 1–4. Free.

The Confederate ironclad C.S.S. *Neuse*, built at Whitehall on the Neuse River, was intended to recapture New Bern. The *Neuse* was one of 22 ironclads commissioned by the Confederate navy. It was 158 feet long and resembled a river barge with a wide, flat bottom. Completed in 1864, albeit without its full complement of armor, the ironclad was kept from entering the war by the low water of the Neuse River. On March 12, 1865, Commodore Joseph Price ordered the gunboat scuttled rather than allowing it to fall into Union hands. The C.S.S. *Neuse*, raised in 1963, is one of only three recovered Civil War ironclads. An audiovisual presentation in the visitor center tells the story of the C.S.S. *Neuse*.

891 Wyse Fork Battlefield (site)

Route 70, 3½ miles east of town.

This outdoor display details the action in this area in March 1865, when Confederate troops tried to halt General Schofield's march on Goldsboro. Unable to do more than delay the Union movement, the Confederates left the scene to join the attack at Bentonville.

Kure Beach

892 Fort Fisher State Historic Site (site)

Route 421; 910-458-5538; Apr–Oct: Mon–Sat 9–5, Sun 1–5; other times: Tues–Sat 10–4, Sun 1–4. Free.

The largest earthwork fort in the Confederacy was constructed here to keep Wilmington open to blockade runners; it stayed open until late in the war. Until July 1862, Fort Fisher was little more than several sand batteries mounting fewer than two dozen guns. Colonel William Lamb, working on designs created in Russia for the Crimean War, employed as many as 1,000 men, many of them slaves, to create one mile of sea defense and one-third of a mile of land defense.

The Union had long planned an assault on Fort Fisher but did not feel confident to do so until December 24, 1864. For two days the sand and earth fortifications absorbed Union shells and the force withdrew. On January 12 the fort was bombarded by land and sea and finally capitulated after six hours of fierce fighting. Federal losses were about 1,300, but the Union fleet held Cape Fear and with it, the Southern supply line. It was considered the greatest land-sea battle of the Civil War and helped seal the fate of the Confederacy.

A path atop the formidable earthwork mounds gives a clear view of the Cape Fear River and the strategic importance of the site. A reconstructed gun emplacement and relics recovered from sunken blockade runners are among the exhibits in the visitor center.

Manteo

893 Battle of Roanoke Island (site)

Route 64 and Route 158.

General Ambrose Burnside and 7,500 men overwhelmed a force of 2,000 Confederate defenders on February 8, 1862. Only 60 men were killed in the engagement, but the sandy, tree-covered island in Pamlico Sound gave the Federals a first-rate base on the Atlantic coast for operations against North Carolina — and a back door to Richmond. A marker commemorates the significance of the Battle of Roanoke Island.

New Bern

894 New Bern Academy (col)

508 New Street; 919-514-4900; Mon–Sat 11–5, Sun 1–5. Admission charged.

This 1809 brick building on the grounds of Tryon Palace, the colonial capitol of North Carolina and the home of royalist governor William Tryon, is a museum that explores the occupation of New Bern by Union forces after the Battle of New Bern in March 1862.

895 The New Bern Civil War Museum (col)

301 Metcalf Street; 919-633-2818; Tues–Sun, 10–4. Admission charged.

The town was occupied by Union forces early in the war, on March 14, 1862, and many ante-bellum homes remain since it was not burned. The Union army took possession of New Bern, using the town as a base from which to conduct operations in North Carolina. The Union held New Bern for the duration of the war despite Confederate attempts to retake the city in March 1863 and February 1864. The museum maintains an in-depth collection of Civil War artifacts.

Newton Grove

896 Bentonville Battleground State Historic Site (site)

Route 701 to Route 1008; 910-594-0789; Apr–Oct: Mon–Sat 9–5, Sun 1–5; other times: Tues–Sat 10–4, Sun 1–4. Free.

The last full-scale Confederate offensive took place here on March 19–21, 1865. Some 25,000 Confederates under General Joseph Johnston opposed 60,000 of Sherman's men in the largest action in North Carolina. At first the Confederates crashed through the Federal breastworks, but after withstanding the initial burst, reinforcements arrived to stem any further advance. When Johnston withdrew, Sherman's Carolina Campaign ground on to its inevitable conclusion.

The 6,000-acre battlefield has well-preserved earthworks. Harper House, which houses the visitor center, served as a Union hospital during the battle; there were more than 4,000 Union and Confederate casualties during the skirmishing. An audiovisual show at the visitor center points out a history trail through the area.

Plymouth

897 Port-O-Plymouth Museum (col)

302 East Water Street; 919-793-1377; Tues–Sat 9–12, 1–6. Admission charged.

One of the most daring adventures of the entire Civil War occurred here on October 27, 1864. Twenty-one-year-old Union naval lieutenant William Barker Cushing slipped into the Roanoke River on a steam launch with a torpedo strapped on the end of a pole. His target was the Confederate ironclad *Albemarle*, which lay outside Plymouth. Cushing made it to the log boom protecting the ram before being fired upon. He smashed through the boom and exploded the torpedo against the hull, sinking the gunboat. The 15-man crew of the launch plunged into the river, and Cushing and one other man managed to swim to safety. General Robert F. Hoke then captured Plymouth. The museum exhibits artifacts from the *Albemarle* and the Battle of Plymouth.

Raleigh

898 North Carolina Museum of History (col)

Five East Edenton Street; 919-715-0200; Tues–Sat 9–5, Sun 12–5. Free.

A display in the chronological gallery examines North Carolina's role during the Civil War.

899 North Carolina State Capitol (site)

One East Edenton Street; 919-733-4994; Mon–Fri 8–5, Sat 9–5, Sun 1–5. Free.

Completed in 1840, the building is virtually unchanged from its Civil War appearance when Sherman's army occupied the capitol in April and May 1865. The capitol dome was the site of one of the last U.S. Army signal stations. Among the statuary on the grounds is a monument to Henry Lawrence Wyatt, the first North Carolina soldier killed in the war, at Bethel Church, Virginia, on June 10, 1861. *Women of the Confederacy* was sculpted by Augustus Lukeman and dedicated on June 10, 1914. The *Confederate Monument*, by Ferdinand von Miller II, soars 75 feet in the air; it was unveiled on May 20, 1894.

900 Oakwood Cemetery (site)

701 Oakwood Avenue; 919-832-6077.

Established in 1869, this is the final resting place for 2,800 Confederate soldiers, five Civil War generals, seven North Carolina governors, and many United States senators.

Roxboro

901 Confederate Monument (mem)

Courthouse Yard.

The memorial honors Person County soldiers and Captain E. Fletcher Satterfield, who was killed at the Battle of Gettysburg.

Salisbury

902 Confederate Monument (mem)

Innis and Church streets.

This allegorical monument to the Rowan County Civil War soldier was erected in 1909.

903 Hall House (site)

226 South Jackson Street; 704-636-1502; Thurs–Sun, 1–4. Admission charged.

Dr. Josephus Hall was drafted by the Confederacy to serve as chief surgeon for the Salisbury Confederate prison. In April 1865 his house, built in 1820, became the headquarters for Union officers under General George Stoneman.

904 Rowan Museum (col)

116 South Jackson Street; 704-633-5946; Thurs–Sun, 2–5. Admission charged.

The museum is housed in an 1819 Federal townhouse and includes the original flag from the Salisbury Confederate prison.

905 Salisbury Confederate Prison Site and National Cemetery (site)

202 Government Road; 704-636-2661; Mon–Fri 9–5, Sat 10–4, Sun 1–4. Free.

This Confederate prison was relatively benign until October 1864 when 10,000 men were brought here. Disease flourished, and the cemetery filled with over 5,000 unknown Union soldiers buried in 18 trenches, each 240 feet long. When Stoneman marched through Rowan County, he torched the prison and many military targets but refrained from destroying the courthouse and private residences because, it is believed, the mayor of Salisbury was a fellow Mason.

Weaverville

906 Zebulon B. Vance Birthplace State Historic Site (site)

911 Reems Creek Road; 704-645-6706; Apr–Oct: Mon–Sat 9–5, Sun 1–5; other times: Tues–Sat 10–4, Sun 1–4. Free.

In the log cabins north of town North Carolina wartime governor Zebulon Vance was born on May 13, 1830. He attended the University of North Carolina in homemade shoes and homespun breeches but became one of the most colorful statesmen of his era. Vance was arrested on his 35th birthday and imprisoned in the Old Capitol in Washington until paroled; he later governed the state again and became a United States senator. Vance is buried in Riverside Cemetery on Birch Street in Asheville with other notable North Carolinians, and a monument to him is at Civic Center in Pack Square.

Wilmington

907 Bellamy Mansion (site)

503 Market Street; 910-251-3700; Wed–Sat 10–5, Sun 1–5. Admission charged.

This ante-bellum house was used as Union military headquarters following the surrender of Wilmington in 1865; it has been restored as a museum of North Carolina history.

908 Cape Fear Museum (col)

814 Market Street; 910-341-4350; Tues–Sat 9–5, Sun 2–5. Admission charged.

This museum dates back nearly 100 years, having been established in 1898 to display Confederate relics. The exhibits tell the story of Civil War Wilmington and include a 17' × 20' scale model of Wilmington in 1863. Other war highlights are a detailed diorama of the Battle of Fort Fisher and an explanation of blockade running.

909 National Cemetery (site)
Market Street at 20th Street.
Union soldiers, many from Michigan and Wisconsin, who fell at Fort Fisher are buried here.

North Dakota

Civil War Status: Part of Dakota Territory
1860 Population: 4,837
Troops Provided: Negligible outside territory

Fargo

910 Commemorative Monument to the Civil War Dead (mem)
Island Park; Broadway and 1st Avenue South.
This male figure, standing in full Civil War dress with both hands around the barrel of his rifle, was dedicated to veterans in 1916.

Grand Forks

911 Civil War Memorial Monument to the Grand Army of the Republic (mem)
Sixth Street and Belmont Road.
The census of the Dakota Territory in 1860 showed only 2,402 white settlers; this memorial is to 168 North Dakota Civil War soldiers. Their names are engraved on a bronze tablet. This sculpture made of Vermont granite was dedicated on June 22, 1913.

Ohio

Civil War Status: Union
1860 Population: 2,339,511
Troops Provided: 319,000

Ashtabula

912 Hubbard House/Underground Railroad Museum (site)
Northwest corner of Lake Avenue and Walnut Boulevard; 216-964-8168; Jun–Aug: Fri–Sun, 12–6; Sept–Oct: Fri–Sun, 1–5. Admission charged.
Hubbard House, built by early settlers William and Catharine Hubbard, was used as a northern terminus of the Underground Railroad. Its code name was "Mother Hubbard's Cupboard." The museum contains period artifacts from the work on the railroad.

Carrollton

913 McCook House (site)
Public Square; 216-627-3345; Jun–Oct: Fri–Sat 9–5, Sun 1–5. Admission charged.
Two branches of the "Fighting McCook" family produced 14 Union soldiers. At roll call there were four major generals, three brigadier generals, one colonel, two majors, three lieutenants, and one private. Four lost their lives in the Civil War. The house features mementos of the family saga.

Chillicothe

914 Ross County Historical Society Museum (col)
45 West 5th Street; 614-772-1936; Apr–Nov: Tues–Sun, 1–5; Dec–Mar: Sat–Sun, 1–5. Admission charged.
Chillicothe was Ohio's first capital. During the war word spread that raider John Hunt Morgan was riding toward the town, and guards were hastily assembled at the covered bridge on Paint Street. When a local scouting party returned to town, they were mistaken for Morgan's raiders and the bridge was burned down in a defensive ploy. Not only did Morgan never appear, but it is lucky he didn't — there was scarcely a foot of water in Paint Creek at the time. The museum features a Civil War room.

Cincinnati

915 Abraham Lincoln Statue (mem)
Reading Road and Forest Avenue.
This 1902 bronze by W. Granville Hastings features a female figure of Victory inscribed with the words: "With malice towards none."

916 Lincoln — The Man (mem)
Lytle Park; 421 East 4th Street.
The beardless Lincoln created by George Grey Barnard was so bitterly received when the statue

was unveiled on March 31, 1917, that it was called a "calamity in bronze." Once criticized for its realism, with clumsy hands and feet, the warm bronze of Lincoln is now much beloved and considered a masterpiece.

917 The Sentinel (mem)

Spring Grove Cemetery and Arboretum; 4521 Spring Grove Avenue; 513-681-6680.

This bronze was the first of many Civil War monuments the prolific Randolph Rogers created. The standing Union soldier holding a rifle diagonally across his chest was cast in 1865. Among the 999 Civil War soldiers buried in this beautifully landscaped burial ground are 40 generals.

918 Harriet Beecher Stowe House (site)

2950 Gilbert Avenue; 513-632-5120; Tues–Thurs, 10–4. Free.

Stowe moved to Cincinnati from Connecticut when her father became president of the Lane Seminary, which built the house in 1833. It was here that Stowe was first exposed to slavery, which led her to write *Uncle Tom's Cabin*, the novel that riveted world attention on the "peculiar institution."

Cleveland

919 Lincoln Delivering Gettysburg Address (mem)

Downtown Mall.

The statue was executed by Max Kalish in 1932, and the famous speech is inscribed below. The memorial was purchased in part with the pennies of schoolchildren and unveiled in 1931.

920 Soldiers' and Sailors' Monument (mem)

Public Square.

This massive monument was created by Captain Levi Schofield, who drew upon his own Civil War battlefield experience to create dramatic sculptural groups on each side of the base. The artillery and infantry scenes flank the round black granite shaft that soars 125 feet high.

Clyde

921 McPherson Cemetery (site)

Routes 20 and 101.

The well-respected Brigadier General James Birdseye McPherson, 36 years of age and on the eve of his wedding, was killed in the Battle of Atlanta by a Confederate force under the command of his West Point classmate, John Bell Hood. He is buried in his hometown cemetery.

Columbus

922 Camp Chase Confederate Cemetery (site)

2900 Sullivant Avenue; 614-276-0060.

Camp Chase was the largest training camp in the area and was later used as a prison for captured Confederates. There are 2,260 Southern soldiers buried here. Near the entrance is a stone arch surmounted by the *Confederate Soldier* statue. A Union soldier, William H. Knauss, contributed a considerable amount of money to beautify the cemetery, and he erected the statue.

923 Ohio State Capitol (mem)

High, Broad, State and 3rd streets; 614-752-9777; Mon–Fri 8–7, Sat–Sun 11–5. Free.

One of the finest examples of Greek Revival architecture in the United States, the building is in the middle of a ten-acre park in downtown Columbus. Among the memorials here is the Lincoln Monument, a bust of Lincoln by T. D. Jones. Lincoln visited here twice and was laid in state in the rotunda. Near the northwest corner is *These Are My Jewels*, a tribute to seven Ohioans who rose to prominence in the Civil War: Ulysses S. Grant, Philip Sheridan, Edwin Stanton, James A. Garfield, Rutherford B. Hayes, Salmon P. Chase, and William Tecumseh Sherman. The work of Levi T. Schofield, this monument was exhibited by the state of Ohio at the World's Columbian Exposition in Chicago in 1893 and then moved here.

Fremont

924 Rutherford B. Hayes Presidential Center (site)

Spiegel Grove State Park; 1337 Hayes Avenue; 419-332-2081; Mon–Sat 9–5, Sun 12–5. Admission charged.

The center includes the first presidential library with works of American history dating to the Civil War and was the residence of the nineteenth president of the United States. This is the final resting place for Rutherford B. Hayes, decorated as a Union general, and his wife Lucy. A small museum contains relics of Lincoln and the war.

925 Memorial Monument (mem)

Birchard Library Park; 423 Croghan Street.

The memorial is dedicated to the soldiers and sailors of Sandusky County who fought in America's wars. The single cannon was used by the Americans in their 1813 victory at Fort Stephenson.

Georgetown

926 Grant Homestead (site)

219 East Grant Avenue; 513-378-4222.

Ulysses S. Grant's father Jesse built a small two-story brick house here in 1823. While growing up in this house, Grant was given an application for West Point by a local congressman. This was the beginning of a career that was to carry him to the White House. Also in town on Water Street is the school Grant attended.

Hamilton

927 Soldiers', Sailors', and Pioneers' Monument (mem)

Monument Street.

The two-story structure of limestone block has the names of all Hamilton war dead inscribed in marble walls and a library with the names of all Ohioans who served in the Civil War. Above the entrance are two art glass Civil War scenes: *Army Nurse* and *Our Loyal Mothers and Sisters*. A 17-foot bronze Civil War private surmounts the building. It was designed and modeled by Hamilton sculptor Rudolph Theim and cast at Hamilton Metal Works.

Lakeside-Marblehead

928 Johnson Island Cemetery (site)

Johnson Island; Sandusky Bay.

The United States government leased the island in 1861 and built an 18-acre prison camp, which housed as many as 15,000 Confederates, many of them officers. The cemetery holds the graves of 206 men who died while imprisoned here.

Lancaster

929 The Sherman House (site)

137 East Main Street; 614-687-5891; Apr–Nov: Tues–Sun, 1–4. Admission charged.

William Tecumseh Sherman was born here on February 8, 1820. His brother John, who was a U.S. senator during the Civil War, was born here three years later. The house was built in 1811. The boys lived here until orphaned by the death of their father in 1829 when they were adopted by Thomas Ewing, who lived at 163 East Main Street. Artifacts from the general's life are on display here.

Lisbon

930 Site of Morgan's Surrender (site)

Route 518, eight miles south of town.

A simple stone monument marks the northernmost penetration made by the Confederates during the Civil War. Morgan made some 49 raids into Ohio before being cornered here on July 26, 1863. On a Sunday near the Pennsylvania border, Morgan turned himself and 364 men over to Major George W. Rue. His raid had been spectacular but of little strategic value, and many considered it a foolhardy waste of Southern manpower. Morgan was imprisoned at the Ohio State Penitentiary in Columbus but escaped with six of his officers several months later. He was later killed in action in Greeneville, Tennessee.

Massillon

931 Ohio Society of Military History (col)

Lincoln Way East; 216-832-5553; Tues–Fri 10–5, Sat 10–3. Free.

Clothing, weapons, and other items in this collection date from the Civil War.

New Rumley

932 Custer Monument (site)

Route 646; 614-297-2630.

This eight-and-a-half-foot bronze state statue marks the 1839 birthplace of George Armstrong Custer. It was sculpted by Edwin F. Frey of Ohio State University and dedicated in 1932. Despite graduating at the tail end of a class of 34 at West Point, Custer became the youngest major general in the army at the age of 25.

Niles

933 McKinley Birthplace National Memorial (site)

40 North Main Street; 216-652-1704; Sept–May: Mon–Thurs 8:30–8, Fri–Sat 8:30–5:30, Sun 1–5; other times: Mon–Thurs 8:30–8, Fri–Sat 8:30–5:30. Free.

The twenty-fifth president of the United States was a young Union soldier. William McKinley was born here on January 29, 1843. The museum contains Civil War artifacts.

Oberlin

934 Underground Railroad (mem)

Oberlin College campus.

An unknown sculptor created this modern work of outdoor sculpture, a symbolic piece of steel rail emerging from the ground.

Point Pleasant

935 Ulysses S. Grant's Birthplace (site)

Route 52 at Route 232; 513-553-4911.

Grant was born in this one-room dwelling on April 27, 1822. Nearby, the Grant Memorial Bridge features approaches marked with Civil War guns mounted on stone pillars; the general is commemorated in a bas-relief sculpture on the pillars.

Portland

936 Buffington Island State Monument (site)

Route 124; 614-297-2630.

The only battle of consequence in Ohio took place on the river here. In July of 1863 Confederate general John Hunt Morgan and 2,460 men dashed across southern Ohio after raids in Indiana, avoiding the major cities, while being pursued by some 50,000 Ohio militiamen. The Confederate cavalry reached the West Virginia border where they were surrounded by Union gunboats. On July 19 Morgan was prevented from reaching Kentucky and suffered about 820 casualties. His remnant force of little more than 350 men escaped, but the raid was effectively over, and Morgan and his men surrendered shortly thereafter near Lisbon. A freestone pillar commemorates the battle fought on this four-acre spit of land.

Ripley

937 Rankin House State Memorial (site)

Rankin Hill Road of Route 52; 513-392-1627; Summer: Wed–Sun, 12–5; Sept–Oct: Sat–Sun, 12–5. Admission charged.

The Presbyterian minister John Rankin and his wife sheltered more than 2,000 slaves in this Underground Railroad station from 1825 until 1865 without ever losing a "passenger."

Salem

938 Edwin Coppock Monument (mem)

Hope Cemetery; North Lincoln Street.

A 12-foot sandstone shaft bears the inscription: "Edwin Coppock, a martyr to the cause of liberty." Coppock was 24 when he was hanged for his part in John Brown's raid at Harpers Ferry.

Somerset

939 General Philip Sheridan Monument (mem)

Town Square; Route 22 and Route 13.

This work by Carl Herber honors Union general Philip Sheridan, who came to Somerset at the age of one after his birth in Albany, New York. He graduated from West Point in 1853 and was a captain when Fort Sumter was bombed, but his daring on the battlefield led to a command of his own cavalry and a place among Grant's most trusted leaders. The bronze portrays a mounted Sheridan in cavalry uniform. His house is nearby on Columbus Street.

Steubenville

940 Edwin M. Stanton Monument (mem)

Courthouse Yard; 301 Market Street.

Lincoln's secretary of war was born in Steubenville on December 19, 1814. The 18-foot bronze was sculpted by Alexander Doyle of Steubenville. A marker two blocks away indicates the site of Stanton's birth, and the Jefferson County Historical Association Museum on 426 Franklin Street has his desk in its collection.

941 Union Cemetery (site)

1720 West Market Street.

Edwin Stanton is buried in this graveyard with many Civil War veterans, including three of the four "Fighting McCooks" who perished in the war.

Toledo

942 General James B. Steedman (mem)

Riverside Park; Galena at Summit.

Born in Pennsylvania, Steedman (1817–1863) came to Ohio as a canal-builder and settled in Toledo. He formed the 14th Ohio Volunteer Infantry and distinguished himself on the field of battle at Perryville, Nashville, and Chickamauga. This standing figure of General Steedman with field glasses in hand was sculpted by Alexander Doyle and unveiled on May 26, 1887.

Urbana

943 Soldiers' Monument (mem)

Monument Square.

This 1871 sculpture was sculpted by John Quincy Adams Ward, a leading American artist who depicted a Civil War veteran returning home. Ward was born and is buried in Urbana.

Wooster

944 Civil War Monument (mem)

Town Square.

This standing soldier at rest with the gun butt on the ground was sculpted by Alcock and Dorald and unveiled on May 5, 1892.

Youngstown

945 Soldiers' Monument (mem)
Public Square.

The 47-foot granite shaft was dedicated on Independence Day 1870, donated by the town's citizens to those who gave their life in the Civil War. Around the base are four cannons given as a gift by Union general James A. Garfield, then a member of Congress from the Youngstown district on his way to the White House.

Oklahoma

Civil War Status: Indian Territory known as Five Civilized Indian Tribes
1860 Population: Not subject to census
Troops Provided: Many fought with the Confederacy
Known Scenes of Action: 89

Civil War Timeline
December 9, 1861: Engagement at Chusto-Talasah

December 26, 1861: Engagement at Chustenahlah

July 17, 1863: Battle of Honey Springs

June 23, 1865: Surrender of Brigadier General Stand Waite's Confederate Indian forces at Doaksville

Ardmore

946 Military Memorial Museum (col)
31 Sunset Drive; 405-226-5522; Tues–Sat 10–5, Sun 1–5. Free.

Military artifacts from the Civil War are part of the extensive collection.

Atoka

947 Confederate Memorial Museum (site)
Route 69, one mile north of town; 405-889-7192; Mon–Sat, 9–4. Free.

The Confederacy operated camps along the Middle Boggy River. The Rebels were surprised on February 13, 1864, by Colonel William Phillips and 350 Union troops who ambushed 90 Confederates on the Texas Road where it crossed the river. More than half of the Confederate force was killed.

Those who died in battle and from disease were buried here at Oklahoma's only Confederate cemetery. The museum includes artifacts from the Battle of Middle Boggy.

Fort Gibson

948 Fort Gibson Military Park (site)
Route 80; 918-478-2669; Mon–Sat 9–5, Sun 1–5. Free.

Fort Gibson was constructed in 1824 as part of a network of fortified positions to quell uprisings of the Osage Indians. In 1857 it was deeded to the Cherokee Nation but reactivated by the United States Army in 1863.

From Fort Gibson, Major General James Blunt led a force of 3,000 troops against 6,000 Confederates under Brigadier General Douglas Cooper at the Battle of Honey Springs on July 17, 1863. It was to be the largest battle ever fought in Indian territory. Honey Springs was one of the first conflicts to feature all-black units for the North as well as the largest in which American Indians fought on both sides. The Union prevailed when the Confederates ran out of ammunition.

Fort Gibson remained active until 1890. Seven original buildings remain, including a log stockade, blockhouses, and a guardhouse. Civil War entrenchments are still visible on the grounds. One mile north is the Fort Gibson National Cemetery, established in 1868.

Reenactment: The three most important engagements in Indian territory—Honey Springs, Middle Boggy, and Cabin Creek—are recreated every three years on a rotating schedule.

Fort Towson

949 Fort Towson Military Park (site)
Off Route 70, one mile northeast of town; 405-873-2634; Mon–Fri 8–5, Sat 9–5, Sun 1–5. Free.

This frontier post was established in 1824 but abandoned in 1854 after the Mexican War. The Confederates operated the fort for periods during the Civil War. On June 23, 1865, Cherokee leader Brigadier General Stand Watie surrendered the Cherokee, Creek, Seminole, and Osage Battalion to Lieutenant Colonel Asa Mathews at Fort Towson. As the regal Indian general signed the surrender, he represented the last formal submission of any sizable regiment of Confederate troops.

Some masonry ruins remain on the site, and artifacts are displayed. A sutler's store that peddled supplies to traveling armies has been replicated.

Grove

950 Poison Cemetery (site)
Off Route 59.
The graveyard contains the grave of Confederate brigadier general Stand Watie.

Madill

951 Fort Washita Historic Site (site)
Route 199, 15 miles east of town; 405-924-6502; Mon–Sat 9–5, Sun 1–5. Free.
Fort Washita was created in 1842 as a staging ground for the Mexican War and spawned several future Civil War leaders, including George Mc-Clellan. The United States Army abandoned Fort Washita in 1861, and the Confederates occupied the garrison in the Civil War. Today the site is well-preserved with partially restored barracks, ruins, and the parade ground.

Oklahoma City

952 State Museum of History (col)
2100 North Lincoln Boulevard; 405-521-2491; Mon–Sat, 8–5. Free.
The Oklahoma historical depository features rooms for both the Union and the Confederacy. There are relics, paintings, and interpretations of the Civil War in Indian territory. Also housed here is the Oklahoma Historical Research Library, with extensive holdings on the Indian units that engaged in Civil War battle.

Pensacola

953 Cabin Creek Battlefield (site)
Off Route 82, three miles northeast of town.
Twice Confederate raiders under Stand Watie attacked Union supply trains at Cabin Creek. On July 1, 1863, little damage was done, but on September 18, 1864, the rebels captured 740 mules, 130 wagons, and more than $1 million in supplies. Monuments to both sides in the Second Battle of Cabin Creek are at the battle site.

Rentiesville

954 Honey Springs Battlefield Park (site)
Route 69, north of town.
The First Kansas Colored Infantry carried the day in the Battle of Honey Springs as one of the first all-black fighting units in American history. With the victory here on July 17, 1863, the Union controlled the upper Arkansas River and most of the Indian territory for the remainder of the war. Monuments recall the rout of the Confederates across the Elk Creek.

Oregon

Civil War Status: Union
1860 Population: 52,465
Troops Provided: None outside the West

Portland

955 Lincoln Statue (mem)
Square at S.W. Main and Madison streets.
This portrayal of a standing Lincoln at the time of his Gettysburg speech was unveiled in 1928. It was sculpted by George Fite Waters, a student of Rodin, who completed the work in his Paris studios.

Pennsylvania

Civil War Status: Union
1860 Population: 2,906,215
Troops Provided: 338,000
Known Scenes of Action: Fewer than 20

Civil War Timeline
July 1–3, 1863: Battle of Gettysburg
November 19, 1863: Lincoln delivers his Gettysburg Address

Allentown

956 Soldiers' and Sailors' Monument (mem)
Center Square; 7th and Hamilton streets.
On the site of Allentown's first taverns and trading posts rises a 100-foot shaft of Barre granite, topped with a figure of Liberty. Life-size figures of Civil War veterans surround the base.

Boalsburg

957 Pennsylvania Military Museum (col)
Route 322; 814-466-6263; Tues–Sat, 9–5. Admission charged.
Benjamin Franklin organized Pennsylvania's first

volunteer unit in the Revolutionary War. The tradition of the Pennsylvania citizen-soldier, carried through the Civil War, is illustrated in the exhibits at this museum. The 66-acre park around the museum also features monuments and memorials.

Carlisle

958 Civil War Monument (mem)

Old Courthouse; Courthouse Square; High and Hanover streets.

The monument honors Cumberland County's Civil War dead. Confederate troops, on their way to Gettysburg, shot up the town, and the 1845 courthouse bears shell scars on one of its columns.

959 U.S. Army Military History Institute (site)

Upton Hall, Building 22, Carlisle Barracks; Route 11; 717-245-4131; Mon–Fri 8–4, weekends in the summer. Free.

The Carlisle Barracks, built in 1751, were George Washington's choice for his army's first arsenal and school. The barracks were a recruiting center during the Civil War until the installation was burned by the Confederates led by General J. E. B. Stuart. General Richard S. Ewell's Corps camped on the Dickinson College grounds after General A. G. Jenkins and 500 cavalry took the town following the victory at Chambersburg in 1863. The Confederate occupation lasted three days, after which the town was shelled in retreat. The library has personal letters and diaries.

Chambersburg

960 John Brown's Headquarters (site)

225 King Street.

Mary Ritner's boardinghouse was a known stop on the Underground Railroad. When abolitionist John Brown came to town in the summer of 1859, purportedly as a prospector, he rented a room from the widow Ritner, registering as "Isaac Smith." He received boxes stamped "tools," which were in reality carbines, as he assembled a band of followers to attack the Union arsenal at Harpers Ferry. A state historical marker is in front.

961 Cannon Ball House (site)

Northeast corner of Lincoln Way West and Garber Street.

Stars on the west wall of this private home mark the entry points of Confederate artillery, fired as warning shots on July 30, 1864, before the town was burned. Chambersburg was the only northern town to be so destroyed during the Civil War.

962 Cedar Grove Cemetery (site)

Franklin Street.

The first person was buried here on November 3, 1854. Chambersburg citizens took refuge in the cemetery during the town's burning and a baby named George Gibbs was born here. Near the main gate there are two close rows of twenty graves of Civil War soldiers. More than half are marked only as "U.S. Soldier." They are believed to have died at one of the three church-hospitals set up in the area after the Battle of Antietam.

963 Memorial Fountain (mem)

Memorial Square.

J. W. Fiske of New York designed this fountain, which was christened on July 17, 1878, in front of 15,000 people. A statue of a Union soldier is next to the fountain, facing south to guard against the return of Southern raiders.

Confederate generals Robert E. Lee and A. P. Hill met in the town square, known as "The Diamond," on June 26, 1863, to discuss an invasion of either Harrisburg or Gettysburg. They chose to advance east to Gettysburg. A star on the pavement south of the fountain marks the spot of the Confederate council.

On July 30, 1864, Confederate general John McClausland demanded a ransom of $100,000 in gold or $500,000 in United States currency or the town would be burned. When his demands were not met, Chambersburg was incinerated and looted, leaving some 550 buildings in ruins. A stone in the southwest corner of Memorial Square commemorates the burning of the town. It was dedicated in 1893.

964 The Old Jail (col)

175 East King Street; 717-264-1667; Apr–Dec: 9:30–4. Free.

The Franklin County jail was built in 1818 and was one of the few buildings to survive the torching of Chambersburg in 1864. Abolitionist John Cooke was interned here after the Harpers Ferry raid before being taken south for trial and execution. Union and Confederate prisoners were kept here. Today the building is the home of the Kittochitinny Historical Society and contains relics from the burning of the town.

965 Strite Murder Site (site)

2999 Country Road.

On June 20, 1863, Isaac Strite was shot and buried in a manure pile by Confederate stragglers when he refused to tell where his money was kept. Strite was the only Pennsylvania civilian deliberately killed by Confederates during the Gettysburg Campaign. The farm is now privately owned.

Chester

966 Civil War Soldier (mem)

Chester Rural Cemetery; Soldier's Circle.

This monument to the Union soldiers of Delaware County was dedicated on September 17, 1873. The standing soldier holding a rifle vertically was sculpted by Martin Milmore.

Easton

967 Soldiers' and Sailors' Monument (mem)

Circle; 3rd and Northampton streets.

The tall shaft, erected in 1899 on the site of Northampton County's first courthouse, was dedicated to the area's Civil War dead.

Fayetteville

968 Thaddeus Stevens Iron Works (site)

Caledonia State Park; Route 30, east of town.

A mass of crumbling masonry is all that remains of an iron foundry erected in 1837 by Thaddeus Stevens. On June 26, 1863, Confederate general Jubal A. Early ordered his men to burn the furnace, going some distance out of his way to destroy the property of Stevens, a "radical" Republican abolitionist. When told of the destruction of his property, Stevens is said to have asked, "Did they burn the debts, too?"

The 1830 blacksmith shop, which survived, is now a museum and part of a short interpretive trail at the entrance to the park. Stevens, who died in 1868 at the age of 76, is considered the "father of public education in Pennsylvania."

Gettysburg

969 Confederate States Armory and Museum (col)

529 Baltimore Street; 717-337-2340; Apr–Oct: Wed–Mon, 12–8. Admission charged.

This small brick museum displays a variety of Confederate edged weapons and small arms, along with some Union swords and guns. Many of the carefully displayed relics are quite rare.

970 "The Conflict" Theater (col)

213 Steinwehr Avenue; 717-334-8003; Summer: daily, 9–9; other times: daily, 10–7. Admission charged.

Altogether, six multimedia presentations explain not just the events at Gettysburg but the entire Civil War. Included are *Three Days at Gettysburg*, a definitive study of the battle; *The War Within*, which chronicles the entire war; and *Adventure at Gettysburg*, a program for children.

971 Farnsworth House (site)

401 Baltimore Street.

Now a bed-and-breakfast and tavern, this house was one of many used by Confederate sharpshooters during the Battle of Gettysburg. Over 100 bullet-scarred bricks attest to the desperate attempts to dislodge these deadly snipers.

972 Gettysburg Battle Theater (col)

571 Steinwehr Avenue; 717-334-6100; Daily, 9–5. Admission charged.

A 50-foot diorama gives an overview of the battlefield as the events leading to the ultimate conflict are laid out. The film and multimedia reenactment offer a human perspective on the Battle of Gettysburg.

973 Gettysburg National Military Park (site)

97 Taneytown Road; 717-334-1124; Daily, 8–5; park roads open 6 A.M.–10 P.M. Free.

On July 1, 1863, the Union Army of the Potomac, 92,000 men under General George Meade, met the invading Confederate Army of Northern Virginia, 70,000 troops led by General Robert E. Lee in Pennsylvania farm country. The fighting raged for three days over 25 square miles, culminating in a desperate Confederate charge across an open field into the center of the Union line under deadly fire. When the disastrous charge ended, the South's ranks were shattered, and the outcome of the war was never in doubt again.

Lee had pressed the attack onto Northern soil and had been repulsed. It was his last major offensive of the Civil War. More men fought and more men died at Gettysburg than in any other battle before or since on North American soil. There were 51,000 casualties here. It was the bloodiest battle of the war. Four months later, on November 19, 1863, Abraham Lincoln dedicated the Gettysburg National Cemetery on the battlefield with his most famous speech.

America's most famous battlefield is now speckled with 1,400 monuments, statues, and markers. There are three observation towers, and 31 miles of roads wind through the park. The visitor center, just south of town, serves as the starting point for guided and self-guided tours of the battlefield.

A perpetual flame burns on Oak Hill, site of the first day's fighting on July 1. Outnumbered, the Union defenders were driven back through town to the south. Devil's Den is a group of huge boulders from which Union troops were driven by Confederate general James Longstreet on July 2. Just south of the visitor center is Missionary Ridge, where

10,000 men fell in 50 minutes as Confederate general George Pickett's final assault failed on July 3. It became known as the "High Water Mark of the Confederacy." Pickett's Charge is dramatized in a 356' × 26' painting in the nearby Cyclorama Center.

The Gettysburg National Cemetery, covering 21 acres, contains the graves of 3,706 Civil War dead, 1,664 of them unknown. The *Soldiers' National Monument* stands near the spot where President Lincoln spoke humbly for two minutes, delivering the immortal Gettysburg Address.

Reenactment: Gettysburg Civil War Heritage Days take place on the last weekend in June and the first weekend in July. In addition to the living history encampment and battle recreation, there are military band concerts and a Civil War lecture series. A memorial service is held on November 19, the anniversary of Lincoln's Gettysburg Address.

974 Lee's Headquarters and Museum (site)

401 Buford Avenue; 717-334-3141; Apr–Oct: daily, 9–9; other times: 9–5. Admission charged.

One of the few historic houses in Gettysburg open to the public, this old stone house was where Lee and his lieutenants made plans for the Battle of Gettysburg. Among the Civil War relics are photographs and documents.

975 Lincoln Room Museum (col)

Wills House; 12 Lincoln Square; 717-334-8188; Daily, 9–7. Admission charged.

This historic home on Gettysburg's main square has been transformed back to its appearance on November 18, 1863, as Abraham Lincoln prepared his thoughts before the delivery of his Gettysburg Address. The house was used as a hospital after the Battle of Gettysburg. A modern interpretation of Lincoln is on the street out front, and a bust and the text of the address are displayed at the original entrance.

976 Lincoln Train Museum (col)

Steinwehr Avenue; 717-334-5678; Mar–Nov: daily, 9–7. Admission charged.

A replica 1863 passenger coach and 1890 caboose offer a simulated trip to Gettysburg with President Lincoln and reporters in sight, sound, and motion. Also on display is a military rail collection.

977 National Civil War Wax Museum (col)

297 Steinwehr Avenue; 717-334-6245; Summer: daily, 9–9; other times: 9–5. Admission charged.

A Civil War audiovisual presentation includes more than 200 life-size figures in 30 scenes, plus a battleroom auditorium. An animated Abraham Lincoln delivers the Gettysburg Address.

978 National Tower (site)

999 Baltimore Pike; 717-334-6754; June–Aug: daily, 9–6:30; Apr–May and Sept–Oct: daily, 9–5; Nov: Fri–Sun, 10–4. Admission charged.

The 307-foot tower offers 360-degree views of the battlefield from enclosed and open decks. A 12-minute audio program describes the fighting. (site)

979 Soldiers' National Museum

777 Baltimore Pike; 717-334-4890; Daily, 9–5. Admission charged.

Lifelike dioramas and displays depict ten major battles of the Civil War. The museum features the largest private collection of battlefield relics from Gettysburg.

980 Jennie Wade House (site)

548 Baltimore Street; 717-334-4100; Daily, 9–5. Admission charged.

The story of Jennie Wade, Gettysburg's only civilian killed in the battle, is recounted in this restored house, riddled with more than 200 bullet holes. A stray bullet passed through two doors and struck the young woman while she was baking bread for convalescing troops.

Greencastle

981 Dolly Harris Site (site)

Citizen's National Bank; Antrim Street.

On June 22, 1863, young Dolly Harris waved the Union flag as General Pickett and his division marched by her home. He saluted and the troops cheered her bravery. The incident inspired many subsequent poems. A historical marker tells the story.

982 Greencastle Raid (site)

Town Square.

In June of 1863 most of the Army of Northern Virginia (over 65,000 men, 200 cannon, 2,000 vehicles, and 10,000 horses and mules) passed through Greencastle. On July 2, 1863, Union captain Ulric Dahlgren attacked a larger Confederate force and captured messages bound for General Robert E. Lee at Gettysburg. The next time the Confederates marched through town, after the battles at Gettysburg on July 5–6, the wagon train of wounded was 17 miles long. A marker in the southeast corner of the square tells of the action.

983 Rihl Monument (mem)

Route 11.

On June 22, 1863, Corporal William Rihl of Company C, 1st New York Lincoln Cavalry, was killed in skirmishing here. Rihl was the first Union soldier killed in Pennsylvania during the war. His body was placed in the town's Lutheran cemetery and in 1886 reinterred at the site where he fell. In 1887 an obelisk was erected in his memory. A historic marker is across the highway.

Hanover

984 Hanover Battlefield (site)

Route 194.

The first Civil War battle north of the Mason-Dixon line was fought here on June 30, 1863, when General James E. B. Stuart's cavalry rode into town just as a Union cavalry division was leaving. The Union generals, Kilpatrick and Custer, were at the head of the column three miles northeast of Hanover when they heard the noise of the battle in the town behind them. Kilpatrick wheeled his horse around and led a mad charge back across fields and over fences. Custer set up batteries on the hills north of town to answer the Confederate cannon booming from the hills south and southwest. Horsemen charged and countercharged through the town's streets. Some 11,000 soldiers were engaged in the conflict, which ended at nightfall when Stuart withdrew, leaving more than 100 dead, wounded, or missing; the Northern forces suffered approximately 200 casualties. The battle prevented Stuart from reaching Gettysburg until the day after the major engagement had begun there, thus depriving Lee of "the eyes of his army."

Harrisburg

985 Capitol Preservation Committee's Civil War Flag Project (col)

908 Market Street, 2nd Floor; 717-783-6484. By appointment.

Pennsylvania's 400 Civil War battle flags are housed a short distance from the capitol in the Capitol Preservation Committee's conservation facility. Included in the tour is a discussion on the conservation of historic flags.

986 John Harris/Simon Cameron Mansion (site)

219 South Front Street; 717-233-3462; Mon–Fri, 11–3. Admission charged.

Built by the city's founder in 1766, the home was remodeled in 1863 by Simon Cameron, a former United States senator and President Lincoln's first secretary of war. Cameron was forced to resign amidst the swirl of controversy created when he advocated the arming of blacks during the conflict. Exhibits include Cameron's career at the beginning of the Civil War.

987 Soldiers' and Sailors' Memorial Bridge (mem)

Eastern approach to Capitol Hill.

The structure of 17 spans, with a facing of Indiana limestone and a granite base, was erected in 1930 as memorial to Pennsylvania's veterans in the wars of the nation. At the western end of the bridge two great columns, each topped with the figure of an American eagle, rise to a height of 145 feet.

988 State Museum of Pennsylvania (col)

3rd and North streets; 717-787-4978; Tues–Sat 9–5, Sun 1–5. Free.

Three floors of exhibits preserve the history of Pennsylvania, including its military history. One of the world's largest framed paintings, *The Battle of Gettysburg: Pickett's Charge*, is displayed here. The state archives are also housed here.

Lancaster

989 Wheatland (site)

1120 Marietta Avenue; 717-392-8721; Apr–Nov: daily, 10–4:15. Admission charged.

James Buchanan conducted his presidential campaign from the library of this 1828 Federal mansion. His success landed him in the White House in 1856 as the country lurched toward the Civil War. Tours are conducted by costumed guides.

Lemoyne

990 Fort Washington (site)

8th and Ohio streets.

A small marker indicates the northernmost penetration of the Confederate invasion. In 1863 Lee's advancing army created a panic, and embankments were thrown up along the western and southern sides of the town known as Washington Heights.

Media

991 Soldiers' Monument (mem)

County Courthouse.

This granite infantryman stands as a memorial to the Delaware County artillery, navy and cavalry — and the "patriotic women who aided the defenders of our country." The monument was dedicated in 1885.

Mercersburg

992 Black Cemetery (site)

Bennet Avenue.

The town was the birthplace of James Buchanan, president of the United States before Lincoln, and site of many Confederate raids. This burial ground contains the graves of numerous veterans from the United States Colored Troops, including the famous 54th Massachusetts.

Philadelphia

993 All War Memorial to Colored Soldiers and Sailors (mem)

Winter and 20th streets.

Below the torch of life, to the left and right, are placed groups of black soldiers and sailors, enlisted men and officers. J. Otto Schweizer created this recognition of black military service in 1934.

994 City Hall (mem)

Broad and Market streets.

Conceived as the tallest building in the world when proposed after the Civil War, the city hall was not completed in time to garner the honor. It was designed to incorporate over 200 works of art, including two Civil War monuments, both in the North Plaza. The first, completed in 1884, honors Major General John Fulton Reynolds, who fell at Gettysburg. Joseph Temple offered $25,000 toward the sculpture to recognize Reynolds and Pennsylvania's participation in the conflict. The equestrian statue portrays a startled horse in danger at the front of the battlefield; the General is pointing in the direction of the horse's agitation.

The second statue is of Philadelphia-born General George McClellan, an engineer by training, who once led the Army of the Potomac. A brilliant tactician, the overcautious McClellan was commemorated by the Grand Army of the Republic, who commissioned the bronze by Henry Jackson Ellicott in 1894.

995 Civil War Library and Museum (col)

1805 Pine Street; 215-735-8196; Mon–Sat 10–4, Sun 11–4. Admission charged,

Founded in 1888, the Civil War Library and Museum is the oldest Civil War museum in the country. Three floors of exhibits include extensive holdings from Pennsylvanian George Meade. The research library includes more than 2,000 photographs and 12,000 books.

996 Civil War Soldiers' and Sailors' Monument (mem)

Benjamin Franklin Parkway and 20th Street.

Two marble and granite pylons open the city of Philadelphia from this spacious parkway, one dedicated to sailors, the other to soldiers. Above the group of sailors is inscribed: "In giving freedom to the slave we assure freedom to the free"; above the straining soldiers: "one country, one Constitution, one destiny." On the back of the monuments are listed great sea and land battles leading to the war's conclusion. The 40-foot monuments were completed by Herman Atkins MacNeil in 1927.

997 Civil War Soldiers' and Sailors' Monument (mem)

Germantown Avenue between Church and School House lanes.

This 1883 mustachioed soldier with gun in hand, by John Lachmier, rests on a historic spot. It marks the center of the British line during the Battle of Germantown in the American Revolution.

998 General Ulysses S. Grant (mem)

Kelly and Fountain Green drives.

Famed sculptor Daniel Chester French won the commission for this work over seven other artists and insisted his former student Edward Potter work with him. Together they created a vision of the general surveying a battlefield from an eminence. Potter, whose interest was primarily in horses, created a steed obedient to the will of the rider. The sculpture was dedicated on April 27, 1899, the seventy-seventh anniversary of Grant's birth.

999 Grand Army of the Republic Civil War Museum and Library (col)

4278 Griscom Street; 215-289-6484; limited hours vary, and by appointment. Free.

The veterans who formed Post 2 of the Grand Army of the Republic donated many personal Civil War memorabilia and relics, which are displayed here.

1000 Historical Society of Pennsylvania (col)

1300 Locust Street; 215-732-6201; Tues, Thurs–Sat 10–5, Wed 1–9. Admission charged.

Included in these extensive holdings are artifacts relating to the Civil War and the Underground Railroad.

1001 Independence Hall (site)

Sixth and Chestnut streets.

Lincoln spoke here on February 22, 1861, on his way to his inauguration in Washington; his body lay in state here for two days when being returned to Illinois. More than 85,000 people filed by in respect.

1002 Johnson House (site)

6133 Germantown Avenue; 215-843-0943; Apr–Oct: Sat, 1–4. Admission charged.

The Johnson House, a former Underground Railroad station, is the only site in Philadelphia to interpret the city's active role in the secret slave escape route.

1003 Abraham Lincoln (mem)

Fairmount Park; Kelly Drive at Sedgely Drive.

This statue by Randolph Rogers of a seated Lincoln with a quill in hand, having just signed the Emancipation Proclamation, is a nine-foot, six-inch bronze on a granite pedestal. It was unveiled on September 22, 1871, the anniversary of the proclamation.

1004 Major General George Gordon Meade (mem)

West Fairmount Park; Lansdowne Drive north of Memorial Hall.

Meade commanded Pennsylvania reserves at Gettysburg and served as commissioner of Fairmount Park, one of the largest city parks in the world. Meade was directly responsible for the layout of the park, with its winding drives and bridle paths. Alexander Milne Calder did his rendering of Meade on horseback from memory, using recollections by friends and family. When the statue was unveiled on October 18, 1887, more than 30,000 people attended.

1005 General Galusha Pennypacker Memorial (mem)

Logan Square; 19th and Benjamin Franklin Parkway.

A native of nearby Chester County, Pennypacker became the youngest Union general at age 22. The memorial is a youthful, energetic figure striding forward on top of a gun carriage and flanked by two tigers. The ten-foot, eight-inch bronze by Albert Lacassle was dedicated in 1934.

1006 Smith Memorial Arch (mem)

West Fairmount Park; North Concourse Drive.

Richard Smith, a Philadelphian who had made his fortune as a founder of electroplate and type, bequeathed half a million dollars to build a monument to Pennsylvania's naval and military heroes of the Civil War. In 1897 a call to artists attracted 59 entries, and 15 artists, among the most distinguished of the time, were selected. Two were women and four were Philadelphians.

Completion of the project, one of the most ambitious of its time, took 15 years. When it was dedicated in 1912, it was with little fanfare — the enthusiasm for the Smith Memorial Arch having waned considerably. The gateway to West Fairmount Park features two equestrians — Major General Winfield Scott Hancock and Major General George B. McClellan — three figures — Major General George Gordon Meade, Major General John Fulton Reynolds, and Richard Smith — and nine busts — Admiral David Dixon Porter, Major General John Hartranft, Admiral John A. B. Dahlgreen, James H. Windrim, Major General S. H. Crawford, Governor Andrew Gregg Curtin, General James A. Beaver, John B. Gest, and *Two Eagles and Globes*.

1007 Spirit of 61 (mem)

Union League of Philadelphia; 140 South Broad Street.

The First Regiment Infantry of the National Guard of Pennsylvania was the first regiment from the Keystone State called to action after Fort Sumter. Henry Kirke Bush-Brown's portrayal shows a First Regiment soldier marching in full uniform, a unique rendering at the time, in 1911, the 50th anniversary of the unit.

1008 The Woodlands Cemetery (site)

The Woodlands and Clark Park; 4000 Woodland Avenue; 215-386-2181.

The grounds overlook the spot where the Schuylkill River and the Mill Creek converge. Union wounded from Gettysburg were transported by river to the nearby Satterlee Hospital, the largest United States Army hospital in the Civil War. Clark Park is on the site of the former hospital, marked by a stone removed from the Gettysburg battlefield in 1916.

Pittsburgh

1009 Allegheny Arsenal (site)

Northwest corner of 40th and Butler streets.

This was the site of one of America's leading arsenals during the Civil War. It had been designed between 1813 and 1815 by Benjamin Henry Latrobe, who worked on the United States Capitol.

1010 City-County Building (mem)

Grant Street.

In the rotunda are presidential portraits in bronze relief; the first, in 1915, was the Abraham Lincoln likeness from the one-cent piece by Victor Brenner.

1011 Hampton Battery Memorial (mem)

East Park; Cedar Avenue near Anderson.

This work, by an unknown sculptor, honors the Pennsylvania Independent Light Artillery, known as Hampton's Battery after their first captain, Robert B. Hampton. Eighty local men were mustered into the unit on October 8, 1861, and only 28 returned home. All the first officers — Hampton, Geary, Todd and Miller — were killed. Their names are on the rim.

1012 Soldiers' and Sailors' Memorial Hall (col)

Fifth Avenue and Bigelow Boulevard; 412-621-4253; Mon–Fri 9–4, Sat–Sun 1–4. Free.

The 1910 building was modeled after the Mausoleum of Halicarnassus, one of the seven ancient wonders of the world. The massive base covers an entire city block and is made of Rhode Island granite. Two bronze relief tablets can be seen. One tablet is dedicated to the Civil War Corps of Telegraphers from Allegheny County. The corps' organizer, Andrew Carnegie, is surrounded by 27 members. The other tablet is a memorial to Civil War soldiers.

Inside are historical military exhibits, including black military history. Artifacts range from shell fragments collected at Gettysburg to duplicate sets of the War Department's official Civil War records.

1013 Soldiers' Monument (mem)

West Park.

This soaring stone monument honors 4,000 Allegheny County Civil War dead. Created by Peter C. Reniers, it was dedicated in 1871. Civil War cannons were placed at each corner of the fortresslike base in the 1890s.

Pottstown

1014 Grand Army of the Republic Fountain (mem)

High and Washington streets.

This ornately decorated fountain was dedicated on July 4, 1893, and features a soldier dressed in Civil War uniform.

Rouzerville

1015 Monterey Pass (site)

Old Route 16.

Along this road on the night of July 4 and the morning of July 5, 1863, Union cavalry attacked the advance of Lee's army as he retreated from Gettysburg. In one of the largest military actions in Pennsylvania during the Civil War, Union forces captured over 1,000 prisoners and many supply wagons.

Scranton

1016 Soldiers' and Sailors' Monument (mem)

Courthouse Square; Spruce Street between Washington and Adams avenues.

Dedicated on November 15, 1900, this monument features the figure of Victory atop a 60-foot granite shaft.

Washington

1017 LeMoyne House and Military Museum of Southwestern Pennsylvania (site)

49 East Maiden Street; 412-225-6740; Feb–Dec: Wed–Fri, 12–4. Admission charged.

Built in 1812, this stop on the Underground Railroad was once the home of Dr. Francis Julius LeMoyne, a vocal antislavery politician. The Washington County Historical Society now operates here. The military museum takes up one room in the house.

Waynesboro

1018 Cooke Monument (site)

Penn State Mont Alto Campus entrance; Route 997.

On this spot Captain John Cooke, abolitionist John Brown's "secretary of war," was captured by local men on October 25, 1859. After a brief stay in the Franklin County Jail he was taken to Charles Town and executed in December.

1019 Early's Camp (site)

Waynesboro Hospital; East Main Street.

A state historical marker identifies the site of General Jubal Early's camp on June 23, 1863.

West Chester

1020 Civil War Monument (mem)

Marshall Square Park; North Matlack and Biddle streets.

This granite Civil War soldier at parade rest was erected by the surviving members of the 97th Regiment on October 29, 1887. A brief history of the unit is inscribed on the base.

1021 Old Glory (mem)

Chester County Courthouse; High and Market streets.

The bronze by Harry Raul, depicting a man in Civil War uniform striding forward, was dedicated on May 30, 1915, to the sacrifices of Chester County men for the Union.

Rhode Island

Civil War Status: Union
1860 Population: 174,620
Troops Provided: 24,000

Cranston

1022 War Veterans Memorial Flag Pole
(mem)

Rolfe Street, Pontiac and Park avenues.

All of the nation's wars, including the Civil War, are paid tribute to by this flagpole with a standing eagle spreading its wings in front of the pole base. Below is a three-sided base. Two of the three large sides depict soldiers, and the third side identifies those honored by the memorial.

East Providence

1023 Memorial to Bucklin Post No. 20
(mem)

East Providence City Hall; Grove and Purchase streets and Taunton Avenue.

A standing bronze soldier mounted on a large natural boulder honors the Civil War veterans who "offered their lives that this Union might be preserved." The names of soldiers and sailors are listed, albeit badly worn.

Newport

1024 Fort Adams (site)

Fort Adams Road; entrance to Newport Harbor.

Newport was a bustling seaport as early as 1646, rivaling New York and Boston prior to the Revolution. The fortress, erected to protect Newport Harbor in 1799 and one of the largest bastioned forts in America, launched the military careers of many notable Civil War personalities.

1025 Newport Historical Society Museum and Library (col)

82 Touro Street; 401-846-0813; Summer: Tues–Sat, 9:30–4:30; other times: Tues–Fri 9:30–4:30, Sat 9:30–12. Free.

Newport was the site of the United States Naval Academy during the Civil War, and the Naval War

College was established here in the 1880s. The society preserves that history in a library and three museums.

Pawtucket

1026 Freedom Arming the Patriots
(mem)

Wilkinson Park; Park Place.

In this statue by William Granville Hastings, a kneeling farmer takes a sword from a standing female figure. It was dedicated in 1897 to the soldiers and sailors of the Civil War.

Providence

1027 Brown University (col)

John Hay Library; 20 Prospect Street.

The McClellan Lincoln Collection, considered one of the great Lincoln collections at the turn of the century, was acquired for Brown University by John D. Rockefeller; it includes more than 15,000 volumes and related material.

1028 Rhode Island Historical Society Library (col)

121 Hope Street; 401-331-8575; Summer: Wed–Fri 9–5:45, Tues 12–8; other times: Wed–Sat, 9–5:45. Free.

The society has Civil War relics, manuscripts, and regimental histories. The Harris Collection on the Civil War and Slavery is maintained at the Providence Public Library on Empire Street.

1029 Soldiers' and Sailors' Monument
(mem)

Providence Mall.

This memorial to Rhode Island's Civil War warriors was designed by Randolph Rogers, cast in Munich, Germany, and dedicated in 1871.

1030 State House (col)

Smith Street between Francis and Gaspee streets.

The building was constructed between 1895 and 1904, and it is said that only St. Peter's in Rome has a larger marble dome. The collection contains a number of Civil War flags, and in the front is the "Gettysburg Cannon," a bronze Napoleon 12-pounder used by the Rhode Island Light Artillery, Battery B, at the point where Pickett made his famous charge at the Union line.

1031 Swan Point Cemetery (site)

Blackstone Boulevard.

Among the Union veterans interred here is General Ambrose E. Burnside.

Westerly

1032 Westerly Memorial Building and Library (col)

Broad Street.

Erected in 1894 as memorial to Civil War veterans, this is considered to be the first living memorial in the country. The desk used by Union commander George Meade at Gettysburg is among the items in the collection.

South Carolina

Civil War Status: Confederacy; seceded from the Union on December 20, 1860
1860 Population: 703,708
Troops Provided: 63,000
Known Scenes of Action: 239

Civil War Timeline

April 12–13, 1861: Bombardment and surrender of Fort Sumter
November 7, 1861: Battle of Port Royal Sound
April 7, 1863: Federal ironclads attack Charleston
July 11 and 18, 1863: Assaults on Fort Wagner
November 30, 1864: Engagement at Honey Hill

Abbeville

1033 Burk-Stark Mansion (site)

306 North Main Street at Greenville Street; 864-459-4600; Fri–Sat, 1–5, and by appointment. Admission charged.

Abbeville is often referred to as the "birthplace and the deathbed of the Confederacy." The first meeting to discuss a possible secession from the United States of America was held here on November 22, 1860. Scheduled for Court Square, the meeting was moved to a nearby hillside, known since as Secession Hill, as the crowd grew to be thousands. Secession Hill is now inaccessible.

On May 2, 1865, Confederate president Jefferson Davis held his final cabinet meeting in this mansion. After the fall of Richmond, the government convened here where it was decided that Davis should continue to Washington, Georgia, where conditions would dictate his further course of action. Meanwhile the wagon train of specie would be divided, with $25 each going to the officers and men. Davis's flight lasted only another eight days before he was apprehended on the anniversary of Stonewall Jackson's death, a date still celebrated in the South as Memorial Day.

Davis's host for the final war council was ex-congressman Armistead Burt, who lived in this 1841 plantation house for six years in the 1860s. A granite monument and cannon commemorate this historic meeting.

1034 Confederate Monument (mem)

Monument Square, between Pickens and Washington streets.

Erected in 1906, this tall obelisk has suffered serious damage over the decades, most recently by a fire in 1991. It commemorates the Confederate cause and the "Five Colonels" who met here in the dying days of the rebellion.

Beaufort

1035 Baptist Church (site)

600 Charles Street between King and Prince streets.

This Greek Revival church was built in 1844. By 1857 the membership consisted of 182 whites and 3,317 slaves. During the Civil War the church was used as Union Army Hospital Number 14.

1036 Beaufort Museum (col)

713 Craven Street; 803-525-7077; Daily, 10–5, except Wed and Sun. Admission charged.

All the men in this wealthy ante-bellum area volunteered for service at the outbreak of the war, and the town was looted before Union occupation on November 7, 1861. General Isaac Stevens, who despised looters, ran them out of town. Over Stevens's strenuous objections, the Beaufort library, established in 1802, had its books shipped to New York for auction. Many were sold until Chief Justice Chase, secretary of the treasury, stopped the sale, saying, "We do not war on libraries." The books were moved to the Smithsonian for safekeeping until they could be returned when the authority of the Union was reestablished in South Carolina. Tragically, they burned in a fire in 1868. In 1940 Congress appropriated $10,000 to pay for new books. The Beaufort Museum, located in a 1798 arsenal, features 6,000 artifacts, many from the days of the Civil War.

1037 Beaufort National Cemetery (site)

1601 Boundary Street at northwest entrance to town.

This was one of the first United States national cemeteries designated by President Abraham Lincoln. There are more than 9,000 Union soldiers buried here as well as a small group of Confederates.

1038 St. Helena's Episcopal Church (site)

Church Street between King and North streets; 803-522-1712; Mon–Fri, 10–4. Free.

The tombstones of the graveyards were pressed into emergency service as operating tables during the war. Buried here is Lieutenant General R. H. Anderson, veteran of Fort Sumter, who served under Lee and was reduced to toiling as a day laborer after the war.

Camden

1039 Battle of Boykin's Mill (site)
Route 261, south of town.

The last battle of the Civil War in South Carolina took place here when 2,500 Federal troops battered local Confederate resistance in February of 1865.

1040 Pantheon to Confederate Generals (mem)
Kershaw Square on Chestnut Street between Lyttleton and Fair streets.

The vine-covered pergola is supported by six concrete columns with bronze tablets in honor of Camden's Confederate generals: James Cantey, James Chestnut, Zack Cantey Deas, John D. Kennedy, Joseph B. Kershaw, and John Villepigue.

Charleston

1041 Battery #5, James Island Siege Line (site)
1251 Marsh View Drive; 803-762-3563.

The earthworks here, still well-preserved, were the eastern terminus of the Confederate defenses of James Island, constructed under the direction of General P. G. T. Beauregard.

1042 General P. G. T. Beauregard (mem)
Washington Square; Broad and Meeting streets.

One of several monuments in the square to honor prominent South Carolinians, this monument is to the leader of the city's defense during the Civil War.

1043 Confederate Defenders of Charleston (mem)
Battery Park; East Battery Street and Murray Boulevard.

Hermon Atkins MacNeil created this bronze monument to the Confederate soldiers who served in the defense of Charleston during the Civil War.

1044 Drayton Hall (site)
Ashley River Road, Route 61, nine miles northwest of town.

Built in 1738 by John Drayton, this house remained in the family for seven generations. It was the only house in the area not burned by the Union in 1865 because a Confederate officer moved a number of slaves, ill with smallpox, into the house.

1045 Fort Sumter National Monument (site)
Accessible only by boat; boat trips leave Charleston City Marina on Lockwood Boulevard; 803-883-3123; varying boat schedule. Free; admission charged for boat ride.

The fort was named for General Thomas Sumter, the "Gamecock of the Revolution," and begun in 1829 but still unfinished in 1860 when South Carolina seceded from the United States of America. The first shots of the Civil War were fired when the steamer *Star of the West*, bringing troops and supplies to Fort Sumter, was shelled on January 9, 1861, by a Confederate battery on Morris Island across the bay.

Three months later the Confederate commander General P. G. T. Beauregard bombarded the fort for 34 hours on April 12–13 until Major Robert Anderson surrendered. The Confederates occupied and held Fort Sumter until 1865 despite many desultory attacks and three long bombardments in 1863–1864. An ironclad squadron was repulsed, and when the fort was finally deserted on February 17, 1865, there had been 567 days of continuous military operations against Charleston, the longest siege in modern history.

The fort was replaced but never built to its original height after the war ended. Fort Sumter has been restored and is among the most historic of all American military sites. From Fort Sumter you can see Forts Johnson and Moultrie, which fired on the Union position here.

1046 Magnolia Cemetery (site)
70 Cunnington Avenue; 803-722-8638.

The graves of influential Confederate civilian leaders are included with those of military heroes in this cemetery, established on the banks of the Cooper River in 1849. Buried here are Captain Horace Hunley and the crew of the C.S.S. *H. L. Hunley*, the Confederate submarine that was the first to sink a warship.

1047 Marion Square (mem)
Calhoun Street between King and Meeting streets.

The public green, also known as Citadel Green, has monuments to John C. Calhoun, eloquent defender of the Southern cause, and a shaft honoring Wade Hampton, Confederate general and governor of South Carolina.

Cheraw

1048 Enfield (site)
135 McIver Street.

This house, fronted by a row of cedars, was built in 1815 as a wedding present. Union general Oliver Otis Howard used this upcountry plantation house as his headquarters.

1049 Hartsell House (site)
143 McIver Street.

The downstairs portion of this 1790 home of South Carolina Chief Justice Henry McIver was the personal headquarters for General William T. Sherman. More of his Union troops were quartered here than in any other town in South Carolina.

1050 Lyceum Museum (col)
Town Green. Open on request.

An explosion on Front Street by the Pee Dee River during the Civil War leveled most of the government buildings on this square. The town hall next door to the museum was used as a war hospital and still stands. On the other side, the Merchant's Bank Building at 232 Market Street was the last bank to honor Confederate currency. The museum depicts the history of Cheraw, a town that became a haven for refugees and a storage place for valuables during the Civil War.

1051 Matheson Memorial Library (site)
612 Kershaw Street.

Built in 1810 as a private school, this building was General Sherman's official headquarters in 1865. The town now utilizes the building as a library.

1052 St. David's Episcopal Church (mem)
First and Church streets.

This was the last Anglican Church built in South Carolina under King George III in the 1770s. It was used by both the Confederate and Union armies. The *Confederate Monument* was the first ever erected in memory of those who had fallen in the Civil War. Erected on July 26, 1867, when Union forces still occupied the area, the original inscription did not mention Confederate soldiers directly. Sculpted by J. H. Villeneuve, it is a square, white tapered shaft on a square, gray base.

Columbia

1053 Archives Building (col)
1430 Senate Street; 803-734-8577; Tues–Fri 9–9, Sat 9–6, Sun 1–6. Free.

This repository for South Carolina government records dates back to 1871. Quarterly exhibits display South Carolina and Civil War history.

1054 Chestnut Cottage (site)
1718 Hampton Street.

Chestnut Cottage was the home of General James Chestnut, who entertained Confederate president Davis here in 1864. His wife, Mary Boykin, wrote an influential diary, *Mary Chestnut's Civil War*, about the South during the war years.

1055 Crawford-Clarkson House (site)
1502 Blanding Street.

John Crawford hired a guard to protect his 1838, two-story yellow frame house from burning in 1865; a mahogany secretary bears two scar marks from bayonet thrusts by Sherman's soldiers.

1056 DeBruhl-Marshall House (site)
1401 Laurel Street.

This house dating from 1820 is thought to have been the headquarters for Confederate colonel James Johnstone prior to 1865. Mrs. John S. Wiley, the widow DeBruhl, persuaded Sherman's soldiers to extinguish the flames they had set to the house.

1057 First Baptist Church (site)
1306 Hampton Street.

The first Secession Convention was held here in December 1860, a year after the church was built. The business of secession was then moved to Charleston. The pulpit furnishings, slave gallery, and brick-pillared portico are as they were then.

1058 Guignard House (site)
1527 Senate Street.

John Guignard, one of the surveyors who laid out the city of Columbia, owned this 1813 house. It was saved from burning by a slave cook named Dilcie, who went to meet Sherman and promised the best cooking in Columbia after its tenants had fled. The Union officers established headquarters here and presented her with the house and its contents after they left, which she guarded for her white employers.

1059 Hampton-Preston Mansion (site)
1615 Blanding Street; 803-252-1770; Tues–Sat 10:15–3:15, Sun 1:15–4:15. Admission charged.

This substantial city home of General Wade Hampton, the Confederate leader who became one of South Carolina's most popular governors, was built about 1818 and was occupied by Union officers in 1865.

1060 Palmetto Armory (site)
1802 Lincoln Street.

The armory produced large supplies of arms issued to Confederate troops during the Civil War. Muskets, rifles, and pistols bore the palmetto tree insignia.

1061 South Carolina Confederate Relic Room and Museum (col)

University of South Carolina; 920 Sumter Street; 803-734-9813; Mon–Fri, 8:30–5. Free.

Both Federal and Confederate wounded were nursed in dormitories here, which saved the campus, dating from 1835, from a torching. The collection of artifacts from the Civil War era is considered South Carolina's greatest.

1062 South Carolina State Museum (col)

301 Gervais Street; 803-737-4595; Mon–Sat 10–5, Sun 1–5. Admission charged.

Once the world's first all-electric textile mill, this is one of the South's largest museums with four floors of exhibits, including much on Civil War history.

1063 State Capitol Building (site)

Main and Gervais streets.

Sherman left most of Columbia in 1865 in smoldering rubble as he took the capital, but he spared complete demolition of this building, which had then been under construction for ten years, because he admired it as a beautiful work of art. Bronze stars on the south and west facades mark scars made by Sherman's shells.

Three Confederate monuments are on the grounds; north of the State House is the *Monument to the Confederate Dead*, a tall, white marble shaft surmounted by a figure in Confederate uniform; to the east is the *Wade Hampton Equestrian*, a bronze statue of General Wade Hampton by F. W. Ruckstull, and also Ruckstull's bronze group, *Monument to the Women of the Confederacy*. A majestic dogwood is marked in memory of Robert E. Lee.

Ehrhardt

1064 Rivers Bridge State Park and Battlesite (site)

Route 64, seven miles southwest of town; 803-267-3675.

At the main crossing of the Savannah River, 1,200 Confederates from South Carolina, Georgia, and Tennessee, under the command of Major General Lafayette McLaws, held 22,000 men of Sherman's invading army in check for two days. The swampy terrain did as much to impede Sherman's advance as the sniping Confederate bullets, but the delay gave the defenders time to mass their strength

and families in the invasion line a chance to conceal their possessions. Battle breastworks are still intact, and a Confederate museum and monuments are at the site.

1065 Broxton Bridge Plantation (site)

Route 601, six miles south of town; 800-437-HUNT. Tours by appointment.

Another site of battle as Sherman crossed into South Carolina; the breastworks here have been perfectly preserved.

Florence

1066 Florence National Cemetery (site)

Route 301S, one mile east of town; 803-669-8783.

During the Civil War Florence developed into a shipping center and later a hospital town. Three miles south of town a "prison pen" was constructed in September 1864 and eventually held as many as 12,000 Union soldiers. Before the stockade was complete, the incoming stream of prisoners was herded into an improvised camp, and unsanitary conditions led to an outbreak of typhoid fever. The daily procession of wagons hauling the dead, piled with 100 bodies at a time, overwhelmed coffin makers, and some of the corpses were simply wrapped in blankets and buried.

The prisoner cemetery became the nucleus of the national cemetery. The six-acre national shrine is often referred to as South Carolina's "Little Arlington."

1067 War Between the States Museum (col)

107 South Guerry Street; 803-662-1471; Wed and Sat, 10–5. Admission charged.

Relics and treasures from the Civil War include flags, money, bayonets, and sabers.

Georgetown

1068 Battery White (site)

Belle Isle Yacht Club off Route 521; 803-546-1423.

The Battery White was constructed on Myrant's Bluff to defend the Santee River in 1862 under the direction of General John C. Pemberton. The remains are excellent examples of Civil War earthworks.

Greenville

1069 Greenville Womens College (site)

College Street.

Strong Unionist sentiment existed in this area, which became an important hospital center for Confederate soldiers. The library building for the school was one such important hospital.

Hartsville

1070 Jacob Kelley House (site)

2585 Kelleytown Road, three miles west of town; 803-332-4508; Mar–Dec: first Sun, 3–5. Free.

This home, dating back to circa 1820 and now restored, was taken over briefly as a headquarters for Sherman's army during the Civil War.

Pageland

1071 Five Forks Cemetery (site)

Route 9.

Buried under a stone engraved "Murdered in Retaliation" is James H. Miller, a cavalryman under General Wade Hampton, executed by firing squad at the order of General Sherman in 1865. Legend has it that after leaving South Carolina following the burning of Columbia, the Federals swarmed the countryside, foraging for supplies. Hampton's men, too few in number to stage a battle, took potshots at the invaders, killing some. Sherman sent a warning to Hampton that the next raider killed would mean a Confederate death. Hampton replied that such an act on a prisoner would be murder.

A few days later, Northern raiders looted a farm, drove off livestock, and kidnapped Dick Sowell, a slave. When the band stopped for dinner, Sowell crushed a sleeping sergeant's head with a lightwood knot, rounded up the animals, and headed home. Sherman learned of the incident and ordered his Confederate prisoners to draw lots to be shot in accordance with the threat. Miller lost.

St. Helena Island

1072 York W. Bailey Museum (col)

Route 21; 803-838-2235; Tues–Fri, 11–4. Free.

When the plantation owners abandoned the island in the Civil War, their former slaves took over their residences, and it became one of the most purely African communities in America. The museum depicts the history and culture of the island.

Sullivan's Island

1073 Patapsco Monument (mem)

Fort Moultrie; 1214 Middle Street.
The monument marks the mass grave of five crewmen whose bodies were recovered when the U.S.S. *Patapsco* was raised after the Civil War. It commemorates the 65 crewmen the ship had when it sunk and lists their names on the four sides of the granite obelisk.

Yemassee

1074 Sheldon Church Ruins (site)

Route 17, south of town.
These graceful remains are a haunting monument to war. Built in 1753, the church was burned by the British in 1779. Rebuilt, the church was burned again by Sherman in 1865.

South Dakota

Civil War Status: Part of Dakota Territory
1860 Population: 4,837
Troops Provided: Negligible outside territory

Keystone

1075 Mount Rushmore National Monument (mem)

Route 16, two miles southwest of town.
This is the world's largest sculpture and is carved in solid granite. Creator Gutzon Borglum intended to sculpt the four presidents to the waist but died before he could complete the work. The dedication of Abraham Lincoln, whose face measures 60 feet from chin to forehead, was on September 17, 1937, on the 150th anniversary of the signing of the Constitution.

Milbank

1076 Civil War Soldiers' Monument (mem)

Grant County Courthouse.
This 20-foot monument was erected on May 30, 1904, in memory of Union soldiers. A bronze Civil War soldier, sculpted by T. H. Jennings, stands atop a multitiered base inscribed with the names of Civil War sites.

Tennessee

Civil War Status: Confederacy; seceded from the Union on June 8, 1861

1860 Population: 1,109,801
Troops Provided: 31,000— Union
186,000— Confederacy
Known Scenes of Action: 1,462

Civil War Timeline

February 6, 1862: Battle of Fort Henry
February 13–16, 1862: Battle of Fort Donelson
April 6–7, 1862: Battle of Shiloh
April 7, 1862: Capture of Island No. 10
June 6, 1862: Battle of Memphis
December 31, 1862–January 2, 1863: Battle of Stones River
October 28–29, 1863: Wauhatchie Night Attack
November 17–December 4, 1863: Siege of Knoxville
November 23–25, 1863: Battle of Chattanooga
April 12, 1864: Fort Pillow Massacre
November 29, 1864: Affair at Spring Hill
November 30, 1864: Battle of Franklin
December 15–16, 1864: Battle of Nashville

Athens

1077 McMinn County Living Heritage Museum (col)

522 West Madison Avenue; 423-745-0329; Mon–Fri 10–5, Sat–Sun 2–5. Admission charged.

Included among the 26 permanent exhibit areas are displays on Tennessee's secession from the Union, the Civil War in the state, and its economic aftermath.

Blountville

1078 Battle of Blountville Monument (mem)

Courthouse Yard.

The historic district includes 20 buildings, many of which are Civil War survivors. The memorial is dedicated to Sullivan County soldiers in the Battle of Blountville on September 22, 1863.

Bolivar

1079 Monument to the Memory of the Fallen Confederate Sons (mem)

Hardeman County Courthouse; Main Street.

The Union army occupied this town several times during the Civil War and burned the courthouse, which was replaced in 1868 with the present building. This marble obelisk was one of the first memorials to volunteers and was dedicated in 1873.

Bristol

1080 Bristol War Memorial Park (mem)

Cumberland Street.

Bronze statues and brick markers and an eternal flame honor the veterans of America's wars.

Brownsville

1081 Lincoln Museum/Haywood County Museum (col)

127 North Grand Avenue; 901-772-4883; Mon–Fri 10–4, Sun 2–4. Free.

Located in the Brownsville Historic District, this collection of books and memorabilia concerning Abraham Lincoln was owned by a local resident, Morton Felsenthal.

1082 To the Confederate Dead of Haywood County (mem)

County Courthouse.

The inscription on this granite monument makes mention of the nearly four-to-one advantage in troop strength the Union enjoyed over the Confederacy. It was dedicated on January 19, 1909, to the memory of the Haywood County war dead. The significant area battles are listed on the base.

Buckminster Hollow

1083 A Confederate Memorial (mem)

Buck Smith Hill Road.

Enoch Wickham crafted this sculpture of Bill Marsh and Sam Davis shaking hands. Davis was hanged as a Confederate spy and Marsh was hanged for being sympathetic to the Union.

Chattanooga

1084 Battles for Chattanooga Museum (col)

3742 Tennessee Avenue; 423-821-2812; Summer: daily, 8:30–8:30; other times: daily, 9–5. Admission charged.

Collectively the battles fought around Chattanooga in the autumn of 1863 spelled the beginning of the end for the South. Grant's triumph was so crushing that Confederate leader General Braxton Bragg asked to be relieved of his command. This museum at the foot of Lookout Mountain describes the fighting that took place here with a three-dimensional electric battle map featuring 5,000 miniature soldiers and light effects while "Dixie" plays in the background.

1085 Chattanooga Regional History Museum (col)

400 Chestnut Street; 423-265-3247; Mon–Sat 10–4:30, Sun 11–4:30. Admission charged.

Part of the museum collection is an extensive repertoire of more than 500 Civil War pieces. There are weapons, hundreds of photographs and original documents, and a chair from Grant's headquarters, which was on East 1st Street, one of the highest spots in town.

1086 Cravens House (site)

Route 148; 423-821-6161; Apr–Oct: daily, 9–4. Admission charged.

This home near Lookout Point was the center of desperate fighting in the Battle Above the Clouds on November 24, 1863. It was known as the "White House" during the struggle when both sides used it as a headquarters. The Cravens family rebuilt the house after the war.

1087 *The General* (mem)

Chattanooga National Cemetery; 1200 Bailey Avenue, Holtzclaw Street between Main Street and Bailey Avenue; 423-855-6590.

On April 12, 1862, at Big Shanty, Georgia, Andrews' Raiders, disguised as civilians and led by Federal spy James J. Andrews, seized the wood-burning locomotive *The General* and headed north in a scheme to cut the Confederacy in half by destroying communications between Chattanooga and Atlanta. Deposed *General* conductor William A. Fuller and another employee gave chase on foot until they found a handcar.

At Etowah River Fuller found a yard engine, the *Yonah*, and gave chase while Andrews was stalled waiting for a southbound train to pass. Almost catching up at Kingston, the *Yonah* became snarled in yard traffic and the chase continued. After abandoning another engine, Fuller found the *Texas* and took up the chase again. As his dogged pursuer gained, Andrews set a boxcar aflame on a wooden bridge on the Tennessee line and rushed into the woods. Captured a week later, some of the raiders were exchanged for Confederate prisoners, but Andrews and seven others were executed in Atlanta and their bodies removed to Chattanooga — the destination they had not reached.

A bronze miniature coal-burning locomotive, a reproduction of the engine seized on April 12, 1862, by Andrews' Raiders, sits atop a three-tiered marble base. A brick walk encircles the monument and the graves of Andrews and seven soldiers executed as Union spies. The sculptor was R. D. Barr; the sculpture was dedicated in 1890. The Raiders were the first soldiers to receive the Congressional Medal of Honor; Andrews, a civilian, was not eligible.

The national cemetery was established in 1863 by General Thomas in an effort to collect and bury over 2,000 bodies of the Union soldiers who had died in the fighting at Chattanooga.

1088 Missionary Ridge (site)

South Crest Road.

This was the site of the headquarters of Confederate commander General Braxton Bragg until Ulysses S. Grant broke through the Army of Tennessee on November 25, 1863, in ferocious and decisive fighting. The Union hold on Chattanooga was secure.

1089 National Medal of Honor Museum of Military History (col)

4th Street and Georgia Avenue; 423-267-1737; Mon–Sat, 9–4:30. Free.

The museum features an audiotape of the Great Locomotive Chase, the incident that inspired the Medal of Honor. History and artifacts from other Medal of Honor recipients are exhibited.

1090 Orchard Knob (site)

Orchard Knob Street.

Rising abruptly from the valley, Orchard Knob is one mile west of Missionary Ridge, and from it the movements of the Union army in any direction were visible. The attack here in November 23, 1863, opened the three-day battle for Chattanooga. Later, generals Thomas and Grant watched the attack on Missionary Ridge from here.

The earthworks, behind which Federal cannon were placed after the hill was seized from the Confederates, are well preserved. The guns are mounted as nearly as possible in the position of Grant's signal guns. An account of the military movements is on historical markers.

1091 Read House/Crutchfield House (site)

Martin Luther King and Broad streets; 423-266-4121.

Jefferson Davis made his second secession speech from the balcony of the original 1847 hotel, then known as Crutchfield House. It was the first local building occupied by Union forces and served as a hospital in 1863. Now a restored Radisson hotel, the new owners have memorialized the building's past by featuring a different battle of the Civil War on each of 13 floors, showcasing museum-quality art, battle information, and profiles of the commanding officers.

1092 Signal Mountain (site)

Route 127, up the mountain, following signs.

No fighting occurred here, but the mountain's commanding view of the city, the rivers, and the surrounding mountains made it a crucial signaling point in the battle for control of Chattanooga.

1093 A. P. Stewart (mem)

Hamilton County Courthouse.

Belle Kinney portrayed Lieutenant General A. P. Stewart standing in full military uniform. The statue was dedicated in 1911.

Clarksville

1094 Confederate Monument (mem)

Greenwood Cemetery; Greenwood Avenue.

A Confederate monument rising almost 50 feet was unveiled on October 25, 1893. Built at a cost of $7,500, the bronze statue atop the monument is of a Confederate infantryman. The two granite statues on the base represent the cavalry and the artillery.

1095 Fort Defiance/Fort Bruce (site)

200 South 2nd Street; 615-648-0001; Daily, 8–5. Free.

During the capture of Clarksville, Fort Defiance was burned by retreating Confederates. When the city was retaken in August 1862, it was reactivated under the command of Colonel Sanders D. Bruce, of Kentucky, for whom it was renamed.

1096 Don F. Pratt Museum (col)

Route 41A North; Fort Campbell Military Installation, Gate 4; 502-798-3215; Daily, 9:30–4:30. Free.

Military uniforms, weapons, and other memorabilia relating to the history of the United States Army in Kentucky and Tennessee, dating from the Civil War, are displayed here. The base straddles the Kentucky-Tennessee line.

Cleveland

1097 Confederate Monument (mem)

190 Church Street.

This figure of a Confederate soldier at rest is crafted from Italian marble and stands on a base of Elberton gray granite. The total height of the monument is 28 feet. It was dedicated to the unknown Confederate dead on May 31, 1911.

Columbia

1098 Confederate Monument (mem)

Cemetery Avenue; 3rd Avenue, between C and B streets.

This statue of a Confederate soldier at funeral parade rest is dedicated to "our fallen heroes."

1099 Rippavilla (site)

Route 31N; 800-381-1865; Mon–Sat 9–4, Sun 1–4. Admission charged.

Columbia changed hands several times during the Civil War, and several of the area's ante-bellum homes retain scars of the occupation. This 1852 plantation serves as headquarters for the Tennessee Ante-bellum Trail. A museum of the Civil War Armies of Tennessee is also here.

Covington

1100 Tipton County Confederate Soldiers' Monument (mem)

Tipton County Courthouse; No. 1 Liberty Avenue.

The monument to Tipton County Confederate soldiers stands atop an elaborate granite base; it is a Southern cavalryman. It was dedicated on May 29, 1895.

Dandridge

1101 Battle of Dandridge (site)

Courthouse Yard.

A self-guided walking tour includes 30 sites on the National Historic Register. This marker identifies the site of the action on December 24, 1863, when the right flank of General James Longstreet's army defeated Union forces under General Gordon Granger.

Dover

1102 Fort Donelson National Battlefield (site)

Route 79, one mile west of town; 615-232-5706; Daily, 8–4:30. Free.

On February 13, 1862, General Ulysses Grant began to move on the critical Confederate stronghold at Fort Donelson, which controlled the Cumberland and Tennessee Rivers. For four days Grant orchestrated a land and river assault before the fort capitulated. Confederate general Simon Bolivar Buckner asked for terms of surrender, and Grant sent back the famous reply that made him a hero in the North: "No terms except unconditional and immediate surrender can be accepted. I propose to move immediately upon your works." The defeat was crushing for the Confederacy. The whole state of Tennessee was wide open, Kentucky was in the Union fold, and the loss of the two rivers broke the Confederate defense line. Psychologically, the euphoria over the Southern victory at Manassas was squelched, and Lincoln had found in "Unconditional Surrender" Grant a general in whom he had confidence.

The 536-acre park includes examples of the defenses used in the Civil War, including a river battery, earthworks, and rifle pits. The Dover Hotel, where Buckner surrendered 13,000 men, 3,000 horses, and 20,000 muskets, is in the park. The national cemetery, established in 1867, overlooks the old fort and both water batteries. The Confederate monument was erected in 1933 on the western edge of the park to honor the Confederate soldiers who defended Fort Donelson. The visitor center offers an audiovisual slide program and self-guided tours of the field.

Dresden

1103 Confederate Memorial Statue (mem)

Courthouse Square, southwest corner.

A marble Confederate soldier at parade rest commemorates the Weakley County soldiers of the Civil War. Around the base, companies and regiments are listed and the battles in which they fought. The statue was dedicated on June 7, 1915.

Dyer

1104 Forrest's Raid (site)

Routes 77 and 45W.

A historical marker in Dyer reads: "December 21, 1862. During its intensive operations against Federal communications in this area, a detachment of Forrest's Brigade captured here Company K, 119th Illinois Infantry, burned stores and tore up track to north and south of town. By noon the next day destruction was completed and the Brigade moved on to Union City."

Dyersburg

1105 Confederate Monument (mem)

Dyer County Courthouse; Veterans Square.

The battles fought by the "faithful Confederate soldiers of Dyer County" are chronicled on this stone monument erected by the United Confederate Veterans and dedicated on April 6, 1905.

Eva

1106 Nathan Bedford Forrest State Park (site)

Eva Road; 901-584-6356; Park: daily, dawn — dusk. Free.

On November 4, 1864, Confederate general Nathan Forrest lined the Tennessee River near the town of Eva at the mouth of Trace Creek with batteries. Large wooden cannon, camouflaged in the

trees, were deployed here to give the impression of extensive fortifications. He shelled Federal gunboats, wagon trains, barges, warehouses, and the supply base of Johnsonville. From his observation point at Pilot Knob, the highest elevation in West Tennessee, Forrest watched what is considered the first defeat of a naval force by a cavalry force in military history. The Federals withdrew after six boats had been sunk. Confederates estimated the damage inflicted here at nearly seven million dollars. The General Nathan Bedford Forrest Park, covering 86 acres, was established in the audacious cavalry officer's honor in 1929. A marble shaft commemorates the Confederate victory, and a monument to Forrest is adjacent to the visitor center.

Farragut

1107 Farragut Folklife Museum (col)

11408 Municipal Center Drive; 423-966-7057; Mon–Fri, 2–4:30. Free.

Located in the Farragut Town Hall, the museum features an extensive collection of personal belongings from United States Admiral David Farragut, hero of the Union conquest of the Gulf of Mexico region. Farragut was born near here on July 5, 1801, in a log cabin. His parents later moved to New Orleans.

Fayetteville

1108 United Daughters of the Confederacy Monument (mem)

Fayetteville Courthouse Square.

Dedicated in 1904, this stone Confederate soldier honors the 3,000 Confederate soldiers of Lincoln County.

Franklin

1109 Carnton Plantation and Confederate Cemetery (site)

1345 Carnton Lane; 615-794-0903; Apr–Oct: Mon–Sat 9–5, Sun 1–5; other times: Mon–Sat 9–4, Sun 1–4. Admission charged.

During the afternoon of the Battle of Franklin, Carnton's doors were opened to wounded and dying soldiers. By evening the floor of the long back porch held the bodies of four Confederate generals, and the 25 rooms were stuffed with wounded. By morning an estimated 150 more soldiers had died. A year and a half after the battle, the McGavocks, whose father, Randal, a former mayor of Nashville, had built the house in 1826, set aside two acres as a Confederate cemetery and, at their own expense, had the bodies of 1,481 dead moved to the plot. It is the largest private Confederate cemetery in the country and is open free to the public all year long.

1110 The Carter House (site)

1140 Columbia Avenue; 615-791-1861; Apr–Oct: Mon–Sat 9–5, Sun 1–5; other times: Mon–Sat 9–4, Sun 1–4. Admission charged.

This little, one-story house, built by Fountain Branch Carter after coming to Franklin in 1830 from Fairfax, Virginia, was caught in the center of the Battle of Franklin. Some of the bloodiest and most desperate fighting of the entire war took place in the Carters' front yard on November 30, 1864. Although the fighting lasted only five hours, some 8,578 Americans were killed, wounded, or captured. More high staff officers were killed or wounded in this conflict than in any other major battle. The Confederates lost six generals, the most famous being the dashing Pat Cleburne. Also killed were S. R. Gist, H. B. Granbury, John Adams, O. F. Strahl, and John C. Carter.

The Battle of Franklin brought personal tragedy to the Carters as well, who had three sons join the Confederate cause. Their youngest, Tod, a Confederate captain, returned home for the first time in three years to see his house behind Union lines. After the Carters emerged from hiding in the cellar they found Tod dead in the yard.

Original buildings from Fountain Carter's 200-acre farm bear the scars of battle and are designated as the most heavily damaged buildings still standing from the Civil War. A visitor center includes a military museum, battlerama, and video presentation.

1111 Confederate Monument (mem)

3rd Avenue and Main Street.

Nearly 10,000 people witnessed the unveiling of this monument in the center of town on November 30, 1899, the 35th anniversary of the Battle of Franklin. The Italian marble statue depicts an infantryman at rest.

1112 Fort Granger (site)

Route 31; 615-791-3217.

In February 1863 General Rosecrans ordered Major General Gordon Granger to fortify Franklin. On November 30, 1864, Confederate general John Bell Hood attacked, and the Federals abandoned the garrison in flight to Nashville. The fort was reoccupied two weeks later as Hood's army withdrew from Tennessee.

1113 Harrison House (site)

Route 31.

In the library of this house dating from 1810, Hood devised the battle plan for the attack of Franklin. Earlier that summer, during the engagement at Perry Station, John Herbert Kelly, then the youngest general in the Confederate army, was brought here with mortal wounds.

1114 Lotz House War Between the States And Old West Museum (col)

1111 Columbia Avenue; 615-791-6533; Mon–Sat 9–5, Sun 12–5. Admission charged.

The Lotz House, crafted by German woodworker Albert Lotz in 1858, was a hospital after the Battle of Franklin. Many rare Confederate and Federal war relics are on display.

1115 Winstead Hill (site)

Route 31, two miles south of town.

From this knoll Hood surveyed the positions of the Federal troops occupying Franklin. His decision to attack the heavily fortified Union army led to one of the bloodiest confrontations of the Civil War. Several markers interpret the events prior to and during the battle.

Gallatin

1116 Trousdale House (site)

South Locust Avenue and West Main Street; 615-452-5648; Tues–Sat 9–4:30, Sun 12:30–5:30. Admission charged.

This was the home of Brigadier General William Trousdale, who served in the War of 1812, the Seminole War, the Mexican War, and later as governor of Tennessee; it contains Confederate artifacts. A monument, *Confederate Soldiers*, was dedicated in the front yard in 1903.

Greeneville

1117 Dickson-Williams Mansion (site)

Irish and Church streets.

This showplace of East Tennessee was coveted as a headquarters for generals of both the Confederate and Union armies. It was built by William Dickson, Greeneville's first postmaster.

1118 Greeneville Cumberland Presbyterian Church (site)

Main and Church streets.

Skirmishing took place in town on several occasions — as testified to by the Civil War cannonball lodged in the brick facade of this downtown church. General John Hunt Morgan was killed across the street after hiding in St. James Episcopal Church.

1119 Andrew Johnson Historic Site Visitor Center (site)

Depot and College streets; 615-638-3551; Daily, 9–5. Admission charged.

Several locations in town relate to the seventeenth President and Lincoln's vice president, all accessible from this visitor center. Johnson emigrated to Greeneville from Raleigh, North Carolina, in 1826 at the age of 17. He was the only Southern senator to remain in Congress at the outbreak of the Civil War. After serving out his term as president, he returned to the United States Senate, the only former president to do so.

The visitor center complex includes a museum and two Johnson sites. The future president was the only tailor in town during the 1820s. It is said that there was much more political debate than fashion talk in the small frame tailor shop now enclosed in a brick building. The two-story brick house across from the tailor shop was the Johnson family home for more than a decade until there was money for a permanent home on South Main Street in 1851.

That homestead two blocks away was Johnson's home until his death in 1875. The house was desecrated by Confederate forces during the Civil War because of Johnson's Union sympathies. It has been restored with Johnson possessions. The third site, the Andrew Johnson National Cemetery, is on a hill picked out by President Johnson. Around an imposing white monument the Johnson family is buried.

1120 Old Harmony Graveyard (site)
Church Street.
Greeneville's oldest cemetery dates to the 1790s and features graves and monuments from the Civil War.

1121 Monument to the Union Soldiers
(mem)
Greene County Courthouse; Depot and Main streets.
The statue of the Union soldier standing at parade rest attests to the fact that many soldiers from Greene County served in the Union Army during the Civil War. The bronze was installed in 1916.

1122 General Morgan Monument (mem)
Courthouse Square; Depot and Main streets.
General John Hunt Morgan, famed Confederate raider and despised in the North, was ambushed and killed in Greeneville during a morning raid on September 4, 1864. He was said to have been shot by Private Andrew G. Campbell of the 13th Tennessee Cavalry. A tablet memorial on a rose-speckled marble monument commemorates his cavalry career. Sam Highbarger was the sculptor.

Harrogate

1123 The Abraham Lincoln Museum
(col)
Lincoln Memorial University; Cumberland Gap Parkway; 615-869-6235; Mon–Fri 9–4, Sat 11–4, Sun 1–4. Admission charged.
The school was founded as a memorial to Abraham Lincoln in 1897, and this museum houses one of America's largest Lincoln collections. There are thousands of artifacts relating to his personal life and the Civil War, including relics of military surgery. A bust of Lincoln by Gutzon Borglum is in the museum.

Henning

1124 Fort Pillow State Historic Park
(site)
Route 87 off Route 51.
Built during the Civil War at the mouth of Cole Creek near the Mississippi River bluffs, the fort was defended by a garrison of black soldiers and Tennessee Unionists, called "home-made Yankees" by West Tennesseans. Early on the morning of April 13, 1864, General Nathan Bedford Forrest and his Confederate cavalry surrounded the garrison. From this point on the history of Fort Pillow is clouded by conflicting accounts.

The Federals contended that Forrest slaughtered an unnecessary number of their men, 262 black and 295 white. A Congressional Committee on the Conduct of War called it an atrocity in the killing of black soldiers. Southerners, however, maintained that the heavy losses were a result of the fort not surrendering. General Sherman was ordered to investigate and retaliate but did nothing, lending credence to the story that the so-called Massacre of Fort Pillow was propaganda.

The earthworks of Fort Pillow, named for General Gideon J. Pillow, still remain in this 1,646-acre park on the Chickasaw Bluffs.

Humboldt

1125 Confederate Monument (mem)
Bailey Park.
Beginning the march north through Gibson County, a detachment of General Nathan Bedford Forrest's brigade captured both railroads running into Humboldt, destroyed track, trestles and rolling stock, and burned stores of ammunitions. A granite Confederate soldier stands here at parade rest, dedicated on September 24, 1914.

Jackson

1126 Britton Lane Battlefield (site)

Britton Lane.

Pre–Civil War Jackson grew into a railroading center for the shipment of cotton and was a critical supply depot during the conflict. Grant made the town his headquarters in the days before Shiloh, and Jackson remained in Union hands until Nathan Forrest stormed the town in early 1863 along the Mobile & Ohio Railroad. General John P. Hatch seized the town again for the Union in July of 1863.

The Battle of Britton's Lane cost the Union a large wagon train and 213 prisoners. After the battle, 87 Union prisoners were detained in the Denmark Presbyterian Church near the Britton Lane. Their graffiti can still be viewed today. Confederates killed in the battle were hastily buried in a mass grave, marked by a monument. A restored Civil War cabin, used as a hospital by both sides, is located on part of the original battlefield.

1127 Memorial to Confederate Dead (mem)

Madison County Courthouse; Main Street and Highland Avenue.

A Confederate soldier at parade rest, rendered in marble, was installed in 1888. The inscriptions point out that many counties in the South supplied more soldiers than they had voters to the Confederate cause.

Kenton

1128 Forrest's Raid (site)

Routes 89 and 45W.

A historical marker in town reads: "December 21, 1862. At Kenton, a detachment from Forrest's Brigade, coming north from Rutherford, captured a Federal garrison of 250 men, including Colonel Thomas J. Kinney, 122nd Illinois Infantry. They also tore up five miles of track between the two towns."

Knoxville

1129 Confederate Memorial Hall (site)

3148 Kingston Pike; 615-522-2371; Tues–Fri, 1–4. Admission charged.

Confederate General James Longstreet used this brick Victorian mansion, built in 1858, as his headquarters during the Siege of Knoxville in November 1863. Three Confederate sharpshooters using the house's tower were killed by Federal cannon fire. Artifacts from the Confederacy are on display.

1130 Confederate Monument (mem)

Bethel Cemetery; 1917 Bethel Avenue.

A segmented gray marble shaft thrusts 48 feet into the air in honor of more than 1,600 soldiers of the South who gave their lives in the mountain passes in the area. A standing private at rest stands atop. This monument by Lloyd Branson was dedicated on May 19, 1892.

1131 Fort Dickerson (site)

Off Route 441.

Fort Dickerson commanded the high ground atop a 300-foot-high ridge across the Tennessee River from Knoxville. It was one of a ring of 16 earthen forts constructed by the Federal army to protect the town during the Civil War. Confederate cavalry under General Joseph Wheeler rode against the fort in the early days of its construction in November 1863, but the troops were turned back by the difficult terrain and by Federal resistance that was stronger than expected. A marker identifies the spot of the fort.

1132 Mabry-Hazen House (site)

1711 Dandridge Avenue; 615-522-8661; Apr–Oct: Mon–Fri 10–5, Sat–Sun 12–5; other times: closed Sunday. Admission charged.

Joseph Mabry, a prominent Knoxvillian, built this two-story frame house in 1858. It was used by both sides during the Civil War as a headquarters, and mementos of this period are on exhibit.

1133 Museum of East Tennessee History (col)

600 Market Street; 615-544-4318; Tues–Fri 10–4, Sun 1–5. Admission charged.

The museum celebrates the region's peculiar history — a Union stronghold in a secessionist state. Artifacts and exhibits tell of the impact of this position on the region's development.

1134 Union Soldiers' Monument (mem)

Knoxville National Cemetery; 939 Tyson Street.

This monument, dedicated in 1906 to the Union soldiers of Tennessee, consists of a miniature fortress. At the top of the central turret is a Union soldier standing at parade rest.

1135 Volunteer State War Era Veterans Hall of Honor (col)

4000 Chapman Highway; 615-577-0757; Tues–Sat 10–4, Sun 1–4. Free.

Tennessee earned its nickname, the "Volunteer State," with its contributions to the Mexican War. This collection of Tennessee's military history includes over 2,000 items, many pertaining to the Civil War.

Lebanon

1136 General Hatton (mem)

Town Square.

The Confederate general is portrayed in stone, standing with his arms crossed. He gazes from atop a tiered base made of blocks of rough-surfaced stone, imbedded with inscriptions to the memory of Wilson County Civil War veterans. The statue was unveiled in 1912. A monument to Confederate dead is in Cedar Grove Cemetery.

Lewisburg

1137 Confederate Soldier Monument (mem)

Marshall County Courthouse; Commerce Street.

This monument honors the men who served in the Confederate army and the women who served at home. A metal infantryman stands on a stone base, on which are listed the names of those who died in the Civil War from Marshall County.

Lexington

1138 Battle of Parker's Crossroads (site)

I-40 and Route 22, Exit 108; 901-968-5533.

After a successful raid to destroy Union rail communications, Confederate general Nathan Bedford Forrest surrounded Union colonel Cyrus L. Dunham's brigade near Parker's Crossroads on December 31, 1862. While negotiating for surrender, Forrest in turn was surrounded by Federal reinforcements. When told he was sandwiched between two Union forces, Forrest ordered, "Charge them both ways!" Taking a skeleton force of 75 men, he stunned his prospective captors with an offensive charge and escaped south of town.

Reenactment: A self-guided driving tour provides a complete view of Parker's Crossroads Battlefield, although all the stops are on private property, except for the beginning point in City Park. A Tennessee Historical Marker tells the story of the fighting here. The Battle of Parker's Crossroads is reenacted on the second weekend in June biennially, every even year.

Maryville

1139 Blount County War Casualties (mem)

Blount County Courthouse.

The names of Blount County war dead from all wars, from the War of 1812 through the Persian Gulf War, are listed on bronze plaques around this 1966 monument, sculpted by James Tipton. A bronze statue of a soldier dressed for battle is perched atop a large marble and concrete base.

Memphis

1140 Confederate Park (site)

Front Street at Madison Avenue.

The ramparts used in the defense of Memphis from Federal gunboats in 1862 are still visible. Facing Front Street is a statue of Jefferson Davis, who lived here following his internment after the Civil War.

1141 Forrest Park (site)

Madison Street between Dunlap and Manassas streets.

General Robert E. Lee was once asked to identify the greatest soldier under his command. He replied, "a man as I have never seen sir … Forrest." General Nathan Bedford Forrest died in 1877 two blocks from this site, where he is buried. Sherman had called him "the most remarkable man our Civil War produced on either side." The large bronze equestrian statue was erected in 1905.

1142 Hunt-Phelan Home (site)

533 Beale Street; 901-344-3166; Summer: daily, 9–6; other times: daily, 10–5. Admission charged.

This oldest home in Memphis, recently opened for tours, was the headquarters for Ulysses S. Grant as he planned the assault on Vicksburg. Earlier, General Leonidas Polk had planned the Battle of Corinth in the home. It was built over five years from 1828 until 1832 by slaves and Chickasaw Indians.

1143 Memphis Pink Palace Museum and Planetarium (col)

3050 Central Avenue; 901-320-6320; Mon–Sat 10–5, Sun 1–5. Admission charged.

This wide-ranging collection emphasizes the cultural and natural history of the mid–South and includes an excellent Civil War collection.

1144 Mississippi River Museum at Mud Island (col)

125 North Front Street; 901-576-7232; Summer: daily, 10–5; Spring and Fall: Tues–Sun, 10–5. Admission charged.

Control of the Mississippi River was a primary Federal objective during the Civil War, and five galleries of this museum are dedicated to its role in the conflict. A life-size replica of a Union City ironclad warship is displayed.

1145 To the Heroes of Illinois (mem)

Memphis National Cemetery; 3568 Townes Avenue, Section B.

This monument is a bronze figure of a soldier lying in state on a pink and black marble sarcophagus. Created in 1928 by Leon Hermant, it commemorates the contributions of Illinois volunteers who fell here.

Of the 13,965 soldiers buried in this graveyard, 8,866 are unknown. Many from the crew of the U.S.S. *Sultana* are also interred here. On April 27, 1865, hundreds of paroled Federal soldiers were on this ship on their way home from Vicksburg after enduring Confederate prison camps. In the darkness of early morning a defective boiler exploded on the overcrowded ship, hurling soldiers and wreckage into the air. Fire burst out immediately, and the river was filled with struggling men, horses, and mules. The loss was officially put at 1,238 killed, but estimates range as high as 1,900. It remains one of America's most lethal maritime disasters.

Mount Pleasant

1146 Confederate (mem)

Town Square; Main Street.

The stone Confederate soldier standing atop a 20-foot base was erected by the Bigby Gray Chapter of the United Daughters of the Confederacy on September 27, 1907.

Mulberry

1147 Confederate Memorial (mem)

Mulberry Town Square.

A youthful Confederate soldier was installed on September 27, 1909, in remembrance of the "300 Confederate unconquered soldiers who went out from Mulberry."

Murfreesboro

1148 Civil War Monument (mem)

Murfreesboro Town Square.

This bronze soldier on a base of granite blocks honors the "valor of Confederate soldiers who fell in the great Battle of Murfreesboro."

1149 Oaklands Historic House Museum (site)

900 North Maney Avenue; 615-893-0022; Tues–Sat 10–4, Sun 1–4. Admission charged.

This restored Italianate plantation house was occupied by both Southern and Northern officers during the Civil War. Jefferson Davis stayed here in December 1862 while visiting troops, and the house was also the setting for the surrender of Murfreesboro.

1150 Stones River National Battlefield (site)

Route 41/70S; 615-893-9501; Daily, 8–5. Free.

On December 31, 1862, on a foggy, wet winter morning, more than 83,000 men from the Confederate and Union armies met west of Murfreesboro along the meandering Stones River. C.S.A. general Bragg carried the fighting this day, but Union General Rosecrans chose to stay on the battlefield rather than retreat north to Nashville. After a day of posturing, with both sides hoping the other would withdraw, fighting resumed on January 2. Nearly 3,000 men were killed on the battlefield, and the total casualty rate soared to over 35 percent. In the end the Federals claimed a victory that split the Confederacy and paved the way for General Sherman's "March to the Sea."

A self-guided auto tour departs from the visitor center, which features an 18-minute slide program and museum exhibits. Remnants of Fortress Rosecrans, one of the largest earthen forts constructed during the war, are visible. One of the nation's oldest intact Civil War monuments marks Hell's Half-Acre, where Union soldiers held the ground against fierce Confederate attacks. More than 6,000 Civil War soldiers are buried in the National Cemetery. A Civil War encampment takes place in July.

Nashville

1151 Belle Meade Mansion (site)

5025 Harding Road; 615-356-0501; Mon–Sat 9–5, Sun 1–5. Admission charged.

During the Battle of Nashville in December of 1864, Confederate general James R. Chalmers made his headquarters at Belle Meade plantation. Out front, bullet scars from a cavalry skirmish that took place on the lawn are still visible on the limestone columns.

1152 Belmont Mansion (site)

1900 Belmont Boulevard; 615-386-4459; Jun–Aug: Mon–Sat 10–4, Sun 2–5; Sept–May: Tues–Sat, 10–4. Admission charged.

From this house, built in 1853, General Thomas J. Wood directed the Battle of Nashville during the first day.

1153 Confederate Memorial (mem)

Mount Olivet Cemetery; 1011 Lebanon Road.

A Confederate soldier of marble stands atop a 36-foot shaft of granite in tribute to the sacrifice of the soldiers of Tennessee in the Civil War. A broken shaft holding a Confederate battle flag is carved in relief around the shaft. Carlo Nicoli carved the sculpture, which was dedicated on May 16, 1899. The cemetery is the burial site for nearly 1,500 Confederate soldiers, including seven generals.

1154 Confederate Women (mem)

Legislative Plaza; 7th Avenue and Union Street.

The inscription reads: "To commemorate the heroic devotion and self-sacrifice of the women of Tennessee." Belle Kinney sculpted three figures — a male dying against a broken cannon, a classical Greek goddess, and a woman in Civil War era dress. The monument was dedicated on October 10, 1926.

1155 Sam Davis Monument (mem)

Centennial Park; West End Avenue.

George Zolnay interpreted Sam Davis, "boy hero of the Confederacy," seated in this 1909 sculpture. The monument of the executed spy was meant to symbolize the heroism of the Confederate private soldier.

1156 Sam Davis of Tennessee (mem)

Tennessee State Capitol; 7th and Charlotte streets.

Another rendering of Davis stands on the south lawn of the capitol. He wears a short jacket and his buckle marked with "C.S.A." This bronze monument was dedicated in April 1909 and bears the inscription: "The boys will have to fight the battles without me."

1157 Minnesota Monument (mem)

Nashville National Cemetery; 1420 Gallatin Road.

A monument with a standing woman by John Karl Daniels is dedicated to the state of Minnesota's soldiers who lost their lives here.

1158 The Peace Monument (mem)

Franklin Road near Woodmont Boulevard.

This monument was dedicated on November 11, 1927, to remember the Battle of Nashville. Giuseppe Moretti sculpted a straining youth holding back two rearing horses, symbolic of the will of both sides.

On December 15 and 16, 1864, the Confederacy's last offensive action ended in the loss of the Army of Tennessee at the Battle of Nashville. It has been called one of the most decisive battles of the entire Civil War. A driving tour of the Battle of Nashville can be picked up at the Cumberland Science Museum at 800 Fort Negley Boulevard.

1159 Tennessee State Museum (col)

James K. Polk Cultural Center; 5th and Deaderick streets; 615-741-2692; Tues–Sat 10–5, Sun 1–5. Free.

A large section of the 60,000 square feet of Tennessee history exhibition space is devoted to the Volunteer State's role in the Civil War. The state capitol on the site, completed in 1859, was known as Fort Andrew Jackson during the Civil War.

1160 Travellers' Rest (site)

636 Farrell Parkway; 615-832-8197; Tues–Sat 10–5, Sun 1–5. Admission charged.

The original four-room house, built in 1799, is one of Nashville's oldest. Union troops camped on the lawn during the Federal occupation of Nashville, and for two weeks before the Battle of Nashville, Travellers' Rest was the headquarters of Confederate commander John Bell Hood. On the second day of the battle, December 16, 1864, Federal forces charged the Confederate right flank on Peach Orchard Hill on the property.

Paris

1161 The Confederate Soldier (mem)

Courthouse Square; Washington Street.

This stone monument to the Confederate soldiers of Henry County was dedicated on October 13, 1900.

Pulaski

1162 Sam Davis (mem)

Courthouse Square; Public Square–1st Street.

The revered Confederate spy is memorialized in stone in the town where he was executed by the Federals on November 27, 1863. The standing figure of a boy was dedicated on October 11, 1906, by Giles County. On the base are inscribed his final words, which rang through the Confederacy: "If I had a thousand lives, I would lose them all here before I would betray my friend or the confidence of my informer."

A small museum devoted to Davis can be visited through arrangement with the Giles County Chamber of Commerce. In the collection are the leg irons worn by Davis as well as other Civil War memorabilia. The museum is free.

Savannah

1163 Cherry Mansion (site)

101 Main Street.

This private residence is the oldest structure in Savannah and was built around 1830. Major General Ulysses S. Grant made his headquarters here from March 17, 1862, until the Battle of Shiloh. He pitched his headquarters tent in the yard and took his meals with the Cherry family. He was eating breakfast on the morning of April 6 when a courier arrived with the news that the battle had begun. Grant immediately left for Pittsburgh Landing by steamer.

1164 Tennessee River Museum (col)

507 Main Street; 800-552-3866; Mon–Fri 9–5, Sat 10–5, Sun 1–5. Admission charged.

The Tennessee River was the invasion route for Union armies into the Confederate west, a history of which is presented in the exhibit *The War on the River*. *The Army* presents the most complete projectile collection from the Shiloh battlefield.

Shelbyville

1165 Confederate Monument (mem)

Lane Parkway; Confederate Square.

The white marble statue dedicated on October 17, 1899, is inscribed to those who "rose to defend their homes and firesides, they endured every hardship without complaint."

Shiloh

1166 Shiloh National Military Park (site)

Route 2; 901-689-5696; Summer: daily, 8–6; other times: daily, 8–5. Admission charged.

The first major western battle of the Civil War was fought along the Tennessee River on April 6 and 7, 1862. The prize was the possession of major railroads and control of the lower Mississippi River valley.

General Albert Sidney Johnston led 44,000 Confederates in a surprise attack on Ulysses S. Grant's 40,000 Union troops in the forests and fields surrounding a small log church called "Shiloh meeting house." The Confederates pushed Grant back two miles that first day, but Johnston was mortally wounded near Peach Orchard.

Grant's reinforcements arrived at Pittsburgh Landing the next day, enabling him to overwhelm new commander General P. G. T. Beauregard, who retreated to Corinth, Mississippi. The two-day carnage claimed 23,746 men recorded killed, wounded, or missing. Shiloh was the bloodiest battle since the war began, forcing Grant to conclude, "I gave up all idea of saving the Union except by complete conquest."

A 25-minute movie, *Shiloh: Portrait of a Battle*, is shown every half hour, tracing the events leading up to the battle and describing the fighting. Out on the battlefield a nine-and-a-half-mile auto

tour has stops with taped messages about the battle. The Shiloh National Cemetery, established in 1866, contains 1,227 known and 2,416 unknown Northern dead. Mass burial trenches located throughout the battlefield contain the majority of the 1,728 Confederate soldiers killed at Shiloh.

Smyrna

1167 Sam Davis Home (site)

Sam Davis Road; 615-459-2341; Summer: Mon–Sat 9–5, Sun 1–5; other times: Mon–Sat 10–4, Sun 1–4. Admission charged.

Captured as a Confederate spy, 21-year-old Sam Davis chose to give his life rather than divulge the name of his accomplice. His frame home is on this 168-acre plantation and has been called "the most beautiful shrine to a private soldier in the country."

Spring Hill

1168 Spring Hill Battlefield (site)

2870 Lee Lane; 615-791-9136; Daily, dawn–dusk. Free.

On November 29, 1864, Confederate general Hood's army tried to capture Federal general Schofield's army. Schofield slipped away in the night, and the Spring Hill affair became one of the most controversial events of the war, resulting in the disastrous Battle of Franklin.

Trenton

1169 The Confederate Monument (mem)

Courthouse Square.

This imitation granite Confederate soldier was dedicated on May 31, 1907, "lest we forget."

1170 Trenton Battlefield (site)

Route 77.

Confederate general Nathan Forrest's experience at Trenton is commemorated with a historical marker: "Advancing along this route from Spring Creek, December 20, 1862, part of Forrest's brigade under his command captured the Federal garrison of Trenton, entrenched around the station on the west side of town. Meanwhile a detachment had taken Humboldt and wrecked both railroads there. The day's bag of prisoners was 700. He paused here for regrouping."

Tullahoma

1171 Tullahoma Confederate Cemetery (site)

Southwest of Tullahoma Square; 615-455-5497.

Tullahoma was the winter headquarters for the Confederate Army of Tennessee for six months after the three-day struggle at Stone's River — the bloodiest battle west of the Appalachians. While the army camped here, one of the earliest Confederate cemeteries was established early in 1863. Here, 407 unmarked graves hold the remains of those who died due to sickness and wounds. That July, General Braxton Bragg removed the Army of Tennessee under Federal pressure, leaving the area in Union hands.

Union City

1172 Civil War Monument (mem)
Kiwanis Park.

A tall obelisk with a standing Confederate soldier was dedicated in 1909 to those veterans of Obion County who "starved in Federal prisons."

Winchester

1173 Franklin County Old Jail Museum (col)
400 Dinah Shore Boulevard NE, US 41; 615-967-0524; Mar–Dec: Tues–Sat, 10–4:30. Admission charged.

Six rooms of artifacts, including one on the Civil War, preserve the history of Franklin County in the town's original jail cells, two blocks east of the town square.

Texas

Civil War Status: Confederacy; seceded from the Union on January 28, 1861
1860 Population: 604,215
Troops Provided: 2,000 — Union
90,000 — Confederacy
Known Scenes of Action: 90

Civil War Timeline
January 1, 1863: Battle of Galveston
September 8, 1863: Battle of Sabine Pass
May 12–13, 1865: Battle of Palmitto Ranch; last Civil War land engagement

Austin

1174 Lorenzo de Zavala State Archives and Library Building (col)
Twelfth Street, east of Capitol; 512-463-5455; Mon–Fri, 8–5. Free.

The records of the state of Texas include documents on Texas state troops and militia.

1175 Littlefield Memorial Fountain (mem)
21st Street and University Avenue.

A double walk from this fountain by Pompeo Coppini at the entrance to the University of Texas features statues of Lee, Albert Sidney Johnston, and Davis.

1176 State Capitol (mem)
Congress Avenue.

There are three Civil War memorials on the Capitol grounds. A monument to Confederate dead is at the south entrance, on the center walk. Erected in 1901, it features bronze figures on a granite base representing President Jefferson Davis and three Confederate soldiers and one sailor. Designed by Pompeo Coppini, the memorial was executed by Frank Teich. A monument to Hood's Texas Brigade on the east lawn was also designed by Coppini, as was the *Terry's Texas Rangers* on the center walk. The latter monument was unveiled in 1907 in commemoration of the Eighth Texas Cavalry, an independent unit in the Confederate Army. The work portrays one of Terry's Texas Rangers astride a spirited horse.

1177 State Cemetery (site)
East 7th and Comal streets.

The "Arlington of Texas" has monuments marking the graves of 2,000 noted Texans, including Stephen F. Austin. The reclining marble figure of Confederate general Albert Sidney Johnston, killed while leading a charge at Shiloh, was sculpted by Elizabet Ney.

Brownsville

1178 Fort Brown (site)
Terminus of Taylor Avenue.

Now a part of Texas Southmost Junior College, this fort was built in 1846 to defend the Mexican border. On March 2, 1861, the Federals burned military supplies and abandoned the fort. The Union once again controlled Fort Brown in 1863 and once again ceded control to the Confederates in 1864.

1179 Palmitto Hill Battlefield (site)
Route 4, twelve miles east of town.

The last land engagement of the Civil War was fought on May 12 and 13, 1865, more than a month after the surrender at Appomattox. Whether either side, or both, knew of Lee's capitulation is unknown. Lieutenant Colonel David Branson, who commanded the Union force, stated that the battle was imminent when he learned of the surrender but that he could not get word to the Confederates because they refused to honor any flag of truce from a unit with blacks, and his troops consisted in part of blacks.

The Texas version of Palmitto Hill holds that both sides knew of the truce and that as the Confederate troops were disbanding the Union decided to assault Brownsville and capture hundreds of bales of cotton there. Colonel John S. "Rip" Ford gave chase and a running encounter ensued that scattered the Union force.

Whichever version contains more truth, a few days after the battle Branson and Ford posed together in Brownsville for a tintype photograph. A historical marker commemorates the battle.

Camp Verde

1180 Camp Verde (site)
Route 689.

A small community with a population less than 100 is on the approximate site of Camp Verde, a U.S. Army frontier post established on July 8, 1855, and famous as the home of Jefferson Davis's camel corps. Seeking a dependable means of transportation of army supplies to the remote arid regions of the southwest, Davis, then secretary of war, imported a camel herd and native herders. The corps of men were made up of cavalrymen who were taught the art of handling camels by the herders. Known derisively as "camelteers," few harbored any warm sentiment for their temperamental new mounts. Camp Verde was surrendered to the Confederates in 1861, and the camels were left without any supervision. Many wandered into the hills, and survivors were found periodically for years afterward.

The Confederates maintained the fort until 1865, keeping prisoners in a walled canyon nearby. Union soldiers were allowed to build shacks and exercise in fresh air with no chance of escape up the steep walls. As many as 600 men were detained here. The only remaining structure of Camp Verde is the main ranch house of Nowlin Ranch, not open to the public.

Comfort

1181 German Settlers Monument (mem)
High Street and Route 27.

This town was established by German settlers in 1854. They were so pleased with the picturesque area and pure water that they ended their migration and named their new home "Camp Comfort." The Germans were openly sympathetic to the Union and rather than serve forced enlistments in the Confederate army, fled toward Mexico. Fritz Tegener and some 65 men were surprised and attacked by mounted Confederate soldiers on the west bank of the Neuces River about 20 miles from Fort Clark. In the fighting that followed nineteen settlers were killed and nine wounded. The nine wounded prisoners were executed a few hours after the battle.

After the Civil War the survivors and friends of the slain gathered the remains and returned them to Comfort, where they lie beneath this monument. It is the oldest Civil War monument in Texas and was dedicated on August 10, 1862.

Corpus Christi

1182 Centennial House (site)
411 North Upper Broadway; 512-882-8691; Wed, 2–5 (when flag is flying). Free.

The city's oldest existing home is built of "shell-crete"— shell mixed into concrete. It was built in 1848 and served as a hospital during the Civil War.

In August of 1862 Union gunboats established a land base on the outlying islands from Corpus Christi and demanded the surrender of the town. The Texans refused and shelling began on August 16. Tradition has it that some Union troops had spirited away a barrel of whiskey and stowed it away in empty shells. When the order to attack was given there was no time to reload the charges without revealing the theft so the "whiskey bombs" were launched. The town soon succumbed anyway.

Dallas

1183 The Confederacy (mem)
Fair Park; Centennial Building.

This cast stone monument to the time Texas spent in the Confederate States of America was created by Lawrence Tenney Stevens for the Texas Centennial Exposition in 1936.

1184 Confederate Monument (mem)
Pioneer Park; 1400 Marilla.

The central obelisk of this monument stands 51½ feet high and faces south. A Confederate soldier surmounts the shaft, which is surrounded by four figures at the corners — Robert E. Lee, Stonewall Jackson, Albert S. Johnson, and Jefferson Davis. Dedicated on April 29, 1897, this sculpture was created by Frank Teich.

1185 Robert E. Lee and the Confederate Soldier (mem)
Lee Park; Turtle Creek Boulevard and Hall Street.

Alexander Proctor sculpted General Lee and his steed, Traveller, amid a bronze figure group on a base of Texas pink granite. The monument was dedicated on June 12, 1936.

Eagle Pass

1186 Fort Duncan (site)
Route 277.

This settlement started with the temporary Camp Eagle Pass, which became the permanent Fort Duncan in 1849. Garrisoned by the Confederate troops of the Frontier Regiment in the Civil War, it kept open one of the few outlets for Southern cotton during the war. On July 4, 1865, General Joseph O. Shelby and his 500 veterans gathered solemnly around their battle flag and four colonels at last lowered it, and cast it, weighted, into the muddy waters of the Rio Grande. General Shelby tore the plume from his hat, and floated it into the river. Theirs was the last flag to fly over an unsurrendered Confederate force, and the spot where it was buried has been called the "Grave of the Confederacy."

El Paso

1187 Fort Bliss Museum (col)
Pleasanton Road and Sheridan Drive; 915-568-4518; Daily, 9–4:30. Free.

Fort Bliss was established in 1848 to reign over the lands ceded after the Mexican War. During the Civil War the U.S. Army post was the headquarters for Confederate troops in the Southwest. A replica of the original adobe fort is maintained as a museum of frontier military life. The Museum of the Noncommissioned Officer on the grounds also contains Civil War artifacts.

Fairfield

1188 Val Verde Cannon (mem)
Freestone County Museum; 302 East Main Street.

The cannon on the courthouse lawn is a relic of the Texan Confederate force that made an unsuccessful attempt to drive the Federals from New Mexico. The museum is in the nineteenth century jail.

Fort Davis

1189 Fort Davis National Historic Site (site)
Route 17; 915-426-3224; Daily, 8–5. Admission charged.

Once the largest and most important frontier fort in western Texas, Fort Davis, named for then sec-

retary of war Jefferson Davis, was established in 1854 to protect the 600 miles of wilderness between San Antonio and El Paso known as the Overland Trail. Federal troops abandoned the fort on March 13, 1861, to return east to the Civil War. After failing to conquer New Mexico, the Confederates evacuated Fort Davis as well. By the time Federal troops returned in 1867, the bulk of the installation needed to be rebuilt. A museum in reconstructed barracks displays cavalry relics and souvenirs of the Camel Corps.

Franklin

1190 Walter Williams Grave (site)
Mount Pleasant Church; Route 2446, four miles southeast of town.

In a rural church cemetery in this small community is the grave of Walter Williams, said to be the last survivor of the Civil War.

Galveston

1191 Rosenburg Library (col)
2310 Sealy Avenue; 409-763-8854; Tues–Sat, 9–5. Free.

This first public library of Texas contains Civil War artifacts and documents, maps, and manuscripts.

Gonzales

1192 Confederate Fort (site)
Intersection of Routes 90A and 183.

Earthworks remain here from a Confederate fort in southeast Texas.

Hempstead

1193 Liendo Plantation (site)
Wyatt Chapel Road; 800-826-4371; First Saturday of the month, 10, 11:30, 1. Admission charged.

The first cotton plantation in Texas was built in 1853 on 67,000 acres obtained from a Spanish land grant assigned to Justo Liendo. Converted to a prison camp during the Civil War, it housed soldiers captured at the Battle of Galveston. Now a private residence, it is open for tours one Saturday a month.

Hillsboro

1194 Harold B. Simpson Confederate Research Center (col)
Hill College; 817-582-2555; Mon–Fri, 8–12 and 1–4. Free.

More than 3,000 volumes, photographs, correspondence, and dioramas are devoted to the Civil War, especially the Confederate general John Hood's Texas Brigade. The museum features historic firearms, edged weapons, artifacts, and an art collection.

Laredo

1195 Fort McIntosh (site)

Foot of Washington Street.

The star-shaped earthworks from the frontier were established by the United States Army in 1848 and remained in continuous use until May 1946. Fort McIntosh was evacuated on April 11, 1861, by the Union when the Department of Texas was surrendered. Federal troops made an unsuccessful attempt to retake the Confederate garrison by advancing up the Rio Grande River in 1863, but the United States did not regain the fort until October 23, 1865. The old guardhouse, chapel, warehouse, and commissary remain, parts of which are used for the Laredo Junior College and Laredo State University.

Longview

1196 Our Confederate Heroes (mem)

Gregg County Courthouse; 101 West Methvin Street.

The statue of a Confederate soldier was erected on June 3, 1911, to honor the men who fought for the Confederacy. Frank Teich created the life-size figure on a 34-foot shaft of Texas granite. At the base of the shaft is an allegorical female figure, perhaps representing Liberty.

Mason

1197 Fort Mason (site)

Route 87, south of courthouse.

A four-room officers' quarters has been reconstructed from its original foundations on the crest of Post Hill, marking a former cavalry post that was Robert E. Lee's last command in the United States army. A number of crumbling foundations still indicate the sites of some of the 23 original buildings that included barracks, storehouses, stables, and a hospital.

Mexia

1198 Confederate Reunion Grounds State Park (mem)

Route 2705 off Route 14, six miles south of town.

The park was the site of Confederate States of America veterans reunions from 1889 until 1946. A Confederate cannon is on the grounds.

Newcastle

1199 Fort Belknap (site)

Route 251, three miles south of town; Daily except Wednesday, 9–5.

Six original buildings and one replica remain from a frontier fort where Civil War notables such as Albert Sidney Johnston, Earl Van Dorn, George Thomas, and George McClellan were stationed. Union troops abandoned the fort early in the war.

Paris

1200 Sam Bell Maxey State Historic Structure (site)

812 South Church Street; 214-785-5716; Wed–Sun, 10–5. Admission charged.

The two-story, white Victorian home was built by Confederate general Sam Bell Maxey in 1868. The restored building contains Civil War mementos.

Port Arthur

1201 Sabine Pass Battleground State Historical Park (site)

Route 3322 off Route 87, 15 miles south of town.

In the summer of 1863 General Benjamin Butler, in command of the Department of the Gulf, was ordered to attack Texas. He chose Sabine Pass and Fort Griffin, a mud fortress guarding the Texas coast. Lieutenant Dick Dowling held fire until three Union gunboats reached close range on September 8. Two gunboats were sunk, another captured, and the remainder driven off—all in 45 minutes. The 5,000-man invading force could not land, and the invasion of Texas was thwarted. Dowling had at his disposal all of 42 men and six cannon.

Dominating the park is a heroic statue of Dick Dowling on a wide base of Texas pink granite, erected by the state he defended in 1936. The men who fought with Dowling are listed. The inscription: "Texas remembers the faithfulness and valor of her sons and commends their heroic example to future generations."

Richmond

1202 Confederate Museum (col)

2740 F.M. 359, north of town; Tues, Thurs 10:30–3, Sun 2–4. Free.

Displays include weapons and swords, pictures of battles, and artifacts. Tape-recorded histories document the ante-bellum era.

1203 Fort Bend County Historical Museum (col)

500 Houston Street; 713-342-6478; Tues–Fri 10–4, Sat–Sun 1–5.

This small museum traces the development of the area from the first colonists in 1822; one special exhibit is on the Civil War.

Rio Grande City

1204 Fort Ringgold (site)

Route 83, east side of town limits.

Among the officers who saw service in this 1848 fort, one of Texas' best preserved old military posts, were Ulysses S. Grant, Jefferson Davis, and Stonewall Jackson. Landmarks include the old post hospital and the Lee House, occupied by Colonel Robert E. Lee when he commanded the Department of Texas before the Civil War.

Tyler

1205 Camp Ford (site)

Route 271, two miles northeast of town.

The Confederate prison here, named for Colonel John "Rip" Ford, was established in 1863, and by the following year it was the largest prisoner of war compound west of the Mississippi River. More than 6,000 Union soldiers and sailors were stockaded here, with many digging caves in the hillside and constructing primitive mud-and-stick huts for shelter. A historical marker in a roadside rest area describes the prison.

1206 Confederate Soldier Monument (mem)

Oakwood Cemetery; 400 Ellis Street.

A marble Confederate soldier on a tiered base honors 231 fallen Smith County soldiers who died of disease while training in Tyler. The monument was dedicated on July 6, 1909.

Vermont

Civil War Status: Union
1860 Population: 315,098
Troops Provided: 35,000

Brandon

1207 Civil War Monument (mem)

Routes 7 and 73.

Stephen A. Douglas was born here in 1813. This memorial is a granite shaft with a figure of a Civil War soldier. On the base are the names of 54 soldiers who died in service to the Union.

Brattleboro

1208 Civil War Monument (mem)

Town Common; Putney Road and Linden Street.

This eight-foot standing figure of a Civil War soldier commemorates the 385 Brattleboro men who enlisted in the Union Army, 31 of whom died. The dedication of the design by George Hines was on June 17, 1887.

1209 Military Hospital Monument (site)

Brattleboro Union High School; Fairground Road.

The two bas-relief panels, representing a soldier going out to fight and one coming home from the war, were dedicated on September 12, 1906. The monument marks the location where more than 10,000 Vermont men were enlisted into the Union army and where 4,000 soldiers were hospitalized and/or mustered out of the service.

Bennington

1210 Civil War Memorial (mem)

West Main Street.

On a rough-hewn granite block is a bronze plaque depicting four officers, including James Hicks Wallbridge, mounted on horses and reviewing the 2nd Vermont Regiment. This memorial to Vermont's Civil War volunteers was created by William Gordon Huff and dedicated in August 1930.

Burlington

1211 General George Jerrison Stannard (mem)

Lakeview Cemetery; 455 North Avenue.

The war exploits of General Stannard, a Georgia, Vermont, native, are recounted on the granite base at his gravesite. He was wounded several times in Virginia and lost his arm at Fort Harrison. His likeness is portrayed in bronze by Karl Gerhardt.

Chester

1212 Soldiers' Monument (mem)

Town Green, opposite cemetery.

This monument to "her patriot sons" features a bronze Civil War soldier by Heinrich Manger. It was dedicated in 1884.

Chittenden

1213 Grand Army of the Republic Civil War Monument (mem)

Town Square.

This granite Civil War sentry, facing south, surmounts a granite base, which is inscribed with the names of 86 Chittenden soldiers enlisted in the Civil War.

Coventry

1214 Soldiers' Monument (mem)

Town Green.

A crowd estimated at 2,000 turned out for the dedication of this white bronze infantryman on August 14, 1912. The memorial was donated to Coventry by Riley Wright, former captain of the 15th Vermont. A tablet on the monument lists the names of 125 Coventry Civil War soldiers.

Derby

1215 Civil War Monument to Honor Derby Soldiers (mem)

Derby Center; Main Street.

A simple tapered shaft by Daniel Chandler is split to symbolize the splintering of the Union during the Civil War. Some 240 names are listed on three plaques. It was dedicated on October 31, 1866, and was reportedly the first monument erected to the Civil War dead in Vermont.

East Poultney

1216 Civil War Monument (mem)

East Poultney Town Cemetery.

This generic Union soldier was dedicated to Colonel Judson A. Lewis by his widow and given to the town to be placed next to Green Mountain College in 1915. The granite monument was moved to this location in 1959.

Franklin

1217 Franklin Monument (mem)

Carmi Marsh-Veteran's Park; Main Street.

James Walling designed this bronze infantryman to "the memory of the boys who went from this town to the battlefields of the Civil War." It was dedicated on September 10, 1910, with the names of 130 Franklin soldiers listed on the base.

Hartland

1218 Hartland Civil War Soldier (mem)

Hartland Green; Route 12.

This granite work by Adams McNichol features a Civil War soldier, outfitted in a Union uniform, standing at rest.

Highgate

1219 Soldiers' Monument (mem)

Main Street Park.

The white bronze soldier in Civil War uniform was dedicated on July 12, 1911. On the base are inscribed major battlefields on which Vermont soldiers fought. Also inscribed are the names of 196 Civil War soldiers.

Lunenburg

1220 Lunenburg Civil War Monument (mem)

Lunenburg Common.

The names, by rank, of Lunenburg's Civil War soldiers are listed on this granite monument of a soldier, installed in 1904.

Middlebury

1221 Middlebury to Her Soldiers (mem)

Triangle at Merchants Row and South Pleasant Street.

The monument, which covers a fire protection cistern that became obsolete when piped water came to town, was donated to Middlebury by Colonel Silas Ilsley. Marshall Jones created a standing color-bearer atop a multitiered base. It was dedicated to Middlebury soldiers on May 30, 1905.

Middlesex

1222 Union Soldier (mem)

Camp Meade Motor Court and Bunker House Restaurant.

This recent vintage Union soldier was carved from wood by Milo Marshall in 1987. The standing figure has a blue uniform with a double-breasted coat.

Middletown Springs

1223 The Hoadley Monument (mem)

Village Green, in front of Congregational Church.

The Union soldier at parade rest was a gift of blacksmith and carriage builder Francis Hoadley, who enlisted for the Civil War at the age of 15 and rose to the rank of captain. The white bronze was dedicated on May 30, 1904.

Milton

1224 Civil War Monument (mem)

River and Main streets.

The granite infantryman is inscribed: "To our soldiers, erected 1909 by Town of Milton in Memory of the Boys in Blue who Marched from this town to the battlefields of the Civil War." The names of 200 Milton soldiers who served in the Civil War are inscribed on the four sides of the monument.

Montpelier

1225 State Capitol (col)

State Street; 802-828-2228; Mon–Fri, 8–4. Free.

The restored Vermont State House features portraits of people and events that shaped the state's history, including battle flags and silver plaques listing Civil War engagements in which Vermont men participated.

Morrisville

1226 Soldiers' Monument (mem)

Morristown Elementary School; Route 12 and Route 15A.

This sheet copper standard-bearer wearing a Civil War uniform was dedicated on May 30, 1911, 50 years after the outbreak of the war at Fort Sumter.

Newfane

1227 Civil War Memorial (mem)

The Common at Newfane; Main Street.

This Civil War soldier on a pedestal holds a musket and was dedicated on May 30, 1916. Although worn, plaques on two sides of the base list Newfane soldiers killed in the conflict.

Northfield

1228 Civil War Memorial (mem)

Town Square.

Founded in 1819, Norwich University, the Military College of Vermont, is dedicated to the development of the "citizen-soldier." It was relocated here in 1866.

Royalton

1229 Royalton Civil War Monument (mem)

The Green.

A Civil War soldier clasping a musket stands in tribute to the soldiers of Royalton. Dedication was on September 26, 1919.

St. Albans

1230 St. Albans Historical Museum (col)

Church and Bishop streets; 802-527-7933; July–Sept: Tues–Sat, 1–4. Admission charged.

On October 19, 1864, 22 Confederate soldiers held up three St. Albans banks and fled into Canada with $200,000. One townsman reportedly fired on the invaders with a long rifle from the War of 1812 and was slain by return fire. The town eventually recovered about $70,000 of the money, but the perpetrators were freed by a Canadian tribunal that ruled the robbery an act of war. Civil War relics are on display in the town's museum.

St. Johnsbury

1231 The Soldiers' Monument (mem)

Courthouse Park; Main Street and Eastern Avenue.

This standing female figure of America is carved in Carrara marble and holds a sword. Vermont sculptor Larkin Goldsmith Mead created the memorial, which was dedicated on August 20, 1868.

Swanton

1232 Civil War Monument (mem)

Junction of Grand Avenue and Canada Street.

Dedicated in 1868, this white marble *Goddess of Liberty* by Daniel Perry was erected by the town in honor of the Swanton soldiers "who fell in the War of the Rebellion." The base was originally inscribed with the names of 29 soldiers, their rank, regiment, and place and time of death, but the carving is almost worn away.

Tunbridge

1233 The Soldiers' and Sailors' Monument (mem)

Tunbridge Memorial Park; Route 110.

This granite soldier, standing properly in full military uniform, was designed by John Anderson following a gift of $5,000 by Homer Hoyt, a Civil War veteran, in 1921. It was dedicated to Tunbridge veterans in July 1924.

Wallingford

1234 Boy with the Boot (mem)

Northeast corner of Route 7 and Route 140.

Once dubbed "The Most Mysterious Statue in the World," this monument was dedicated on April 3, 1898, to Civil War veteran Arnold Hill by his family. The standing boy depicted, with rolled up pants, represents a drummer boy who brought water in his boot to dying soldiers. Beyond that, the origin of the statue is unknown.

Westford

1235 Reverend John Woodward Statue (mem)

Brookside Road, just past west end of town common.

John H. Woodward joined the First Vermont Cavalry as its chaplain in 1861 after two stints in the Vermont Senate. The granite figure of Woodward, wearing a long coat barely longer than his beard, also honors 108 Civil War veterans.

Williamstown

1236 Civil War Soldiers Monument (mem)

Congressional Meeting House Common; Main Street.

A vertical, tapered marble shaft is topped with a perched eagle with wings spread. The granite base is inscribed with the names of Williamstown soldiers "who lost their lives in the defense of their country." The monument and surrounding fence cost $2,000 when installed in 1869.

Wilmington

1237 Civil War Statue (mem)

Pettee Memorial Library; South Main Street.

A gray-veined, white marble standing figure of a soldier was erected in Wilmington "in memory of our country's defenders."

Woodstock

1238 Civil War Memorial (mem)

Tribou Park; Pleasant and Central streets.

This standing Civil War soldier of granite honors the "boys of Woodstock and vicinity who served in the army and navy of the nation in the War of the Rebellion." It was dedicated on May 30, 1909.

Virginia

Civil War Status: Confederacy; seceded from the Union on April 17, 1861
1860 Population: 1,596,318; State split in 1863
Known Scenes of Action: 2,154

Civil War Timeline

June 10, 1861: Engagement at Big Bethel
July 21, 1861: First Battle of Manassas (Bull Run)
October 21, 1861: Battle of Ball's Bluff
March 9, 1862: Battle of Hampton Roads between the U.S.S. *Monitor* and the C.S.S. *Virginia*, the first naval battle between ironclad vessels
March 23, 1862: Battle of Kernstown
April 5, 1862: McClellan's Army of the Potomac besieges Confederate forces at Yorktown
May 8, 1862: Battle of McDowell
May 15, 1862: Battle of Drewry's Bluff
May 23, 1862: Battle of Front Royal
May 25, 1862: First Battle of Winchester
May 31, 1862: Battle of Seven Pines (Fair Oaks)
June 1, 1862: Robert E. Lee assumes command of the Army of Northern Virginia
June 8, 1862: Battle of Cross Keys
June 9, 1862: Battle of Port Republic
June 25, 1862: Battle of Oak Grove
June 26, 1862: Battle of Mechanicsville
June 27, 1862: Battle of Gaines' Mill
June 29, 1862: Battle of Savage's Station
June 30, 1862: Battle of Glendale (Fraser's Farm)
July 1, 1862: Battle of Malvern Hill
August 9, 1862: Battle of Cedar Mountain
August 28, 1862: Battle of Second Manassas (Bull Run)
September 1, 1862: Battle of Chantilly (Ox Hill)
November 7, 1862: Ambrose E. Burnside replaces McClellan as commander of the Army of the Potomac
December 11, 1862: Battle of Fredericksburg
January 19, 1863: Burnside begins "Mud March"

January 26, 1863: Joseph Hooker succeeds Burnside as commander of the Army of the Potomac

April 11, 1863: Confederate siege of Suffolk begins

May 1, 1863: Battle of Chancellorsville

May 3, 1863: Second Battle of Fredericksburg

May 3, 1863: Battle of Salem Church

May 10, 1863: Stonewall Jackson dies at Guinea
Station from wounds received at Chancellorsville

June 9, 1863: Battle of Brandy Station

June 13, 1863: Second Battle of Winchester

June 28, 1863: George Meade replaces Hooker
as commander of the Army of the Potomac

October 14, 1863: Battle of Bristoe Station

November 7, 1863: Engagement at Rappahannock Station

November 26, 1863: Mine Run Campaign begins

May 5, 1864: Battle of the Wilderness

May 8, 1864: Battle of Spotsylvania Court House

May 15, 1864: Battle of New Market

May 16, 1864: Second Battle of Drewry's Bluff

May 23, 1864: Battle of North Anna River

May 31, 1864: Battle of Cold Harbor

June 5, 1864: Battle of Piedmont

June 11, 1864: Battle of Trevilians

June 15, 1864: Battle of Petersburg

June 17, 1864: Battle of Lynchburg

June 18, 1864: Siege of Petersburg begins

July 24, 1864: Second Battle of Kernstown

July 30, 1864: Battle of the Crater

September 19, 1864: Third Battle of Winchester
(Opequon Creek)

September 22, 1864: Battle of Fisher's Hill

September 29, 1864: Battle of Chaffin's Farm
(Fort Harrison)

October 19, 1864: Battle of Cedar's Creek

April 1, 1865: Battle of Five Forks

April 2, 1865: Petersburg lines breached as siege
ends and Confederates abandon Richmond

April 6, 1865: Battle of Sailor's Creek

April 9, 1865: Lee surrenders at Appomattox
Court House

April 26, 1865: John Wilkes Booth killed at Garrett house in Port Royal Crossroads

---

Abingdon

1239 Confederate Monument (mem)

Sinking Spring Cemetery; Alternate Route 58
West.

A large tombstone to the "Unknown Confederate Dead" stands in a stone-walled area of the graveyard. The burial plot originated in September 1861
when 17 Louisiana soldiers were killed in a train
wreck on the edge of town. Three governors of Virginia are also interred here.

1240 Martha Washington Inn (site)

150 West Main Street.

Abingdon was an important Confederate railroad
depot and supply base during the Civil War when
all the church bells in town were melted down for
cannon. The town was the headquarters for Confederate generals John Hunt Morgan and John C.
Breckinridge. Union general Stoneman burned
most of the town in 1864. One building that survived was this inn, still in use today and restored
to its original appearance. This hostelry was used
as a military hospital.

Aldie

1241 First Massachusetts Cavalry Mon-
ument (mem)

Country Road 734, north of Route 50.

Fierce mounted engagements peppered this area
from June 17 through June 21, 1863. Total cavalry
losses were higher than those at Gettysburg two
weeks later. Three junior Federal officers were promoted to brigadier general after these battles:
George Armstrong Custer, William Averell, and
Elon Farnsworth. The monument to the First Massachusetts is the only reminder of the bloody events
of those five days. Said one of its captains, Charles
Francis Adams, "My poor men were just slaughtered and all we could do was to stand still and be
shot down."

Alexandria

1242 Alexandria National Cemetery
(site)

Payne and Wilkes streets.

More than 3,000 Civil War soldiers, both Confederate and Union, are buried in one of the first
of America's national cemeteries.

1243 Boyhood Home of Robert E. Lee
(site)

607 Oronoco Street; 703-548-8454; Feb–
Dec: Mon–Sat 10–4, Sun 1–4. Admission charged.

Lee spent many of his formative years in this
house, twice living here for five-year periods before
leaving in 1825. Celebrations are held regularly in
the 1895 home to commemorate famous people and

events connected with the residence, especially in January on the anniversary of Lee's birth.

1244 Christ Church (site)

118 North Washington Street; 703-549-1450; Mon–Fri 9–4, Sat 9–1, Sun 2–4:30. Free.

The present building was completed just prior to the American Revolution. George Washington paid 36 pounds, 10 shillings for Pew 60. Robert E. Lee was confirmed here. The white Lee pew and the Washington pew are marked with silver plates. Confederate officers and a mass Confederate grave are on the grounds.

1245 Confederate War Memorial (mem)

Washington and South Prince streets.

This standing male figure, with lowered head and hat in hand, sculpted by Casper Buberl, marks the place where the 17th Virginia Regiment assembled on May 24, 1861. The poignant memorial to Alexandria's 97 war dead was dedicated on May 24, 1889, but now constitutes a small traffic hazard in the middle of the busy road. The statue was once ringed by a 40' × 60' fence with ornamental gas lights, but as the road was widened, the fence was removed to let more cars by. The statue is still close enough to the highway to have been clipped by the occasional careening auto. But a Virginia Assembly statute passed in 1890 assures it "shall perpetually remain at the site" and, furthermore, that the location can never be changed by any future government statute.

1246 Fort Ward Museum and Historic Site (site)

4301 West Braddock Road; 703-838-4848; Tues–Sat 9–5, Sun 12–5. Free.

The fifth largest and best preserved of the 68 forts that once ringed Washington features interpretive programs and tours. This defensive position was buttressed by 36 gun emplacements. A museum in the fort headquarters offers a 12-minute video, *Fort Ward and the Defenses of Washington, D.C.*

Reenactment: The Civil War Union Army Garrison Day recreates military life each September. Evening tours of the site are offered on that day.

1247 The Lyceum (col)

201 South Washington Street; 703-838-4994; Mon–Sat 10–5, Sun 1–5. Free.

The museum of Alexandria history was a hospital during the Civil War. The Lyceum was established in 1839 as a cultural and science center.

1248 Stabler-Leadbeater Apothecary Museum and Shop (col)

105 South Fairfax Street; 703-836-3713; Mon–Sat 10–4, Sun 1–5. Admission charged.

A pantheon of America's greatest statesmen had their prescriptions filled here. Among the famous names in the account books is that of Robert E. Lee. In October 1859 United States Army colonel Lee was shopping in the drugstore when Lieutenant J. E. B. Stuart handed him an order to report to western Virginia and suppress John Brown's raid on the Federal arsenal in Harpers Ferry.

Amelia

1249 Confederate Memorial (site)

Amelia County Courthouse; Business Route 360.

After Grant broke through the defenses at Petersburg and captured Richmond, Lee's scattered army numbered only 30,000 men. He planned to follow the railroad to Danville, Virginia, and meet up with General Johnston's troops in North Carolina. By a narrow margin of only a few hours the Amelia Courthouse escaped both a final battle of the Civil War and surrender.

On April 4, 1865, Lee's harassed army arrived here on its retreat from Petersburg, failed to find expected provisions, and remained a day while foraging parties had frequent clashes with Federal cavalry and lost about 200 wagons. On the evening of the 5th, with Grant at Nottoway Courthouse blocking the route to Danville, Lee circled north, then west. From Nottoway, Grant sent the greater part of his army against Lee here only to find the town evacuated.

At Sailor's Creek that afternoon three Federal columns struck Lee's moving lines, captured 7,000 men, but failed to stop the retreat. The present building was built in 1924; the Confederate Memorial is a stalwart bronze soldier. A Coehorn mortar, captured near Flat Creek during the fighting, is displayed on the grounds.

Appomattox

1250 Battle of Appomattox Station (site)

Main and Church streets.

A marker identifies the station of the South Side Rail Road where, on April 8, 1865, three trains unloading supplies for the Army of Northern Virginia were captured by units of Sheridan's Union cavalry under General George Custer. This action marked the last strategic use of the railroads by Confederate forces. Lee surrendered the next day.

Appomattox Court House

1251 Appomattox Court House National Historical Park (site)

Route 24; 804-352-8987; Summer: 9–5:30; other times: 8:30–5. Free.

On April 7, 1865, Robert E. Lee clashed with Sheridan's cavalry near Appomattox Station and, faced with more of the same, sent a rider with a white towel between the lines with a message to Grant. On Sunday morning, April 9, Lee, somberly attired in a new uniform, waited for Grant in the parlor of the Wilmer McLean House. Ironically, McLean had moved to this remote spot after his farm had been overrun earlier in the war during the Second Battle of Manassas.

Grant and Lee had known each other slightly over the years; Lee had once reprimanded Grant for his unkempt appearance in Mexico. Now Grant arrived in dusty fatigue clothes, without side arms. He apologized for his dress, saying he was some miles from his headquarters and believed Lee would rather receive him as he was than be detained. After some casual conversation Lee requested terms for surrender. Grant wrote out his terms, discussed weeks earlier at City Point with Lincoln, and handed Lee a piece of paper: officers and men would be paroled, only public property was to be surrendered and officers were allowed to retain their sidearms and horses. Lee was pleased and asked if men could keep their horses to retill their farms. Grant agreed and ordered three days of rations sent to Lee's ragged troops. After the negotiations Union batteries began to fire salutes, but Grant ordered them stopped in deference to their countrymen. It was to be a surrender of honor.

After the surrender the country knew the name "Appomattox," but the town was far from prospering. The railroad passed to the south, and in 1892 the courthouse burned and the county seat moved to Appomattox. Appomattox Court House no longer even had that.

In the spring of 1893 the McLean House was dismantled with the intention of taking it to Washington, D.C., as a war museum. But the pile of bricks and lumber was never moved. The village that had riveted America's attention in 1865 was disintegrating. In 1930 the United States Congress passed a bill to build a monument on the site of the historic surrender 65 years earlier. The monument was never built, but in 1935 work began on restoring the dilapidated village. On April 6, 1954, it was designated a national historical park, and much of the village now looks as it did in April 1865. All the 27 structures and memorial tablets are easily reached on a self-guided walking tour.

Arlington

1252 Arlington National Cemetery (site)
Memorial Drive; 202-554-5100; Apr–Sept: 8–7; other times: 8–5. Free; fee for motorized tram tour.

The largest of the more than 100-plus national burial grounds, Arlington includes more than 400 landscaped acres and the graves of 225,000 war veterans. By the end of the Civil War, more than 16,000 graves were here. Arlington is the final resting spot for 81 Union generals, and a monument stands over the mass grave of 2,111 Union soldiers. Jackson Circle, near the rear of the cemetery, marks the graves of 250 Confederates.

The land for the cemetery was confiscated from Robert E. Lee after the war began. When the Marquis de Lafayette visited this 1,000-acre estate of George Washington Parke Custis, the step-grandson of George Washington, in 1824, he declared the view across the Potomac River the finest in the world. In 1831 it became the Lee family home. Although Robert E. Lee spent much of his married life traveling to various military posts, six of his seven children were born here. After Lee decided to accept the command of Virginia's forces, the family left, never to return.

The house subsequently became the headquarters for Union officers planning the defense of the capital. The estate was then used as a training camp, and the title passed to the Federal government in 1864 when the land was seized for nonpayment of taxes. In 1882 Custis Lee, the general's oldest son, successfully sued the United States for return of the property, but by now much of the hillside was covered with headstones. He accepted $150,000 for the property. Arlington House, restored to the way Lee left it, can be visited on a self-guided tour.

Among the Civil War monuments on the grounds are the Confederate Memorial and the Major John Rodgers Meigs Monument. Thirty-five years after the war ended, as a gesture of goodwill, Congress permitted a Confederate section in Arlington National Cemetery on McPherson Drive. The circular frieze located in the center of the shaft shows 32 life-size figures of Southern citizens sending soldiers off to war. Created by Moses Ezekiel, Virginian sculptor and soldier, it is crowned by a heroic female symbol of peace.

John Rodgers Meigs was a West Point graduate and engineer who quickly distinguished himself by his coolness under fire. He was awarded the ranks of brevet captain and brevet major within a three-week period — honorary promotions on the battlefield since there were no medals to bestow for valor. On October 3, 1864, when still only 22, Meigs was killed by Confederate guerrillas near Harrisonburg, Virginia.

The monument to honor his memory is a high relief tomb effigy, seven inches tall and 39 inches long. It shows Meigs as he was found in death on the field of battle. Theophilus Fisk Mills completed the memorial. Major General Montgomery Meigs, quartermaster of the Union army, is honored with a huge granite monument only feet away from that of his only son. It was his proposal that the property be used for a cemetery.

1253 Fort Myer Old Guard Museum (site)

Building 249; Sheridan Avenue; 703-696-6670. Free.

The only Civil War fortification still in use near Washington provides ceremonial units for Arlington. The entrance to the fort, established in 1863, is directly behind the cemetery. The museum is devoted to the traditions of the army's oldest regiment.

Bailey's Crossroads

1254 Lincoln's Review of Troops (site)

Route 7, 2½ miles west of I-395.

After the Union defeat at the First Battle of Manassas on July 21, 1861, Lincoln appointed Major General George B. McClellan as commander of the demoralized army. A superb organizer, McClellan rebuilt the army and on November 20, 1861, staged a formal military review here, with Lincoln and his entire cabinet in attendance. The army — 50,000 strong — spread over 200 acres; this was the largest review ever held in America up to that time. A historical marker commemorates the occasion.

Bedford

1255 Bedford City/County Museum (col)

201 East Main Street; 703-586-4520; Feb–Dec: Mon–Sat, 10–5; other times: 9–4. Admission charged.

The 1895 building houses exhibits on the area's local history, including Civil War artifacts.

1256 Confederate Memorial (mem)

Bedford County Courthouse; Main Street.

The red brick building now standing here was built in 1930 and is the third on this ground since 1782. The Confederate monument is an obelisk in the courthouse square, honoring the Bedford County Civil War volunteers. The county supplied 600 men, a large percentage of its population in the 1860s.

1257 Confederate Memorial (mem)

Longwood Cemetery; Bridge Street.

During the Civil War five Confederate hospitals were established around Bedford. Years after the war, the remains of soldiers who died of sickness and wounds were placed in a mass grave in the cemetery. A tall obelisk marks the burial site of 192 Southern soldiers and a Confederate nurse.

Berryville

1258 Crook and Early (site)

Route 7, eight miles east of town.

Confederate general Early, passing through this gap on his return from his Washington raid, was attacked here by General George Crook's cavalry on July 16, 1864. Crook, who after the war became one of the most formidable Indian fighters, earning the nickname "Gray Fox," destroyed a few wagons. Early captured a cannon. A marker recounts the action.

Brandy

1259 Battle of Brandy Station (site)

Route 29, one mile north of town.

One of America's greatest cavalry battles raged in these woods on June 9, 1863, between J. E. B. Stuart, who was screening Lee's advance toward Gettysburg, and Hooker's Union cavalry. Hooker surprised Stuart here, and the largest cavalry battle of the Civil War was unexpectedly underway. There were approximately 17,000 horsemen from both sides slashing through the woods and galloping across the fields. The Confederates managed to hold the field, but in any other respect the battle resulted in a Federal victory — the first major Union success of the war. Prior to the Civil War the Confederates had been much the better horsemen, and this engagement gave the Federals needed confidence for future engagements.

The battlefield is undeveloped and virtually unchanged from its 1863 appearance. Two historical markers stand on Fleetwood Hill, the center of the saddled action. Other roadside markers in the area relate to the great cavalry clash.

1260 Lee's Grand Review Site (site)

Route 342, Virginia State Police parking area.

General Lee reviewed his cavalry here on June 8, 1863. Ewell's corps broke camp two days later for the march to Pennsylvania.

Buena Vista

1261 Moomaw's Landing (site)

Route 60, west end of town.

Moomaw's Landing on the North River Canal was an important shipping route for the Confederacy. A historical marker indicates that the packet *Marshall* passed here bearing the body of General Thomas "Stonewall" Jackson to its final resting place in Lexington.

Burke Station

1262 Burke Station Raid (site)

Route 645 at Route 652.

A historical marker recounts the aftermath of a Confederate raid in December, 1862, led by Confederate general J. E. B. Stuart. From this site, originally the railroad depot, Stuart wired Washington to complain about the poor quality of the mules he had just captured.

Burkeville

1263 Davis Escape Route (site)

Route 360.

On April 3, 1865, Jefferson Davis and his cabinet passed through Burkeville as they fled from Richmond to Danville, and three days later Union troops, pursuing the retreating Confederates, camped here.

Burrowsville

1264 Coggins Point (site)

Route 10, eight miles northwest of town.

From this bluff on the James River, General D. H. Hill shelled McClellan's camp on the north side of the river on July 31, 1862.

Cape Charles

1265 Union Occupation (site)

Route 13 near Route 184.

The area was occupied by Federal forces early in the Civil War as a precaution against the Confederacy establishing a base from which to attack Washington. When the Federal troops landed here, the residents, thinking there was to be a battle, armed themselves with whatever weapons they could lay hands on, only to find that no fighting was contemplated. The false alarm has been called the Battle of Three Ponds. Though General H. H. Lockwood, who commanded the Federal forces, established friendly relations with the people, most men of the Eastern Shore who enlisted in the Civil War chose the Confederate side.

Carmel Church

1266 North Anna Battlefield (site)

Route 684, three miles south of town off Route 1.

Grant's troops took a small Confederate earthworks in the angle between Long Creek and the North Anna River on May 23, 1864. A historical marker notes the troop movements here. Lee's army was camped on the south side of river; another marker is half a mile south in Hanover County. Part of the battlefield and some of the Confederate earthworks have been preserved.

Cedar Mountain

1267 Cedar Mountain Battlefield (site)

Route 657.

On August 9, 1862, an exhausted Confederate army under General Stonewall Jackson stumbled onto Union cavalry and artillery blocking the road near Cedar Run. Confederate Brigadier General Jubal Early hastily assembled an artillery line and the gunneries spilled shells across both sides of the road.

Jackson led 22,000 men, and the Union, under Nathaniel Banks, could call on only 12,000 forces but the Federals were having the best of the fray until late in the day when Jackson rode into the center of the field defying fire on three sides. Brandishing his sword, rusted uselessly to its scabbard, and waving a battle flag, Jackson rallied his troops to victory as A. P. Hill arrived to reinforce the lines.

Two days later Jackson joined with Lee at the Second Manassas and would never again direct a campaign as an independent commander. Cedar Mountain would always remain to Jackson "the most successful of my exploits."

The battlefield has changed little but is completely in private hands and difficult to see. Area roadside markers indicate the lines of attack during the Battle of Cedar Mountain.

Chancellorsville

1268 Chancellorsville Battlefield Visitor Center (site)

Route 3, 12 miles west of Fredericksburg; 540-786-2880; Summer: 8:30–6; other times: 9–5. Free.

Chancellorsville was the last of a series of Federal failures in Virginia, after each of which Lincoln changed commanders. General Joseph Hooker, who had supplanted General Ambrose E. Burnside, was placed in command of 130,000 men north of Rappahannock River. General Lee had 57,000 Confederates on the south bank. Beginning an offensive on April 29, 1863, Hooker sent his cavalry raiding toward Richmond and placed a corps near Fredericksburg. Then, hurriedly moving the greater part of his army up the river, he crossed to the south side and entrenched here.

Lee was now opposed by two forces, either of which outnumbered his army. While retaining 14,000 men to oppose the Federal front, Lee sent Stonewall Jackson on a counterflank march. On

May 2, Jackson's corps surprised the Union rear and routed the main body. While riding across the front of his lines at dusk to bolster his tired and scattered troops, Jackson was shot down by Confederate bullets. He was removed to the Wilderness Tavern to have his left arm amputated. Lee sent word: "You have lost your left arm, I have lost my right." He died eight days later.

At dawn the next morning General Stuart attacked from the west and Lee from the east. The Union army, caught between these forces, fell back across the Rappahannock River. The Federals lost 17,000 men and the Rebels about 13,000. The Union forces did not cross the river again until Gettysburg had been fought. Lee had his finest victory.

The visitor center has a museum and a 12-minute videotape on the Battle of Chancellorsville. The self-guided battlefield tour includes a 12-mile recreation of Jackson's daring flank march. Among the sites are restored gun pits; the Catharine Furnace remains, where Confederate munitions were manufactured; remains of the critical Chancellorsville Tavern site, the site of Jackson's amputation; and the Lee-Jackson bivouac where the generals spent their last evening together plotting their bold flanking plan.

The Jackson Monument behind the visitor center marks the approximate spot where Stonewall Jackson was felled. Confederate veterans had originally marked the area with a large boulder in the 1880s. Information on visiting the site of Jackson's amputation, where his arm is buried in the Lacy family cemetery at Ellwood, can be obtained in the visitor center.

Chantilly

1269 Chantilly Battlefield (site)
Route 50 and West Ox Road.

Stonewall Jackson arrived here on September 1, 1862, and fought a spirited skirmish that left two promising Union generals dead—the able Philip Kearny and Isaac Stevens. The tiny Ox Hill Battlefield is surrounded by modern development; written information on the battle can be picked up at the Manassas National Battlefield Park.

Charles City

1270 Berkeley Plantation (site)
Route 5; 804-829-6018; Daily, 8–5. Admission charged.

This regal plantation is the birthplace of President William Henry Harrison and was selected by George McClellan as his headquarters in the summer of 1862. Union general Daniel Butterfield composed the bugle call that later became "Taps" while stationed here. The brick house dates to 1726.

1271 Charles City Courthouse (site)
Route 5.

A historical marker notes that Grant's army was stationed here in June 1864. A Confederate monument is across the way.

1272 Salem Church (site)
Route 5, six miles west of town.

The site of this church, no longer standing, four miles north, was used as a field hospital in June 1864, following the action at Nance's Shop, where Confederate general Hampton attacked a train of 800 wagons led by General D. M. Gregg. Gregg's cavalry was driven from the field, but the wagons escaped to the James River. The wounded soldiers were brought to the church here and some were buried in the churchyard.

Reenactment: A Civil War encampment is set up at Evelynton Plantation (800-473-5075) in August.

Charlottesville

1273 Confederate Monument (mem)
University Cemetery; Alderman and McCormick roads.

The bronze statue of a bareheaded sentry pays tribute to the remains of 1,200 Confederate soldiers, most of whom perished from disease.

1274 Stonewall Jackson on Little Sorrel (mem)
Northeast corner of Jefferson and East 4th streets.

This exceptionally vigorous figure of Stonewall Jackson charging forward on Little Sorrel, bending forward in the saddle, chin thrust forward, is the vision of Charles Keck. Unveiled in 1921, the statue is regarded as one of the most impressive equestrian statues in America.

1275 Lee Monument (mem)
Lee Park; Jefferson Street between 1st and East 2nd streets.

Begun by H. M. Schrady and finished after his death by Leo Lentilli, this equestrian statue of the Confederate commander was dedicated in 1924. The figure with Traveller convincingly portrays Lee's calm and serenity and patient wisdom.

1276 University of Virginia (col)
Alderman Library; Route 29 and Route 250 business routes.

One of the great Civil War repositories, the university owns nearly 2,000 different collections about the war in Virginia.

Claudville

1277 Stuart's Birthplace (site)

Route 773, ½ mile from North Carolina border.

James Ewell Brown Stuart, who became major general commanding the cavalry of the Army of Northern Virginia, was born near here on February 6, 1833. The site of the house and several buildings have been relocated at the roadside marker; a self-guided walking tour is available.

Clover

1278 Staunton River Battlefield State Park (site)

Route 600, north of town; 804-454-4312.

On June 25, 1864, a marauding Union cavalry corps attempted to burn the high railroad bridge over the Staunton River and sever the railroad line between Danville and Richmond. For a defense the Southerners could muster only a small Confederate force, bolstered by 500 "Old Men and Young Boys." Still, the Federals were repulsed in fierce fighting.

The remnants of earthworks, rifle pits, and a planked railroad bridge remain along the river. The visitor center of the 87-acre park includes exhibits on the battle and home life in Southside, Virginia, during the Civil War.

Colonial Heights

1279 Fort Clifton (site)

White Bank Park.

Fort Clifton was constructed during the winter of 1863-1864 on a high elevation near the junction of the Appomattox River and Swift Creek. The fort controlled navigation on the river north of Petersburg and proved impregnable during the Civil War. The most serious attempt to breach its defenses took place on May 9, 1864, in the Battle of Swift Creek, when a coordinated naval and land assault of 20,000 Federals was repulsed by 4,200 Confederates under Brigadier General Bushrod Johnson.

1280 Violet Bank Museum (site)

303 Virginia Avenue; 804-520-9395; Tues–Sun 10–5, Sun 1–6. Free.

Lee made his headquarters here from June 17 to November 11, 1864, pitching his tent beneath the famous cucumber tree, the second largest of its kind in the world. Here he learned about the daring Union attack in Petersburg at "The Crater." The museum interprets the period from 1815 to 1873 and includes Civil War relics.

Columbia

1281 Lee's Stopping Place (site)

Route 690 at Route 612, nine miles south of town.

After surrendering his Army of Northern Virginia, Lee stopped at Flannagan's (Trice's) Mill and there spent the night of April 13-14, 1865, on his journey to Richmond. A historical marker indicates the location.

Comorn

1282 Cleydael (site)

Route 206, west of Route 218.

This T-shaped house was built as a summer home in 1859 for Dr. Richard H. Stuart. It was here that John Wilkes Booth and three companions came at dusk on April 22, 1865, to beg food and medical aid. The doctor, becoming suspicious, declined to admit them to the house but gave them permission to rest at the barn. The following morning Booth sent the doctor a note, contemptuously thanking him for "what we did get" and enclosing $5. Dr. Stuart threw the note into the fire, but his son-in-law recovered it. Later the doctor was imprisoned for complicity in the assassination, but the note exonerated him.

Criglersville

1283 Jackson's Camp (site)

Route 670, one mile north of town.

Just to the north of this historical marker, on the night of November 25, 1862, Stonewall Jackson camped with his corps. He was on his way to join Lee at Fredericksburg.

Cross Keys

1284 Battle of Cross Keys (site)

Keezletown Road (Route 276).

Major General Richard Stoddert Ewell engaged a larger Union force under General John Fremont here, seven miles southeast of Harrisonburg, to prevent Fremont from hooking up with James Shields at Port Republic to the east. Ewell took the strategic position on the road leading to Port Republic and inflicted heavy losses on the Union during one hour of fighting.

The battlefield has remained virtually untouched since the action here on June 8, 1862. A circle tour map shows the location of the main action, and a bronze memorial describes the conflict. A small cemetery, where snipers took cover behind tombstones, is across from Ruritan Hall.

Culpeper

1285 Confederate Monument (mem)

Fairview Cemetery; Route 522, west of Main Street.

The monument marks a mass grave of unknown Confederate soldiers. The national cemetery in town contains the graves of Union soldiers who died, mostly of illness, during the Civil War.

1286 4th Virginia Cavalry Regiment Monument (mem)

Little Fork Episcopal Church; Route 229, six miles south of Route 211.

The Episcopal Church was built in 1776, and the 4th Virginia Cavalry Regiment organized and drilled here. A unique stone monument to this company has been erected behind the church.

1287 The Museum of Culpeper History (col)

140 East Davis Street; 540-825-1973; Mon–Sat, 11–5. Free.

Appropriately, one of the items in the collection is a Civil War surgeon's kit — most of Culpeper's buildings were pressed into service as hospitals during the several large battles fought in the area.

Danville

1288 Civil War Prison No. 6 (site)

300 Lynn Street.

Danville was an important prison town for the Confederacy, holding as many as 7,000 Union prisoners. This is the only one of the town's prison buildings still standing.

1289 Danville Museum of Fine Arts and History (site)

Sutherlin Mansion; 975 Main Street; 804-793-5644; Tues–Fri 10–5, Sat–Sun 2–5. Free.

This Italian Villa mansion was home to Major William Sutherlin, wartime quartermaster of Danville. For one week, April 3–10, 1865, Jefferson Davis and the remnants of the Confederate government stayed here. Davis, whose upstairs bedroom is restored to its appearance during his visit, met with his cabinet for the final time on April 4. News of Lee's surrender arrived here on April 10, ending the government and sending Davis in flight to Greensboro, North Carolina. Due to these events, Danville has become known as the "Last Capital of the Confederacy." The museum contains Civil War artifacts.

1290 United States National Cemetery (site)

721 Lee Street.

Tobacco warehouses were converted into six Civil War prisons in Danville, where more than 1,000 officers and enlisted men died of smallpox and dysentery. The national cemetery was created in 1867 as a resting place for these soldiers.

Dayton

1291 Shenandoah Valley Folk Art and Heritage Museum (col)

Bowman Road and High Street; 540-879-2681; Jan 16–Dec 14: Wed–Sat 10–4, Sun 1–5. Free.

The red brick museum offers artifacts of Civil War action in the Shenandoah Valley, highlighted by a celebrated electric map providing a strategic view of Stonewall Jackson's Valley Campaign of 1862. The map was developed in 1962 on the centennial of the event.

1292 World War I Cannon (mem)

Corner of Mill and Main streets.

This German cannon was the largest field piece brought back from Europe by the United States government after World War I; it was restored in 1990 as a memorial to area veterans of all wars. On the memorial is a rarity — one of the few markers in the South dedicated to a Union Army officer, Lieutenant Colonel Thomas R. Wildes of the 116th Ohio. Seeking revenge for the death of one of his engineers by a Confederate sniper, General Sheridan ordered the burning of all buildings within five miles of Dayton. George Armstrong Custer assumed the task with relish, but Sheridan changed his mind after Wildes sent a messenger pleading the cause of the citizens. The town was spared.

Dinwiddie

1293 Confederate Monument (mem)

Dinwiddie Courthouse; Route 1.

A tall granite monument dwarfs the brick building, scene of an engagement on March 29, 1865, when Sheridan arrived here while Warren was attacking Anderson about three miles north. Two days later Sheridan moved south but was checked by Pickett and driven back to the courthouse.

Dranesville

1294 Battle of Dranesville (site)

Route 7.

Near here two foraging expeditions came in conflict on December 20, 1861. The Union force commanded by General Ord forced Stuart's cavalry to retire. The next day Stuart returned, reinforced, to carry off his wounded. Later in the war, the fords near Dranesville would be used for Confederate armies marching north. Historic markers are on the sites.

Dublin

1295 Battle of Cloyd's Mountain (site)
Route 100, five miles north of town.

In April 1864 Grant ordered Brigadier General George Crook to cut the Virginia and Tennessee Railroad in southwestern Virginia. Near Cloyd's Mountain on May 9, Crook battled Confederate defenders commanded by Brigadier General Albert G. Jenkins. Crook drove Jenkins from his earthen fortifications as losses were frightful. Jenkins was mortally wounded and 538 of his 2,400-man force were lost. Crook severed the railroad and withdrew on May 11. A marker here describes the battle.

Edinburg

1296 The Edinburg Museum (site)
703-984-8521. Free.

The town was known as the "Granary of the Confederacy." Confederate general Turner Ashby made the town a base of operations in 1862 for some 28 raids in one month. Consequently Union general Sheridan vowed to leave it "so desolate that a crow flying over would need a knapsack." He set the mills on fire but, persuaded by two young women that the people of the community depended on the mills for food, had the flames extinguished. The museum of the small town contains Civil War curiosities.

Elkwood

1297 Battle of Kelly's Ford (site)
Route 620, just past Route 674 at the bridge.

Opposing cavalry forces fought a running battle along the Rappahannock River here through tangled underbrush. It was the first fight of any appreciable size east of the Mississippi River that was fought purely with soldiers on horseback. The Union cavalry had been organized into a separate unit only weeks before.

The tone for the engagement had been established during months of inaction in late 1862 and early 1863 as both sides settled into winter camps. West Point classmates and friends, Brigadier General Fitzhugh Lee of the Confederates and Union brigadier general William Averell continuously exchanged letters during the lull, mostly on the same theme — Lee taunting Averell about the inferiority of the Union cavalry. In late February after a brief raid, Lee left a particularly challenging message: "I wish you would put up your sword, leave my state, and go home. You ride a good horse, I ride a better. If you won't go home, return my visit, and bring me a sack of coffee."

Averell met the challenge on March 17. With 3,000 cavalrymen and a battery of six cannon the Union attacked at the crossing of the Rappahannock. After spirited fighting the Federals withdrew, inflicting 146 casualties while suffering only 85. Although he might have pressed more aggressively for a victory, Averell decided it more prudent to withdraw, but only after leaving behind two wounded Confederate officers, a sack of coffee, and a message: "Dear Fitz, Here's your coffee. Here's your visit. How do you like it?"

The fighting began at Kelly's Ford, 300 yards downstream from the modern bridge. Pathways and roadside stops along Route 674 provide access to the battlefield sites. One trail leads to a marker near the spot where a shell exploded near Major John Pelham, sending a sliver of metal into the back of his head.

1298 Pelham Memorial (mem)
Route 15-29 and County Road 685.

A weathered marble shaft honors Confederate major John Pelham, the 24-year-old chief of Stuart's horse artillery, who was mortally wounded at Kelly's Ford. Pelham had been praised three months earlier by Lee at Fredericksburg as "the gallant Pelham." At that time he employed flying artillery tactics to hold off a Federal force for two hours with only one cannon. Observing from a nearby hilltop, Lee exclaimed, "It is glorious to see such courage in one so young!" Pelham was shot during a cavalry charge and died soon afterward. The 1926 monument is in the yard of a private home.

Fairfax

1299 Confederate Cemetery Monument (mem)
Route 236.

Once a Union stockade during the Civil War, the site is now a Confederate graveyard. Large markers indicate the burial plots of unknown Confederate dead.

1300 Fairfax Museum and Visitor Center (col)
10209 Main Street; 800-545-7950; Daily, 9–5. Free.

In addition to recounting the rich Civil War heritage in Fairfax, the museum features the Colonel John S. Mosby Collection and the James E. B. Stuart Collection.

1301 Ford Building (site)
3977 Chain Bridge Road.

Antonia Ford, a beguiling beauty with a knack for remembering conversations, lived in this building, which currently houses offices. Confederate cavalry leader J. E. B. Stuart awarded Miss Ford a written commission as "my honorary aide-de-camp" in recognition of her recollection of Union secrets. Arrested as a spy when the document was found, Antonia was escorted to a Washington prison by Union major Joseph C. Willard, who fell in love with her. He worked to secure her release seven months later, and they were married.

1302 Dr. William Gunnell House (site)

10520 Main Street.

On the night of March 9, 1863, Union brigadier general Edwin H. Stoughton was rudely awakened by a slap. "Get up, general, and come with me," said the intruder. "What is this? Do you know who I am?" demanded Stoughton. "I reckon I do, general. Did you ever hear of Mosby?" "Yes, have you caught him?" "No, but he has caught you."

Ranger John Singleton Mosby also captured 32 other Union soldiers and 58 horses. Upon hearing of the raid, Lincoln disgustedly observed that he could create another general with the stroke of a pen, but he surely did hate to lose those horses. One officer Lincoln did not have to replace was Colonel Johnstone; he escaped capture by hiding beneath an outhouse, wearing only his nightshirt. Dr. Gunnell's house, built in 1835, is now a private residence; a monument to the raid stands in front.

1303 Marr Monument (site)

Fairfax Courthouse; 4000 Chain Bridge Road.

The monument in front of the courthouse honors John Quincy Marr, the first Confederate officer to die in battle in the Civil War. Marr commanded the Warrenton Rifles during a Union cavalry attack at 3 A.M. on June 1, 1861. His body was found in a clover field 800 feet southwest of the courthouse when dawn broke. Marr was killed by the impact of a minié ball in the chest — without spilling blood. The cannons at the site face north, as do all Confederate cannon monuments. Mathew Brady made this a widely recognized site by using it in many photographic studies. The building was a Union headquarters during the war.

Falmouth

1304 Confederate Cavalry Raids (site)

Route 17, eight miles northwest of town.

Near this historical marker Wade Hampton surprised and captured five officers and 87 men of the Third Pennsylvania Cavalry on November 28, 1862. Three months later Fitz Lee raided a Union camp here.

1305 Chatham (site)

120 Chatham Lane; 540-373-4461; Daily, 9–5. Free.

This eighteenth-century Georgian mansion became a front-line headquarters for various Union generals. Two pontoon bridges spanned the Rappahannock River beneath the estate north of Fredericksburg. Once more than 1,000 acres, only 30 remained after the Civil War. Clara Barton and Walt Whitman worked in a field hospital here.

1306 Mud March (site)

Route 17, four miles northwest of town.

At the site of this marker, on January 20–21, 1863, Burnside sought to drive on Lee at Fredericksburg. A storm created a quagmire, and Burnside's movement was abandoned in the mud.

1307 Sheridan's Raid (site)

Route 1, five miles south of town.

This historical marker identifies the spot where Sheridan, moving from winter camp, came into the Telegraph Road on his raid to Richmond, May 9, 1864, while Lee and Grant were fighting at Spotsylvania. The 10,000 Union cavalry filled the road as far as the eye could see.

Farmville

1308 Historical District (site)

Main Street, Route 45.

Grant sent Lee his first note inquiring about surrender from this town, east of Appomattox. When the note was received three miles north at Cumberland Church — still standing — Confederate general James Longstreet replied simply, "Not yet." This site was part of Lee's retreat tour; there is a short walking trail through the town where Grant camped.

1309 Sailor's Creek Historical Battlefield (site)

Sailor's Creek Road (Route 617), nine miles east of town; 804-392-3435.

On April 6, 1865, Sheridan encircled the rear third of Lee's retreating forces, and after an afternoon of fierce fighting captured 7,000 Confederate troops, including many generals and colonels. Most were artillerymen, sailors, and army clerks forced to fight as infantrymen during the march. The Federals captured more men here than were captured in any other one-day field engagement of the war. As scattered parts of his army caught up with the main column of Lee's force, the general exclaimed, "My God! Has the army dissolved?" Sailor's Creek was the last major battle of the Civil War in Virginia.

Portions of the more than 200 acres of the battlefield have been set aside as a state historical park. An interpretive driving tour covers many sites, including the Hillsman House, on Route 617, which was used as a hospital.

Fort Eustis

1310 U.S. Army Transportation Museum (col)

Besson Hall; Mulberry Island, northwest of Newport News; 804-878-1182; Daily, 9–4:30. Free.

Several Civil War exhibits are included in the museum at Fort Eustis, a star-shaped earthwork fortification that anchored the right flank of the Confederate main defense line across the Virginia Peninsula. Fort Crafford is located on a remote part of the site. The earthworks and gun emplacements are well preserved.

Fort Lee

1311 Quartermaster Museum (col)

Fort Lee, two miles east of Petersburg; 804-734-4203; Tues–Fri 10–5, Sat–Sun 11–5. Free.

Civil War memorabilia are included among the military uniforms, flags, transport, and food service exhibits. Fort Lee was founded in 1775, two days after the United States Army.

Fredericksburg

1312 Fredericksburg and Spotsylvania National Military Park (site)

1013 Lafayette Boulevard; 540-373-6122; Summer: daily, 8:30–6:30; Apr–May and Sept–Oct: Mon–Fri 9–5, Sat–Sun 9–6; other times: daily, 9–5. Free.

On December 13, 1862, the Federals stormed Lee's entrenchments in their first attempt to control this city between Washington and Richmond. The Union was turned away in such gruesome fighting that Lee was moved to remark, "It is well that war is so terrible; else we should grow too fond of it." The slaughter of Ambrose Burnside's troops was Lee's most one-sided victory.

By May of 1863, this area had seen the most intense fighting ever staged on the North American continent. The Federals were finally able to drive the Confederates from their trenches on Marye's Heights on May 3, after Lee left only a token defensive force while he took to the offensive.

Four battlefields are administered by the National Park Service in this area: Fredericksburg, The Wilderness, Spotsylvania Court House, and Chan-

cellorsville. The complete site covers 77,000 acres and includes 16 individual interpretive stops and three buildings. The casualties in the area exceeded 100,000.

At the Fredericksburg visitor center a walking tour leads three blocks down the Sunken Road, which proved to be the most impregnable Confederate defensive position of the war. Part of the original wall remains. Martha Stevens, who remained in her house on the battlefield treating the wounded, is buried in her yard along the road. Another walking tour tracing the assault on Marye's Heights begins in the town at the visitor center.

A driving tour along Lee Drive further emphasizes the strength of the Confederate defensive position. The Southern Memorial Pyramid, 30 feet square and 23 feet high, was built in 1903 by railroad men who piled Virginia granite along the railroad where train passengers could view it.

1313 Fredericksburg Area Museum and Cultural Center (col)

Old Town Hall and Market House; 905 Princess Anne Street; 540-371-3037; Mar–Nov: Mon–Sat 9–5, Sun 1–5; Dec–Feb: Mon–Sat 9–4, Sun 1–4. Admission charged.

The Hall was used as a barracks and a hospital during the Civil War and now features six permanent interpretive history galleries on Fredericksburg, including one on the Civil War and Reconstruction.

1314 Fredericksburg Confederate Cemetery (site)

Washington Avenue and William Street.

Established in 1867, the graveyard contains the remains of more than 3,300 Southern soldiers, 2,184 of whom are unidentified. Although the cemetery is relatively small, six Confederate generals are buried here: Seth M. Barton, Dabney H. Maury, Abner M. Perrin, Daniel Ruggles, Henry H. Sibley, and Stevenson. A monument of a Confederate soldier was erected in 1884.

1315 Fredericksburg National Cemetery (site)

Sunken Road and Lafayette Boulevard.

Of the 15,243 soldiers interred in the trenches on this hillside, only 2,473 are in identified graves. Most are privates, as the higher ranking officers were often transported home by family members. A battle painting and a two-minute audio program recreate the battle scene on December 13, 1862. The national cemetery was authorized in July 1865.

1316 Richard Kirkland Monument (mem)

Sunken Road.

Along the Sunken Road Wall, Richard Kirkland is honored for his heroic efforts on behalf of fallen Union soldiers during the fighting west of Fredericksburg. On December 13, 1862, as the slaughter of Federal troops continued unabated, the 19-year-old Confederate soldier could tolerate it no longer. He scaled the stone wall to bring relief to his suffering enemies at considerable peril to his own life. Realizing what was happening, the Union riflemen ceased firing for an hour while Kirkland moved from soldier to soldier. The monument was crafted by Felix DeWardon, who also produced the World War II Iwo Jima memorial.

Reenactment: On the anniversary of the battle a ceremony takes place at the memorial. Other events in town mark the fighting in Fredericksburg.

1317 Sergeant Kirkland's Museum and Historical Society (col)

912 Lafayette Boulevard; 540-899-5565; Daily, 10–5. Free.

Located near the site where Richard Kirkland gave relief to many wounded Union soldiers during the Battle of Fredericksburg, the museum emphasizes Civil War history.

1318 Old Salem Church (site)

Orange Turnpike, Route 3, three miles west of town.

On May 3, 1864, after leaving Fredericksburg, Lee defeated the Federals at this 1844 Baptist church, which had been a hospital during the Chancellorsville campaign.

Front Royal

1319 Belle Boyd Cottage (site)

101 Chester Street; 703-636-1446; Apr–Oct: Mon–Fri 11–4, weekends by appointment. Admission charged.

Front Royal was once known as "Hell Town" for the unsavory characters who gathered here. The temptress Boyd Belle invited Union general Nathaniel Banks and his officers to a ball here, then sneaked away on horseback to tell Stonewall Jackson of the loose-lipped Federals' plans. The next morning Jackson captured 750 of Banks's 1,000 men. Boyd, born in Martinsburg, West Virginia, in 1843, was arrested twice and released twice. She escaped to England in 1863, where she became a stage performer. She eventually married a Union officer and died in Kilbourne, Wisconsin, in 1900. The house museum depicts the Civil War era.

1320 Confederate Monument (mem)

Warren County Courthouse; Main Street and South Royal Avenue.

On May 23, 1862, Jackson surprised the Federal garrison in Front Royal. No traces of the battle remain, but a stone Confederate monument stands on the lawn to the right of the courthouse.

1321 Execution of Mosby's Men (site)

Route 340, ½ mile north of town.

Near this marker several of Mosby's guerrillas were executed by order of General Custer on September 23, 1864. Later, on November 6, Colonel Mosby, in retaliation, ordered the execution of an equal number of Custer's men near Berryville.

1322 Mosby Monument (mem)

Prospect Hill Cemetery.

This stone monument, flanked by two cannon, honors the seven members of Mosby's Rangers who were illegally executed as spies by the Federals in 1864 in Front Royal. *The Soldiers' Circle Monument* stands over the graves of 276 Confederates.

1323 Warren Rifles Confederate Museum (col)

95 Chester Street; 703-636-6982; Apr–Oct, Mon–Sat 9–5, Sun 12–5. Admission charged.

Memorabilia of such Confederate heroes as Boyd, Lee, Jackson, and Early are on display. The artifacts of Confederate ranger John S. Mosby are particularly interesting.

Gainesville

1324 Thoroughfare Gap (site)

Route 55.

Through this pass in the Bull Run Mountains came Joseph E. Johnston and Thomas Jackson on their way to the First Battle of Manassas on July 19, 1861. By the time Lee sent Jackson through the pass to achieve a smashing victory at the Second Manassas a year later, he was known as "Stonewall."

Glendale

1325 Battle of Glendale (site)

Route 156.

During the Seven Days' Battles, on June 30, 1862, Lee lost a chance to destroy McClellan's army, leaving the Confederate commander bitterly disappointed, despite the fact that he had saved the capitol in Richmond. Markers interpret the battle; a national cemetery is here.

Gloucester

1326 Abingdon Church (site)

Route 17, six miles south of town.

The parish was established in the 1650s; the church was used as a stable during the Civil War. The Federal government later paid to repair some of the damage to the building.

1327 Gloucester Courthouse (site)
Route 17.

The 1766 courthouse was the site of a cavalry skirmish on January 29, 1864. The nearby debtor's prison has been converted to a tourist information center where lists of all known Confederate graves in area cemeteries can be obtained.

Gloucester Point

1328 Confederate Earthworks (site)
Route 17.

The first fort here was built in 1667. The point was fortified by the Confederates in 1861 and occupied by Union troops in 1862. Some remaining earthworks are visible opposite Tyndall's Point Bridge.

Goochland

1329 Goochland Courthouse (site)
Route 6.

Union raiders stormed the town on March 11, 1865, liberating prisoners from the county jail down the street and torching the building. The courthouse was spared.

1330 Pleasants Monument (mem)
County Roads 641 and 670.

A stone marker pays tribute to James Pleasants, a Confederate hero in Goochland County who, it is said, once captured 13 Union soldiers and killed another.

Gordonsville

1331 Exchange Hotel Museum (site)
Route 33; 703-832-2944; Mar–Dec: Tues–Sat 12–4, Sun 12:30–4:30. Admission charged.

This original railroad hotel was a hospital during the war, known as the Gordonsville Receiving Hospital. More than 6,000 men were cared for here in one month after the Battle of the Wilderness in 1864. The restored building now houses an outstanding Civil War exhibit.

1332 Maplewood Cemetery (site)
Route 33.

In the back of the graveyard is a grassy plot, set amid the trees, where about 700 Confederate soldiers are buried, having died in Gordonsville during the war. A bronze marker is here in lieu of individual gravestones.

1333 Presbyterian Church (site)
Route 33.

The church looks much as it did during the Civil War, when esteemed Confederate minister Daniel B. Ewing was pastor. A historical marker indicates that Stonewall Jackson, an extraordinarily pious man, visited the town 18 times during the Civil War and worshiped here.

Guinea Station

1334 Stonewall Jackson Shrine (mem)
County Road 606; Summer: daily, 9–5; Apr–May and Sept–Oct: Fri–Tues, 9–5; other times: Sat–Mon, 9–5. Free.

On May 2, 1863, General Thomas "Stonewall" Jackson was wounded by his own men while surveying his position on the field at Chancellorsville. After having his left arm amputated he endured a 27-mile ambulance ride to T. C. Chandler's Fairfield Plantation at Guinea Station, well behind Confederate lines.

In a small, one-story, white clapboard office, the general died on May 10, 1863. The room, in which he died with the words "Let us cross over the river and rest under the shade of the trees," is maintained as it was that day.

Hampton

1335 Fort Monroe (site)
804-727-3391; Daily, 10:30–4:30. Free.

The fort, begun in 1819 and named for James Monroe, took 15 years to build. Robert E. Lee assisted in the construction. Known as "The Gibraltar of Chesapeake Bay," Fort Monroe was one of the few United States forts not to fall into Confederate hands at the start of the Civil War.

Wrongly accused in the assassination plot against Abraham Lincoln, Jefferson Davis was imprisoned here after his capture, first in a casement (a chamber in the wall of the fort) and then in Carroll Hall when his health failed. Davis stayed until his parole in 1867.

Fort Monroe was the largest stone fort ever built in the United States. The seven-point fort, surrounded by a water moat, can be viewed on a self-guided tour. The Casement Museum includes Davis's cell, models of the ironclads *Monitor* and *Merrimac*, and other Civil War artifacts pertaining to the defense of the Virginia coast. Its sister fort, Fort Wool, is an island fortress open to boaters.

Harrisonburg

1336 Turner Ashby Monument (mem)

Port Republic Road (Route 659), one mile east of I-81.

Brigadier General Turner Ashby, the Confederate cavalry commander in the Shenandoah Valley, led the fight to an easy victory here on June 6, 1862. Sensing the outcome, Union general John Fremont reinforced his command with the "Pennsylvania Bucktails," a regiment known for its sharpshooting skills. As the Bucktails penetrated the rear guard of the Confederates, Ashby charged to the front of the line only to have his horse shot out from under him. He continued on foot until a bullet tore through his chest. Rallied by his death, the Confederate troops subdued the Bucktails and captured commander Colonel Thomas Kane.

The monument atop a hill on the undeveloped battlefield reads: "General Turner Ashby, C.S.A., was killed on this spot, June 6, 1862, gallantly leading a charge." A battle map and historical markers are also at the site.

1337 Confederate Monument (mem)

Woodbine Cemetery; 150 Ott Street.

The obelisk stands in honor of the soldiers of the Confederate States of America. Memorials stand on the graves of Civil War soldiers from Rockingham County.

High Bridge

1338 High Bridge (site)

Route 619 at Route 688.

One mile north of this historical marker stood the Southside Railroad Bridge, spanning the 75-foot-wide Appomattox River. On April 6, 1865, 900 Union soldiers attempted to burn the 2,500 foot-long, 126-foot high structure and were captured by Confederate cavalry. Crossing on April 7, retreating Confederates burned four spans but failed to destroy the lower wagon bridge, thus allowing Union soldiers to continue their pursuit of Lee's army.

Hopewell

1339 City Point National Cemetery (site)

Terminus of Memorial Avenue.

The national cemetery was established in 1868; the *Monument to Union Dead* pays tribute to over 6,000 Union soldiers. Included are more than 1,000 graves of black soldiers as well as those of 100 Confederates.

1340 City Point Unit (site)

Cedar Lane; 804-458-9504; Daily, 8:30–4:30. Free.

Placed in charge of all Union armies on March 9, 1864, General Ulysses S. Grant chose to make his headquarters in the field with the Army of the Potomac rather than in Washington. After failing to destroy Lee's army north of Richmond and abandoning the drive for Petersburg after four days of bloody fighting, he settled into siege warfare with his base here. He selected the estate of the Eppes family, Appomattox Manor, for his camp. He erected tents and later timber-and-mortar cabins on the front lawn of the plantation, established in 1635. By the Civil War the plantation covered 2,300 acres on the Appomattox and James rivers.

President Abraham Lincoln visited Grant twice at City Point. It was during his second visit, aboard the president's ship, *River Queen*, on March 28, 1865, while conferring with Grant, William Sherman, and Admiral David Porter, that Abraham Lincoln set the tone for the country's healing when he ordered, "Let them surrender and go home, they will not take up arms again. Let them all go, officers and all, let them have their horses to plow with, and, if you like, their guns to shoot crows with. Treat them liberally. ... I say, give them the most liberal and honorable terms." Both Petersburg and Richmond fell during his two-week stay, and Lincoln visited both cities before returning to Washington on April 8. He lived only six more days.

City Point tells how the Civil War was waged. Rivers and railroads were necessary to supply troops in the field. The exhibits and a model of the old town demonstrate the logistics of outfitting an army. A short slide program is also offered. Appomattox Manor is partially restored and features period furnishings of the Eppes family.

Nothing remains of the bustling wooden wharves that pumped life into the Union army. A short walking tour includes General Grant's wooden cabin, earthworks, and the spot on the James River where a Union powder barge was blown up by a Confederate saboteur, killing 42 men.

1341 John Randolph Hospital (site)

Route 10.

On this site were seven hospitals during the siege of Petersburg, covering 200 acres. The compound of log barracks and 1,200 tents ministered to as many as 10,000 patients at times. Each patient had his own bed and washbasin, regularly received fresh pillows and linen, and had an abundance of fresh water pumped up from the Appomattox River. This made the Depot Field Hospital not only the largest facility of its kind in America but also the finest.

1342 Union Fort (site)

Appomattox Street.

A historical marker indicates the site of one of several forts built during the Civil War to protect the supply depot. The Federals conducting the siege of Petersburg, the longest of the war, needed to be supplied, and overnight the tiny village of City Point became one of the busiest ports in the world as hundreds of ships brought food, clothing, ammunition, and other goods to the Union army. An astounding 1,500 tons of supplies were unloaded at the half-mile wharf every day, and more than 275 boxcars arrived daily. On an average day during the siege, the Union army had thirty days of food and twenty days of forage stored in City Point—9,000,000 meals of food and 12,000 tons of hay and oats.

1343 Weston Manor (site)

Weston Lane and 21st Avenue; 804-458-4682; Apr–Oct: Mon–Fri 9–5, Sun 1–5. Admission charged.

General Philip Sheridan used this plantation house, which has been restored, as his headquarters. Furnishings include Sheridan's signature windowpane.

Jarratt

1344 Jarratt's Station (site)

Route 139.

A marker here commemorates the Civil War when the village was little more than a stop on the Petersburg Railroad. On May 8, 1864, Union brigadier general August V. Kautz burned the town as part of his campaign to stem the flow of supplies to Lee at Richmond.

Jetersville

1345 Union-Confederate Skirmish (site)

Route 360.

The Union forces chasing Lee on his final retreat on April 5, 1865, were entrenched in this railroad town. Remains of the trenches are inaccessible; the site is interpreted by markers.

Kenilworth

1346 Battle of Stephenson's Depot (site)

Route 11 at Route 664.

Jackson camped at this gray stone house, the home of Quaker William Stephenson, after the Battle of Winchester on May 25, 1862. On June 15, 1863, General R. S. Ewell, commanding a corps of Lee's army, captured wagons, cannon, and more than 2,300 of General R. H. Milroy's force, which was retreating from Winchester. The Confederate victory cleared the Shenandoah Valley of Union troops and allowed Lee to formulate his plan for invading Union territory and thus, if successful, induce England to aid in the conflict.

1347 Fort Collier (site)

Route 11 at Route 764.

A marker identifies the site of the fort that was thrown up around the home of Isaac Stine in 1861 by General Joseph E. Johnston, then Confederate commander in the valley. From here a semicircle of defenses went up around Winchester.

King and Queen Court House

1348 Dahlgren's Raid (site)

Route 631, 2½ miles northwest of town.

Young colonel Ulric Dahlgren, a Federal cavalry officer, was mortally wounded in a skirmish with a home guard unit, which had gathered during the night on March 2, 1864. In February 1864 Dahlgren and H. J. Kirkpatrick had attempted to enter Richmond to release Federal prisoners. Frustrated and separated from most of his command, Dahlgren, with 165 officers and men, made his way to this vicinity, pillaging and destroying property. Dahlgren died 300 yards north of this marker.

Lacey Springs

1349 Night Attack at Lacey Springs (site)

Blue Stone Inn Restaurant; Route 11.

In December 1864 Major General George Armstrong Custer was moving along the Valley Pike in the Shenandoah Valley to distract Jubal Early's men encamped for the winter in Staunton. On the night of December 21 Custer gave orders for a 4:00 A.M. reveille to prepare for a 6:00 A.M. departure. It proved to be an order of good fortune.

During the night, traveling in rain and snow, Confederates under Brigadier General Thomas Lafayette Rosser had moved into position for what they assumed would be a surprise attack and easy victory. Already awake, however, the Union easily repulsed the invasion and suffered only two casualties while the Confederates suffered more than 50 killed.

The incident was not without drama. When the first shots were fired, Custer was still in bed. Fearing capture if he left his quarters, he slipped into a Confederate general's dress coat and jumped on a horse to slip by the enemy and begin directing the battle. The dress coat had been taken at the Battle of Tom's Brook from his old West Point roommate, Thomas Rosser.

The battle map of Lacey Springs is in the parking lot of the restaurant.

Leesburg

1350 Battle of Ball's Bluff (site)
Small dirt road off Route 15 Bypass.

On October 21, 1861, a Union force of 1,000 crossed the Potomac River here and met one of the North's first disasters of the Civil War. Oregon senator Edward Baker, a close friend of Abraham Lincoln, led his command foolishly under the bluffs controlled by the Confederates. Rifle fire from above killed Baker and half his force, many of whom were trapped between rifle fire and unscalable cliffs. Others drowned and their bodies floated down the river to Washington.

Reenactment: The smallest United States national cemetery and stone markers remain in this quiet field. The calamity is reexamined in August at the nearby Oatlands Plantation (703-777-0519).

1351 The Loudoun Museum (col)
16 Loudoun Street; 703-777-7427; Mon–Sat 10–5, Sun 1–5. Free.

Many Civil War artifacts are here, especially those pertaining to Loudoun's war hero, Confederate "Gray Ghost" John Singleton Mosby. In addition to the history presented on Loudoun County, the museum is a departure point for a self-guided walking tour of the historic district. Many of the houses served as hospitals during the war; a Confederate monument is on the courthouse grounds.

Lexington

1352 Lee Memorial Chapel (site)
Washington and Lee University; 703-463-8768; Apr–Oct: Mon–Sat 9–5, Sun 2–5; other times: Mon–Sat 9–4, Sun 2–5. Free.

The school was founded in 1740 as Liberty Academy and saved from bankruptcy by George Washington, who donated $50,000 worth of James River Canal stock in 1796. Robert E. Lee served as president of the then Washington Academy for five years after the Civil War, and the school was renamed Washington and Lee after his death on October 12, 1870. His office remains as he left it in Lee Chapel. Lee and many of his family are buried here; a recumbent statue by Edward Valentine, rich in texture, resides over the crypt. His horse Traveller is buried outside the chapel.

The building itself was built in 1867–68 under the close supervision of Lee and his son, George Washington Custis Lee, a professor at neighboring Virginia Military Institute. A museum in the basement has artifacts relating to his career at the school.

The James G. Layburn Library has extensive Lee and Civil War holdings. Also on campus, up the hill west of the Chapel, is the Lee-Jackson home, where both Stonewall Jackson and Robert E. Lee lived at different times.

1353 Maury Monument (mem)
Goshen Pass; Route 39, northwest of town.

An anchor monument honors C.S.A. commodore Matthew Fontaine Maury, who was an instructor at the Virginia Military Institute after war. The "Pathfinder of the Seas," as Maury was known, considered Goshen Pass the loveliest spot in Virginia.

1354 "Stonewall" Jackson House (site)
Eight East Washington Street; 703-463-2552; Mon–Sat 9–5, Sun 1–5. Admission charged.

This modest brick and stone structure, built in 1801, was the only home Thomas Jonathan Jackson ever owned. He lived a quiet life in Lexington as a professor for a decade before the Civil War. He married, mourned the death of his young wife, traveled abroad, and married a second time. Around Lexington he was involved in the Presbyterian Church, joined a debating society, and was elected director of a local bank. The building has been restored to its appearance in 1859, the year Jackson and his second wife, Mary Anna, moved here.

1355 "Stonewall" Jackson Memorial Cemetery (site)
300 block of South Main Street.

Jackson and his family are surrounded by more than 100 Confederate soldiers in this graveyard. A statuary portrait by Edward Valentine, dedicated in 1891, stands over the gravesite. It faces Jackson's beloved South, said to be the only time he ever turned his back on the enemy. Also in the cemetery is the gravesite of the Civil War's "poetess of the South," Margaret Junkin Preston.

1356 Virginia Military Institute Museum (col)
Jackson Memorial Hall; 703-464-7325; Mon–Sat 9–5, Sun 2–5. Free.

Virginia Military Institute, established in 1839, contributed a great number of officers to the Confederate States of America. Thomas "Stonewall" Jackson taught natural philosophy and artillery tactics here for ten years; he was known to his students as "Old Tom Fool." During the Civil War the campus was virtually demolished by Union general David Hunter after the Battle of New Market in 1864.

The campus is graced by a number of Civil War monuments. On the grounds is an unusual statue of Jackson standing in the wind by Sir Moses

Ezekiel. The cannon in back of the statue were cast in 1848 and used by Jackson in cadet artillery training. For generations they were known as "Matthew, Mark, Luke, and John."

On the east side of the parade ground is Ezekiel's statue *Virginia Mourning Her Dead* dedicated to the cadets who fell at New Market. Six of the ten who died are buried behind the monument. Ezekiel, an 1866 VMI graduate, was a member of the corps of cadets recruited for the battle. An oil painting of the heroic cadet charge hangs here. It was completed by B. West Clinedinst. A statue of Commodore Maury is in the Preston Library on Letcher Avenue.

The museum of military history is loaded with Jackson memorabilia, foremost being his bullet-pierced raincoat worn at Chancellorsville and his horse, Little Sorrel, now stuffed. Little Sorrel's gentle nature was particularly suited to Jackson, who was not an accomplished equestrian.

Locust Grove

1357 Germanna Ford (site)

Route 3, five miles west of town at the Rapidan River.

This had been the principal crossing of the Rapidan River since colonial times. Three times the Federal Army of the Potomac crossed the river at the site identified by the historical marker here to launch offensives against Lee's Army of Northern Virginia.

On May 4, 1864, Union soldiers crossed for the final time as Grant began his Overland Campaign, which is marked as a 100-mile interpretive trail toward Petersburg. The first markers are just west of Germanna Community College. The route uses the same roads as the soldiers used.

1358 Robinson's Tavern (site)

Route 20.

Near this historical marker stood ancient Robinson's Tavern. Around this tavern in November 1863, Meade gathered his troops for a campaign in which he planned to surprise Lee in his winter quarters to the west. Confusion in assembling the troops gave Lee time to entrench on Mine Run and the plans were ruined.

Louisa

1359 Battle of Trevilians (site)

Route 33, 4½ miles west of town.

As the Union army lay at Cold Harbor in June 1864, Grant sent Sheridan with two cavalry divisions to cut Lee's communications and join General David Hunter, then advancing eastward from the Shenandoah Valley. General Wade Hampton overtook Sheridan here, and after two days of confused and indecisive fighting on June 11 and 12, the Federals retired eastward. Nearly 2,000 men were lost. Markers recount the action.

Lynchburg

1360 Confederate Monument (mem)

Monument Terrace; 9th Street between Church and Court streets.

At the top of the 70-foot hill is the bronze statue of a Confederate infantryman with bayonet fixed, designed by James O. Scott of Lynchburg and erected in 1898. Across the street is the 1855 Old City Courthouse, which is a city museum that includes Civil War memorabilia.

1361 Daniel Monument (mem)

Triangle bounded by 9th and Floyd streets and Park Avenue.

A unique monument to "The Lame Lion of Lynchburg," this statue was designed by Moses Ezekiel and erected in 1913. It depicts Major John Warwick Daniel, seated and holding a crutch. Daniel served in the Confederate army and a wound at the Battle of Wilderness left him a cripple. He later became a four-term United States senator.

1362 Fort Early (site)

Fort and Vermont avenues.

With three rail lines and a major canal, this was a major supply point during the Civil War. On June 17, 1864, General Jubal Early arrived with the Second Corps of Lee's army and erected a redoubt. Union troops commanded by General David Hunter arrived the following day and were repulsed. There are markers throughout town pertaining to the Battle of Lynchburg, but only the partially restored earthworks remain.

The monument to Early is a tall granite obelisk dedicated in 1920 and is near the redoubt. After commanding the town's defenses, Early returned to live in Lynchburg from 1869 until his death in 1894.

1363 Jackson Funeral Boat (mem)

Riverside Park; 2240 Rivermont Avenue.

A fragment of the hull of the canalboat *Marshall* has been salvaged and put in this public park on a scenic bluff overlooking the James River. The *Marshall* carried General Stonewall Jackson's body from Lynchburg to its final destination in Lexington.

1364 Old City Cemetery (site)

4th and Taylor streets.

Founded in 1806, the Confederate section of the graveyard contains 2,200 soldiers from 14 states.

Information tablets at the entrance describe Lynchburg's role as a hospital during the Civil War, and a kiosk lists the names and location of all that are buried here. A monument stands in tribute to the 365 soldiers who died of smallpox during the war.

The Pest House Medical Museum depicts conditions in Lynchburg's "House of Pestilence" during the Civil War. The museum emphasizes the work of physician Dr. John Jay Terrell, who took responsibility for creating humane conditions. Tours of the exterior are self-guided; tours of the interior are offered by appointment.

1365 Mustering and Disbanding Site (site)

Rivermont Avenue and Monsview Drive.

A historical marker identifies the point where the Second Virginia Cavalry was mustered into service on May 10, 1861. At the same place the remnant of the regiment was disbanded on April 10, 1865, having completed four years of service minus one month.

1366 Spring Hill Cemetery (site)

Fort Avenue between Lancaster Street and Wythe Road.

Here are the graves of three generals from the Confederate States of America: James Dearing (1840–1865), Jubal Early (1816–1895), and Thomas Taylor Mumford (1831–1918).

McDowell

1367 McDowell Battlefield (mem)

Route 250, one mile east of town.

Stonewall Jackson began his Shenandoah Valley Campaign by besting the Federal troops under Milroy and Schneck on May 8, 1862. Jackson controlled the high ground just to the south. More than 180 men were killed and over 600 wounded in four hours of fighting.

Reenactment: Some breastworks and interpretive signs for the battle are located in the national forest here. The McDowell Presbyterian Church bears the scars of a cannonball hit, and names and dates were carved into the bricks on the front of the building. The Battle of McDowell is reenacted on the first weekend in May. In addition to the demonstrations, in the Civil War camp there are period medical reenactments.

Madison

1368 Cavalry Engagement at Jack's Shop (site)

Route 231, 6½ miles south of town.

This cavalry skirmish on September 22, 1863, received its name from a blacksmith shop that stood nearby. Stuart's Confederate cavalry got trapped between Union horsemen led by John Buford and H. Judson Kilpatrick. Stuart's horse artillery fired and charged in both directions, finally breaking through Kilpatrick's line to escape.

Malvern Hill

1369 Battle of Malvern Hill (site)

Route 156.

Before abandoning his assault on Richmond for the safety of Harrison's Landing on the James River south of the city, McClellan made a final stand on Malvern Hill. Rather than dig trenches, the Federals massed artillery and infantry along the ridge, which fell away sharply to the left. To the right the flank was protected by swampland. Any Confederate assault would have to cross open ground in front of the Union guns.

On July 1, 1862, Lee ordered just such an attack. By nightfall, more than 5,000 Confederates lay in the field between the woods on the left and the Union position. According to one Confederate officer, "It was not war — it was murder." The Army of the Potomac was safe at its new supply base. The Seven Days' Battles were over.

Cannons stand guard over the field as they did during the Civil War under Union artillery commander Adelbert Ames, the last Civil War general to die, in 1933. A short walking trail follows the steep slopes that protected the Federal left flank.

Manassas

1370 Confederate Monument (mem)

Confederate Cemetery; end of Church Street.

Among the speakers at the 1889 dedication of the red sandstone monument was General W. H. F. Lee, son of Robert E. Lee. The bronze statue atop the memorial, added in 1909, is entitled *At Rest*. The cemetery was started in 1867 with the donation of one acre of land; by the next year 250 Southern soldiers were interred here.

1371 The Manassas Museum (col)

9101 Prince William Street; 703-368-1873; Tues–Sun, 10–5. Admission charged.

Civil War artifacts and lithographs tell the story of the fighting at Manassas and the importance of the railroads to both sides. Included in the exhibits is a commemoration of the 1911 Peace Jubilee, a half-century reunion of Civil War veterans who had fought in Manassas. The reunion occurred at the courthouse on Lee Avenue. A video program, *A Community at War*, is screened, and self-guided tours, which explain the things that are no longer there to see, leave from the museum.

1372 Manassas National Battlefield Park (site)

Route 234; 703-361-1339; Summer: 8:30–6; other times: 8:30–5. Admission charged.

The Manassas Gap and the Orange and Alexandria railroads crossed in Manassas, a surveyor's decision in the 1850s that transformed this small farming community into one of America's best-known towns in the Civil War. In an attempt to control that railroad junction the Northern and Southern armies clashed twice in the first two years of the war five miles north of town near a creek called Bull Run, resulting in 30,000 casualties.

On July 21, 1861, the Civil War was expected to end. The fully equipped Union army under General Irvin McDowell was prepared to take the field for the first time at Bull Run. The complete submission of the rebels was considered such a certainty that the Federal troops were accompanied by picnickers and sightseers. After ten hours of bloody fighting, the Union army was in retreat toward Washington, and it was apparent this was not going to be a one-battle war.

The armies returned to Bull Run a year later, seasoned and spirited. Robert E. Lee's Army of Northern Virginia was at the peak of its power, and he outmaneuvered General John Pope's Union army in three days of struggle beginning on August 28. With his masterful victory here, Lee was able to carry the war to the North for the first time.

Reenactment: The Manassas Battlefield is perhaps the Civil War site most affected by the encroachment of modern development. A walking trail on Henry Hill is the best way to view the First Battle of Manassas, including an equestrian statue of Confederate general Thomas Jackson where he earned the nickname "Stonewall." A driving tour encompasses both battles. A Civil War weekend takes place on the last weekend in August on the anniversary of the Second Battle of Manassas.

Mechanicsville

1373 Battle of Beaver Dam Creek (site)

Route 156, south of town.

Heavy fighting engulfed this swampy bog under a ridge on June 26, 1862. The Confederates lost three times as many men as the Federals, and only Stonewall Jackson's nighttime arrival kept the Union from advancing on Richmond from this point. Roadside markers and a turnout off the road interpret the battle.

1374 Chickahominy Bluff (site)

Route 360, south of town.

This bluff overlooking Mechanicsville witnessed the beginning of the Union Seven Days' struggle to conquer Richmond in 1862. This first stop on the Richmond National Battlefield driving tour is interpreted with signs and a short walking trail. Earthworks remain.

Middleburg

1375 Mosby's Rangers (site)

Route 50, four miles west of town.

Here at Atoka (Rector's Crossroads), on June 10, 1863, Company "A," 43rd Battalion of Partisan Rangers, known as "Mosby's Rangers," was formally organized. A historical marker identifies the site.

Middletown

1376 The Battle of Cedar Creek (site)

Route 11; 540-869-2064; Apr–Nov: daily. Free.

Confederate general Jubal Early surprised two larger Union corps and nearly routed them on October 19, 1864, but starving soldiers broke ranks to loot abandoned camps. Union general Philip Sheridan was at Winchester, on his return from a War Department strategy meeting in Washington, when he learned of the battle. He mounted his horse and raced to the battlefield to rally Union troops to victory. This was the last battle fought for control of the Shenandoah Valley, and it helped insure a second term in office for a grateful President Lincoln.

Reenactment: The 158 acres of the battlefield are undeveloped, but a recently opened visitor center interprets the Battle of Cedar Creek where the Federals endured nearly 6,000 killed and wounded and the Confederates 3,000. Each October one of America's largest reenactments is held here incorporating infantry, cavalry, and artillery, and recalling 15 hours of carnage, which littered these wide fields.

1377 Belle Grove (site)

Route 11, one mile south of town; 540-869-2028; Mar 15–Nov 15: Mon–Sat 10–4, Sun 1–5. Admission charged.

Sheridan made his headquarters here, and at 5 A.M. on October 19, 1864, Early's attack on sleeping troops near the mansion was an almost complete rout until the Union general arrived to effect a complete reversal of the day's events, a ride immortalized in a poem by Thomas Buchanan Read. Tours interpret the house, finished in 1797, and its role in the Battle of Cedar Creek.

1378 Tomb of an Unknown Soldier (site)

Route 11, one mile south of town.

On the highest mountain to the southeast of this marker is the grave of an unknown soldier. The mountaintop was used as a signal station by both armies in the Civil War.

Monterey

1379 Confederate Monument (mem)
Court Square.

This is an unusual monument in that the soldier shades his eyes with one hand and grips his weapon with the other.

Mount Crawford

1380 Sheridan's Last Raid (site)
Route 11, south of town.

On March 1, 1864, Major General Phillip Henry Sheridan began his final march through the Shenandoah Valley on a mission to destroy railroads, capture Lynchburg, and join Sherman in North Carolina. In the cavalry raid at Mount Crawford, Sheridan captured 30 men and seized 20 ambulances and wagons filled with much needed supplies. A highway marker identifies the site.

Mount Jackson

1381 Confederate Monument (site)
Confederate Cemetery.

The western terminus of the Manassas Gap Railroad, one of only two rail lines connecting the Shenandoah Valley with the rest of Virginia, was at Mount Jackson. A cavalry engagement occurred south of here between the 1st Virginia and 1st New York. The obelisk in the graveyard marks the graves of 112 unknown Confederate soldiers.

New Cold Harbor

1382 Battle of Gaines's Mill (site)
Route 718.

The heaviest fighting of the Seven Days' Battles around Richmond in 1862 took place along the heavily fortified Union lines at the Boatswain Creek on June 27. Pushing their way up a heavily forested hill, the Confederates suffered 9,000 casualties while the Union lost 7,000 before retreating.

An interpretive trail follows the Confederate attack, including the site where Texas and Georgia troops broke through the Union line. The Watt House, restored to its 1835 appearance, was used as a headquarters and hospital during the action. It is private and viewed from the outside.

New Market

1383 The Museum of the American Cavalry, 1607–1946 (col)
George Collins Parkway (Route 305); 703-740-3959; Apr–Nov: daily, 9–5. Admission charged.

During the first two years of the American Civil War, over a quarter of a million horses were supplied to the United States cavalry. During the war there were more than 60,000 cavalry troops in the field. The collection covers the entire history of the American cavalry, with particular emphasis on the exploits of the horsemen in the Civil War.

1384 New Market Battlefield Historical Park (site)
George Collins Parkway (Route 305); 703-740-3102; Daily, 9–4:30. Admission charged.

One of the most dramatic — and telling — episodes of the Civil War occurred here on May 15, 1864. Only a threadbare Confederate force was left to defend Staunton from a marauding Union army commanded by General Franz Sigel. Confederate general John Breckinridge, a former United States vice president under James Buchanan, despairingly called upon 257 teenage cadets from the Virginia Military Institute. Breckinridge did so with the utmost reluctance, saying, "Major, order them up, and God forgive me for the order." The cadets, as young as 14, entered the fray fearlessly, captured a battery, and took nearly 100 prisoners. Ten cadets were killed and 47 wounded. This was to be the final Southern victory in the Shenandoah Valley.

The 280 acres of the Battle of New Market are administered by the Virginia Military Institute. A walking tour of the battlefield traces the charge of the cadets around the restored Bushong farmhouse and into the "Field of Lost Shoes," an open expanse that had become a quagmire from three days of hard rain prior to the battle.

In addition to the battlefield, the Hall of Valor is one of the finest of Civil War museums, featuring life-size dioramas and a history of the war in the eastern theater of the war. There are two special films, one on Stonewall Jackson's 1862 Shenandoah Valley Campaign and the other on the VMI cadets at New Market.

Reenactment: The battle is restaged on the weekend in May closest to the anniversary of the VMI cadet charge at New Market.

1385 New Market Battlefield Military Museum (col)
George Collins Parkway (Route 305); 703-740-8065; Mar–Dec: daily, 9–5. Admission charged.

Situated on a hilltop where the Battle of New Market began, this museum building, fashioned after Robert E. Lee's home in Arlington, contains more than 2,000 military artifacts. The memorabilia, which cover all American wars but are predominantly from the Civil War, are chronologically arranged in 108 displays. A 30-minute film on the Civil War is screened. Fifteen monuments on the grounds mark Union and Confederate positions during the fighting.

New Post

1386 Jackson's Headquarters (site)

Route 17, six miles southeast of town.

A historical marker at the location indicates that in an outbuilding here at Moss Neck, Stonewall Jackson had his headquarters from December 1862 to March 1863. He was engaged in guarding the line of the Rappahannock River with his corps of Lee's army.

Newport News

1387 Battle of Dam No. 1 (site)

Newport News Park; 13564 Jefferson Avenue; 804-888-3333; Daily, dusk–dawn. Free.

Confederate major general John Bankhead Magruder prepared defensive lines here early in 1862. He also installed levees to flood the lowlands in the event of a Union incursion. The attack came on April 16, 1862, at Dam No. 1, as General McClellan launched his Peninsula Campaign against Richmond. The Federal force was stymied and never attempted to break through the Confederate defenses along the Warwick River.

Newport Park is the largest municipal park east of the Mississippi River. Over five miles of continuous earthworks remain in pristine condition.

1388 Battle of Lee's Mill (site)

Route 60, just east of Route 105.

A historic marker is at the spot of Magruder's second line of defense. Heavy rains and massive Confederate earthen fortifications defending the river crossing stopped a Union advance on April 5, 1862. Magruder's defenses caused McClellan to initiate his month-long Warwick River Siege, the first siege of the Civil War. On May 3, the Confederates finally abandoned the earthworks and withdrew to Williamsburg.

Reenactment: The battle is reenacted at Endview Plantation (804-247-8523) on the weekend closest to April 5.

1389 Mariners' Museum (col)

100 Museum Drive; 804-596-2222; Mon–Sat 9–5, Sun 12–5. Admission charged.

A minor part of this sprawling museum is devoted to Civil War naval history, but it is a significant part. The museum is the official curator of the Monitor Collection, and the *Clash of Armor* exhibit tells the tale of the U.S.S. *Monitor* and C.S.S. *Virginia*, formerly the *Merrimac*. A video shows the *Monitor* as it appears today, sunken off the coast of Cape Hatteras, North Carolina.

1390 Monitor-Merrimac Center and Museum (col)

917 Jefferson Avenue; 804-245-1533; Daily, 9–5. Free.

The highlight of the museum devoted to the Civil War's most famous naval battle features the world's largest diorama of the Battle of Hampton Roads. The exhibits not only feature explanations of the battle but describe the 100-day race to get the two ironclads built and into action.

Reenactment: Harbor cruises explore the scene of the engagement. The battle is remembered with activities and reenactments in early March.

1391 Monitor-Virginia Overlook (site)

16th Street off Jefferson Avenue.

The ironclad C.S.S. *Virginia* gained the Confederacy's greatest naval victory when it sank the U.S.S. *Cumberland* and *Congress* on March 8, 1862, in Hampton Roads. When the *Virginia* set sail the next morning it was with the full expectation of finishing the destruction of the wooden Union fleet. Instead, it met the U.S.S. *Monitor*, another ironclad.

People gathered on shore to watch the battle that would forever change naval warfare. After three hours, the *Virginia* retired, the battle a draw. They never fought again.

The overlook is located near the site of Camp Butler, a Union installation used as a prisoner camp in the last months of the war.

1392 War Memorial Museum of Virginia (col)

9285 Warwick Boulevard; 804-247-8523; Mon–Sat 9–5, Sun 1–5. Admission: $2.

More than 60,000 artifacts, including weapons, uniforms, vehicles, and posters, are displayed from all wars, including the Peninsula Campaign and the War of the Sea during the Civil War.

Norfolk

1393 Camp Talbot (site)

Oak Grove Road and Granby Street.

The Confederate Camp defending Norfolk was located about a half mile west of this historical marker. Georgia and Virginia troops were stationed in Norfolk from April 1861 until the evacuation of the city on May 10, 1862.

1394 Confederate Flag Site (site)

Market Street at Monticello Avenue.

A marker identifies the spot where the Confederate Stars and Bars was unfurled for the first time in Norfolk, from a housetop a block-and-a-half east of this corner. It was April 2, 1861, two weeks before the secession of Virginia from the Union.

1395 Confederate Monument (mem)

Main Street and Commercial Place.

This towering pedestal of white Vermont granite is surmounted by the bronze figure of a Confederate soldier, sculpted by William Couper. The pedestal was erected in 1889 on a center lot of the original town of Norfolk, but the monument was not completed until 1907 when more funds became available.

1396 McArthur Memorial (site)

City Hall Avenue.

The former 1847 city hall was the scene of an elaborate flag raising of "Old Glory" when the city was surrendered by Confederate major W. W. Lamb in 1862. The Federal force of 6,000 landed on May 10 under Major General John E. Wood, with Lincoln and key cabinet members watching the movement from a ship in the harbor. A historical marker on West Ocean View Avenue near Mason Creek Road identifies the location of the landing.

1397 Nauticus, the National Maritime Center (col)

One Waterside Drive; 800-664-1080. Hours vary; Admission charged.

One section of the Maritime Center is the Hampton Roads Naval Museum, with paintings and models and artifacts of the area's naval history.

1398 Selden's Home (site)

Freemason and Botecourt streets.

A marker here indicates the house that was seized and occupied as the headquarters of the Federal military government between 1862 and 1865. The house was built in 1807 as the country residence of Dr. William B. Selden. Robert E. Lee visited Selden's son William, a friend and surgeon for the Confederacy, in 1870, his last visit to Norfolk.

Nottoway

1399 Confederate Monument (mem)

Nottoway County Courthouse; Route 460, west of town.

Near here the Confederate cavalryman, W. H. F.

Lee, interposed between Wilson and Kautz raiding to Burkeville and fought a sharp action on June 23, 1864. Wilson then started on his return to Grant's army. Grant passed through here with part of his army in pursuit of Lee on April 5, 1865. The *Confederate Monument* is a little soldier leaning wearily on his gun.

Old Cold Harbor

1400 Battle of Cold Harbor (site)

Route 156, west of town.

Midway between two shabby taverns, Old Cold Harbor and New Cold Harbor, the Confederates dug in on June 1–2, 1864, to await Grant's attack. It came on June 3, a frontal assault on a narrow section of the Confederate line. Knowing the odds they were facing, the Union soldiers pinned bits of paper bearing their names and those of their next of kin to the backs of their uniforms. This was the beginning of dog tags later issued routinely to the military. Some 7,200 Federals were shot down in 20 minutes in what has been referred to as the worst slaughter of Americans in history.

After the disastrous frontal assault Grant resumed his flanking movements and swung around to lay siege to Petersburg. That evening, conferring with his staff, Grant said, "I regret this assault more than any one I have ever ordered."

Part of the Richmond National Battlefield Park, Cold Harbor features its own interpretive shelter with battle exhibits and an electronic map. A self-guided walking tour of the battlefield includes fine examples of Civil War fortifications. Across the road is Garthright House, a Union field hospital during the fighting, which is viewed from the outside. Next to the battlefield is Cold Harbor National Cemetery, with the remains of more than 2,000 Union soldiers, over 1,300 of them unknown.

Orange

1401 Clark Mountain (site)

Route 697, northeast of town.

Now a commercial orchard, the top of Clark Mountain was a Confederate lookout in 1864 where Southern commanders could track Union troop movements prior to their Overland Campaign.

1402 Confederate Monument (mem)

Orange County Courthouse; Route 15.

The county seat was never invaded, and the courthouse has changed little since the Civil War. The basement was used as a Confederate arsenal; the Confederate memorial stands on the front lawn.

1403 Jackson's Crossing (site)

Route 15, 7½ miles north of town.

The historical marker here identifies the spot at Locust Dale where Stonewall Jackson's army crossed the river moving north to the battle of Cedar Mountain on August 9, 1862. The battle was fought a few hours later.

1404 Saint Thomas's Episcopal Church (site)

Route 15, south of town; 703-672-3761.

Lee made his headquarters in Orange from December 1863 to May 1864, and the town became a favorite Confederate rendezvous point. The pew where Lee and Jefferson Davis worshiped during services here is marked. Lee is said to have hitched Traveler to the locust tree out front.

Paris

1405 Delaplane (site)

Route 17, 6½ miles south of town.

On July 19, 1861, Stonewall Jackson marched his corps to this railroad station from Winchester, crowded into cattle and freight cars, and traveled to the First Battle of Manassas, contributing significantly to the Confederate victory there. With the movement of more than 10,000 troops by rail it was clear a new era of military transport had arrived.

Petersburg

1406 Edge Hill (site)

Route 1, at southern city limits.

To the right of the historical marker stood Turnbull House, headquarters of Robert E. Lee from November 23, 1864, until April 2, 1865. After Lee's evacuation to Cottage Farm, Federal artillery destroyed the house.

1407 Fort Sedgwick (site)

Crater Road and Morton Avenue.

This Union fort was named for General John Sedgwick, who was killed at Spotsylvania. Fort Sedgwick, the key eastern link in the siege line at Petersburg, earned the name of "Fort Hell" because of heavy Confederate mortar and sniper fire. This was the site of the final major assault by the Union Ninth Corps on April 2, 1865. A nearby marker identifies the site of Rives Salient, which was defeated by local militia in the first attack on Petersburg ten months earlier; the site, identified by a marker, was leveled in the late 1960s.

On the remnants of the fort is a tall stone monument to the memory of the Third Division of the Federal Ninth Corps. The Confederate Fort Mahone was lost during Grant's drive that morning of April 2, 1865.

1408 Old Blandford Church and Reception Center (site)

319 S. Crater Road; 800-368-3595; Daily, 10–5. Admission charged.

Since 1901, this eighteenth-century parish church has been a memorial to the Southern soldiers who died during the Civil War. In honor of the Confederate dead, states each contributed a stained glass window designed by Louis Comfort Tiffany. Over the main door is the only Tiffany window in the world that features the Confederate battle flag. The weathered tombstones of Blandford Cemetery date to the early 1700s, and are surrounded by locally made ornamental ironwork. Some 30,000 Confederate soldiers are buried here, where local tradition insists the first Memorial Day was observed on June 9, 1866. Also here is the mausoleum of General William Mahone, who led the Crater charge.

1409 Pamplin Park Civil War Site (site)

6523 Duncan Road; 804-861-2408; Daily, 9–5. Free.

A modern interpretive center describes the decisive battle on April 2, 1865, that ended the siege of Petersburg. There are pathways among the original Civil War fortifications and interactive exhibits in the display areas.

1410 Petersburg National Battlefield (site)

Route 36; 800-368-3595; Summer: daily, 8:30–5:30; other times: 8–5. Admission charged.

Despite heavy losses in the fighting early in 1864, Ulysses S. Grant pushed on to Richmond, intending to cut off its supply line from the south at Petersburg. Four days of sharp fighting beginning on June 15, 1864, pushed the Confederate lines back one mile, where both armies entrenched. The longest siege on American soil began.

Almost immediately the 48th Regiment of Pennsylvania Volunteers, comprised mostly of coal miners, began digging a 511-foot mine shaft into the Confederate line, quietly carrying out tons of soil in cracker boxes. On July 30, after a month of digging, the Federals exploded four tons of powder under the Confederate battery, blowing 278 Southern defenders into the air.

In the confusion that followed, the Union troops storming the line plunged directly into the massive crater created by the explosion rather than advancing around it. The Confederates were able to seal their defensive line and inflicted horrible casualties in a determined counterattack. The siege was to last nine more months. Before it ended on April 2, 1865, a total of 42,000 Union and 28,000 Confederate troops were killed or captured in the Petersburg campaign.

The Petersburg National Battlefield comprises five major units across 1,531 acres. At the visitor center is an hourly, 17-minute lighted map presentation that describes the battle and complexities of the siege. A walking tour at the center includes well-preserved earthen defenses and a replica of the Union mortar "Dictator," capable of lobbing shells two miles into Confederate defenses. The full self-guided driving tour covers 16 miles.

The Crater, which measures 170 feet by 60 feet and was 30 feet deep when blown apart, can be visited on a walking tour. The trail follows the mine shaft and explains the engineering complexities involved in executing the treacherous plan.

1411 Poplar Grove National Cemetery (site)

Route 675, ½ mile south of town.

The national cemetery was established in 1868 for those who died at Appomattox and Petersburg. Of the 6,178 interments 4,110 are unknown; 36 are Confederate soldiers. Heavy fighting occurred on this ground in 1864, with the prize being a nearby railroad.

1412 Siege Museum (col)

15 West Bank Street; 800-368-3595; Daily, 10–5. Admission charged.

The ten-month Union siege of Petersburg was the longest such military operation ever conducted on American soil. The museum portrays the human story of the Civil War as lavish lifestyles gave way to a bitter struggle for survival. Exhibits and a 20-minute film show the people of Petersburg living before, during — when a chicken could only be bought for $50 — and immediately after the siege. The museum itself is housed in the historic Exchange Building, built in 1839 as a commodities market.

Port Republic

1413 Battle of Port Republic (site)

Route 340.

Located at the confluence of the North and South rivers, Port Republic, although small, was an important center of trade on the Shenandoah. Jackson attacked a strong Union position held by James Shields here on June 9, 1862, and twice won and lost Union batteries. Reinforced later in the day, Jackson finally drove Shields from the field, then burned a bridge over the rain-swollen river to prevent General John Fremont's troops from coming with Federal help. Confederate losses were heavy as Jackson's Valley Campaign of 1862 came to an end.

A circle tour map marks the battlefield off the road. In town is a battlemap marker on the spot where the sole remaining bridge over the Shenandoah River stood during the battle. A bronze marker is positioned where the Union battery was defended.

1414 Port Republic Museum (col)

Frank Kemper House; 703-249-4435; Sundays and by appointment. Donations.

Also known as the Turner Ashby House, this is where the Confederate cavalry leader was brought after his death. The primary focus of the museum is Port Republic's Civil War history.

Port Royal Cross Roads

1415 Booth's Death Site (site)

Route 301.

On this road, two miles to the south of the historical marker, is the Garrett place. There, John Wilkes Booth, Lincoln's assassin, was found by Union cavalry and killed while resisting arrest on April 26, 1865.

Portsmouth

1416 Confederate Monument (mem)

Town Square; High and Court streets.

The plain shaft of North Carolina granite stands 56 feet high and is surrounded by four sentinels. The shaft was finished in 1881, the sentinels added later. A single star on the face of the capstone faces south.

1417 Confederate Navy Yard (site)

South end of 1st and 4th streets.

The Virginia militia took control of the naval yard, one of the world's largest, on April 20, 1861. The fleeing federal force destroyed war material worth almost five million dollars. The Confederates salvaged what they could, including a steam frigate that had been burned to the waterline, the U.S.S. *Merrimack*. Raised into a dry-dock and repaired, the *Merrimack* would emerge a year later as the world's first ironclad warship, the C.S.S. *Virginia*.

1418 Portsmouth Naval Hospital (site)

Hospital Point; Effingham Street.

The oldest naval hospital in America was established in 1827 and used by both armies. In the hospital graveyard is a memorial to the 337 dead of the U.S.S. *Cumberland* and the U.S.S. *Congress*, who died under the guns of the C.S.S. *Virginia* in the Battle of Hampton Roads. Fifty-eight Confederates are buried here as well.

1419 Portsmouth Naval Shipyard Museum (col)

Two High Street; 804-393-8393; Tues–Sat 10–5, Sun 1–5. Admission charged.

This museum on the Elizabeth River features a large collection of naval items, including items from the C.S.S. *Virginia*, models, and Civil War naval uniforms.

Powhattan

1420 Lee's Last Camp (site)

Route 711, ten miles north of town.

A marker identifies the spot where Robert E. Lee, riding east from Appomattox to Richmond to join his family, pitched his tent for the final time on April 14, 1865. He stopped here to visit his brother, Charles Carter Lee, who lived nearby at Windsor. Not wishing to inconvenience his brother, Lee camped by the roadside.

Prince George

1421 The Cattle Raid (site)

Route 106, seven miles east of Prince George.

Just to the north of the marker here, at old Sycamore Church, Wade Hampton overpowered a cavalry guarding Grant's beef cattle on September 16, 1864. Hampton rounded up 2,500 beeves and drove them back across the Nottoway River into Lee's lines. Federal troops sent to recapture the herd were repulsed.

Rawlings

1422 Virginia Battlerama (col)

Route 712; 804-478-5781.

On display are realistic miniatures representing ten Virginia Civil War battles, including historical narration. Among the battles recreated are "The Crater," "Fredericksburg," Sailor's Creek," and "Five Forks."

Richmond

1423 Battle Abbey (col)

428 North Boulevard Avenue; 804-358-4901; Mon–Sat 10–5, Sun 1–5. Admission charged.

The present headquarters of the Virginia Historical Society was dedicated as a Confederate memorial hall in 1913. There is a vast collection of Southern battle flags, portraits, Civil War weapons, and equipment. The collected art includes a large gallery of portraits of Southern heroes. The Civil War research library is among the finest anywhere.

1424 Battle of Chaffin's Farm (site)

Fort Harrison; Route 5, eight miles southeast of the city.

A system of permanent defenses south of Rich-

mond was anchored at Chaffin's Farm, a large open bluff. The lines remained untested until September 1864. Federal general Benjamin Butler led the attack that resulted in the capture of only one defensive position, Fort Harrison, on September 29. The Union renamed the earthworks Fort Burnham after the Union general killed in the attack.

The Confederate counterattack, initiated immediately, was under the personal supervision of Robert E. Lee. This effort failed, and the two sides settled into trench warfare until the end of the war.

The National Park Service maintains a small, seasonal visitor center at Fort Harrison, which is toured on a short, interpretive walking trail. Several other Confederate fortifications, including the well-preserved Fort Brady, are easily reached from this site. A national cemetery is on the premises.

1425 Belle Isle (site)

Off 7th Street.

This 60-acre island in the currents of the James River was one of the South's most notorious Civil War prison camps. Gun emplacements can still be seen on the heights of the island. A pedestrian bridge provides access to the site.

1426 Confederate Chapel and the R. E. Lee Camp (site)

2900 Grove Avenue; Sat, 10–2. Free.

This small, white frame chapel is one of two structures surviving from a Confederate soldier's home established here in 1883. Funerals for more than 1,700 veterans and their relatives were held in this chapel still adorned with Confederate symbols. As many as 300 residents lived here, the final veteran moving out in 1947. A cannon used to defend Charleston harbor during the Civil War is on the grounds.

1427 Drewry's Bluff (site)

Bellwood Road, Route 656, off Route 1/301, seven miles south of the city.

This fortification, named for its builder, Captain A. H. Drewry, was erected in 1862 to protect the water approach to the Confederate capital. Located on a bluff overlooking a bend in the James River, the garrison repulsed its first Union attack on May 15, 1862. Included in the fleet was the celebrated ironclad, the U.S.S. *Monitor*.

A Confederate naval academy was established here the following year and Drewry's Bluff, also known as Fort Darling, was the scene of more fighting in May of 1864 during Union major general Benjamin F. Butler's Bermuda Hundred campaign. Confederate general P. G. T. Beauregard bested the Federals again, and the fort never capitulated until the Rebels evacuated Richmond.

The fort is administered by the National Park

Service at the Richmond National Battlefield. A walking tour visits the remains of the fort, which include a huge Columbiad cannon.

1428 A. P. Hill Monument and Grave
(mem)

Intersection of Laburnum and Hermitage roads.

Confederate general Ambrose Powell Hill is buried under this monument in the intersection. After Hill was killed near Petersburg when his lines were broken on April 1, 1865, his body was moved several times before ending up here.

1429 Hollywood Cemetery (site)

Cherry and Albemarle streets; 804-648-8501; May–Oct: daily, 8–6; other times: 8–5. Free.

These 115 hillside acres on the James River are a burial ground for United States presidents James Monroe and John Tyler, and Confederate president Jefferson Davis. A granite pyramid honors more than 18,000 Confederate soldiers interred here, including generals J. E. B. Stuart, Fitzhugh Lee, George Pickett, and Matthew Fontaine Maury.

1430 Lee House (site)

707 East Franklin Street.

Robert E. Lee came to this 1844 Greek Revival house after surrendering his army at Appomattox. It had been the wartime home of his family. He stayed briefly before moving permanently to Lexington.

1431 Libby Prison (site)

Bounded by 20th, 21st, Cary, and Canal streets.

The infamous Civil War prison building was removed from its location for exhibit at the 1892 Chicago World's Fair. During the war Luther Libby's ship chandlery housed Federal officers in various stages of misery. Commemorative plaques are embedded in a modern floodwall that now traverses the site.

1432 Library of Virginia (col)

11th Street at Capitol Square; 804-786-8929; Mon–Sat, 8:15–5. Free.

The focus of the collection is Virginia history, and it includes more than one-and-a-half million books and 22 million documents.

1433 Monument Avenue (mem)

Laid out in 1889 as a ceremonial entry to downtown Richmond from the west, this is considered one of America's most beautiful boulevards. From the city outward the first monument, at Lombardy Street, is the statue of the "Eyes and Ears" of the Confederate Army, General J. E. B. Stuart. Stuart died at the age of 31 after being wounded at the Battle of Yellow Tavern.

Next, at Allen Avenue, is one of the grandest of equestrian statues, a 60-foot rendering by Jean Antoine Mercie of General Robert E. Lee atop Traveler. It is inscribed, simply, "Lee." At Davis Avenue is the 1907 tribute to Jefferson Davis by Edward Valentine. The 13 Doric columns in the sculpture represent the 11 states that seceded and the 2 that sent delegates to the Confederate Congress.

In the Boulevard intersection is a stoic General Stonewall Jackson, unveiled in 1919. The final monument to be dedicated was that of oceanographer Matthew Fontaine Maury, who invented the electric torpedo by experimenting with exploding powder charges in his bathtub. It was erected in 1929, sculpted by F. William Sievers, who also did the Jackson monument.

Stuart and Jackson, both battlefield casualties, face north, while Lee, who survived, faces south.

1434 The Museum and White House of the Confederacy (col)

1201 East Clay Street; 804-649-1861; Mon–Sat 10–5, Sun 12–5. Admission charged.

The museum's galleries on three levels feature the largest collection of Confederate artifacts in the world. Artifacts from every important Southern leader, including Lee's surrender sword at Appomattox, are on display. Also on display is the last Confederate flag, flown by the C.S.S. *Shenandoah*, a warship harassing a United States whaling fleet in the Pacific Ocean when the war ended. Unaware of the fall of the Confederacy until August, the crew then sailed 17,000 miles around Cape Horn to England, finally surrendering to the British on November 6, 1865.

Next door is the executive mansion of Confederate president Jefferson Davis and his family from 1861 to 1865. Accurately restored to its mid–nineteenth century appearance, the house was the political and social hub of the Confederate States of America.

1435 Richmond National Battlefield Park (site)

3215 East Broad Street; 804-226-1981; Daily, 9–5. Free.

The visitor center is in Chimborazo Park, a landscaped promontory overlooking the wharves and many of Richmond's largest factories, and whimsically named for a peak in the Andes. In 1862 Dr. James B. McCaw established a hospital here of 150 buildings and 100 tents — then the largest military hospital in the world. More than 76,000 patients were cared for here with a mortality rate of less than 20 percent — in the days before antiseptic surgery. The park site was purchased by the city in 1874.

At the visitor center is a film presentation and exhibits. A full 80-mile tour of preserved battlefield sites and historic locations detailing the four-year defense of Richmond begins here. Seven military drives were hurled by the North at the beleaguered city. The two most important, McClellan's Peninsular Campaign in 1862 and Grant's Overland Campaign in 1864, are covered on this tour. An audiotape for the tour and booklets are available.

Near the visitor center is Oakwood Cemetery, with 16,000 Confederate interments. Several national cemeteries around Richmond were established to rebury Union dead hastily covered on Richmond battlefields.

1436 St. Paul's Episcopal Church (site)

Southwest corner of North 9th and East Grace streets.

Both Davis and Lee worshiped at the "Church of the Confederacy." Davis was confirmed here and was attending services when he learned that Lee's defensive line at Petersburg had been broken on April 2, 1865, and that the evacuation of Richmond was imminent. The Lee Memorial Window is striking.

1437 Site of J. E. B. Stuart's Death (site)

206 West Grace Street.

A historical marker at the site describes the home of Stuart's brother-in-law, Dr. Charles Brewer, to whose home Stuart was brought after being mortally wounded at the Battle of Yellow Tavern. Dr. Brewer's house was destroyed in 1893.

1438 Soldiers' and Sailors' Monument (mem)

South end of 29th Street.

The base of this monument, dedicated in 1894 to the common Confederate soldier and sailor, affords one of the best views of the James River. Below, the Confederate naval yard was located. It is said that William Byrd II stood on this spot and fancying it like one in Richmond on the Thames in England, gave the town its name.

1439 Tredegar Iron Works (site)

Tredegar Street at the James River.

The buildings here are reminders of what once was the most important iron works in the South. During the Civil War, the Tredegar turned out more than 1,100 artillery pieces for the Confederacy. The iron armor for the C.S.S. *Virginia*, the world's first ironclad warship, was rolled here.

1440 The Valentine, The Museum of the Life and History of Richmond (col)

1015 East Clay Street; 804-649-0711; Mon–Sat 10–5, Sun 12–5. Admission charged.

The Richmond history museum is strong on costume collections, including Civil War period pieces. There is a plaster cast of the famous recumbent statue of Lee at Lexington in this 1812 house.

1441 The Virginia State Capitol (site)

Capitol Square; 804-786-4344; Apr–Nov: daily, 9–5; other times: Mon–Sat 9–5, Sun 1–5. Free.

This building designed by Jefferson was the seat of government for the Confederate States of America. Here Robert E. Lee assumed command of all Virginia forces and Jefferson Davis delivered his inaugural address at the base of the Washington statue. On the grounds are bronze statues of General Stonewall Jackson, Confederate governor William Smith, and surgeon Hunter McGuire.

1442 Yellow Tavern (site)

Telegraph Road, off Route 1, north of the city.

A small park and monuments mark the spot where J. E. B. Stuart received his mortal wound on May 11, 1864.

Salem

1443 Hanging Rock Battlefield (site)

Route 311, ½ mile north of I-81, Exit 41.

Markers and monuments indicate where Union general Hunter was intercepted by Confederate forces as he was retreating from Lynchburg on June 21, 1864. After losing some artillery here, he continued his retreat.

Saltville

1444 Confederate Salt Works (site)

Route 107.

Saltmaking began in Saltville in 1788. During the Civil War the salt wells pumped so much preservative salt to the Confederate government that the town became a target for Union raider Stoneman, who destroyed the salt works in October 1864. A marker indicates the site.

Savage Station

1445 Battle of Savage Station (site)

Route 156.

Hoping to protect a supply line along the Richmond and York River Railroad, the Federals pulled out of their trenches east of Richmond on June 29, 1862. Confederate general John B. Magruder followed and disrupted the Union plans. They set fire to the supplies they couldn't move with them and moved south across the swamp, leaving behind

2,500 sick and wounded men in a field hospital. Markers interpret the events here.

Seven Pines

1446 Battle of Seven Pines (site)
Route 60, east of town.

After sweeping through Yorktown and Williamsburg in 1862, George McClellan was confronted by Confederate commander General Joseph E. Johnston here on May 31. The resulting battle was indecisive, but Johnston was seriously wounded. Robert E. Lee assumed command of the Army of Northern Virginia the next day.

There are no remains of the battlefield, but state historical markers interpret the critical day that catapulted Lee to the command of the Southern forces. A national cemetery is here.

Spotsylvania

1447 Battle of Spotsylvania (site)
4704 Southpoint Parkway; 800-654-4118; Summer: daily, 9–7; other times: 9–5. Free.

After the struggle in the Wilderness, both armies raced east along what is now Route 613 to control the crucial road junction at Spotsylvania Court House. The Confederates arrived first and hastily erected heavy earthworks. From May 8 to 21, 1864, fighting raged along the lines. On May 12 the engagement became so desperate that a break in the northwestern face of the defensive line came to be known as the "Bloody Angle."

A driving tour covers the battlefield, and a numbered walking tour has been developed for the "Bloody Angle." Musket fire was so intense in this area that a marker attests to a 22-inch oak tree that was felled solely by bullets.

1448 Spotsylvania Confederate Cemetery (site)
Route 208.

Local women established a Confederate cemetery on five acres of land, a half-mile east of the courthouse in 1866. Here they reburied nearly 600 soldiers from crudely marked graves on area battlefields. In the center of the cemetery is a granite shaft crowned by a stone Confederate soldier who silently watches over the dead, most of whom are identified.

Stony Creek

1449 Battle of Stony Creek (site)
Route 301 at Stony Creek.

In 1864 supplies for Lee's army were carted from the railroad here to Petersburg. On June 28 the cavalry of General Wade Hampton routed the cavalry of General James H. Wilson, causing them to abandon the spoils of plunder and 1,000 blacks. The pillaging later precipitated a Federal investigation.

Strasburg

1450 Fisher's Hill Battlefield (site)
Route 11, two miles south of town.

Following his defeat by Sheridan at Winchester, Confederate general Early fell back to this position, sometimes referred to as the "Gibraltar of the Valley." Sheridan once again forced him to retreat on September 22, 1864. Early's adjutant general, A. S. Pendleton, was mortally wounded while attempting to check the Union attack. Historical roadside markers recall the events of the day, and a self-guided walking trail winds across the site.

1451 Hupp's Hill Battlefield Park and Study Center (site)
Route 11, southern end of Cedar Creek Battlefield; 703-465-5884; Mon, Wed–Fri 10–4, Sat–Sun 11–5. Admission: $3.50.

Hupp's Hill was the site of a sharp skirmish between Early's army and members of the 8th Corps of Sheridan's army on October 13, 1864, that resulted in nearly 400 casualties. Six days later more than 9,000 men fell at nearby Cedar Creek, and Hupp's Hill became virtually forgotten.

Original trenches and lunettes dug by Sheridan's men are still visible. The Study Center is a unique Civil War museum that encourages hands-on activities to interpret the war. There is a 100-foot hand-painted mural of the history of the Civil War and the world's largest map of the Battle of Cedar Creek. Among the exhibits is the third largest known collection of Confederate currency. Guided tours of the area's battlefields are offered.

Stratford

1452 Stratford Hall Plantation (site)
Route 214; 804-493-8038; Daily, 9–4:30. Admission charged.

Thomas Lee, a prominent Virginia planter, built Stratford in the 1730s, using brick made on the site and virgin timber from his 1,670 acres. Lee raised eight children here, including Richard Henry Lee and Francis Lightfoot Lee, the only brothers to sign the Declaration of Independence. In 1807 Robert Edward Lee, the most prominent of the distinguished Lees, was born here.

Reenactment: The plantation is still managed as a farm today, and each year in early June a Civil War Living History Encampment and Battle Reenactment takes place here.

Suffolk

1453 Confederate Monument (mem)

Cedar Hill Cemetery; Main Street and Constance Road.

On April 11, 1864, Confederate general James Longstreet laid siege to Suffolk, hoping to thwart a northern push to Richmond by Union general John Peck and his 25,000-man army. The offensive never materialized and the siege was largely ineffective. The monument is the most prominent of the markers of Confederates graves in this burial ground.

Sutherland

1454 Battle of Five Forks (site)

Routes 613 and 627.

By the spring of 1865 the last remaining supply line to Lee's fatigued troops in Petersburg was the South Side Railroad, protected by the Confederates at a critical junction called Five Forks. Sheridan and Warren attacked Lee's extreme right defenses on the afternoon of April 1, 1865, and overwhelmingly defeated infantry and cavalry under generals George E. Pickett and Fitzhugh Lee.

The next day Grant assaulted Petersburg, and the Confederates abandoned Richmond that night. Five Forks became known as the "Waterloo of the Confederacy."

Five Forks is administered by the Petersburg National Battlefield. Most of the battlefield is on private property, and the key points of action are described along the area roadways.

1455 Battle of Sutherland Station (site)

Routes 460 and 708.

After the fall of Richmond on April 2, 1865, Lee and the remains of his army — only 30,000 strong — began a retreat westward in hopes of joining Johnston's troops in North Carolina. The 1803 Fork Inn features an exhibit room with relics and an explanation of the skirmishing at Sutherland Station.

This is the first stop on a 100-mile, 20-stop tour of Lee's retreat route, which has been developed. Narration at the stops can be heard on the car radio.

1456 Namozine Church (site)

Route 708, ten miles west of town.

Confederate and Union cavalry, the latter under George Armstrong Custer, skirmished at this two-story, white frame church on April 3, 1865, before engaging in a running battle along Lee's retreat route. The Union captured 350 men. The church was used as a hospital and Sheridan's headquarters.

Talleysville

1457 Stuart's Ride Around McClellan (site)

Route 33.

A historical marker indicates where Confederate cavalry commander J. E. B. Stuart, coming from Hanover Courthouse on his famous ride around McClellan's army, arrived on the early night of June 13, 1862.

Tobaccoville

1458 Derwent (site)

Route 13, two miles east of town.

Ten miles north of this historical marker is where Robert E. Lee brought his family in the summer of 1865, leaving postwar Richmond far behind. The Lees stayed in this modest, two-story frame house as the guests of Mrs. E. R. Cocke. While there, Lee was offered the presidency of Washington College in Lexington, which he accepted on August 24, 1865. On September 15, he left Derwent for his final home in Lexington.

Tom's Brook

1459 Battle of Tom's Brook (site)

Route 11.

After his rout of General Early's troops at Fisher's Hill on September 22, 1864, Union general Sheridan chased the Confederates up the Valley Pike through Tom's Brook, south to Woodstock. Thinking his campaign won, Sheridan turned back north to Winchester, burning mills and military targets along the way. Angered at the desecration, Early sent his cavalry under General Thomas Rosser back at Sheridan. The Federal horsemen, under Generals Alfred Torbert and George Armstrong Custer, won a smashing victory and drove the Rebels far south in retreat. So fast was their withdrawal after two hours of fighting that the skirmish came to be known as the "Woodstock Races." The field can be viewed from a historical marker.

Unionville

1460 Mine Run Campaign (site)

Route 20, 6½ miles east of town.

A historical marker identifies where Meade, advancing south from the Rapidan River to attack Lee, found him in an entrenched position on November 28, 1863. Heavy skirmishing lasted until December 1, when Meade retreated back across the Rapidan.

Vienna

1461 Freedom Hill Fort (site)

Old Court House Road, off intersection of Routes 7 and 123.

Unique interpretive markers describe this fortified picket enclosure used to protect Federal camps from raiding Confederate cavalry.

Warrenton

1462 Mosby Monument (mem)

Old Courthouse.

After a fire in 1890 the courthouse was restored as a replica of the Civil War building. Portraits, including Civil War figures from Fanquier County, hang on interior walls. A roughhewn, red stone obelisk to Colonel John Singleton Mosby, Confederate ranger, stands on the lawn. Mosby came to Warrenton after the war and practiced law; he lived in one of the most gracious residences in town at 173 Main Street, which is now a private residence.

1463 Old Jail Museum (col)

Main and Ashby streets; 540-347-5525; closed Mondays. Free.

The Black Horse Cavalry was conceived at a gathering of Warrenton lawyers in 1858. The Black Horse led a successful charge against the Union forces at the First Battle of Manassas and later served as bodyguard escorts for the ranking Confederate generals. Following the war, a number of the men in the Black Horse became prominent leaders in Virginia. The museum features Civil War material.

1464 Warren Green Hotel (site)

Hotel Street.

From the upper porch of this prominent nineteenth-century hostelry, in November 1862, General George B. McClellan delivered his farewell address to the Federal Army of the Potomac that he had created. The restored building now houses county offices.

1465 Warrenton Cemetery (site)

Lee Street.

Colonel John Mosby is buried here, the grave marked by a tall shaft. Some 600 unknown Confederate soldiers are interred here.

Waterford

1466 Waterford Baptist Church (site)

Routes 665 and 783.

On August 27, 1862, a company of Federal cavalry took cover in the church during a firefight with Confederate troopers. The bricks in the front of the church are still pockmarked from careening bullets.

Waynesboro

1467 Harman Monument (mem)

Route 250, off Route 340.

A simple stone marker stands at the spot where Colonel William H. Harman was felled at the Battle of Waynesboro. Harman was a local attorney for the county.

1468 Riverview Cemetery (site)

Route 340, south of Route 250.

Sheridan and Early clashed on a ridge west of town on March 2, 1865. Custer led the attack, encircling the enemy, and captured some 1,600 men and claimed 17 flags, 11 guns, and all the Confederate supplies. Early and his staff escaped into the woods. This was the last important battle fought in northern Virginia. An obelisk in the graveyard honors soldiers from four states who were killed here.

Wilderness

1469 Wilderness Battlefield (site)

Route 20, south of Route 3.

Here for the first time Robert E. Lee was pitted against Ulysses S. Grant in the field. President Lincoln had just appointed Grant as commander of the Federal forces with one objective — defeat Lee in the field, continue south, and end the war. Grant massed 120,000 troops near Culpeper Courthouse to attempt to accomplish what six other generals of the Army of the Potomac before him could not.

From his position at Orange Courthouse atop Clark's Mountain, Lee could easily see that his force of 65,000 was no match for Grant's army. He elected on May 5, 1864, to negate the numerical advantage by starting the fight in dense, tangled woods. Small squads became disoriented in two days of fighting through the forest as musket fire set underbrush ablaze and indeed Lee, although narrowly avoiding capture, was able to battle Grant's superior forces to a draw.

But it was only a momentary check as Grant, unlike his predecessors, continued his drive to Richmond. And the losses were frightful — 17,000 men killed and wounded for the North; 11,000 men killed and wounded for the South. The tide of the war had swung to the Federals.

Reenactment: Little of the battlefield remains today, and what survives can be reached only by car to see roadside markers. Exhibits and information on the Battle of the Wilderness can be found at the nearby Chancellorsville Battlefield Visitor Center on Route 3. The battle is recreated in May on a private farm open to the public that weekend. In addition to a major clash each day, there are authentic encampments featuring music, demonstrations, and sutlers, "the traveling salesmen of the Civil War."

Williamsburg

1470 Battle of Williamsburg (site)

Route 60, ½ mile southeast of town.

On May 5, 1862, the first battle of the Federal Peninsular campaign was fought. The heaviest action was at Fort Magruder, but there was skirmishing in the streets and on the campus of the College of William and Mary as well. The Wren Building, the main building on campus, was burned, and in 1895 the United States government paid partial restitution. Markers detail the Confederate defenses and the Union attack.

Winchester

1471 Battles of Winchester (site)

Kurtz Cultural Center; 2 North Cameron Street; 540-722-6367; Mon–Sat 10–5, Sun 12–5. Free.

Four major engagements were fought in and around town: Kernstown (March 23, 1862); First Winchester (May 25, 1862); Second Winchester (also known as Stephenson's Depot, June 14–15, 1863); and Third Winchester (also called Opequon Creek, September 19, 1864). Winchester was a major supply route: the town lay on the Valley Pike and was served by east-west and north-south railroads and the Potomac River. Not surprisingly, from the spring of 1862 until the fall of 1864 Winchester changed flags 70 times.

No traces of these battles, which all drew Union strength away from Richmond, remain. The center features a permanent exhibit, "Shenandoah: Crossroads of the Civil War," which provides an overview of 15 battles and sketches of the leaders in the Shenandoah Valley campaigns. A series of historical markers along Route 11 trace the movements of the armies in these battles.

1472 Confederate Memorial (mem)

County Courthouse; Loudoun Street Mall.

This sculpture of a Virginia infantryman standing at rest, dedicated in 1916, was created by Frederick Cleveland Hibbard.

1473 Confederate Monument to Unknown Dead (site)

Stonewall Cemetery; entrance off Kent Street at the end of Boscawen Street.

The tall shaft in the center of the graveyard, part of the Mount Hebron Cemetery, honors 829 unknown soldiers killed in fighting around Winchester. It is one of the earliest Civil War monuments, dedicated in 1866. More than 3,000 identified soldiers also buried here, including cavalry commander Turner Ashby. Across Woodstock Lane is a national cemetery, five acres purchased by Federal government in 1866, where 2,110 known and 2,381 unknown soldiers are buried.

1474 Handley Library (col)

Braddock and Piccadilly streets; 703-662-9041.

The Archives Room is an excellent source of correspondence, diaries, and records of Winchester and Frederick Counties during the war.

1475 Stonewall Jackson's Headquarters (site)

415 North Braddock Street; 703-667-3242; Apr–Oct: daily, 9–5; Mar, Nov–Dec: Fri–Sun, 9–5. Admission charged.

Jackson made his headquarters in this small, French-style house between November 1861 and March 1862. Now a museum, the house has Jackson artifacts and other relics from the fighting in the Shenandoah Valley.

1476 Sheridan's Headquarters (site)

Braddock and Piccadilly streets.

The Union general directed his Second Valley campaign from this imposing home. On October 19, 1864, Sheridan began his famous ride to Cedar Creek from here to rally his troops to victory. The building is now a private club.

Wytheville

1477 Toland's Raid (site)

Route 52 at Bland County Line.

Over this pass, Union cavalry under Colonel John T. Toland raided to Wytheville to destroy the Virginia and Tennessee Railroad in July 1863. Mary Tynes, a girl of the neighborhood, rode ahead to warn the people. When the raiders reached Wytheville, a town prized for its lead and salt mines, they were repulsed by home guards and Toland was killed. A marker commemorates Tynes' heroic action.

Yorktown

1478 Colonial National Historical Park (site)

Colonial Parkway and Old Route 238; 804-898-3400; Daily, 9–5. Admission charged.

Best known for its climactic Revolutionary War battle, Yorktown also has a Civil War history. Confederate general Magruder built fortifications here during the war, and McClellan laid siege to the town as he marched to Richmond. The national park has developed a self-guided Civil War tour, which includes the park and the town. The national cemetery has 2,200 Union dead, and also features a small Confederate burial ground.

Reenactment: A Civil War weekend is staged on each Memorial Day weekend in the historical park.

West Virginia

Civil War Status: Broke from Virginia to become the thirty-fifth state on June 20, 1863
1860 Population: Part of Virginia
Troops Provided: 32,000— Union
10,000— Confederacy
Known Scenes of Action: 632

Civil War Timeline
April 19, 1861: Confederates occupy Harpers Ferry
June 3, 1861: Engagement at Philippi; first land action of the war
July 11, 1861: Engagement at Rich Mountain
September 12–15, 1862: Siege and capture of Harpers Ferry
November 6, 1863: Battle of Droop Mountain

Ansted

1479 Contentment (site)
Route 60, one mile northwest of town; 304-574-3354; Summer: Mon–Sat 10–4, Sun 1–4. Admission charged.

Contentment was built in 1830 and purchased in 1872 by Colonel George Imboden, who served on the staff of General Robert E. Lee, for his 15-year-old bride. It is furnished with period pieces and contains Civil War memorabilia.

Bartow

1480 Camp Allegheny (site)
Off Route 250; 304-799-4636.

This camp in the Potomac Highlands was one of the highest (4,400 feet) of the Civil War. Established by Confederate forces in the summer of 1861, it was unsuccessfully stormed by the Federals in December of that year. But the coming harsh winter and the logistical nightmare of keeping the garri-

son supplied led to its abandonment in April 1862. Camp remnants are visible today.

Beverly

1481 Rich Mountain Battlefield (site)
Old Staunton-Parkersburg Pike, five miles west of town; 304-637-RICH.

In an apple orchard on the hillside, Confederate breastworks were thrown up in an attempt to block General George B. McClellan's relentless advance into western Virginia early in the Civil War. On July 11, 1861, McClellan moved forward quickly, leaving an artillery unit to bombard nearby Laurel Hill as he hurried his main force southward against Lieutenant Colonel John Pegram's smaller force on Rich Mountain. The ruse deceived General Robert S. Garnett, in command at Laurel Hill, who did not discover until too late that he had been outflanked. He retreated to the east and north, but when the weary survivors of the Confederate rout at Rich Mountain fell back to Laurel Hill, they found the fortified camp abandoned. Cut off from supplies, faced with the prospect of hunger and a dangerous retreat through hostile territory, 555 soldiers and officers of Colonel Pegram's command surrendered to McClellan when he offered them wagonloads of bread.

This decisive victory catapulted McClellan to the command of the Army of the Potomac. The Confederates withdrew from northwestern Virginia, allowing the formation of the state of West Virginia two years later. The battlefield is now a boulder-strewn hillside. Visitor information is available in the town of Beverly.

Charleston

1482 Capitol Complex (mem)
Kanawha Boulevard East.

Facing the Kanawha River is *Lincoln Walks at Midnight*, a sculptural rendition of a poem by Vachel Lindsey. The statue was dedicated in 1974. On the west lawn are two Civil War monuments standing side by side. One, a bronze statue of Stonewall Jackson facing south, by Sir Moses Ezekiel, was erected as a memorial to the Confederate Soldiers. The other, the symbolic figure of a mountaineer, sculpted by Rimfire Hamrick, is dedicated to the "brave men and women who saved West Virginia to the Union." In the southwest corner of the grounds is a Union soldier, dedicated in 1930 with a base sculpted by Roy Stewart. That base bears an inscription to the 32,000 soldiers, sailors, and marines contributed by West Virginia to the Union. In the northeast corner is the *Mountaineer Soldier*, by Henry Kirke Bush-Brown, where a Union soldier emerges from a mountain cabin.

1483 The Cultural Center (col)

Greenbrier and Washington streets; 304-558-0220; Mon–Fri 9–5, Sat–Sun 1–5. Free.

A part of the capitol complex, the museum features exhibits on the Civil War and John Brown's operations in western Virginia.

Charles Town

1484 Jefferson County Courthouse (site)

George and Washington streets.

Here, in this town named for George Washington's younger brother, abolitionist John Brown and his band of followers were tried and sentenced for treason. The room in which Brown was tried is part of the present courthouse, which was rebuilt after having been shelled in the war. The site of the gallows where he was hanged on December 2, 1859, is on South Samuel Street between McCurdy Street and Beckwith Alley.

Clarksburg

1485 Stonewall Jackson (mem)

West Main and 3rd streets.

This equestrian statue of General Jackson by Charles Keck depicts a determined rider surveying the field past the horse's right ear.

1486 Stonewall Jackson Birthplace (site)

Edel Building; 324 Main Street.

A bronze tablet marks the site of Thomas Jonathan Jackson's birth on January 21, 1824. One of four children, he was three years old when his father died of fever. In 1830 he went to live on his grandfather's farm in Weston.

1487 War Memorial (mem)

General Nathan Goff Armory; Armory Road, off Route 19.

A stone Civil War sentry stands on a massive base in tribute to the citizens of Harrison County. It was dedicated on May 30, 1908.

Durbin

1488 Cheat Summit Fort (site)

Off Route 250, north of town; 304-799-4636.

This pit-and-parapet fort at the summit of White Top Mountain, reached by footpath, was built by General George McClellan to secure the railroad and turnpike running through western Virginia. When in the fall of 1861 Confederate forces were unable to dislodge the Federals from this position, the region was secured for the Union.

Elkwater

1489 J. A. Washington Memorial (mem)

Route 219.

Colonel John Augustine Washington, great-grandnephew of President George Washington and aide-de-camp to General Robert E. Lee, was killed here on September 13, 1861. Washington was out on patrol, scouting Federal positions near the Elkwater Bridge while accompanied by W. H. F. Lee, the son of Robert E. Lee. Federal earthworks from the skirmish here are still visible.

Fairmont

1490 Pierpont House (site)

Northeast corner of Pierpont Avenue and Quincy Street.

On April 29, 1863, Confederate general William E. "Grumble" Jones and his cavalry attacked the city, took 260 prisoners, and destroyed the railroad bridge across the Monongahela River. This former home of Governor Francis H. Pierpont was raided by Jones's troops. Pierpont was active in the Wheeling conventions and was elected governor of the Restored Government of Virginia at the second Wheeling convention. After the state was admitted to the Union, he moved the government to Alexandria, Virginia, until after the war.

Falling Waters

1491 Pettigrew Monument (mem)

Apple Pie Ridge; Route 11.

This granite column, on which rest four stacked cannonballs, commemorates the fact that in the Boyd House, once located 200 yards to the west, was the site where Brigadier General James Johnston Pettigrew of North Carolina, a Confederate leader in the assault on Cemetery Ridge during the Battle of Gettysburg, died. In the retreat southward, General Pettigrew was fatally wounded in the Battle of Falling Waters on July 14, 1863; a bronze plaque on the monument is inscribed with the tribute paid him by his superior, Robert E. Lee.

Fetterman

1492 Brown Monument (mem)

Route 50, west of town.

This granite marker was erected to T. Bailey Brown, considered the first Union soldier to be killed in the Civil War. Brown was cut down by a Confederate sentry on the night of May 22, 1861. The dedication of this marker was on the actual site of Brown's death when it was unveiled on May 16, 1928, but the monument has since been relocated.

Grafton

1493 Grafton National Cemetery (site)

431 Walnut Street; 304-265-2044.

This strategic town on the Baltimore and Ohio Railroad was occupied at various times by both sides during the war. The graves of more than 2,000 soldiers are here, including the first Union army mortality, T. Bailey Brown. The inscription on his marker reads: "T. Bailey Brown of Co. B. 2nd W. Va. Vol. Inft. Capt. George R. Latham, Comdg. The First Union Soldier Killed in the Civil War at Fetterman, W. Va., May 22, 1861 by Daniel Knight of Co. A 25th Va. C.S.A. Capt. John A. Robinson, Comdg."

Harpers Ferry

1494 John Brown Wax Museum (col)

High Street; 304-535-6321; Mar–Dec: daily, 9–5; other times: Sat–Sun, 10–5. Admission charged.

The life of America's most controversial abolitionist is portrayed with sight and sound animation.

1495 Harpers Ferry National Historical Park (site)

Visitor Center off Route 340; 304-535-6029; Daily, 8–5. Admission charged.

There were few more strategic towns in the 1800s than Harpers Ferry. Not only was it located at the confluence of the Shenandoah and Potomac rivers, but it was also a converging point for the Baltimore and Ohio Railroad, the Winchester and Potomac Railroad, and the Chesapeake and Ohio Canal. The town changed hands eight times during the Civil War, often with its industry crippled by withdrawing forces.

The industry of particular interest was the United States Armory and Arsenal, established in the closing years of the eighteenth century. It was this arsenal abolitionist John Brown planned to capture in order to seize 100,000 weapons to arm a Southern slave revolt. Brown's 21-man "army of liberation" raided the arsenal and other strategic points on Sunday evening, October 16, 1859. Thirty-six hours later most of his men were killed or wounded, and U.S. Marines under Colonel Robert E. Lee had captured Brown.

The park covers 2,300 acres of land in three states. The ruins of the arsenal and the armory fire enginehouse, known as "John Brown's Fort," where the abolitionist was apprehended, can be visited off Shenandoah Street. Civil War museums are on High Street. On the hills outside of town, in a separate area of the park, are the remains of Civil War fortifications.

Hillsboro

1496 Droop Mountain Battlefield State Park (site)

Route 219; 304-653-4254; Park: daily, 6–10; museum: daily, 8–5. Free.

Due to the state's mountainous terrain, the fighting in West Virginia was intended to disrupt enemy communications and supplies rather than to destroy armies. So when the state's largest battle of the Civil War took place here on November 6, 1863, the forces numbered about 1,700 for the Confederates and 3,000 for the Union under General William Averell. A Federal force led by Colonel Augustus Moor pestered the Confederate left flank while Averall collapsed the right. After five hours of fighting, Confederate general John Echols was forced to retreat off the mountain summit rather than surrender his entire command. With this the last serious Southern resistance in West Virginia was crushed.

Footpaths lead to graves, monuments, and Confederate earthworks. A small museum displays artifacts from the battle.

Hinton

1497 Confederate Monument (mem)

Memorial Building; Park Avenue and James Street.

The 16-foot gray bronze statue of a Confederate soldier, mounted on a granite base, was dedicated in May 1914 to the Confederate soldiers of Greenbrier and New River alleys who followed Lee and Jackson. The monument bears an embossed likeness of General Robert E. Lee.

Kingwood

1498 Civil War Monument (mem)

Preston County Courthouse; Corner of Price Street and Route 7.

This monument for Preston County's Civil War veterans is carved from white beryl granite and was dedicated on October 31, 1903. It depicts a soldier standing at parade rest.

Lewisburg

1499 Confederate Cemetery (site)

McIlhenney Road.

A cross-shaped common grave contains the remains of 95 unknown Confederate soldiers who died in the Battle of Lewisburg on May 23, 1862. The graveyard lies within the perimeter of the Union camp before the attack.

1500 Confederate Monument (mem)

Courtney Drive and Washington Street.

The standing soldier in bronze was designed by William Ludlow Sheppard and dedicated on June 14, 1906, to the Confederate dead of Lewisburg.

1501 Greenbrier County Library (site)

301 Courtney Drive.

The building was erected in 1834 as a library for visiting jurists staying at the North House across the street. During the Battle of Lewisburg it was used as a hospital, like other buildings in town, and inside is a section of old plaster where soldiers scratched their names.

1502 Lewisburg Visitor Center (site)

Carnegie Hall; 105 Church Street; 304-645-1000; May–Oct: Mon–Sat 9–5, Sun 1–5; other times: daily, closed Sunday. Free.

Union and Confederate forces clashed for an hour in Lewisburg on May 23, 1862. The Confederates under Brigadier General Henry Heth failed to dislodge the Union from town, losing more than 300 men. Union colonel George Crook was to be best remembered as the captor of Apache chief Geronimo, but on this day he led the 3rd Provisional Ohio Brigade to victory.

The visitor center provides brochures for a walking tour of the historic district and the Battle of Lewisburg. Skirmish sites are marked with bronze plaques.

1503 North House Museum (col)

101 Church Street; 304-645-3398; Mon–Sat, 10–4. Admission charged.

This brick tavern dating from the 1820s now houses the Greenbrier Historical Society, which has a collection of Civil War artifacts and documents relating to Lewisburg.

Marlinton

1504 Pocahontas County Historical Museum (col)

Route 219; 304-799-4973; Summer: Mon–Sat 11–5, Sun 1–5. Admission charged.

On January 1, 1862, some 738 Federal troops under Major G. Webster launched a raid against the Confederate supply center at nearby Huntersville. The Union force was intercepted in Marlinton by a Confederate militia half its size. The action resulted in one Federal and eight Confederate casualties as Webster captured large supplies of food and weapons. The museum displays Civil War artifacts.

Martinsburg

1505 Belle Boyd House (col)

126 East Race Street; 304-267-4713; Wed–Sat, 10–4. Free.

This Greek Revival house dating from 1853 was built by Ben Boyd, father of beautiful 17-year-old Confederate spy Belle Boyd. It is now home to the Berkeley County Historical Society. A Civil War museum features Berkeley County people and artifacts from the 1860s. Belle Boyd, after her arrest for shooting a Union soldier in her parents' home for having made threats against her mother, was held prisoner in the Berkeley County courthouse.

Mingo

1506 Confederate Soldier (mem)

Mingo Flats Road off Route 219.

This monument was originally unveiled on July 23, 1913, on Valley Mountain, near Mingo, in the proximity of where General Robert E. Lee's army was encamped for 30 days half a century earlier. The memorial is a stone Confederate soldier at parade rest, dedicated to the memory of the men from Randolph County who served in the Civil War.

Moundsville

1507 Civil War Soldier (mem)

Marshall County Courthouse; 7th and Tomlinson streets.

This deteriorating bronze is of a Civil War soldier standing at parade rest. It was unveiled on Decoration Day, 1909, in memory of the soldiers of Marshall County.

New Cumberland

1508 Union Soldier Monument (mem)

Hancock County Courthouse; Court Street.

Holding the barrel of a rifle with both hands, this bronze Union soldier stands as a tribute to the "defenders of the Union." It was dedicated on May 30, 1886.

Parkersburg

1509 Confederate Soldier (mem)

City Park; Park Avenue and 19th Street.

This bronze was dedicated to Parkersburg's Confederate dead on July 21, 1908. Leon Hermant created a Confederate soldier standing at the ready atop a rectangular obelisk of rough textured granite.

Parsons

1510 Battle of Corrick's Ford Monument (mem)

Courthouse Lawn; Route 219.

On July 13, 1861, Union forces overtook the Confederate troops retreating from Laurel Hill and routed them in a fierce battle south of town. General Robert S. Garnett, Confederate commander, was wounded, and after the battle he died in the arms of Union general Thomas A. Morris, who had been a classmate of his at West Point. Garnett was the first Confederate general to die in the Civil War.

Philippi

1511 Barbour County Historical Society Museum (col)

146 North Main Street; 304-457-4846; May–Oct: Mon–Sat 11–4, Sun 1–4. Free.

This museum was opened in 1985 in a restored train depot, east of the Philippi Covered Bridge. Civil War memorabilia from strategic Barbour County are a prominent part of the collection. The museum is a good departure point for a Civil War walking tour of the town.

1512 Blue and Gray Park (site)

West end of the Philippi Covered Bridge; Routes 119 and 250.

On June 3, 1861, the Federals launched a surprise attack here on Confederate troops under the command of Colonel George Porterfield in an effort to remain in control of the Baltimore and Ohio Railroad, the main link of communications between Washington and the West. The Confederates retreated and did so in such haste the affair is known as the "Philippi races." Total casualties were five for the Union and two for the Confederates, none of whom were killed.

Once secured, the bridge was used by the Union as barracks and a crucial transportation link. The Battle of Philippi was the first land battle between the North and the South in the Civil War. The Union victory helped discourage secessionist movements in western Virginia.

The Philippi Covered Bridge across the Tygart Valley River was established in 1852 and remains the longest two-lane, "double-barrel" covered bridge serving a federal highway. The mini-park features a flag circle displaying three-foot-by-five-foot replicas of the five flags that flew over Philippi during the Civil War. Nearby, two cannons mark the spot where the first land shots were fired at half past four on the morning of June 3, 1861.

Reenactment: Each year on the weekend closest to June 3 the Blue and Gray Reunion is staged to commemorate the Battle of Philippi.

1513 Site of Hanger's Amputation (site)

Church Street.

At this location Dr. James D. Robinson of the 16th Ohio Volunteers performed the first amputation of the Civil War, removing the leg of James E. Hanger of Mount Hope, Virginia. Hanger's leg had been shattered by a six-pound cannon ball early in the Battle of Philippi. He survived the emergency operation and later invented an artificial limb. After the war he organized a company that became one of the world's largest manufacturers of prosthetic devices, J. E. Hanger, Inc.

Ripley

1514 Union Soldier (mem)

Jackson County Courthouse; 112 Court Street.

A tiered granite base supports a West Virginia soldier at parade rest. This memorial was dedicated on June 25, 1915.

Romney

1515 Fort Mill Ridge Trenches (site)

Off Route 50.

Romney changed hands 56 times during the Civil War. General Lew Wallace's Union occupation was the first of the 56 changes on June 11, 1861. There was scarcely a family that did not lose a man, and all bridges in the area were destroyed. The battle trenches are well-preserved and interpreted with signs.

Ronceverte

1516 Organ Cave (site)

Routes 219 and 63, three miles south of town; 304-647-5551; May–Oct: daily, 9–7. Admission charged.

This limestone cavern was the site of a Confederate munitions factory. The factory and 37 original saltpeter hoppers are still intact.

Shepherdstown

1517 Pack Horse Ford (site)

Route 45.

This strategic river crossing has been used for centuries by Indians and wild game. During the Civil War a wooden toll bridge was destroyed by Confederate forces fearing a Union invasion. In September 1862, after the battle of Antietam, Lee retreated to Shepherdstown, crossing the river at

Pack Horse Ford as the town, once considered by George Washington for the nation's capital, was converted into a sprawling hospital.

Summersville

1518 Carnifex Ferry Battlefield State Park (site)

Route 23; 304-872-0825.

On September 10, 1861, Union troops under the command of Brigadier General William S. Rosecrans engaged the Confederates on the Henry Patterson farm overlooking Carnifex Ferry on the Gauley River. The Southerners, led by Brigadier General John B. Floyd, were forced off their entrenched position, and their drive to regain control of the Kanawha Valley was thus ended. The movement for West Virginia statehood could proceed without serious opposition.

Reenactment: The Battle of Carnifex Ferry is restaged each September.

Sutton

1519 Battle of Bulltown (site)

Route 19 at Little Kanawha River.

On October 13, 1863, the Battle of Bulltown occurred near the Union trenches. The Federal forces repulsed the attack after 12 hours of skirmishing. The Confederates were led by Colonel William L. "Mudwall" Jackson, a first cousin of Stonewall. Each side suffered casualties, and one civilian, a farmer named Moses Cunningham, was clipped by a Union bullet when he raced from his farmhouse into the line of fire yelling, "Hurrah for Jeff Davis." He recovered.

Fortifications dug to protect the fort are still visible. The Cunningham House, today at the center of Historic Bulltown Village, was a Confederate retreat. Seven unknown Confederates are buried at the site.

1520 Monroe County Confederate Soldier (mem)

Highway 219.

The monument was dedicated on September 5, 1901. It was built outside the town limits, with the intention that the town would grow and the statue would then mark the town square. At present the marble soldier still looks longingly toward Union while standing in a cow pasture.

Weston

1521 Jackson's Mill Historic Area (site)

Jackson's Mill Road, off Route 19, north of town; 304-269-5100; Summer: Tues–Sun, 12–5. Admission charged.

Thomas "Stonewall" Jackson grew into adulthood working in this mill for his uncle Cummins. The museum is the focal point for the historic area.

Wheeling

1522 Soldiers' and Sailors' Monument (mem)

Wheeling Park; National Road.

On opposite sides of the shaft are the figures of a sailor and a soldier; at the top is a draped female figure of Liberty holding a sword and shield. Dedication of the monument was on May 30, 1883.

1523 West Virginia Independence Hall (site)

1528 Market Street; 304-238-1300; Mar–Dec: daily, 10–4; other times: Mon–Sat, 10–4. Free.

Originally designed as a federal Custom House, the building served as capitol for the Restored Government of Virginia from 1861 to 1863, as debates raged on the matter of West Virginia's independence. This pivotal time in West Virginia history is interpreted by costumed guides through the restored rooms. An interpretive video, *For Liberty and Union*, is available.

Wisconsin

Civil War Status: Union
1860 Population: 775,881
Troops Provided: 91,000

Baraboo

1524 Sauk County Historical Museum (col)

531 4th Avenue; 608-356-1001; May–Sept: Tues–Sun, 2–5. Admission charged.

The military room on the second floor has Union photographs and Confederate currency and bonds. The museum is housed in a 14-room mansion dating from 1906.

Berlin

1525 Berlin Soldiers' Monument (mem)

Nathan Strong Park; Huron, State, Park, and Church streets.

This monument to the volunteer soldiers and

sailors of the Civil War gradually evolved from an idea in the 1870s, to a granite base in the 1880s, to a bronze Union soldier on the base in the 1890s.

Cassville

1526 Governor Nelson Dewey Home-site (col)
Route 133; 608-725-5210; Summer: daily, 11–4. Admission charged.

There are Civil War artifacts in this former estate of the first Wisconsin governor, Nelson Dewey. The family settled here in 1836, and he died in 1889.

Columbus

1527 Civil War Monument (mem)
West James and South Dickson Boulevard.

This life-size standing soldier was erected for the area soldiers that fill unknown graves around the country.

Janesville

1528 The Lincoln-Tallman Restorations (site)
440 North Jackson Street; 608-752-4519; June–Sept: Tues–Sun, 11–4; other times: Sat–Sun 11–4. Admission charged.

The Lincoln-Tallman House is the largest antebellum restoration in the Midwest. Built in 1857, this Italianate villa was visited by Abraham Lincoln for a weekend in 1859. The future president was able to enjoy such nineteenth-century innovations as indoor plumbing and central heat.

Kenosha

1529 Palumbo Civil War Museum (col)
Carthage College, Lenz Hall; 2001 Alford Park Drive; 414-552-8520; Mon–Fri, 8–4. Free.

Located on the shores of Lake Michigan, this museum on campus features a permanent display of Civil War relics and books.

Kewaunee

1530 War Monument (mem)
Courthouse Square; Juneau and Kilbourn.

A stone sentry loading a rifle stands in honor of the soldiers and marines of Kewaunee County.

Madison

1531 Camp Randall site (site)
University Avenue to Monroe Street between Breese Terrace and Randall Avenue.

During the Civil War 42 acres of land were donated by the Wisconsin State Agricultural Society to the state legislature for use as drill grounds for Union soldiers. The camp was named in honor of the wartime governor, Alexander W. Randall. The camp quickly became the center of Wisconsin's military activities — 70,000 men were drilled and quartered here. Local newspaper accounts recall complaints about the rowdies who led brewery tours in the area.

After the war Camp Randall was used as a fairgrounds and later as athletic fields. In 1911 a section was set aside as Camp Randall Memorial Park, and a memorial arch, 36 feet high and 36 feet wide, was completed in 1912 and dedicated to Civil War soldiers.

1532 Wisconsin Veterans Museum (col)
30 Mifflin Street; 608-264-6086; Apr–Sept: Tues–Sat 9:30–4:30, Sun 12–4; other times: closed Sundays. Free.

This wide-ranging collection covers America's wars since the Civil War, mementos and displays of which are in the Nineteenth Century Gallery.

Mayville

1533 Civil War Monument (mem)
Mayville Middle School; North Main Street.

The Woman's Relief Corps of Mayville dedicated this stone monument to Union soldiers and sailors in May 1928.

Ripon

1534 Little White School House (site)
Blackburn Street; 414-748-4730; Mon–Sat 10–4, Sun 12–4. Free.

The mass meeting here on March 20, 1854, resulted in a new political party — to be called "Republican." Abraham Lincoln was to be the new political organization's first president.

Waukesha

1535 Soldiers' Monument (mem)
Cutler Park.

This Civil War memorial consists of a Vermont granite soldier standing at parade rest on a 30-foot-high shaft. Dedicated on September 20, 1911, it is missing two of its original four cannons at the corners of the base.

1536 Waukesha County Historical Museum (col)

101 West Main Street; 414-548-7186; Tues–Sat 9–4:30, Sun 1–4. Free.

Among the displays is one of the first Civil War uniforms issued in the North.

Wisconsin Rapids

1537 Victorious Charge (mem)

Court of Honor; West Wisconsin Avenue, between North 9th and North 10th streets.

John Servino Conway sculpted this dramatic bronze of a bearded standard-bearer having fallen in the course of a victorious charge. The rest of his unit continues the charge. This memorial to those who fought for the Union was dedicated on June 28, 1898.

Wyoming

Civil War Status: Pieced together from several territories as the Wyoming Territory on July 25, 1868

1860 Population: Not recorded

Troops Provided: Negligible outside territories

Laramie

1538 Abraham Lincoln Memorial Monument (mem)

Ten miles southeast on I-80 at edge of rest area.

The three-and-a-half-ton bronze bust, some 42½ feet tall, was sculpted by Robert Russin. It originally commemorated the sesquicentennial of Lincoln's birth in 1959 and was situated at the highest point on the Lincoln Highway, U.S. Route 30, the nation's first transcontinental road.

APPENDIX: GRAVESITES

Significant individuals, showing city

Allen, Henry Watkins (Baton Rouge, LA)
Andrews, James J. (Chattanooga, TN)
Austin, Stephen F. (Austin, TX)
Bates, Edward (St. Louis, MO)
Blair, Francis, Jr. (St. Louis, MO)
Boone, Daniel (Frankfort, KY)
Booth, John Wilkes (Baltimore, MD)
Brady, Mathew B. (Washington, DC)
Breckinridge, John Cabell (Lexington, KY)
Brown, John (Lake Placid, NY)
Brown, T. Bailey (Grafton, WV)
Buchanan, Franklin (Easton, MD)
Buell, Don Carlos (St. Louis, MO)
Burnside, Ambrose (Providence, RI)
Carson, Kit (Taos, NM)
Carter, Samuel P. (Washington, DC)
Clay, Henry (Lexington, KY)
Cooper, Mark (Cartersville, GA)
Davis, Jefferson (Richmond, VA)
Davis, Sam (Smyrna, TN)
Dearing, James (Lynchburg, VA)
Dodd, David Owen (Little Rock, AR)
Dodge, Grenville (Council Bluffs, IA)
Douglas, Stephen A. (Chicago, IL)
Douglass, Frederick (Rochester, NY)
Eads, James (St. Louis, MO)
Earle, R. G. (Adairsville, GA)
Ezekiel, Moses (Arlington, VA)
Forrest, Nathan Bedford (Memphis, TN)
Fritchie, Barbara (Frederick, MD)
Gamble, Hamilton (St. Louis, MO)
Granger, Gordon (Lexington, KY)
Grant, Ulysses S. (New York, NY)
Hayes, Rutherford B. (Fremont, OH)
Hill, Ambrose Powell (Richmond, VA)
Jackson, Thomas (Lexington, VA)
Johnson, Andrew (Greeneville, TN)
Johnson, George (Georgetown, KY)
Johnston, Albert Sidney (Austin, TX)
Johnston, Joseph (Baltimore, MD)
Key, Francis Scott (Frederick, MD)
Lee, Fitzhugh (Richmond, VA)
Lee, Robert E. (Lexington, VA)
LeFlore, Greenwood (North Carrollton, MS)

Lincoln, Abraham (Springfield, IL)
Lincoln, Robert (Arlington, VA)
Lincoln, Thomas (Charleston, IL)
McPherson, James Birdseye (Clyde, OH)
Mahone, William (Petersburg, VA)
Maury, Matthew (Richmond, VA)
Meigs, John Rodgers (Arlington, VA)
Miller, James H. (Pageland, SC)
Mitchell, Margaret (Atlanta, GA)
Montgomery, James (Mound City, KS)
Morgan, John Hunt (Lexington, KY)
Mosby, John Singleton (Warrenton, VA)
Mumford, Thomas Taylor (Lynchburg, VA)
Mundy, Sue (Franklin, KY)
Pelham, John (Jacksonville, AL)
Pettigrew, John Johnston (Crewsell, NC)
Pickett, George (Richmond, VA)
Preston, Margaret Junkin (Lexington, VA)
Price, Sterling (St. Louis, MO)
Rihl, William (Greencastle, PA)
Rogers, William (Corinth, MS)
Saint-Gaudens, Augustus (Cornish, NH)
Seward, William (Auburn, NY)
Sherman, William Tecumseh (St. Louis, MO)
Shields, James (Carrollton, MO)
Sibley, Henry H. (Fredericksburg, VA)
Shorter, John Gill (Eufala, AL)
Stephens, Alexander Hamilton (Crawfordville, GA)
Stevens, Martha (Fredericksburg, VA)
Stuart, James E. B. (Richmond, VA)
Truth, Sojourner (Battle Creek, MI)
Tubman, Harriet (Auburn, NY)
Twain, Mark (Elmira, NY)
Vance, Zebulon (Asheville, NC)
Wallace, Lew (Crawfordsville, IN)
Ward, John Quincy Adams (Urbana, OH)
Watie, Stand (Grove, OK)
Wesson, Laura (High Point, NC)
Whitney, Eli (New Haven, CT)
Wofford, William T. (Cassville, GA)
Young, P. M. B. (Cartersville, GA)
Zollicoffer, Felix (Somerset, KY)

INDEX

References are to entry numbers